Shoeless

For Deborah

Shoeless

The Life and Times of Joe Jackson

by DAVID L. FLEITZ

McFarland & Company, Inc., Publishers
Jefferson, North Carolina, and London

Acknowledgments: I would like to thank many people without whom this book would never have been possible.

Bruce Markusen, researcher at the National Baseball Library in Cooperstown, New York, made many useful items available to me from the files of the Baseball Hall of Fame. Steven Gietschier of the *Sporting News* also provided me with timely and valuable data, as did Keisha Whitehead of the Chicago Historical Society and the photographic department of the Cleveland (Ohio) Public Library. Also, the Eugene C. Murdock Collection at the Cleveland Public Library is one of the best collections of baseball reference materials available anywhere, and this proved a fruitful source of information.

I am also indebted to many people in Joe Jackson's hometown of Greenville, South Carolina, for their contributions. The staff members of the Greenville Public Library and the Greenville County Historical Society have been most helpful, as has Jonathan Pait of Bob Jones University, where the photographic collection of the Greenville County Historical Society is housed. Mike Nola, who runs the Shoeless Joe Jackson Virtual Hall of Fame on the Internet, has been a valuable source of information, as has Mrs. Ethel Jackson Copeland, the daughter of one of Joe Jackson's cousins. Mrs. Copeland provided me with the first two photographs that are reproduced in this book.

Eliot Asinof, author of *Eight Men Out*, kindly allowed me to ask about some of the details of the book that he wrote nearly forty years ago, and Furman Bisher, who interviewed Jackson in 1949, was also most generous with his recollections. I also appreciate the time and attention that I received from Mike Veeck, the son of the former owner of the Chicago White Sox.

Most of all, I am indebted to my wife Deborah, as much for her moral support as for her editing skills.

Library of Congress Cataloguing-in-Publication Data

Fleitz, David L., 1955–
    Shoeless : the life and times of Joe Jackson / by David L. Fleitz.

      p. cm.
    Includes bibliographical references and index.
    ISBN 0-7864-0978-9 (softcover : 50# alkaline paper) ∞
    1. Jackson, Joe, 1888–1951.   2. Baseball players—United States—Biography.   3. Chicago White Sox (Baseball team)—History.   I. Title.

    GV865.J29F54 2001
    796.357'092—dc21
    [B]   2001018318

British Library cataloguing data are available

Manufactured in the United States of America

McFarland & Company, Inc., Publishers
  Box 611, Jefferson, North Carolina 28640
  www.mcfarlandpub.com

Contents

Introduction

I spent a lot of time in libraries when I was a kid.

I'd make a beeline over to the shelves where books with the Dewey number 796.357 were kept. Here were housed all the baseball books. I read Ty Cobb's autobiography. And Babe Ruth's. And Frankie Frisch's, and Ted Williams', and Stan Musial's, and those of three dozen other players. I also devoured every book I could find about the history of the American and National leagues by writers like Fred Lieb, Lawrence Ritter, Lee Allen, and many others.

I realized that there was precious little information about the man with the greatest baseball nickname ever. All I knew of Shoeless Joe Jackson was that he once hit .408, hit .356 lifetime, was illiterate, and dropped out of sight after the Black Sox scandal. That's all. Oh yes, and everyone called him "the greatest natural hitter that ever lived."

Why was there so little information on the man with the third highest lifetime batting average in the history of the game? I found that Joe Jackson was relegated to a kind of baseball netherworld after his banishment from the game in 1920. Cobb, Ruth, Mathewson, Aaron—all had scores of books and articles written about them, meticulously detailing their lives and careers. Of course, they are all in the Baseball Hall of Fame, and their names are kept alive for each generation of baseball fans. Shoeless Joe, by contrast, is not in the Hall of Fame, and he seemed to drop out of the consciousness of baseball writers nationwide.

However, there were tidbits here and there. Lawrence Ritter's *The Glory of Their Times* (for my money, the greatest baseball book ever written) contained interviews with old-time ballplayers who remembered

Jackson and recounted some of his feats. Ty Cobb, a fellow Southerner, maintained friendly relations with Jackson and talked about Joe in his autobiography. Babe Ruth patterned his powerful swing after Jackson's. However, such mentions were few and far between, compared to the voluminous data on other players. Shoeless Joe remained a distant, ghostly figure, lost in time, who became legendary by the very dearth of information about him.

I read Eliot Asinof's fine treatment of the Black Sox scandal, *Eight Men Out*, and Victor Luhrs' *The Great Baseball Mystery*, on the same subject. Excellent books, both of them, but I wanted to know more about the man himself. What was Joe Jackson like? How many of the myths about him are true, and which ones are false? Did he like the name Shoeless Joe? Did some kid really ask him, "Say it ain't so, Joe"? Why would he throw his career away on such a foolish scheme, the rigging of the 1919 World Series? How guilty, in fact, was he? Should he have been banned for life, or was he more sinned against than sinning? Did he ever learn to read and write?

In 1989, the movie *Field of Dreams*, based on the novel *Shoeless Joe* by W. P. Kinsella, was released. The ghost of Shoeless Joe Jackson figures prominently in the story. "I loved the game," says Kinsella's Jackson in the book. "I'd have played for food money. I'd have played free and worked for food. It was the game, the parks, the smells, the sounds. Have you ever held a bat or a baseball to your face? The varnish, the leather...." This romantic image of Joe Jackson became so ingrained in the public imagination that sometimes you see quotations from Kinsella's novel attributed not to Kinsella, but to Jackson himself. Kinsella's ghostly invention, waxing poetic about the game of baseball, became the public image of the long-dead Jackson.

New attention came Shoeless Joe's way with the great success of *Field of Dreams*. Most of the clamor was of a maudlin, sentimental type — poor Shoeless Joe, an innocent man wronged, booted out of the game he loved in the prime of his career, and all that. Soon a movement to elect Joe Jackson to the Baseball Hall of Fame began to take shape, along with a wave of historical revisionism about the Black Sox. The eight banned players seemed to grow haloes above their heads. Somehow, the scandal became the fault of the greedy club owners, or the vicious new Commissioner Landis making a show of his power, or the nasty Chicago sportswriters.

My interest in writing this book is to find out the truth about Shoeless Joe Jackson. I won't dwell on the particulars of the Black Sox scandal in great detail, since other authors have already covered that same territory, and covered it very well. I'm not really interested in discussing which bagman delivered what amount of money to which middleman, or how each group of mobsters and gamblers double-crossed each other. I'm interested in Shoeless Joe Jackson—who he was, and why he did what he did. I will, however, tell the story of the scandal and its aftermath as it relates to Jackson himself.

I also want to separate the truth about the man from the myths that surround him. For example, one oft-told story about Jackson's days with the Philadelphia A's starts out with "Jackson stood on third base after slamming a mighty triple…" It doesn't take much effort to find out that Jackson hit no triples for the A's at all. Every one of his six hits in a Philadelphia uniform was a single. The other stories about him—that he played in his stocking feet, that he wound up scraping out a living as a pants presser, that he signed his contracts with an X, that he tried to warn the White Sox management about the fix before it happened—deserve to be examined also.

In recent years, several fine biographies of baseball personages have been published. These well-researched, even scholarly works were penned by men such as Charles Alexander (Ty Cobb, John McGraw) and Robert Creamer (Babe Ruth, Casey Stengel). These fine writers raised the bar of the baseball biography and proved that the term "sports journalism" is no longer an oxymoron. I think that Joe Jackson's life deserves the same biographical treatment.

Does Shoeless Joe Jackson belong in the Hall of Fame? I'll answer that in the last chapter.

Several other books have emerged in recent years about Shoeless Joe, all of which are more concerned with expanding on the myths than in examining them, and are more interested in getting Joe Jackson into the Hall of Fame than in telling his story. Jackson's life is interesting enough without all the sentimental embellishments that have grown up around his legend. It is not my intent to write a piece of campaign literature. I want to find out the truth.

David Fleitz
February 2001

Chapter 1

The Kid from Brandon Mill

> [Greenville County, South Carolina,] was a county of corn whiskey and ignorance. If a man learned to read and write, he was looked on as a freak.
> —*Eliot Asinof*[1]

South Carolina, the first Southern state to leave the Union in 1860, suffered bitterly during the Civil War. General Sherman and his army put Atlanta, Georgia, to the torch, and then hacked their way up the Atlantic coast, burning South Carolina's cities, destroying its factories and bridges, leaving devastated towns and ruined farms in their wake. At war's end in 1865 the once-proud state which led its neighbors out of the Union lay in ruins.

Plantation agriculture, while never really profitable, had been the foundation of the state's economy from Revolutionary times. In fact, in the mid–1700s two-thirds of the state's residents were African-American slaves. The state had never bothered to diversify its economy, and so the end of slavery and the Union army destroyed the entire economic base of the state. The large landowners and Confederate officials lost most of their property, and the plantations broke apart into small parcels of land for tenant farming. The proud jewel of the South became a state of share-croppers.

The carpetbaggers kept control until 1876, when a hotly disputed presidential election threatened to plunge the nation into chaos once again. The Republican candidate, Rutherford B. Hayes, secured his election with a promise to end Reconstruction. Soon Federal troops left South Carolina, and a terrorist organization called the Red Shirts drove freed blacks out of office, away from the ballot box, and even out of their own homes and communities with shootings and lynchings. The old white aristocracy, called the Bourbons, grabbed control of the state government once again. Violence, corruption and poverty sank South Carolina into an economic slump that it would not escape for decades.

Joseph Jefferson Wofford Jackson was born on July 16, 1888, in the most backward, depressed area of this state.[2]

Joe Jackson was born in Pickens County, located in the extreme northwest part of the state at the edge of the Blue Ridge Mountains, in what the South Carolinians call the "up country." George Elmore Jackson, Joe's father, worked as a sharecropper on a run-down former plantation, paying his rent with the crops he grew, hoping for enough extra to feed the family. The name of George Jackson's landlord has been lost to history, but the man was once described as "an eccentric old fire-eater" who quarreled regularly with his tenants. Storms, drought, and the many disagreements with the landlord drove George Jackson off the land. He found work at a cotton mill in the town of Pelzer, but he didn't stay there long. A few years after Joe's birth, George moved his family again, to Brandon Mill, about 12 miles away.

Brandon Mill was a company town that grew up around a huge, five-story textile factory of the same name, on the outskirts of the city of Greenville in Greenville County. Greenville, South Carolina, emerged from the Civil War as a major processor of cotton into cloth, and no fewer than eleven large cotton mills ringed the environs of the city. Brandon Mill stood on the west side of Greenville, and there George Jackson and his wife Martha set up a household in one of the small company-owned houses. George found work at the mill, and at a very young age, so did Joe.

Mill work was not much of a step up from sharecropping, but the pay was more regular, and a man like George Jackson could put his younger family members to work and earn more money for the household. As soon as the Jackson children were able, each in turn took on a shift at the mill. Joe Jackson's biographies usually say that he began work at the mill at age 13, but children as young as six might be assigned to work on an as-needed basis. Joe and the other Jackson children often accompanied their father to the mill, performing some of the less-demanding tasks and freeing the adult workers for the more demanding ones. Joe took on a full-time shift at 13, but he began his career in the mill at the age of six or seven.

Most of the men of Brandon Mill and many of the children worked 12-hour days, usually in dangerous conditions. School attendance was out of the question; for several generations, education remained a luxury that poor families like the Jacksons could ill afford. George and Martha Jackson's family grew almost yearly and totaled eight children by the time Joe turned 18. Mouths need to be fed, and the work at the mill, depressing as it was, paid the bills.

South Carolina's main economic resource seemed to lie in its huge pool of unskilled manual laborers. Poor whites from England had settled in the state since the 1700s, while others arrived later from Oglethorpe's former penal colony of Georgia. When its agricultural economy collapsed at the end of the Civil War, South Carolina became a state of itinerant former farm laborers, all desperately looking for work. This is where the cotton mills came in.

After the war, Northern business giants viewed the ruined South as fertile ground for exploitation, much as multinational corporations view third-world countries today. Northern textile manufacturers, looking to reduce the cost of doing business, found that these poor, underemployed Southerners would toil in factories for lower wages than people would accept in New England. During the Reconstruction era the textile industry moved south, closer to the cotton fields and the cheap labor, away from the unions and the pesky child labor laws. To this day the textile industry employs half of the workforce in South Carolina.

Few of these unskilled laborers could read, write, or manipulate numbers beyond the simple arithmetic of their meager pay and expenses. They fought dutifully in the Civil War, a conflict fought to preserve the economic privileges of the rich "low country" plantation owners, though the reasons for that conflict wholly eluded these simple mountain folk. Few of these poor people, except for the former Confederate soldiers among them, ever traveled more than a few miles from their homes in their lifetimes. In short, this part of South Carolina was about as poor and destitute as any part of America could possibly be.

Brandon Mill employed more than 800 people, and George Jackson worked as a tender of the engine. In those days, one giant engine powered a mill, and if the engine failed, the entire mill was shut down and no one got paid. Tending the engine was important work, but also hot, sweaty, and dangerous. George and the other adults in the mill worked 60 to 70 hours per week, six days a week, in hot, humid, and noisy conditions. The 40-hour work week was still decades away, and so were laws governing pollution. Mill workers like George Jackson breathed dirty, lint-filled air all week long, and respiratory infections and lung diseases were everyday hazards to which all the workers were exposed. Many of them would succumb to lung problems later in their lives.

Mill workers in the 1880s and 1890s earned very little money. A wage of a dollar a day sounded good to the unskilled former farm workers clamoring for jobs, but in reality, the mills wound up paying somewhat less than that. Some of the mills in Greenville depended upon the Reedy River for their power, and when the river ran low in the heat of summer, the mill simply sent everyone home. If the great engine failed, the mill might be closed for repairs for several weeks, and none of the workers would be paid. Not until about 1900, when the mills started running out of laborers, did the factories start paying anything resembling a living wage, in an effort to keep a stable work force at hand. By 1905 the daily adult wage at Brandon Mill was $1.25. That doesn't sound like much, but it was a 25 percent increase from the dollar a day of the previous decade.

Not much is known about George Jackson, who was 32 years old when his first son was born. The few photographs that exist of him reveal a mustachioed man with the same facial features as his son Joe, though he may have been a bit shorter than his oldest son. George was described as "one of the wiry type of South Carolina backwoodsmen,"[3] a whiskey-drinker and tobacco-chewer. Many people who knew him remarked on one physical feature that he shared with his oldest son. Both George and Joe Jackson had unusually long arms. George, as far as is known, never showed an interest in athletics, but his son used the arms that he inherited from his father to great advantage on the playing field.

George Jackson seems to have possessed a restless spirit, always looking over the horizon for a better deal in life. He left tenant farming to work in the mill, and in the passage of time George grew dissatisfied with the mill as well. Mill work was hard and sweaty, but the growing Jackson family needed food, clothing, and shelter, so George and his children trudged to the mill every day, rain or shine, winter and summer.

Martha Jackson, Joe's mother, was eight years younger than her husband. She was the rock of the family, a stout, no-nonsense woman who loved her family and struggled to keep the household afloat. Martha was the one who made sure that the family did no work on Sunday; though the Jacksons were not churchgoers, they considered themselves good Baptists. Martha was also fiercely protective of her children, and most of the neighbors considered Joe, her oldest son, to be Martha's favorite. Joe was the first of the Jackson children to go to work at the mill, and he was the first to contribute to the household expenses.

A boy of six or seven would start work in the textile mill as a "lint-head," sweeping lint and dust off the floors or dragging bags of cotton from one place to another. He would graduate to machine feeding and off-bearing tasks as soon as he could physically handle the work. Older, stronger boys could be utilized to carry large rolls from one place to another in the factory, or loading heavy materials onto carts. A child might earn about 25 to 50 cents per day at the mill; only when he was able to perform adult tasks would he be eligible for the full $1.25 per day adult wage.

Feeding the machines often proved dangerous, as a piece of clothing or a body part might become caught in the machinery. Dave Jackson, Joe's brother, suffered a series of such accidents. One day the conveyor belt carried him almost to the factory ceiling, then dashed him to the floor, breaking both an arm and a leg. On at least five other occasions, Dave broke his right arm when it became entangled in the rotating machinery. Dave was a fine baseball player, but by his early twenties his right arm was stiff from repeated mill injuries.

Joe Jackson was a quiet kid, big for his age, with brown hair and deeply set, penetrating brown eyes. He also had large hands, but the first thing most people noticed about him was the length of his arms. He had his father's unusually long arms, and Joe excelled at throwing and hitting in the makeshift ball games that the boys of the town enjoyed in the few hours of daylight left after their shifts ended. Sometimes the children would sneak off when no one was looking and play ball during lulls in their shifts. Joe Jackson found that he enjoyed playing ball a lot more than he enjoyed sweeping lint off the floors of the Brandon Mill.

Joe was a healthy boy, for the most part, but at about the age of ten an attack of the measles left him paralyzed. For two months he lay in bed, unable to move, with his legs tightly scrunched into his chest. Eventually the feeling in his limbs came back, as Martha Jackson nursed her oldest son back to health. Joe resumed his mill job and went back to playing ball after the end of his shift. The older men at the factory started to notice the tall kid with the long arms at this time. When Joe was only 13, they approached Martha Jackson about letting her oldest son play on the mill team.

Small towns in South Carolina were built around their mills and factories, and at the turn of the century, the mill owners cast about for activities to keep their workers interested and involved. Saturday afternoon baseball games became the most successful of these activities, so each mill sponsored a baseball team. The Brandon Mill team paid its players $2.50 per game, double a day's pay in the factory itself. There were no movies or vaudeville theaters in the area at this time, and these Saturday ball games provided virtually the only outlet of much-needed entertainment to the hard-working, poorly paid mill hands and their families. Thirteen-year-old Joe Jackson, a switch-hitter and a right-handed thrower, earned a place on the Brandon Mill team.

They put Joe Jackson on the mound, because he could throw a ball harder than any of the full-grown men in the entire mill. One day, in a practice game, Joe let loose with a fastball that broke a batter's arm; after that none of the other mill hands wanted to bat against him, so Joe had to find another position. They tried Joe at catcher, but he didn't like it there, especially after a throw smacked into his mask and bent the metal bar backwards into his forehead, leaving a scar that stayed with him the rest of his life. Martha Jackson wouldn't let Joe catch after that, so the manager placed him in the outfield. Soon the teenager was batting cleanup, belting line drives all over the park, making incredible throws, catching everything hit his way.

The kid emerged as the star of the team, and his batting talent made him a local celebrity around Brandon Mill. Every Saturday, it seemed, Joe would belt a line drive between the outfielders and make it all the way around the bases for an inside-the-park homer. Sometimes he even walloped the ball clear over the fence, an even rarer sight in those days. Joe Jackson became known all through the mill league for his home runs, which the locals called "Saturday Specials." He was only 14 or 15 years old when people started comparing him to Champ Osteen, a mill league legend from nearby Piedmont who by 1904 had graduated to a career in the major leagues. Osteen was the greatest ballplayer ever to come out of the mills, but there already were those who insisted that young Joe Jackson was a better player.

By age 15 Joe Jackson's ball-field exploits were already well known throughout the Carolina hill country. A local fan named Charlie Ferguson made bats in his spare time, and he chose a four-by-four beam from the north side of a particularly strong hickory tree to make one for young Joe Jackson. Ferguson turned a bat in his shop that measured 36 inches long and weighed about 48 ounces. It was a man-sized bat, far bigger than any bat used in the major leagues today, but Joe at 15 was the strongest man on the team. Ferguson darkened the bat with tobacco juice because he knew Joe liked black bats. Joe liked this one, too. He called it "Black Betsy" and he eventually took it to the major leagues.

Players at that time often jumped from one mill or factory to another, chasing better offers, and Joe was no exception. In 1907 Joe played for the Victor Mills team, representing a large factory in Greer, South

Joe (left) and his cousin William (Pink) Jackson in a photograph taken around 1903. Joe and his cousin played for the Tucapua Mill team in Spartanburg, South Carolina, in Joe's early teenage years (courtesy of Mrs. Ethel Jackson Copeland).

Carolina, a few miles north of Greenville. Joe also played for a semipro outfit called the Near Leaguers, managed by a local entrepreneur hoping to capitalize on the baseball fever sweeping the area. The Near Leaguers got their name from the fact that their league was as close to the ranks of organized baseball as it was possible to get without actually being in it. Joe often played for other teams in 1906 and 1907, depending on who paid the best at a particular time, and every now and then he'd return to West Greenville and play for Brandon Mill. Joe Jackson's services were highly in demand, especially when a game attracted a lot of betting interest between two towns or factories.

One day in 1907 a former big leaguer named Tom Stouch played second base in a game against the Victor Mills team in Greer and saw Joe Jackson for the first time. "This tall skinny-looking kid stepped up to the plate," recalled Stouch several years later. "He didn't appear to have much in him, but he drove the ball on a line to a spot where I was standing, like a bullet out of a gun." Stouch had no time to react. The ball ricocheted off his shins. "I thought to myself, if this rube hits 'em like that every time, he must be some whale.... When he hit, he left a trail of blue flame behind them as they shot through the air." Jackson hit a line drive back at the pitcher like "a shell out of a Krupp mortar," according to Stouch. "'Did you discover his weakness?' I asked [the pitcher]. 'No [said the pitcher] but he discovered mine!'"[4] Stouch's club played Victor Mills five times in a row, and they couldn't find a way to keep Joe Jackson off the bases. Tom Stouch made sure to remember Joe Jackson's name.

Joe was a dedicated ballplayer, but he had some of his father's traits in him. Joe, like his father, enjoyed his tobacco and his whiskey. Joe, in fact, liked his liquor so much that he often carried a flask of clear corn whiskey with him. This certainly didn't set Joe apart from his friends in Brandon Mill, but drunkenness was a serious problem in baseball in the early part of century. Joe was still only a teenager, and it remained to be seen if Joe's drinking would inhibit his success in the baseball arena. It was a habit that bore watching.

By 1907, Joe Jackson was well known all through the area, and his name began to appear in scouting reports to major league teams. In 1908 Tom Stouch became the player-manager of the Greenville Spinners, a new minor league team in the Class D Carolina Association, on the lowest rung of the organized baseball ladder. He approached Joe Jackson about playing for the Spinners.

"I'm getting along pretty well [at the mill]," Jackson told Stouch. "I get $35 a month from the mill, but I get $2.50 a game on Saturdays for playing ball, so that gives me $45 a month in all.... I think I ought to be worth $65 a month to you."

Stouch replied, "Joe, if you will promise to leave corn whiskey alone and stick to your business, I will pay you $75 a month."

Joe liked what he heard. "I'll play my head off for $75 a month," said Jackson, and he began his career in organized ball for $75 a month, more than twice the salary he was getting at the mill.[5]

No one taught Joe Jackson how to hit a baseball. It seemed to come naturally to him. "I used to draw a line three inches from the plate every time I came to bat," said Jackson many years later. "I drew a right angle line at the end of it, right next to the catcher, and put my left foot on it exactly three inches from home plate."[6] He stood in the box with his feet together, then took one long step into the pitch and ripped at it with his left-handed swing. In his younger days he batted right-handed against the few left-handed pitchers that he encountered, in order to ensure that their curveballs would always break into him and not away from him. However, Joe abandoned this practice when he got to the major leagues. His bat was much quicker from the left side, and he couldn't get the huge bat around as quickly hitting right-handed against major league pitchers.[7]

Hitters didn't uppercut the baseball at that time, since the ball didn't travel as far then, and an uppercut would produce nothing but a long fly out. Most hitters merely poked and slapped at the ball. Some, like Ty Cobb, held their hands several inches apart on the bat, the easier to punch at the ball and "hit it where they ain't," as Baltimore Orioles star Willie Keeler used to say. The outfielders played much closer to the infield than they do nowadays, perhaps 40 feet closer or more, because they knew that the slap-hitters would not often belt the ball over their heads. The fielders would give up the occasional double or triple in order to keep the batters from hitting lots of singles.

Joe Jackson, however, forced the outfielders to back up. He held his hands together near the end of Black Betsy and swung hard and level, unless the pitch looked so fat he could uppercut it over the fence. Onlookers marveled at how young Joe Jackson could swing so hard and strike out only rarely, because of his incredible reflexes and coordination. Most of Joe's hits were sharp line drives ("blue darters," they called them) that would skip between the outfielders and roll to the fence for a double or triple. Joe had grown strong from lifting rolls and hauling materials around the factory, and line drives fairly leaped off Black Betsy. When he got to the majors, players swore that Joe struck the ball so hard that his line drives sounded different from anyone else's.

Throwing, too, came naturally to young Joe Jackson. He liked to plant himself in the deepest part of center field at the Brandon Mill ballpark and thrill the fans by hurling the ball over the backstop behind home plate, especially if he caught a fly ball for the last out of a game. They called such a throw a "show-out" back then, and it kept the fans buzzing on their way out of the ballpark. The local boy could not only hit a ball harder than anyone else, he could throw it farther also.

The Brandon Mill batters didn't want to face the strong-armed Joe in batting practice, but they liked to see him pitch against other teams every now and then. In one game against the team from Sampson Mill, Joe doubled, tripled, homered, and pitched a two-hitter. A few weeks later he shut out a college team from Wake Forest with a four-hitter, though he managed no hits of his own that day.[8] It appeared that the naturally gifted Joe Jackson was one of those rare athletes who could excel no matter what position he played on the field.

Unfortunately, no one ever taught Joe to read or write. As the oldest of eight children, six boys and two girls, Joe was the first to go to work at the mill, and apparently Joe never attended a day of school. In a state that did not make high schools an official part of its educational system until 1907, education didn't seem like much of a priority. Joe couldn't read or write, but neither could many of his fellow mill workers. At the age of 19, Joe started his career in organized baseball unable to write his own name. He signed his playing contract with an X.

There was some grumbling heard around the mill. Sure, the kid was a good ballplayer, the best for miles around, but few young people ever made it out of the mill. Besides, he could only play ball for a few years. The mill paid only a dollar and a quarter a day, but it would be there forever. Where else could a young man go? Back to sharecropping? The options were few for young men with no education and menial skills. "He'll be back," the mill hands said knowingly.

There were, to be sure, very few avenues out of the mill for a young Southern boy in 1908. Northern kids, many of them recent immigrants, might enter show business, but drawling Southerners weren't usually drawn to that arena. The military beckoned, but the army didn't need many soldiers in peacetime, and many Southerners, still smarting from the Civil War, bore strong resentment about wearing Union blue. Colleges didn't give many athletic scholarships then, especially to young mill hands who never attended school. Professional athletics represented the best avenue to success, and in 1908 the sports from which to choose were limited to two: boxing and baseball. Baseball paid better, was much less painful, and offered the option of coaching or managing in an extensive, nationwide minor league network after one's playing days ended.

The Carolina Association featured six teams in the two Carolinas—Greenville, Greensboro, Anderson, Winston-Salem, Spartanburg, and Charlotte. Playing conditions were crude, and the teenaged Joe was as raw and undisciplined a rookie as they come. Several times that season he tried to steal a base that was already occupied by a teammate. He had a lot to learn, but he belted the ball at a .400 clip in the first few weeks of the season. Joe Jackson's spectacular hitting and fielding quickly caught the attention of the fans in the six cities.

Joe also used his superior throwing ability on the mound as a mop-up pitcher when necessary. In one game, manager Stouch watched four of his pitchers give up 15 runs to the Anderson Electricians. Stouch then waved Joe Jackson in from center field, and Joe shut them out for the last three innings. In another game, Joe threw a fastball that rode too far inside and struck the arm of a player named Meyers, who had just signed with the Brooklyn Dodgers of the National League. Meyers' season was over; Joe's pitch had broken his arm.

Greenville enthusiastically supported its new Carolina Association team, and Joe Jackson became one of its two biggest stars. The other was a smooth-fielding infielder-outfielder named Hyder (Scotty) Barr (or Barre), a 22-year-old former Davidson College star, who also took a turn on the mound every now and then. The Greenville Spinners, powered by the hitting and fielding of Jackson and Barr, quickly took first place and held it through the first half of the season.

Joe, a soft-spoken yet fun-loving young man, became a fan favorite. In the early part of the season, before the opposing outfielders learned to back up when Joe came to bat, Joe belted doubles, triples, and the occasional inside-the-park home run over the fielders' heads. The local paper, the *Greenville News*, delighted in Joe's batting prowess. "Watch the fielders get back this afternoon when Barre and Jackson come to the bat," said the *News*. "Laugh at them."[9]

Joe, the local boy, became the most popular member of the Greenville Spinners, and the fans liked to chant, "Give 'em Black Betsy, Joe! Give 'em Black Betsy!" when he came to bat. Often the fans would shower the kid with coins after a long home run or a spectacular catch, as Joe's five younger brothers scurried through the crowd passing the hat and picking up the change on the field. Joe gave this money to his mother, providing even more income for the Jackson household. One day, Joe's brothers collected $29.75 in coins after a Jackson home run. Stouch flipped a quarter into the hat. "Let's make it an even thirty, Joe," said the manager with a smile.

At the same time, Joe's father George quarreled with the mill owners, much as he had quarreled with his landlord on the tenant farm many years before. He quit his own job at the mill and, with financial assistance from his oldest son, opened a butcher shop. This work made George more independent, but it was less regular than the job at the mill, and the money Joe made from his ballplaying became more important than ever to the large Jackson clan. Joe, still a teenager, became the main breadwinner of the Jackson family.

By late June, Greenville opened up a five-game lead on the rest of the league, and Joe Jackson's fame spread through the Carolinas. He continued his "Saturday Special" tradition, earning a bonus of five dollars from the Greenville club owner for each home run, over the fence or inside the park. "It is unofficially stated that Joe Jackson's contract with the local club calls for a home run on every Saturday," said the *Greenville News*.

The Fourth of July fell on a Saturday that year, and the local fans flocked to the Greenville park to see Joe Jackson provide the fireworks. "Joe Jackson says that he is going to celebrate the Fourth in great style," said the *News*. "This rather indicates that the number of home runs will be not less than six." "How many home runs do you suppose Joe Jackson will get on the fourth?" asked the *News* on July 2. "Some of the fans have guessed anywhere from three to eight." Unfortunately, rain washed out the Fourth of July doubleheader; Joe made amends by belting a homer on the following Monday.

Throughout his baseball career, Joe was a creature of habit, and his hitting suffered whenever his normal routine was disrupted. In the second week of July, Joe broke one of his favorite bats and fell into a deep slump, the first of his professional career. The Spinners went into a 2-11 tailspin and fell into second place behind Spartanburg until Stouch righted the ship and got the Spinners winning again. The Greenville nine found themselves in a three-team race for the pennant with Spartanburg and Greensboro, the eventual winner. Joe battled his way out of his funk by late July and got his batting average back up in the .350 range, best in the league.

Joe got his nickname in that first season. One day he played in a new pair of spiked shoes, without breaking them in properly, and got painful blisters on his feet. Joe wanted to sit out the next game, against Anderson, but manager Stouch wouldn't hear of it. There were only 12 men on the roster, so Joe had to play. He solved the problem by playing the game in his stocking feet, and no one noticed until late in the game when Joe slid into third after crashing a triple. An Anderson fan shouted, "You shoeless bastard, you!"[10] and a local sportswriter heard it and gave Joe Jackson a new nickname. From that day forth, he was known as Shoeless Joe Jackson.

Joe didn't like his nickname at all, because he felt that it reflected badly upon his upbringing. All his life Joe Jackson was sensitive to his public image as a barefoot illiterate, whose gift for hitting a baseball seemed to be as randomly bestowed as an idiot savant's ability to play grand-master chess. To this day, many articles about Jackson wrongly state that he often played in stocking feet, or even barefoot. Such a feat would have been impossible on the rocky, debris-strewn outfields of the rural South at the time. In 1949 Joe told an Atlanta reporter, "I've read and heard every kind of yarn imaginable on how I got the name ... I never played the outfield barefoot, and that was the only day I ever played in my stockinged feet, but it stuck with me."[11]

He also started picking up superstitions, as many athletes do. If Joe saw a hairpin lying on the ground, he would always pick it up and put it in his back pocket. No one knows why Joe started doing this, or how he discovered that hairpins were lucky for him, but from his earliest games for the mill team Joe always picked up hairpins. For some reason, the rustiest hairpins brought him the most luck. In the major leagues, his back pocket would be full of them, and when Joe fell into a hitting slump he would throw away his collection of hairpins and start over.

The young slugger also liked to give names to his bats. Black Betsy, his first bat, was always his favorite, but he also liked to use the General, Dixie, Blond Betsy, Big Jim, and several others. Like many players, Joe felt that a bat only had so many hits in it, and he would put a bat away and use another one if he fell into a slump. Joe also broke out of a dry spell at the plate one day after he had accidentally dipped the end of his bat in some tar, and after that, Joe liked his bats to be half black.

By the summer of 1908, Joe Jackson had acquired a good amount of local fame and more money than most young men in the mill towns of South Carolina had at the time. Confident in his ability to earn a regular living in baseball, Joe married a local girl named Katie Wynn on July 19, 1908. Joe had celebrated his 20th birthday three days before. Katie was only 15 at the time, but no one considered this unusual at all in the rural South of that era. Katie had brown hair and blue eyes, and some education, since she could read and write. She remained married to Joe for 43 years, and until the day Joe died she wrote his letters, managed his money, and read his contracts in and out of baseball. Joe never did learn to read, but in the early days of his major league career, Katie helped Joe learn how to sign his name.

Tom Stouch played only four games in the major leagues, but he had contacts. At that time, the major league teams did not own minor league teams as they do today. Minor league clubs existed as independent outfits, making money not only from ticket sales, but also by developing players and selling them to teams higher up in the baseball food chain. The Greenville Spinners had two players, Scotty Barr and Joe Jackson, who could fetch a good price from the major leagues.

Stouch knew that this 20-year-old could go all the way to the big leagues. The Detroit Tigers were interested in Joe; ever since Ty Cobb came out of the South to stardom with the Tigers, the Detroit team had paid special attention to Southern phenoms. Stouch was also aware that the Washington Senators had sent a scout to look at Joe Jackson the previous spring. Joe Cantillon, a former catcher and manager of the Washington team,[12] saw Joe and dismissed him as "a bush leaguer flash in the pan" and stated firmly that Joe "would prove a farce in the big leagues."[13] Nevertheless, Stouch wasn't discouraged. He wrote to Connie Mack, manager of the Philadelphia Athletics of the American League, and told him about Shoeless Joe Jackson.

Managers today direct the team on the field and in the clubhouse, leaving the scouting and signing of players to others in the front office. In 1908, the manager performed all these tasks, and Connie Mack was better at it than almost anybody in the game. Mack, a tall, immensely dignified former catcher, served as the A's field manager, general manager, and scouting director all in one. He also at that time owned 25 percent of the club, and as befitting his station, Mack managed the team in a suit and tie, not in a uniform. He trusted his informal network of minor league scouts, and he decided that this kid tearing up the league down in South Carolina was worth a closer evaluation.

In mid–August of 1908, Mack sent Ralph (Socks) Seybold, an outfielder recovering from an injury, to Greenville for a look at Scotty Barr, who batted .299 that year and had a 12-6 record on the mound. Mack also told Seybold to look at the outfielder named Jackson, who was leading the league at the time with a .346 average. Seybold was impressed with the kid's incredible arm and his beautiful left-handed swing, especially after he saw Joe belt a double, triple, and homer against Charlotte. He wired Mack, who dispatched his aide Sam Kennedy for a second opinion.

"Barr is all right," Kennedy wired Mack, "but there's an outfielder

Joe and Katie Jackson on their wedding day, July 19, 1908 (courtesy of Mrs. Ethel Jackson Copeland).

here named Jackson who is burning up the league with his hits." Mack, whose A's had fallen far out of the pennant race by this time, had nothing to lose by giving the kid a chance. Mack wired back to Kennedy, "Buy both."[14] In August of 1908, Kennedy paid the Greenville Spinners a total of $1,500 for Jackson's and Barr's contracts. The *Greenville News* reported that Tom Stouch received $600 for Barr's services and $900 for Jackson's.[15]

Most young ballplayers would be excited about going from Class D to the major leagues, but Joe Jackson wasn't like most ballplayers. Scotty Barr hopped on a train for Philadelphia right after the Spinners' season ended, but Joe Jackson hesitated, to Stouch's great surprise. What's wrong with you, demanded Stouch. Every ballplayer wants to play in the major leagues. Don't you want to be a major league ballplayer? Stouch worked all his life to make the big leagues, but when he got to the Louisville Colonels of the National League he played only four games and never got close to the majors again. This Jackson kid could last for 15 years, making real money, and he didn't want to go! Stouch couldn't believe that anyone would feel that way. "Jackson is, in many respects, a queer fish, as you know," related Stouch a few years later.[16]

"I hardly know as how I'd like it in those big Northern cities," drawled Jackson. The 20-year-old Jackson was terrified of leaving home, and he was especially unhappy about leaving his bride of only four weeks. Joe's travels with the Greenville Spinners had never led him out of the South before, and the very thought of a city like Philadelphia, with nearly two million people in it, frightened him.

Jackson, being illiterate, never read the sports pages, and it is quite possible that he had never heard of either Connie Mack or the Philadelphia Athletics. The concerned Greenville paper said that Joe "did not much want to go north at this time and bump into strangers by himself."[17]

Tom Stouch decided to deliver Jackson to Connie Mack in person, mostly to protect his $900 sale. Manager and player met at the Greenville train station one warm mid–August evening. Stouch bought Jackson's train ticket, took him to dinner on the train, and even made sure that the kid was safely settled in his berth. The train would arrive in Philadelphia in the morning, and Tom Stouch would take Jackson and Black Betsy to the ballpark himself. The kid's a little scared, thought Stouch as he drifted off to sleep, but it would all work out in the morning.

Chapter 2

From Philadelphia
to Savannah

My other players didn't know what to make of him. He was a
regular sphinx, never entered into conversation with anyone.
—*Connie Mack*[1]

Tom Stouch woke up in Philadelphia to a surprise. Joe Jackson wasn't
in his berth. In fact, Jackson wasn't on the train at all. Stouch panicked,
fearing that Joe had been the victim of foul play, and it wasn't until he
got to Connie Mack's office that he learned what had happened. Stouch
found Mack holding a telegram, which Joe dictated from the Charlotte
train station. The telegram read, "AM UNABLE TO COME TO PHILADEL-
PHIA AT THIS TIME. JOE JACKSON."

"What does this mean?" asked the perplexed Mack.

Joe, as it turned out, had slipped off the train in Charlotte in the middle of the night and bought another ticket on a southbound train to
Greenville. After Stouch explained the situation, Mack sent Socks Seybold back to Greenville to retrieve Joe Jackson. "Go down to Greenville
and get this fellow's brothers and sisters, and his whole family to come
back with you if necessary," ordered Mack. "See that he doesn't give you
the slip on the way!"[2]

Mack couldn't believe the kid's behavior, but he was used to strange
antics from the likes of Rube Waddell, who pitched for Mack for several
years. Waddell was one of baseball's greatest pitchers, but he was also an

emotionally stunted man-child who demanded Mack's almost constant attention. Waddell disappeared in the middle of the season on fishing trips, demanded a contract stipulation that barred his roommate from eating crackers in bed, and enjoyed chasing fire engines, sometimes in the middle of a game. Mack used to dole out Waddell's salary a few dollars at a time, to keep the pitcher from blowing it all at once and going hungry for two weeks. For Connie Mack, managing a homesick Southern kid should be a piece of cake after dealing with Rube Waddell.

Soon after, Seybold arrived in Greenville and found Joe at home in Brandon Mill. According to the Greenville paper, Seybold told Joe that Scotty Barr "had made a good impression on the fans" and that Jackson would certainly do likewise. It took some doing, but in short order Joe Jackson was boarding another northbound train.

Seybold returned to Philadelphia with Jackson in tow, and on August 25, 1908, Jackson checked his bags at the train station and reported directly to the ballpark. On a dark, drizzly Philadelphia day, Mack put Jackson in the lineup against the Cleveland Naps (later known as the Indians). The kid belted the second pitch he saw from spitball artist Heinie Berger for a run-scoring single. He had no more hits in the game, but he drilled two hard liners to third and then drove the right fielder all the way to the wall with a fly ball. Joe also made a fine, over-the-shoulder catch in center field, and impressed the crowd with two long throws to the infield.

The Philadelphia papers covered Joe's first game in detail, since the A's poor performance so far in 1908 gave the papers nothing much else to write about all season. The *Evening Telegraph* devoted more than two whole columns to the new outfielder from South Carolina, and reported that Connie Mack was happy with his new player. "I was both surprised and immensely pleased," said Mack, "to see him do such splendid fielding today. He judges fly balls like a veteran, plays grounders well, and has a great throwing arm. Evidently Jackson is strong in all respects, without a weakness, and will make a great player for us."[3]

The *Evening Times* was even more enthusiastic. "Jackson surely looks as if he will do," said the *Times*. "He has justified the early predictions of his abilities. With experience and the coaching of Manager Mack, he should turn out to be what has been claimed for him, that he is the 'find' of the season."[4]

Joe Jackson, however, had other ideas. That evening he returned to the train station for his bags. As Jackson told the story later, he heard the station announcer call "Baltimore, Washington, Richmond, Danville, Greensboro, Spartanburg, Greenville…" Jackson couldn't resist. He tried to buy a ticket to go back home to Greenville, but the A's staff was watching him, and they talked Joe out of that course of action.

Joe rejoined the team as the A's prepared to face the first-place Detroit Tigers in a four-game series. The Philadelphia writers were so enthusiastic about Mack's new outfielder that they began awarding Joe more nicknames. "Shoeless Joe" was now "General Jackson" and "Stonewall," and when rainfall delayed the start of the series for two days, the papers celebrated the exploits of the kid from Brandon Mill all over again. The newspapers promoted the imminent matchup between the two Southerners, Jackson and Detroit's Ty Cobb, a Georgian who was already the top hitter in the American League at the age of 21.

Joe heard the other players talk among themselves about this strange apparition from South Carolina in their midst. Tom Stouch, who stayed with the Athletics for a few days, reported that Joe sat in the hotel lobby and listened to the other players compare him to the Detroit star. Joe merely sat and said nothing, but before the games could be played, Joe's homesickness got the best of him. The next morning, Joe Jackson slipped out of town and went home to Greenville once more.

Now Joe discovered how fickle the Philadelphia sportswriters could be. The same writers who sang Joe's praises mere days before turned against him viciously. The papers suggested that Joe abandoned the team not because he missed his family, but because he was afraid of competing with Cobb. This only made the fans more vociferous when Joe finally returned. Also, his teammates didn't appreciate being left shorthanded for two doubleheaders in two days, especially since Connie Mack had given some of his veteran players time off so that he could look at the youngsters.

The A's beat the Tigers three games out of four on August 28 and 29, but his new teammates resented the fact that Joe deserted them just before their important battle with the league leaders. Some of them made their feelings known to the local writers, anonymously accusing the young Southerner of cowardice. They apparently also resented the publicity buildup that the papers accorded the green rookie upon his arrival in Philadelphia.

Martha Jackson stoutly defended her son against the charges of cowardice. "Joe is game, and always has been game," said Martha defiantly. "He left Philadelphia because I sent for him." She flatly rejected the notion that Joe was afraid of Ty Cobb and insisted that Joe was called home because of an illness in the family. "I don't see how anyone could criticize Joe for doing what any man with any self-respect could not help doing,"[5] said Martha. Joe needn't have worried about the competition, since Cobb managed only one safe hit in the four game series, but Joe stayed at home in Greenville for the next week and a half.

This time Connie Mack sent his assistant Sam Kennedy to retrieve Jackson. It took a little more effort this time to convince Joe to return. Only after Mack sent Tom Stouch to intercede did Joe finally make his way back to Philadelphia. Joe reported again on September 7, and though the A's watched him closely, Joe would jump the team one more time before the 1908 season ended.

Connie Mack's intentions for Joe Jackson were quite clear. Mack's pennant winners of 1902 and 1905 had turned into an old team by 1908, one of the oldest in the game that year. The long career of third baseman Jimmy Collins was drawing to a close, and 34-year-old Harry Davis was slowing down at first. Jackson, figured Mack, could fill the hole in left field, where Socks Seybold had become injury prone at the age of 37. Pitcher Jack Coombs played left on days that he didn't pitch, but Mack wanted to move Coombs back to the mound permanently. The other two outfielders, Topsy Hartsel and Rube Oldring, hit .243 and .221 that year. Jobs stood wide open for the taking.

Mack, with his team solidly entrenched in the second division, spent the last two months of 1908 auditioning youngsters. New players reported to the aging A's all through August and September. Mack signed and promoted players such as Harry Krause, a left handed pitcher from California; Frank Baker, a third baseman from Maryland; and 19-year-old Amos Strunk, a hard-hitting outfielder. Jack Barry, a 21-year-old infielder, saw action at shortstop, where the incumbent Simon Nicholls batted only .216 that year. Eddie Collins, one year older than Jackson, came to the A's from Columbia University in 1906 and by 1908 seemed ready to plug the hole at second base, where five other players (including Scotty Barr) failed to make an impression.

The A's batted only .223 as a team in 1908, and only their fine pitching staff kept them from falling to seventh or eighth place in the standings. Above all, Mack needed hitters, and Joe Jackson, despite his immaturity, could hit on the major league level. However, Joe's stay in Philadelphia in 1908 became a living hell. Once the other players found out that he couldn't read or write, they razzed him without mercy.

Older players always made life difficult for younger ones in those days. The young guys wanted the older players' jobs, and the competition would usually turn nasty. Ty Cobb, who reported to the Detroit Tigers from Georgia in 1905, told of having his bats sawed in half, his uniform clothing torn up, and other indignities. One can only imagine an immature, homesick Southerner like Joe Jackson finding his way around up

North for the first time, not even able to read the menu in a restaurant or verbally fence with a fast-talking sportswriter. The old guys on the A's, sensing their careers ending as the next wave of stars arrived, lashed out at all the younger players but zeroed in on the immature and frightened Jackson.

The other young players were all Northerners except for Scotty Barr, who had a reputation as a ladies' man, so Jackson wound up alone almost all the time. Of all the players in the starting lineups of the 16 major league teams in 1908, fewer than a dozen were Southerners. Baseball in 1908 was still a Northern game, populated mostly by Irish Catholics from the East and farm kids from the Midwest, many of whom looked upon Joe as if he were some kind of circus freak. Joe Jackson, with his obvious illiteracy and South Carolina drawl, may as well have come to the A's from another planet.

When Joe managed to spend time with his teammates, his country ways and illiteracy stuck out despite his attempts to disguise them. In restaurants, Joe always ordered ham and eggs for breakfast because he knew every restaurant had that on the menu. At dinner he would hold his menu in front of him, make a production of studying it while listening to the other players' orders, and then ask for whatever sounded best from the other guys. This charade fooled no one. No wonder he hopped a train for home once more before the 1908 season ended.

Jackson didn't like the city, but he had nothing against Connie Mack, who had spent his childhood working in a factory just like Joe did. "He was a mighty fine man," Jackson said many years later, "and he taught me more baseball than any other manager I had."[6] Mack liked educated players and at the time had more college men on his team than any other manager. He also believed, however, that young, uneducated guys from the sticks would benefit from the presence of more refined players, that class and character would rub off on the Rube Waddells and Joe Jacksons. At the same time, Mack's gentlemanly demeanor helped him get more out of such players than a bully like New York Giants manager John McGraw ever could. It usually worked, but not with Joe Jackson.

The hazing got worse as the days dragged on. Experienced players liked to talk the green rookies into drinking out of the finger bowls at expensive restaurants, and they found no difficulty at all in getting Joe to embarrass himself thusly. The players didn't even need to award Jackson a nickname like "Rube" or "Cy," usually given to unsophisticates from the boonies. "Shoeless Joe" seemed to say it all, though "Brainless Joe" crossed more than one player's lips.

Joe didn't help matters any. He tried to hide his illiteracy by pretending to read magazines while traveling on the train. He would even exclaim "Wow! That's some story!" loudly enough for the other players to hear. Then he would disappear into the smoking car before the other players could ask any questions about the article he had "read."

Another story, possibly apocryphal, circulated about Joe. The dining room at the players' hotel had their guests write down their orders ahead of time. Each player wrote down the number of eggs he wanted for breakfast. One morning Connie Mack saw Joe with a huge pile of eggs on his plate. "How do you expect to play ball after a meal like that?" demanded the manager.

"I only asked for two, Mr. Mack," insisted Joe. "I don't know why I got so many eggs." A little more questioning on Mack's part revealed the answer. "I don't know how to make a two," admitted Jackson, "so I put down two ones." That's why he had 11 eggs on his plate.[7]

Joe also ran afoul of his teammates on the practice field. Connie Mack wanted his players to report to the ballpark promptly on the morning of a game (there was no night baseball at that time). Joe, like most rural Southerners of the era, was not a clock-watcher. He might show up on time, or he might show up 20 minutes or half an hour late. If Joe was feeling bad over some treatment he received from his teammates the day before, Joe might not appear at the park at all. The Greenville Spinners were a much more relaxed outfit than the Philadelphia A's, and Joe found it difficult to adapt to the more disciplined, businesslike Northern way of doing things in the major leagues.

The kid from South Carolina turned inward, barely speaking to anyone, responding to questions by looking at the ground and giving one-word replies like "sure" and "nope," if he replied at all. The Philadelphia fans, then as now the roughest in the nation, enjoyed roasting the homesick young man's ears with taunts like "Read any good books lately?" Fighting for a place in batting practice every day and listening to jeers from the stands took all the fun out of baseball for Joe Jackson. He missed his home and his new wife. He spent most of his nights alone, drinking in his room.

Connie Mack put Joe back in the lineup on Tuesday, September 8, against the New York Highlanders (now called the Yankees). Joe went hitless in five trips against pitcher Manning, then went 1 for 4 with another single against Lake and Chesbro the next day. In a doubleheader at Washington on Friday, September 11, Joe singled off Walter Johnson in the first game, a 2-1 loss for the A's, but he went hitless in the second contest, which the A's won 7-0 behind Jack Coombs. After that game, the frustrated Jackson went to the Washington train station, bought a ticket for

Greenville, and went home again. Joe remained in Greenville for the rest of the 1908 season.

Joe might not have left if he had known that a delegation of Greenville friends and fans was en route to Washington by train. The Greenville rooters attended Saturday's game between the A's and the Senators and wildly cheered the center fielder and cleanup hitter for the A's. In those days before players wore numbers on their uniforms, the Greenville fans had no way of knowing that they were cheering Danny Murphy, not Joe Jackson.

"Big league life wasn't just to the young man's liking," said the *Washington Post* after Joe's return to Greenville. "The tall buildings, and big crowds, and the clanging of the electric cars had the effect of making Joe long for that noiseless quiet life at home."[8] There was a great deal of truth in that statement.

Joe's first baseball card, an American Caramel card issued in 1909 (author's collection).

Joe found it painfully difficult to adjust to what appeared to him to be a foreign way of life. To Joe, Greenville was a bustling metropolis, compared to the shabby mill towns like Brandon Mill on the outskirts of the city. He had no idea how to get along in a city like Philadelphia, with more than 100 times Greenville's population. He didn't know how to eat in a restaurant, live in a hotel, or get around the city on streetcars.

Most importantly, Joe had never been on his own before. Though he was a married man of 20, he had never been away from his parents or siblings for any length of time. He missed his familiar Southern surroundings much as a homesick college student misses his hometown. Joe would have been perfectly happy to leave the major leagues behind and play ball in Greenville, where he was a local celebrity. "He told Connie

Mack ... that he'd rather be a star in the bushes than struggle for a regular place on a big league team," added the *Post*.[9]

After Jackson's third trip home Connie Mack tried a different tack. He placed his reluctant young slugger on the A's suspended list and told the newspapermen that Joe would play in Philadelphia in 1909 or nowhere at all. Joe would report to the team in spring training, promised Mack, or he would be suspended from organized baseball for life. Joe hated Philadelphia, but there was no way that he could simply return to the Greenville Spinners. The Philadelphia Athletics owned his rights, and they were going to keep him. Most players would have been released after their first trip home, but Connie Mack saw a star in the making, and he didn't have any intention of letting the young man go.

Jackson played in five games for the A's in the 1908 season. He hit only .130 in 23 trips to the plate, but Connie Mack liked what he saw. Mack and his co-owner Benjamin Shibe would have a brand new stadium, Shibe Park, when the 1909 season opened. Mack and Shibe optimistically planned for 20,500 seats in the new edifice, which was the first triple-decked concrete-and-steel stadium in the major leagues. The A's would have to win to fill the new park, and Mack needed a power hitter in the middle of his lineup if the A's were going win. He knew that Jackson could be that power hitter, but he also knew that Jackson needed another year to grow up.

Mack, a keen judge of human character, pinpointed the trouble with Shoeless Joe Jackson. "He was the town hero on his mill team, and thoroughly satisfied with his lot," said Mack. "He was the center of attraction at the village store in the evening and the whole town rang with his exploits. The trouble was that Jackson didn't want to come to the major leagues."[10]

The *Detroit Free Press* offered its own opinion of Jackson's troubles in the big city after he left the A's in late August. "Joseph is some ball player," said the *Free Press*, "but he shies at the cars."[11]

Joe Jackson spent a relaxing winter at home in Greenville, helping his father George operate the butcher shop that Joe had helped him buy. Sam Kennedy came to Greenville in the spring of 1909 to persuade Joe to report to spring training and give the major leagues one more chance. Joe Jackson, now the main breadwinner of the family, realized that the majors offered the best chance to make a livable wage not only for him and Katie, but also for his parents, brothers, and sisters. In March 1909, Joe decided to give the Philadelphia Athletics another try.

At the A's spring training camp at Savannah, Georgia, Connie Mack divided the team into the "Regulars" and the "Yannigans," which included the younger players like Eddie Collins, Frank Baker, and Joe Jackson. The Yannigans beat the aging Regulars all spring long with surprising ease. One day, Mack took his Yannigans to Louisville, Kentucky, to play the local minor league team. The Louisville management wanted to see the Regulars. "We'll murder these kids," complained the president of the Louisville team. He stopped complaining when the Yannigans, led by Joe Jackson's four hits, won the game by a score of 21-2. One of Joe's hits was a tremendous homer over the right field fence, one of the longest blasts ever seen in the Louisville ballpark.

Joe pounded the ball at a .350 clip in the spring games, but he still missed the South. He was understandably apprehensive about the reception he would receive from the hostile fans up North, especially after his disappearing act of the year before. Mack probably wanted Joe to start the season with the A's, but the razzing from the other players intensified, driving Joe even further into his shell. Besides, Joe liked Savannah so much that he decided that he wanted to stay there.

One famous story involves Jackson and a pile of milk cans. En route to Philadelphia prior to the start of the 1909 season, Jackson spied a shipment of empty milk cans at the railroad station. One of the cans had been painted red, indicating that it was to be returned to the plant down South. "I wish you'd tie me to that can and send me down South too," Jackson told Mack.

"All right," said Mack, "Just for that, I will tie that one on you," and sent Jackson back to the minor leagues.[12] Whether the story is true or not, Mack realized that his young slugger wasn't ready for the big time. On March 28 he sent Jackson on loan to the Class C team in Savannah for the 1909 season.

Katie and Joe moved to Savannah in the spring of 1909. Joe, who would turn 21 that summer, had grown even more, and now was about six feet tall and weighed 170 pounds. The South Atlantic League, also called the Sally League, played in Georgia and the Carolinas, Joe's home turf, and Joe felt far more comfortable here than he ever could in Philadelphia. He got off to a great start with the Savannah nine, and his batting average climbed above .450 in the first month of the season. Joe thoroughly enjoyed himself in his native South, and even talked his manager, Bobby Gilks, into letting him pitch in a few games. One day against Macon, Joe pitched three innings, allowing only one hit and striking out two.

Gilks also encouraged Joe by comparing him to Ty Cobb. "You're just as fast [as Cobb]," the manager told Joe, "and you can field and hit just as well. He's got a lot of nerve, and that's all you need to show him up."[13] Soon the papers were calling Joe the "Ty Cobb of the Sally League."

Despite Joe's hard hitting, the Savannah club lost more games than it won, and it settled into the middle of the standings as the local newspapers criticized the team mercilessly. Joe's bat cooled down a bit in midseason after Bobby Gilks was fired. Joe liked Gilks, and all through his career Joe's hitting suffered when his environment changed in any way. By August, the Savannah team was buried in the standings, and the young outfielder went back to his old tricks. Joe began to miss practice and pull stunts during the games.

One incident kept Joe broke for several weeks. In the middle of a game at Columbus, Georgia, late in the season, Joe and a teammate named Ed Luzon ("the official troublemaker," according to Joe) left the field, for no particular reason. They took seats in the stands and began munching on a bag of peanuts. The new manager, Ernie Howard, sent another player over to get the two back onto the field, but this player joined Joe and Luzon. Shortly afterward, Howard, recognizing a losing cause, joined the other three. The umpire, one Fred Westervelt, gave the four two minutes to return to the field. When they refused to do so, he fined Joe 50 dollars and handed out fines and suspensions to the others.[14]

Despite his antics, Joe Jackson held onto the league lead in batting all season long, and wound up with a .358 mark in 118 games. He also stole 32 bases and threw out 25 runners from the outfield. At the end of the Sally League season, Joe went back up to the A's. He reported to Shibe Park on September 4, 1909.

Shibe Park was the first of the new breed of concrete-and-steel stadiums that went up around the country in the years from 1909 to 1915. It had 20,500 seats, with standing-room space for thousands more, and many observers felt that the A's had wildly overestimated their ability to fill the new park. However, the pennant race had drawn thousands of new fans to the park, and the larger crowds brought new electricity to the games that hadn't been there before. Joe Jackson was accustomed to playing before a few hundred people in Greenville and Savannah. Now, he would appear before crowds many times as large.

In Joe's absence, the Philadelphia A's had undergone a significant makeover. Eddie Collins, Frank Baker, and Jack Barry claimed starting positions early in the season, making up three-fourths of a new infield, as 24-year-old John (Stuffy) McInnis waited for Harry Davis to relinquish the other infield slot. Left-handed pitcher Harry Krause cracked the A's formidable starting rotation and won ten games in a row from May to July. Six of those wins were shutouts, and Krause led the American League that year in earned run average.

Big league pitching, however, overmatched Scotty Barr. He played in 22 games and managed only four hits for an average of .078. Connie Mack hoped that Joe Jackson could pick up the slack and provide some much-needed power in the outfield.

This time, the A's were in the middle of a hot pennant race with the Detroit Tigers, winners of the previous two American League flags. The A's entered September four games behind Detroit in the standings, and every game was crucial. Connie Mack decided to pick his spots with Joe Jackson. He didn't want the immature youngster to buckle under the pressure of a pennant race.

Mack put Joe in center field for a game on September 7 against New York. Joe singled in a run his first time up, but he later struck out and misplayed a line drive by Hal Chase into an inside-the-park home run. The A's lost the game by an 8 to 6 score.

For the next three weeks, Joe watched from the bench as the A's tried desperately to claw their way past the Tigers. There was bad blood between the two teams all year long, which intensified when Ty Cobb spiked the A's third baseman Frank Baker in August. Cobb's spikes ripped Baker's shirtsleeve and slashed his arm, drawing a fair amount of blood. The Philadelphia fans nearly rioted, and the police escorted Cobb off the field, back to his hotel, and to the train station for his own protection.

The usually mild-mannered Connie Mack called Cobb a "dirty player" and a "thug" and called upon league president Ban Johnson to suspend Cobb, which only made the situation even more heated. A photo in the *Detroit News* seemed to prove that Baker's awkward tag, not Cobb's slide, caused the spiking, but feelings ran hot all over Philadelphia against the league leaders. If nothing else, the controversy served to heighten fan interest in the pennant race for the last month of the season.

The A's stood four games behind when the Tigers came to Philadelphia on Thursday, September 16, 1909 for a four-game series. Twenty-five thousand fans stormed the gates of Shibe Park, so many that the team had to call out the police to keep order. The huge crowd saw the A's beat the Tigers 2-1, as the distracted Cobb went 0 for 4 and struck out in the fourth inning with the bases loaded. That evening, mobs of angry fans followed Cobb as he took his after-dinner stroll; fortunately, Cobb and the Philadelphia fans exchanged nothing more than angry glares.

On Friday the Tigers struck back with a 5-3 win in front of 28,000 fans and restored their four-game lead. In that game Cobb stole third and then shook hands with Frank Baker, showing the crowd that all hard feelings were forgotten. He also accidentally smashed a spectator's hat while chasing a fly ball. In the next inning, Cobb handed a five-dollar bill to the surprised spectator, while the crowd cheered.

Joe Jackson watched from a corner of the dugout on Saturday, as a record 35,409 fans jammed into the park and overflowed into a roped-off section of the outfield. They saw veteran right-hander Chief Bender shut out the Tigers by a 2-0 score. There was no Sunday ball in Philadelphia at the time, so the two teams waited until Monday to do battle again. The A's beat the Tigers by a 4-3 score behind Eddie Plank in front of 29,000 fans, but the Detroiters left town with a two-game lead.

The September series between the A's and the Tigers demonstrated that Mack and Shibe had, if anything, built their new park too small. Crowds of 30,000 fans had been a great rarity before 1909, but after that date, more people became interested in attending major league games. More cars were appearing on the nation's roads at this time, and a sharp increase in car and train travel meant that fans could come to the games from longer distances. More than half the teams in the major leagues followed the A's lead and built new, larger facilities or remodeled the ones they had. In a few short years, the neighborhood ballpark would give way to the metropolitan stadium.

The Athletics could get no closer to the Tigers for the rest of the season, and on September 30 the Tigers clinched their third American League pennant in a row. On that day, Joe finally entered the lineup for the first time in three weeks, going hitless against the Chicago White Sox in the first game of a doubleheader. He pinch-hit for starting pitcher Harry Krause in the second game and grounded into a forceout, though he later scored a run. Two days later Joe managed only one single in a season-ending twin bill against the Senators.

Chapter 3

Joe Arrives in Cleveland

> Like most young fellows, when they get into the big league, I thought I knew as much as any of the oldsters, and not only that, but I had made up my mind that I'd do as I pleased, regardless of what anyone said. I know now that I was wrong, but I don't suppose that excuses my conduct any.
> —*Joe Jackson, 1912*[1]

If Connie Mack hoped that Jackson had matured with one more season in the minors, he was sorely disappointed. Katie came to Philadelphia this time, but Joe again found only loneliness and ostracism in the big cities of the North. One day Joe stood on third base when a fan shouted, "Hey, Joe, can you spell 'cat'?" to a loud chorus of laughter. Joe, according to onlookers, spat out a stream of tobacco juice and drawled, "Hey mister, can you spell 'shit'?"[2] His teammates gave him no assistance either, since Connie Mack's lineup was almost set, and the rebuilt A's challenged for the pennant in 1909 without Joe Jackson's help. They were filling the new ballpark too; the A's attendance of 675,000 set a new club record that year. The team didn't need Jackson, and the hazing and ridicule intensified.

Joe, an amiable enough if soft-spoken young man ("a friendly, simple, gullible sort of fellow," said Ty Cobb many years later), turned even more inward. His teammates, almost all Northerners, had no use for Joe Jackson, but Connie Mack still tried to get through to him. Mack offered to engage a tutor to teach Jackson to read and write, but the young Southerner's

33

prickly pride would not allow that. "I ain't afraid to tell the world that it don't take school stuff to help a fella play ball," said Jackson.[3]

Joe, though he earned more money than most of his former fellow mill hands could ever dream of making, seemed to lose interest in baseball. He played in only five games for the A's in 1909, with three hits in 17 trips for a .176 average.[4] Joe's attitude also frustrated Connie Mack. The young Southerner didn't always show up for practice in the morning, which endeared him even less to his more businesslike teammates.

Mack finally lost his patience one day in September, at the height of the pennant race. One day Joe was scheduled to play center field for the A's. The streetcar taking Joe to the ballpark rolled past a burlesque house, and without a word to anyone Joe hopped off and spent the afternoon watching the show. After that stunt Joe's goose was cooked in Philadelphia, so Mack shrugged his shoulders and reluctantly decided to part company with Shoeless Joe Jackson. Mack managed to keep Rube Waddell, strange behavior and all, productive for a good six seasons. He gave up on Joe Jackson after only ten games.

According to Joe's recollections a few years later, Mack asked Joe where he'd like to play and promised to do his best to send Joe there, wherever it was.[5] "I'm sorry, Jackson, that you refuse to settle down and take ball-playing seriously, because you have the making of a crackerjack player in you," said Mack to the immature young Southerner. "I believe you said you wanted to play with New Orleans, didn't you? Well, report there at once."[6] With that, Mack sent Joe on loan to the New Orleans Pelicans of the Southern League for the 1910 campaign, and Joe reported to the Pelicans' spring training camp in March of 1910.

The Pelicans had a close relationship with the Cleveland Naps (now called the Indians) of the American League. The New Orleans team was not a farm team of the Naps in the modern sense, but Naps owner Charles Somers owned the Pelicans also, and many Cleveland players arrived in the major leagues via New Orleans. Somers got a good look at Joe Jackson that spring and marveled at the young man's batting and throwing skills. In addition, Bob Gilks, Joe's manager at Savannah, was now a scout for the Naps and raved about the young slugger's potential.

Connie Mack knew that Joe would never succeed in Philadelphia, but he didn't want to trade or sell Jackson to a competitor in the same league. However, trading him to the hated National League was completely out of the question, and Mack would rather send Joe to a friend like Charles Somers. He did so after clearing one final hurdle. Joe had to clear waivers before he could be transferred to New Orleans, and Brooklyn Dodgers owner Charles Ebbets put in a claim for Jackson. Mack wrote

Ebbets a note, stating that Joe would never make it in the major leagues, and Ebbets dropped his claim.[7]

Joe explained his feelings in characteristically few words. "It wasn't anything I had against Mr. Mack or the ball club," said Jackson in 1949. "I just didn't like Philadelphia." However, Joe enjoyed himself in New Orleans. He hooked up with his former Greenville teammate Scotty Barr, whom Mack had released to New Orleans shortly before, and the combination of familiar teammates and Southern living brought Joe's bat to life again.

The 21-year-old Jackson also resolved to "cut out my kiddish ways" and "attend strictly to my knitting," as Joe put it in an interview two years later.[8] He was beginning his third year in professional baseball, and he was responsible for his wife and extended family back home in Greenville. Joe recognized that he needed to change his lackadaisical attitude if he were to succeed at his chosen profession. If he failed, his only other option was to return to South Carolina and find work in a textile mill.

Joe, perhaps taking a cue from the professional example of Connie Mack, became more diligent in his work habits. He knew that his strength was his most important asset, so he devised an exercise to build up his arms and wrists. Joe held the heaviest bat he could find at arm's length, straight out in front of him, for as long as he could stand it. When he finally dropped the bat, he'd repeat the process with the other arm. On the field, Joe followed the lead of Ty Cobb and swung three bats in the on-deck circle, so that one bat would feel lighter at the plate.

Jackson also devised an eye exercise, in which he would stare at a lighted candle in a dark room with one eye closed for as long as the flame remained in focus. When the flame finally disappeared, Joe would repeat the exercise with his other eye. Joe felt that this process helped him to focus on a pitched ball on its way to the plate.

Happily, Joe Jackson finally matured as a ballplayer in New Orleans. He caused no more problems with his behavior, and he impressed onlookers with his dedication to the game. Joe led the Pelicans to the Southern League pennant, and though he suffered a beaning in late August that sidelined him for a few days, he batted .354 to win his third minor league batting title. Joe, who became one of the most popular players ever to appear in a Pelicans uniform, stole 40 bases and led the league with 82 runs scored and 165 hits. The fans in New Orleans chanted "Give 'em Black Betsy, Joe!" when he came to bat, just like Joe's hometown fans in Greenville.

Joe found something else in New Orleans. He became fascinated with vaudeville and went to any show he could find. He knew that men like Christy Mathewson and John McGraw made money in the off-season by delivering monologues on the vaudeville stage, and his fellow southerner Ty Cobb supplemented his baseball salary with public appearances and speeches. Jackson learned that success in the major leagues could translate to much more money than his baseball salary alone.

During his stint at New Orleans, Jackson remained the property of the Philadelphia Athletics, for if Mack had sold him outright to New Orleans Joe would have been subject to the minor league waiver draft in the fall of 1910. This way, Mack was able to get something for his difficult young outfielder. On July 23, 1910, Mack traded infielder Morrie Rath to the Cleveland Naps for an outfielder named Bristol Lord and an unknown amount of cash.[9] Eight days later, the Naps gave the cash to New Orleans in exchange for the rights to Joe Jackson. This deal kept Joe out of the draft and made possible his transfer to the Cleveland club. The Chicago Cubs, and several other teams, had kept an eye on the young slugger's progress in New Orleans, and they almost certainly would have chosen Joe in the draft if he had been available.

Bris Lord, called the "Human Eyeball" for his incredible eyesight, played for the A's for three seasons before going to the Cleveland team in 1909. At the time of the trade, Lord was hitting only .218 in 58 games. Still, Mack needed help in the outfield, as well as another right-handed bat in his lineup, and Lord was a known quantity to him. Mack approached the Naps about Lord in mid–July, but the Naps held firm for Jackson. "Give me a right-handed outfielder for Rath," Mack told the Naps, "and I will surrender my rights to Jackson."[10] Mack gave Jackson's rights to the Pelicans, who then worked out the deal with Cleveland.

Connie Mack parted with Joe Jackson reluctantly. Mack wanted Jackson to succeed in the worst way, but the other A's made their feelings about Jackson known in no uncertain terms. The A's led the American League at the time of the trade (and would win the pennant by the margin of fourteen and a half games over New York) and Connie Mack didn't want his young first-place team disrupted. Lord spelled the weak-hitting Topsy Hartsel in the outfield, batting .278 in 72 games, as the A's cruised to the pennant and a World Series win over the Chicago Cubs that fall.

Mack and Cleveland owner Charles Somers went way back. Somers, a millionaire coal magnate, bought the Cleveland franchise in the new American League in 1901 and provided much-needed funds to several other American League owners during their war against the established National League. In fact, Charles Somers was the financial angel of the American League; at one point Somers owned parts of four of the eight teams in the circuit. The Boston team nicknamed itself the "Somersets" in his honor, several years before they became the Red Sox.

Somers helped Mack's team financially several times in 1901 and 1902, and he took star infielder Napoleon Lajoie off Mack's hands when the rival Phillies obtained a court order prohibiting Lajoie from playing for the A's. However, by 1910 Somers was the man who needed help. It seems that Charles Somers epitomized the phrase "generous to a fault." Most of the other seven teams in the league prospered by 1910, but the Cleveland Naps struggled to stay afloat.

Many years later Mack explained his decision to let Joe Jackson go as a favor to his friend Somers. "I knew exactly what I was doing when I let Jackson go to Cleveland," Mack said. "Lord, of course, helped me at the time. I knew our players didn't like Jackson, but that isn't why I traded him. I also knew Joe had great possibilities as a hitter. But at the same time things were going none too well for Charlie Somers in Cleveland, and I was anxious to do him a good turn in appreciation for the way he had helped us out in Philadelphia in the early days of the league. So I let him have Jackson."[11]

Joe spent the entire Southern League season at New Orleans, since the deal between the A's and Naps specified that Jackson would not report to Cleveland until the Pelicans' season was over. By early September, the Pelicans had clinched the flag, and the Naps sent for the young slugger. The Cleveland papers followed Jackson's exploits in New Orleans and publicized his imminent arrival for weeks, giving the fans up North something to look forward to in the last month of the season.

Predictably, Joe hesitated to go North once again, but Bob Gilks convinced the young Southerner that Cleveland was a much different place than Philadelphia. It was a smaller, more rural city, and the fans were not nearly as vicious as the ones in Philly. After much discussion with Gilks and Katie, Joe agreed to give Cleveland a chance. In September 1910, he joined the Naps. He would find much smoother sailing in Cleveland.

More than 30 years later Connie Mack, still managing the A's, lamented the lack of talent on his team. Ted Williams of the Red Sox battered Mack's pitching staff all season long in 1941, and on the last day of the season Williams went 6 for 8 against the A's to finish the year with a .406 average. "I wish I had a Williams," said Mack. "I had one once and I lost him. Joe Jackson, one of the greatest hitters of all time."

Joe Jackson reported to the Cleveland team on September 15, 1910. He was supposed to arrive a few days earlier, but he missed his train

Joe at the ready (author's collection).

connection in Cincinnati, and Cleveland officials feared that Joe had changed his mind and gone home as he had done with the A's several times before. This report proved to be false, as Joe arrived in Cleveland with his wife Katie and scout Bob Gilks, Joe's manager at Savannah in 1909.

The Cleveland team was known as the Bronchos and the Blues in its early days, but when the popular second baseman Napoleon Lajoie joined the team in 1902 the writers and fans called the team the Naps in his honor. Lajoie was a French-Canadian who grew up in Rhode Island, and like Joe Jackson, Nap Lajoie spent most of his childhood working in a textile mill. Lajoie played on a semipro team in New England, and when the Philadelphia Phillies bought one of Lajoie's teammates in 1896, the semipro team threw the 20-year-old Lajoie into the deal for free. The teammate didn't last, but Nap Lajoie became one of the biggest stars in baseball.

Lajoie, usually called "the Frenchman," became dissatisfied with the Phillies by 1900, especially when the National League instituted a maximum salary of $2,400 for all players. He jumped across town to Connie Mack's A's in the new American League, where he belted the ball for an unbelievable .422 average in the 1901 season. The Phillies obtained a court order barring Lajoie from playing for the A's, and so Connie Mack reluctantly transferred the Frenchman to Cleveland early in the 1902 campaign. The judge who issued the court order in favor of the Phillies was not amused, and he issued a warrant for the Frenchman's arrest. For the rest of the 1902 season, Lajoie stayed out of Pennsylvania, because he could have been arrested if he had set foot in the state. He vacationed at Atlantic City when his Cleveland teammates played in Philadelphia. Fortunately, the two leagues made peace in 1903, and the Phillies dropped their case against Lajoie.

The Frenchman won three of the first four American League batting titles, and in 1905 he became manager of the team that was named for him. Lajoie's team challenged for the pennant in 1908, losing to the Tigers by half a game when Detroit wasn't required to make up a rainout game. Lajoie's hitting suffered in the five years he served as manager, and late in the 1909 season Lajoie stepped down as manager but continued as an active player. The release of responsibility seemed to invigorate the Frenchman, and when Jackson joined the club Lajoie and Detroit's Ty Cobb were locked in a fierce battle for the batting championship. The winner of the title would receive a new Chalmers automobile.

The Naps, like the A's, were going through a transition phase. Cy Young, who began his pitching career with the Cleveland Spiders of the National League in 1890, won only seven games in 1910 after winning 19 the year before. At the age of 30, perennial 20-game-winner Addie Joss nursed a sore arm all year and was also troubled by a sudden and severe loss of weight and strength. Joss, one of the finest pitchers in baseball in the first decade of the century, left the team in late July and went to Sandusky, Ohio, to recuperate on the beaches of Lake Erie. The Naps were far out of the pennant race by this time and spent the last two months of the season auditioning young players, including Joe Jackson.

Nap Lajoie was still hitting as well as ever, but the rest of the roster got old all at once. Third baseman Bill Bradley, a mainstay of the Naps since 1901, batted .196 in 1910. Outfielder Elmer Flick, a future Hall of Famer who joined the Naps in 1902, played only 66 games in 1910 due to illness. The age of key players and lack of starting pitching dropped the team to sixth place by the time Jackson joined the club. Manager Deacon McGuire, a respected old catcher, had the team in the running early in the season, but by July the fans and newspapers openly ridiculed the team, calling them the "Molly McGuires." One sportswriter referred to the team as the Napkins, "because they fold up so easily."

With the attendance falling, team owner Charles Somers, genuinely well liked by the players, began to have financial problems. Somers knew that his aging team needed rebuilding, and he hoped Joe Jackson would add a charge to the middle of his lineup.

Joe Jackson found, to his relief, that the Naps were a much friendlier team than the A's had been. The team had no more internal tensions than any other club, despite the fact that their ex-manager was not only an active player, but also the biggest star on the team. Lajoie was not the field captain of the team that was named for him; George Stovall, a tough, hard-bitten first baseman, filled that role. In 1907 Stovall and Lajoie got into a heated argument in a hotel lobby, which ended when Stovall broke a chair over the Frenchman's head, but that incident didn't harm the relationship between the two men. "George didn't mean anything by it," said Lajoie afterwards, and for the most part manager McGuire, ex-manager Lajoie, and captain Stovall got along just fine.

The Cleveland Naps were not one of the highly professional, businesslike major league clubs, like Connie Mack's Athletics or John McGraw's New York Giants. However, they weren't one of the "joy clubs," either. The "joy clubs," in the parlance of the era, were the teams that had no realistic chance to win the pennant and went about their business lackadaisically. The New York Yankees, after Hal Chase took over as manager in 1910, were well known for singing on the bench between innings and laughing at their own dropped fly balls. The Naps were not as undisciplined as the Yankees—professionals like Nap Lajoie and Cy Young would not allow that—and they could have fun without embarrassing themselves on the field. The Naps appeared to be the perfect kind of team for a young man like Joe Jackson.

The veterans like Lajoie, Joss, and others didn't see young players like Jackson as a threat to their jobs, and they made the young southerner feel welcome. In addition, Jackson's new teammates enjoyed playing for Charles Somers, one of the best-liked owners in baseball. At that time, Washington had no Sunday baseball, and when the Naps played a weekend series there they would return by train to Cleveland for a Sunday game, then hop on the train back to the East on Monday. Somers, to show his appreciation of his team's efforts during the grueling travel schedule, would walk through the train passing out $20 gold pieces to the players.[12]

It is possible that the players accepted Jackson because he took Lord's place without driving another outfielder off the team, unlike the situation in Philadelphia where a young player's success meant an older veteran's failure. It is also true, however, that the Naps had several southerners on the team, and many of the northerners had come to the Naps by way of New Orleans. They had experienced southern life first hand, and so Jackson did not seem as strange to his new teammates as he had to the college men on the A's. The Naps also had their fair share of drinking men, and Joe Jackson, who carried his own corn whiskey with him, fit in with this crowd.

Whatever the reasons, Jackson felt comfortable with the Naps, and he made his Cleveland debut on Friday, September 16, against the Washington Senators. Joe made a great shoestring catch in center field in the third inning and got his first hit in a Cleveland uniform, a sharp single, in the eighth. "Joe Jackson looks good," said a subheadline in the *Plain Dealer* the next morning. The paper added approvingly, "Jackson showed he was not a dirty ballplayer in the fifth inning, when he refrained from sliding into second base on an attempted steal. Had he done so he would have spiked McBride, who overran the bag in taking Ainsmith's throw."[13] In the next day's game, Joe whacked his first major league home run, a two-run shot over the center field fence off the Senators' Bob Groom.

The Naps then traveled to Philadelphia to face Jackson's old team, the first-place Athletics. Joe ignored the taunts of the Philly fans and belted a triple, followed by three fly balls to Bris Lord. Topsy Hartsel, the A's center fielder, was impressed. "Jackson does not look like the same player he was with us," said Hartsel. "He has improved 1,000 percent."[14] The A's clinched the pennant against Cleveland on September 21, when

Napoleon Lajoie, star of the Cleveland Naps from 1902 to 1914.

the A's and Naps played an 11-inning scoreless tie as the second-place New York Yankees lost.

In all, Joe Jackson played 20 games for the Naps in 1910, in both left and center field, and belted the ball at a .387 clip, with 29 hits in 75 trips to the plate. Jackson finished the season with an average two points above that of Detroit's Ty Cobb, though Jackson did not bat enough times to be eligible for the batting title. Still, his name topped the list of averages at the end of the season, and baseball fans around the country started to take note of Shoeless Joe Jackson. The Cleveland papers called Joe the "nominal batting champion of 1910."

Jackson played left field and had four hits in the controversial season-ending doubleheader at St. Louis on October 9, 1910. The well-liked Lajoie and the hated Cobb entered the last day of the season in a near dead heat for the batting title, and the Chalmers automobile company promised a shiny new car to the winner. Most of the players in the American League wanted Lajoie to win the car, so the last-place Browns decided to give him some assistance. After Lajoie slammed a triple in his first time at bat that day, Browns manager Jack O'Connor ordered his rookie third baseman Red Corriden to play Lajoie halfway into the outfield. The Frenchman then laid down eight consecutive bunts, seven of which went for base hits. What's more, Browns coach Harry Howell offered the official scorer a new suit of clothes to change his ruling on another Lajoie bunt that was ruled a fielder's choice.

At day's end, it appeared that Lajoie had overtaken Cobb for the title, and the St. Louis fans cheered the Frenchman at game's end. Lajoie's apparent victory made the front pages of the Cleveland papers, though the league later ruled Cobb the winner (and Browns owner Robert L. Hedges fired both O'Connor and Howell).[15] The Chalmers company, grateful for the publicity, gave a new car to both Cobb and Lajoie. After this, the automaker decided to use a vote of sportswriters to determine the winner of their award in future years, and from this controversy came the Most Valuable Player award that we know today.

In the last weeks of the season the Naps passed the Chicago White Sox to finish in fifth place with a 71-81 record, 32 games behind the A's. In October 1910 the Naps and the Cincinnati Reds, who finished fifth in the National League that year, played an "All-Ohio Championship," a seven-game post-season series. Somers hoped for big crowds, but the weather refused to cooperate and the attendance averaged only about 5,000 per game. Still, the Cleveland players took home $171.30 each from the series receipts, a welcome bonus at a time when most players made only a few thousand a year.

The Reds won the series four games to three (winning $233 per man), but the seven-game set gave the Naps hope for the 1911 season. One reason was the pitching of Addie Joss, who won the second game 5-3 after three months of inactivity. The other reason for optimism was the hard hitting of Joe Jackson. Joe batted third in the lineup and played center field for the Naps, and had ten hits in 28 trips to the plate for a .357 average in the series.

After the last game of the series, Joe went home to Greenville. He took Black Betsy and the rest of his bats with him; as Joe liked to say, "Bats don't like to freeze no more than me." For the first time in three years, he had ended his season on a positive note. No longer the frightened Southern boy wary and distrustful of his teammates, he was now, at age 22, an up-and-coming major league star.

In late September of 1910, Yankee manager George Stallings accused his star first baseman, Hal Chase, of deliberately "laying down" against opposing teams. Rumors had swirled around Chase for several years. Chase, a popular, personable, smooth-fielding first sacker, enjoyed the night life of Manhattan and seemed much too close to the world of gamblers and "sporting men" for the comfort of his manager. The previous two Yankee managers, Clark Griffith and Kid Elberfeld, had voiced the same concerns.

Joe warming up to pitch. Oddly enough, he is wearing street shoes (author's collection).

Stallings brought his suspicions to the Yankee owners, who did not want to part with the most popular player on the team. The Yankee owners not only absolved Chase, but also fired Stallings and hired Chase to replace him as manager. "What a way to run a ball club!" marveled third baseman Jimmy Austin more than 50 years later. The Yankees, who finished a strong second in the league under Stallings, dropped to the second division in 1911 under Chase.

American League president Ban Johnson held a hearing—to which Stallings was not invited—and afterwards praised Chase and roundly criticized Stallings. "Stallings has utterly failed in his accusations against Chase," said Johnson. "He tried to besmirch the character of a sterling player. Anybody who knows Hal Chase knows that he is not guilty of the accusations made against him."[16] For the next decade, baseball's leadership would quickly sweep any suspicions of gambling and game fixing under the rug.

The Chase incident and the batting title controversy should have served as warning signs that all was not right with the national pastime. The *Chicago Tribune* proved to be unusually prescient in writing about the Cobb-Lajoie race:

> What must a meek outsider think
> When tricks like that they put across?
> When at one frameup they will wink
> How do we know what games they toss?[17]

Chapter 4

.408

Anyway, I started out to talk about Jackson the ballplayer. His first year he hit .408. Imagine a busher doing that! And he was swinging against the dead ball, the spitball, the shine ball, and all that sort of trickery. ... Jackson couldn't read or write, but the secret of batting was an open book to him.
—*Joe Williams, 1946*[1]

Joe Jackson spent the winter at home in Greenville with his family, helping his father in the butcher shop and generally enjoying the adulation of the locals. The successful end to Joe's 1910 season made him look forward to the start of the 1911 campaign, and for once he couldn't wait for spring training to begin. In late February of 1911, Joe spent a week in New Orleans practicing with his former Pelicans teammates, sharpening his batting eye by day and enjoying the vaudeville shows at night.

Jackson arrived at the Cleveland Naps training camp in Alexandria, Louisiana, on March 6, 1911. From the first day, Joe was the talk of the camp. He arrived in perfect playing shape, belting line drives all over, and announced his intention to beat both Cobb and Lajoie for the 1911 batting title. "More power to you, old boy," said Lajoie with a laugh when he heard the 22-year-old Jackson's boast.

Joe's words also reached the ears of Ty Cobb, but the hard-fighting Georgian didn't seem to mind. "I am not jealous of Joe Jackson," said Cobb in early April. "I wish him all the luck in the world. I hope he hits .400, for that matter, for if he does, I am going to try to top him a point or two."[2] Indeed, Cobb and Jackson, who grew up within 100 miles of each other down South, became friends and often socialized when their teams met during the season. Cobb got along much better with Jackson than he did with his own teammates. Still, Cobb's ego took a beating in the batting race shenanigans of 1910, and the proud Georgian resolved that no one would get close to him for the 1911 batting title.

In the relaxed atmosphere of training camp, the Cleveland writers got their first good look at Joe Jackson. Joe had already started developing a sense of fashion, since the papers called him the "Beau Brummell" of the Naps upon his arrival. The former Shoeless Joe now owned several pairs of expensive shoes, and he sported a double-breasted suit and a jaunty felt porkpie hat. He also surprised the writers and other players with his choice of lumber. "Joe brought along a young telephone pole, which he says is a bat," said the *Plain Dealer*. "Joe made it himself this winter." Joe explained that he liked a long bat, the better to pick curveballs off the outside of the plate.

Despite Joe's newfound sense of style, the writers couldn't get past his illiteracy and general lack of polish. Southern ballplayers were still rare in the major leagues at the time, and the Northern writers regarded the young South Carolinian with a mixture of apprehension and amusement. *The Sporting News* stated that Joe was "endowed with all the eccentricities that possess many Southerners" and that Cleveland scout Bob Gilks employed "mental suggestion" to get Joe to do his best on the field. The paper also reported that Joe was so superstitious that he had to be cajoled into letting his picture be taken with the Pelicans in 1910.[3]

Joe Williams, who covered Jackson in the Southern League before both writer and player made the majors, wrote in 1946, "He was pure country, a wide-eyed, gullible yokel. It would not have surprised me in those days to learn he had made a down payment on the Brooklyn Bridge."[4] Williams also told his readers that Joe "was a drinker, but not a heavy one," who carried his own jug of clear, "triple-distilled corn [whiskey]." Joe Jackson also traveled with a pet parrot, said Williams, "a multi-colored pest, whose vocabulary was limited to the screeching banality of, 'You're out!'"[5]

Joe Williams genuinely liked Joe Jackson—"one of the nicest fellows I ever met in baseball," said Williams—but veteran Chicago sportswriter Hugh Fullerton was not impressed with Cleveland's newest star. Fullerton was one of the most respected writers of the era. He began his career in the 1890s, and he had seen every great player in the major leagues since Cap Anson. Hugh Fullerton's columns appeared in syndication all over the nation, and his opinions carried a great deal of weight with the fans

and the other sportswriters. "A man who can't read or write," said Fullerton with great authority, "simply can't expect to meet the requirements of
big-league baseball as it is played today."[6] Joe, for his part, saw no problem with his illiteracy. Katie took care of his business matters, and he
turned down Charles Somers' offer to teach him to read and write.

The young slugger enjoyed the camaraderie of the other players, in
sharp contrast to his loneliness with the A's. Manager McGuire wanted
Joe to learn about major league life from a wily veteran, so he roomed Joe
with team captain George Stovall, whom Joe addressed as "Brother
George." Stovall showed Joe the ropes, both on the field and in the restaurants, trains, and hotels off the field.

Joe also made friends with the other young players. Joe and two other
Naps, pitchers Vean Gregg and Specs Harkness, titled themselves the
"Ancient Order of Retired Insects," with the motto "Bugs once, but not
now." The "bugs" were the members of the team who displayed oddball
tendencies or committed infractions of common sense on or off the field.
The three players cavorted in a photo in the *Plain Dealer*, leading some
to marvel at the incredible transformation of Joe Jackson into a confident,
secure major leaguer.

Joe's salary for 1911 is not known, but a rookie ballplayer of that era
would be expected to earn from $1,000 to $1,500 a year. In later life Jackson told an amazing story in which he went to Charles Somers before the
season began and offered to play for $10,000 if he hit .400 and for free if
he didn't. Jackson claimed that after the season ended Somers paid the
$10,000 in a lump sum.[7] This story is often quoted as the truth, but only
Ty Cobb was making that much in the American League at the time, and
Jackson could hardly wait until October to get any of his pay. Still, Joe's
baseball salary far outclassed the $250 to $300 a year that he would be
making at the mill. Compared to his friends and relatives in Greenville,
Joe Jackson was making a lot of money.

By now Joe had grown to his full adult height, six feet and one inch,
and he weighed 178 well-built pounds. Joe, one of the tallest position
players on the Naps, impressed onlookers with his speed. He went from
home to first base in four and one-fifth seconds, an excellent time for anyone in the league in that era. Joe's speed gave the Naps some flexibility
with their outfield defense. He could play center field and cover greater
expanses of ground, or use his powerful throwing arm to its best advantage in right field.

As a big leaguer, Joe could now have his bats professionally made.
In late 1910 he sent a bat to the J. F. Hillerich Company in Louisville,
Kentucky, so the company could make copies for his use. He didn't send

Black Betsy, which was fortunate, since the bat-making plant suffered a damaging fire in early 1911. Joe packaged another bat to send to the plant, leaving him with only one bat with which to play. This bat broke in two on March 23. Joe was upset; the paper said that he had "used no other [bat] the last three years," which seems to indicate that the broken bat was indeed the original Black Betsy.[8]

Joe quickly retrieved the package to Louisville, which hadn't yet been mailed, took his remaining good bat out and put the broken one inside. From then on, Joe used copies of Black Betsy and not the original.

Along with the rest of the Naps, Joe journeyed to New Orleans for six games against the Pelicans in late March. A crowd of nearly 3,000 braved the rain to see Jackson on Sunday, March 25. Ted Breitenstein, the veteran pitcher of the Pelicans, claimed to have found a way to keep Shoeless Joe off the bases. "We know his weaknesses," the old hurler told the *Plain Dealer*. "Throw the ball behind him and he'll never get a hit." From there, the Naps played their way north through Chattanooga, Cincinnati, and Toledo before the season opener in St. Louis on April 12.

The Naps' main worries as the 1911 season dawned centered around the pitching staff. Cy Young announced in spring training that 1911 would be his last season, and the 44-year-old legend worked hard to get in shape for one more campaign. Addie Joss, however, was still too weak to pitch at all down South. Since February Joss had been losing weight, and sometimes he would not eat dinner at all, pleading a loss of appetite. Though Joss traveled with the team, his health continued to deteriorate, and on April 3 he fainted on the bench in Chattanooga. The team doctor diagnosed the illness as pleurisy, since Joss could not draw a breath without a great deal of pain. When the Naps got to Joss' hometown of Toledo for an exhibition game on April 10, Joss took to his bed at his home at 2440 Fulton Street.

The rest of the team traveled to St. Louis to open the season on April 12, which by coincidence was Addie Joss' 31st birthday, but Joss' condition quickly worsened. He could no longer stand unaided, and his speech was slurred. On April 13, another doctor took a sample of fluid from Joss' spine and discovered the worst. The pitcher's illness was not pleurisy, but tubercular meningitis, which had no cure in the days before antibiotics. The disease had spread to Joss' brain, and early on the morning of April 14, 1911, Addie Joss died.

Deacon McGuire got the phone call from Toledo before breakfast on Friday, April 14. His Naps had lost the first two games of the season to the Browns, probably because of the distraction of worrying about their teammate. As the players gathered for breakfast McGuire took them aside, one or two at a time, and broke the sad news.

The Joss family scheduled the funeral for Monday, April 17, in Toledo, at which time the Naps would be playing in Detroit for the Tigers' season opener. The Cleveland players, however, would have none of it. Center fielder Joe Birmingham wrote out a petition demanding that the team postpone the Monday game so that they could attend the funeral.[9] All the members of the team signed it (though Joe Jackson must have done so with an X), and captain Stovall presented the petition to manager McGuire. The Naps then went out and beat St. Louis that afternoon for their first win of the season.

The Tigers, not surprisingly, balked at postponing their home opener, traditionally the best-attended game of the season. Tiger manager Hugh Jennings refused to consider a postponement, and American League president Ban Johnson threatened to suspend any players who refused to play on Monday. Charles Somers offered a compromise, in which ten or so of Joss' best friends would go to Toledo and represent the team. However, the grieving players stood firm, and before the situation could spiral out of control, Johnson changed his mind. On Sunday night he announced that the game would be rescheduled.

Some sources call this incident the first baseball strike, though it didn't quite get to that point. Still, Johnson gave in and rescheduled the game, fearing that the players would ignore him and go to Toledo anyway. Somers and 15 Cleveland players attended the funeral, which was officiated by the former ballplayer turned evangelist Billy Sunday. Detroit's Ty Cobb sent a wreath of spring flowers to the Joss home and mourned with a group of his Tiger teammates. Joe Jackson and some of the younger Naps who didn't know Joss well did not attend the funeral.

Jackson got off to a tremendous start in the 1911 season. After 17 games his average stood at .408, and on April 21 he belted a towering home run over the forty-foot-high fence in right field. Only Detroit's Sam Crawford had ever hit a homer over the wall, and Joe's blast traveled more than 30 feet farther than Crawford's, landing on the far side of Lexington Avenue. Joe displayed his throwing ability the day before, when he caught a would-be sacrifice fly in center field and threw out Jimmy Austin, one of the league's fastest runners, at home by a comfortable margin.

The players around the league marveled at the exploits of baseball's newest star, though they tried to get Joe off his game with taunts and insults. Since Joe had jumped the Philadelphia team when the pressure became too intense, some players around the league believed that it would only be a matter of time before they "got his nerve." Joe took a lot of taunting from the bench jockeys on other teams, mostly things like "Hey, Professor!" or "Joe, why did you run out on Connie Mack by the light of the moon?" but Joe turned a deaf ear and kept hitting. It spoke volumes for Joe Jackson's newfound sense of maturity and confidence that he could answer the most vicious of bench jockeying with a smile and a flurry of base hits.

At the end of April, both Joe and Nap Lajoie were hitting above .400, but the Naps got off to a poor start. They quickly fell far behind the league-leading Tigers, who roared off to a 21-2 start while the Naps fell to seventh place, with a 6-11 record in their first 17 games. On May 3, manager Deacon McGuire resigned and returned to his scouting duties for the club, and Charles Somers named team captain George Stovall as manager.

Stovall, despite his hot temper, was popular with the Cleveland players, especially after he arranged the team trip to Toledo for Addie Joss' funeral. Still, unbeknownst to the public, Charles Somers saw Stovall merely as an interim manager. Somers had his eye on Harry Davis, the long-time first baseman and captain of the Philadelphia A's, for his next manager, most likely at the instigation of Davis' mentor Connie Mack. Mack had the young Stuffy McInnis ready to take over for the 38-year-old Davis at first base, and Mack wanted to reward Davis for his faithful service by landing him in the Cleveland manager's chair. In late May the Cleveland papers revealed a meeting between Somers and Davis to discuss the future of the Naps; there were denials all around, but Somers' courtship of Davis became the worst-kept secret in baseball.

Chicago's Ed Walsh blanked the Naps on May 4, holding Joe Jackson hitless for the first time since April 23, but after that the Naps began to rise in the standings. On May 7 against the Browns, Joe belted an inside-the-park home run with the bases loaded, the first of four grand slams in Joe's career.[10] This blow, in the top of the twelfth inning, gave the Naps a 6-2 victory. Despite Nap Lajoie's abdominal illness that limited the Frenchman to 90 games, the Naps rode Joe's hot bat into the first division by midseason.

On May 14 the Naps played their first ever Sunday game in Cleveland. The fight for Sunday ball had dragged on for years, and in 1900 only the teams in Chicago, St. Louis, and Cincinnati were allowed to play on Sunday. Back in 1898, the National League's Cleveland Spiders, including Cy Young, were arrested en masse after playing on Sunday,[11] and preachers and politicians regularly railed against the breaking of the

Sabbath. In their early years, the Naps evaded the strict Cleveland blue laws by playing occasional Sunday games in Columbus, Canton, Dayton, and Fort Wayne, Indiana.

Many factory workers and day laborers toiled six days a week at the time, and the Sunday blue laws kept these potential fans away from the ballpark. In 1911 the Cleveland authorities finally relented, since the Naps needed big Sunday crowds to compete financially, and the tickets for the game on May 14 warned the fans against "boisterous rooting." The Naps belted out 18 hits and beat New York 16 to 3. By the end of World War I most of the major league teams were allowed to play home games on Sunday, but the Pennsylvania teams (Pirates, Phillies, and A's) would not be permitted to do so until 1934.

If the seven other teams of the American League expected Joe's bat to cool off on his second trip around the circuit, they were sorely disappointed. From July 11 to August 26, Joe hit safely in 36 of the 37 games in which he played, including a 28-game hitting streak from July 11 to August 12. Joe's average rose from .377 to .405 before Jack Powell of the Browns held him hitless on August 13.

The pitchers of the American League tried everything to stop Joe Jackson, and early in the 1911 season they turned to one of the most time-honored tactics in the game. They started throwing at the rookie sensation. Detroit pitcher George Mullin claimed that Joe would not hit .250 in 1911, because if the pitchers started throwing at his head, Joe would "run away from the plate and never come back."[12] They hit Joe with pitches eight times in 1911 and 12 times the next year, and only his superior reflexes kept him from being hit even more often. Joe dug in and held his ground, and after his first few months in the major leagues, the pitchers got the message that they could not frighten the young slugger away from the plate. "I never pulled away from the plate as long as I was in baseball," said Joe with pride more than 30 years later.[13]

Despite Joe's amazing hitting, he had no realistic chance of winning the batting title. In May, Ty Cobb's average rose above .400 and stayed there for the rest of the 1911 season. Playing like a man possessed, Cobb ran off a 40-game hitting streak, a new American League record, from late May until Ed Walsh stopped him on July 4. After 80 games Joe Jackson's average stood at .380, but Cobb's was 70 points higher at .450. Cobb wanted to make sure that no one would be in a position to deny him the title at the end of the season, as the Browns had nearly done in 1910. All Joe Jackson did with his hitting was to make Cobb play harder. In the next three weeks, Joe's average rose to .398, but Cobb still roared along at a .417 clip.

The new "rabbit ball" helped Cobb and Jackson post their gaudy numbers. In late 1910 the Shibe sporting goods concern, which produced baseballs for the American League, introduced their new cork-center ball, which was wound more tightly than the balls that preceded it. The new ball caused the league batting average to jump thirty points from 1910 to 1911. Run production increased by nearly 25 percent, while the number of shutouts decreased from 132 to 79. For the next few years, the batters would have the upper hand over the pitchers, and Cobb and Jackson took full advantage.

No American Leaguer had hit over .400 since 1901, when Nap Lajoie hit .422 for Philadelphia, but both Cobb and Jackson threatened to pass the magic mark. On September 1, Joe's average stood at an even .400, with Cobb still far ahead at .421. Try as he might, Joe never got within nine points of Cobb all season long. However, the rest of the American League found out that Joe could throw as well as hit. Joe's 32 outfield assists in 1911 set a Cleveland team record that stands to this day.

Joe also learned how to take advantage of Cleveland's League Park. The right field fence was only 290 feet from home plate, because when the place was built in 1891 a few property owners in the right field area didn't want to sell their land to the team. The club compensated by putting a huge wall 40 feet high from center field to the right field pole. Joe, a natural pull hitter, became adept at denting the wall with line drives. Joe also found that the ball would bounce differently depending on where it hit the wall. The bottom half of the wall was cement, while the top half was chain-link fencing. Joe Jackson's line drives might ricochet off the cement, drop straight down off the chain-link fence, or bounce crazily off one of the metal fence posts. Joe's speed allowed him to stretch doubles into triples while the outfielders chased down the ball.

Addie Joss' sudden death left his wife and two children without a breadwinner, and the Cleveland players and management decided to help. They scheduled an all-star game to benefit the Joss family for Monday, July 24, on a date when most of the other American League teams would be idle. The idea was met with great enthusiasm by the rest of the league, especially after Ty Cobb wired his agreement to play to the Cleveland management on July 15. Manager Jimmy McAleer of the Washington Senators got the task of managing what one newspaper called "the greatest collection of All-Star players who ever appeared on the field in the history of the game." The Cleveland management absorbed all the expenses of the game, so that all the money raised from ticket sales would benefit the Joss family.

Each of the other seven teams in the league sent their star players to Cleveland to take part in the historic game. From Detroit came outfielders Sam Crawford, a veteran of 14 seasons in the major leagues, and Cobb, whose .438 batting average led the league. The world champion Philadelphia A's sent two heroes of the 1910 World Series, third baseman Frank "Home Run" Baker and second baseman Eddie Collins. The shortstop was Bobby Wallace of the St. Louis Browns, and the first baseman was Hal Chase of the New York Yankees. Philadelphia's Paddy Livingstone and the Washington Senators' Gabby Street handled the catching duties. The pitching staff included fireballers Joe Wood of the Boston Red Sox and Walter Johnson of the Senators, assisted by spitball artists Russell Ford of the Yankees and Ed Walsh of the Chicago White Sox. Boston's Tris Speaker patrolled center field for the All-Stars.

Most of the players mentioned above were named to the Hall of Fame many years later, making this one of the strongest All-Star teams ever assembled. "Leave that combination together," remarked the *Toledo Blade* on the day of the game, "and there would be no American League."

League Park was not draped in black, nor did it show any sign of mourning save for the flag at half-mast in centerfield. The Joss family and the players had decided that the game should be a celebration of baseball itself, and so it was for the 15,000 fans who jammed the park. Addie Joss' friend Cy Young drew the starting assignment for the Naps. One odd note was the sight of Cobb in a Cleveland uniform. He had left his Tiger uniform at home, and he borrowed a gray road uniform from the Cleveland team.

The All-Stars scored first off Young. Speaker, the first batter, singled and scored on Collins' triple. Cobb drove Collins home with a single, and the All-Stars led 2-0 in the first inning. In the second, Chase and Street singled for the All-Stars, and starting pitcher Joe Wood drove Chase home with a sacrifice fly. Young left the game in the second inning, and the All-Stars held control the rest of the way. The Naps scored in the second, but the All-Stars answered in the fourth with singles by Baker and Crawford and a sacrifice fly by Chase.

Walter Johnson came in to pitch for the All-Stars and shut out the Naps for four innings, while Russell Ford allowed two runs to the Naps in the eighth. The All-Stars scored again in the seventh when Collins singled in the Senators' Clyde Milan, who had replaced Speaker in the outfield. The final score was 5 to 3 in the All-Stars' favor. Joe Jackson went hitless in two trips against Wood and Johnson, then retired in favor of rookie Hank Butcher.

"Guess Cleveland couldn't stand for that team," remarked the *Blade*.

"The collective stars didn't need teamwork to bring about a victory. Their fielding brilliance [was] accomplished without the aid of signals or strategy."[14] Ten participants in the contest (Cobb, Speaker, Baker, Collins, Johnson, Walsh, Wallace, Crawford, Lajoie, and Young) eventually were named to the Baseball Hall of Fame; in 1978, Addie Joss joined them in Cooperstown. In all, the teams raised a total of nearly $13,000 for Lillian Joss and her two children.

The Naps benefited from the performances of several of their young players, in addition to Joe Jackson. Vean Gregg, a rookie left-handed pitcher, won 23 games for Cleveland and led the league with a 1.80 earned run average. Gregg also threw five shutouts. Gene Krapp went 13-9 on the mound, while Ivy Olson took over at shortstop and batted .261, a big improvement from Bill Bradley's .196 of the year before. The new blood in the Cleveland lineup helped spark the team into a four-team battle for third place behind Philadelphia and Detroit. A ten-game winning streak from August 31 to September 9 shot the Naps into third place, where they remained for the rest of the season.

The personnel of the team had changed drastically from 1910. Longtime Cleveland stars Bill Bradley, Elmer Flick, and Addie Joss were all gone when the 1911 season started, and Cy Young soon followed them. On August 15 Young, winner of more than 500 major league games, was released by the Naps. He signed on with the Boston Doves (soon to be called the Braves) and went 4-5 the rest of the season. Young then retired to his farm in Tuscarawas County, Ohio. In mid–August the Naps bought Joe's old Greenville teammate Scotty Barr from New Orleans; unfortunately, Barr twisted his ankle and sat out the rest of the 1911 season. Barr never did appear in a major league game for the Naps.

The Cleveland team batted only .244 in 1910, but Lajoie and Jackson sparked a resurgence in hitting for the Naps. Jack Graney lifted his average from .236 to .269, while Joe Birmingham's .304 mark in 1911 was 73 points higher than the year before. The rabbit ball was partially responsible, but the Cleveland team batting average rose to .282 in 1911, the third best mark in the American League.

However, the Cleveland Naps weren't quite ready to contend for the pennant in 1911. Though the Naps were certainly headed in the right direction, they didn't yet have enough talent to challenge Detroit and Philadelphia, the two powerhouse teams of the American League at the time. Connie Mack had built another winning team with the Philadelphia A's, despite the loss of Joe Jackson to Cleveland in mid–1910. Led by second baseman Eddie Collins and a solid pitching staff, the A's won

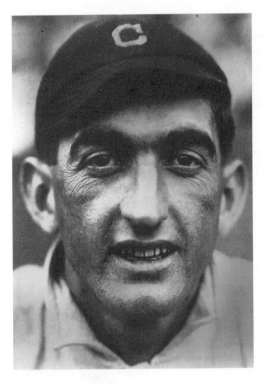

the 1910 pennant and World Series. The Tigers, who won three consecutive pennants from 1907 to 1909, depended mainly upon offensive fireworks as provided by Ty Cobb. Cobb, who was only 18 months older than Joe Jackson, was already being hailed as the greatest player of all time by 1911.

Joe's former team, the A's, took a while to find their stride in 1911. They fell eleven and a half games behind the Tigers in May, but they put on a tremendous charge and won the flag by eight games. The injury-riddled Tigers collapsed to second place despite Ty Cobb's batting heroics. Four other teams—the Red Sox, White Sox,

Face shot of Joe, about 1912 (author's collection).

Naps, and Yankees—battled for third place all season long, with not more than a few games separating third and sixth place. The Cleveland Naps, who went 74-62 under George Stovall after their 6-11 start, finally clinched the third spot in late September. The Naps finished one game ahead of the fourth place Chicago White Sox, and 22 games behind the pennant-winning A's.

Despite the Naps' on-field success, Charles Somers was not impressed with George Stovall's management of the team, and Somers' courtship of the A's captain Harry Davis soon came out into the open. In early September the fans began circulating petitions requesting that Stovall be kept aboard for 1912, but Somers paid no attention. He wanted the respected Davis to manage his team no matter how well George Stovall performed.

The only point of interest for Cleveland fans in September 1911, besides the managerial situation, was Joe Jackson's assault on the .400 mark. Joe's average fell to .398 on September 17, but a four-for-nine performance in a doubleheader on September 20 put him over .400 to stay. Joe was forced to sit out of one game when he crashed into a fence in Washington on September 27, jamming his shoulder, but he played the last few games of the season and kept his average above the magic mark. The final season averages gave Cobb his fifth consecutive batting title with a .420 average, with Joe Jackson second at .408. Though Joe finished second in the 1911 batting race, his .408 average stands as the sixth highest single-season mark of the twentieth century.

Surprisingly, Joe didn't lead the league in any major category in 1911. He finished second to Cobb in batting, and also in hits (233), doubles (45), total bases (337), runs scored (126), and slugging percentage (.590). Joe's only league-leading category was in on-base percentage. Cobb, with one of the greatest offensive seasons in the history of baseball, won the Chalmers Most Valuable Player award unanimously; Joe finished fourth, behind Cobb, Ed Walsh, and Eddie Collins.

Joe's total of 233 hits stands as a Cleveland team record to this day, as do his 32 outfield assists and his .408 average. There was no official rookie-of-the-year award in 1911, but certainly no first-year player in baseball history has ever had such a dominating season.[15] If the award had existed then, Jackson would certainly have won it, and Naps pitcher Vean Gregg, a 23-game winner, would probably have finished second.[16]

Ty Cobb paid tribute to Jackson as the season ended. "Joe is a grand ball player, and one who will get better and better," said Cobb. "There is no denying that he is a better ball player his first year in the big league than anyone ever was."[17] With the batting title secure, Cobb sat out the Tigers' season-ending series against the Browns in St. Louis. One reporter counted only 66 fans in the seats at the Browns-Tigers contest on the last Saturday of the season. Joe also sat out the Naps' season-ending game, one of only six he missed that season, to rest his ailing shoulder.

The Naps and the Cincinnati Reds played another post-season "All-Ohio Championship," but this series failed to interest the fans. The Reds won the first two games of the series by scores of 4-0 and 10-2. Joe Jackson went three for four in the second game, but also committed two errors to open the floodgates for the Reds. The teams then played two doubleheaders on October 14 and 15, both of which the teams split. The Reds won the series four games to two, and Joe batted .333 with seven hits in the six games. Crowds were small, and the Cleveland players earned only $88 apiece for their efforts (the Reds received $127 per man). With poor October weather and little fan interest, the "All-Ohio Championship" series would not be resumed until 1917.

One would think that manager George Stovall would get the credit for the Naps' rise to the first division, but it didn't work out that way. Charles Somers made a secret deal with Connie Mack sometime in 1910 or 1911, in which Somers agreed to hire Mack's first baseman Harry Davis as the Naps' manager for the 1912 campaign.[18] It didn't remain a secret for long, since as early as May the papers reported that Somers and Davis had met to discuss Davis' future as manager of the Naps. George Stovall already knew that he would not return as manager, much to the dismay of the players on the team. By August, Harry Davis was already announcing his plans for the Naps in 1912, which included moving Lajoie to first base, and Stovall spent the rest of the season as a highly successful lame-duck manager.

The saddened players presented Stovall with a silver chest containing $275 in coins as a going-away present. On October 16, the day after the series with the Reds ended, Stovall officially tendered his resignation. Eleven days later, when the World Series ended, Charles Somers hired Harry Davis to manage the Naps for the 1912 season.

One of the most widespread stories about Joe Jackson concerns the race for the batting title in 1911. Ty Cobb won the title that year with a .420 average, while Jackson finished at .408.

Later in his life, Cobb told a story about how he psychologically manipulated the simple-minded Jackson into losing the batting title in the last days of the 1911 season. In his autobiography, published in 1961, Cobb explained how he did it:

> Jackson was a Southerner, like myself, a friendly, simple, and gullible sort of fellow. On the field, he never failed to greet me with a "Hiyuh, Brother Ty." ... So now we were in Cleveland for a season-closing six-game series, and before the first game I waited in the clubhouse until Jackson had taken his batting practice. I had one of the club-house boys tip me off when he was finished, so I couldn't miss him.
>
> Ambling over, Joe gave me a grin and said, "How's it going, Brother Ty? How you been?"
>
> I stared coldly at a point six inches over his head. Joe waited for an answer. The grin slowly faded from his face to be replace by puzzlement.
>
> "Gosh, Ty, What's the matter with you?"
>
> I turned and walked away. Jackson followed, still trying to learn why I'd ignored him.
>
> "Get away from me!" I snarled.
>
> Every inning afterward I arranged to pass close by him, each time giving him the deep freeze. For a while, Joe kept asking, "What's

wrong, Ty?" I never answered him. Finally, he quit speaking and just looked at me with hurt in his eyes.[19]

According to Cobb, Jackson's batting average sank like a rock, enabling Cobb to pass him and win the title by 12 percentage points.

It isn't hard to prove that the incident, as Cobb tells it above, never happened. A quick scan through the newspapers reveals that Cobb never trailed Jackson all season long; in fact, Jackson got no closer to Cobb than nine points in August of 1911. Cobb's average never dipped below .400 at any time after May of 1911, while Jackson didn't climb above .400 for keeps until August.

Also, there was no six-game series to end the season. Cobb's Tigers played the last three games of 1911 in St. Louis, while Jackson's Cleveland Naps ended up with a two-game set in Chicago against the White Sox. Cobb, as usual, didn't even play the last three games of the season. He had a safe lead in the batting race and sat out to protect his .420 batting average.

Though Ty Cobb did often use psychological warfare on his opponents, as many of his contemporaries would testify in their later years, the famous tale of the 1911 batting race, as told by Cobb 50 years later, simply didn't happen.

In truth, the set of circumstances above seems to match the actual events of the 1916 season more closely that they match the events of 1911. In 1916, Cobb trailed Jackson early in the season, but Joe then went into a slump. Cobb beat Jackson by 30 points in the final standings (although Tris Speaker beat Cobb for the crown that year, .386 to .371). In 1925, Cobb related the identical scenario to writer F. C. Lane in describing the batting race of 1916. It seems illogical, however, that by 1916 the 28-year-old Jackson would be so immature as to go into a deep slump after being given the silent treatment by Cobb.

Joe Jackson had his own explanation for the outcome of the 1911 batting race. "A story you now hear from time to time that Ty bulldozed me by getting my goat in a conceived plan to ignore me in Cleveland in that important final series is just a lot of hooey," said Jackson in 1942. "Ty was able to beat me out because he got more hits than I did."[20]

Chapter 5

Baseball's Newest Star

Joe has as level a baseball head as I ever saw in the game. He pulls no bones and I find, the better I know him, that he has a head for things outside of baseball. For instance, he turned a little trick for a few hundred dollars just a few days ago. Those who advised him were good businessmen, but he saw little angles to the deal that others had overlooked. As a result it turned out better for him than the others had figured it.

—Harry Davis, 1912

Harry Davis, the new manager of the Cleveland Naps, began his career with the New York Giants in the National League in 1895. After a few brief stints with other teams (including Connie Mack's Pittsburgh Pirates in 1896), Davis left baseball in 1900 and went to work as a railroad clerk. When Connie Mack needed a first baseman for the A's in 1901, he contacted Harry Davis and offered him the job. Soon Davis was Mack's most trusted lieutenant.

Davis held down the first base position all through the first ten years of the A's and earned a reputation as a solid, dependable workhorse. After the 1905 World Series, which the A's lost to the Giants, Mack made Davis his field captain. Davis also managed the A's on spring training trips and during the season whenever Mack was otherwise occupied.

He didn't hit for much of an average—his lifetime mark was .277—but Harry Davis provided the power for the A's. He led the American League in home runs four seasons in a row from 1904 to 1907, with totals of 10, 8, 12, and 8. In 1911, with young Stuffy McInnis ready to take over at first for the A's, Connie Mack, in appreciation of Davis' faithful service over the years, maneuvered him into the Cleveland manager's chair with the help of Charles Somers. Davis went out in a blaze of glory; after an injury left McInnis unable to play in the 1911 World Series, Davis took over at first and led the A's to victory. Somers hired him as manager the day after the World Series ended.

The Cleveland Naps gathered at Mobile, Alabama, for 1912 spring training without George Stovall. Charles Somers didn't want to enter the season with two ex-managers on the playing roster, so on February 17 he traded Stovall to the St. Louis Browns for pitcher Lefty George.

Harry Davis moved quickly to put his stamp on the Naps. As one of his first acts as manager, he outlawed dice playing in the clubhouse. "I don't object to a small game of poker, but I do draw the line on craps," said Davis. "Some players carry around gambling debts and they cannot do justice to themselves in the games."[1] Davis also banned fraternization between the Naps and opposing players before and during the games, and he tightened the rules on curfew. The new manager promised to lighten up on the spring workouts, after the writers criticized Deacon McGuire the year before for working the players too hard in spring training.

One of the new manager's decisions resulted in bad consequences for the team. Davis announced that he would follow Connie Mack's lead and not use a set pitching rotation; instead, he would use whatever pitcher seemed to have the best "stuff" that day. This system worked for Mack because the A's had several veteran stars on their staff like Chief Bender, Jack Coombs, and Eddie Plank. A young staff like Cleveland's needed a set routine, which Davis would find out as the season progressed.

Davis also surprised the Naps when he named shortstop Ivy Olson as captain. Outfielder Joe Birmingham was the senior Nap starter in time of service aside from Lajoie, but Davis insisted that he needed an infielder to lead the team on the field. Davis admired Olson's "ginger," but Olson's constant chatter got on the nerves of his teammates, and soon Olson and the rest of the Naps were at odds.

Joe Jackson spent a week with the New Orleans Pelicans, getting himself into shape and enjoying the vaudeville shows, before he reported to Mobile on March 5. He arrived with his former Greenville Spinners teammate Scotty Barr, who had played with Joe on the A's in 1908 and with the Pelicans in 1910. Barr and Jackson remained friends, though Barr soon found himself sent back to New Orleans for the 1912 season. After his brief trials with the A's in 1908 and 1909, Barr never played again in the major leagues.

Ty Cobb was on Joe's mind, and Joe announced that he would

challenge Cobb again for the batting title. "I am proud of the fact that I crowded him as a run-getter and a batter," said Jackson. "I don't think it hardly possible for him to bat any better this year than he did last, but he may. I am going to try and beat him." Jackson added, "He sure is an aggravating cuss, beating me out by just a few points."[2] The Cleveland paper also reported that Jackson arrived at the Mobile ballpark and loudly announced, "Here I am, boys. Just give me a bat and I'll put a few over the fence."

Indeed, Joe's self-confidence would have sounded like arrogance from a more worldly, sophisticated player. "Joe Jackson needs no press agent," said the *Plain Dealer* on March 7. "He believes in advertising himself."

Joe, who found it difficult to give one-word answers to reporters in Philadelphia a few years earlier, found a way to communicate with the Cleveland writers. He adopted the persona of the southern storyteller, and the writers enjoyed his colorful, somewhat exaggerated tales of mill life and playing ball down South. "Joe himself has a warm, fervid imagination," said F. C. Lane of *Baseball Magazine*, "which looks upon facts as hurdles to be surmounted by brief but frequent flights of fancy."[3]

Joe arrived at spring training in perfect shape and started hitting right away, but it didn't take long for Harry Davis to grow frustrated with the rest of the Naps. "They haven't any ginger," said Davis on March 19. "They seem to need waking up." Many newspapers picked the Naps to finish as high as third in 1912, but the players began to resent Davis' strictness. Davis, for his part, became more demanding and critical as the weeks of spring training dragged on, almost insuring that the team would struggle when the regular season began.

Davis knew that the Naps had a reputation as a rowdy team. During the previous season, four Cleveland pitchers were arrested after a brawl on a streetcar, and though the authorities dropped the charges, the incident stuck in the minds of the public. Many preachers and politicians still complained about Sunday ball, and Somers may have hired the upstanding Davis as manager in a bid to clean up the team's public image. Davis, a college man himself, came from a team with a large number of college-educated and refined players, and he found that his imitation of Connie Mack didn't play well among the more fun-loving and hard-drinking Naps.

The Naps moved to New Orleans for a series of games in the Pelicans' home park, and the fans came out to see Joe Jackson. Joe was probably the most popular player the Pelicans ever had, and the Naps drew big crowds for their games in New Orleans whenever Joe Jackson appeared in the lineup. On March 24, 1912, Joe belted a home run over the center field fence that observers called the second longest ever hit in the Pelicans' park. In a 13-0 win against Louisiana State University in early April, Joe smashed two homers far over the fence. In league games Joe used a hard, level swing, but in exhibitions Joe liked to entertain the fans by swinging from the heels and uppercutting the ball, driving the ball long distances in the smaller Southern ballparks.

Jackson began to find out what it was like to be a celebrity. In Memphis, the Naps' exhibition game was rained out, but the people still wanted to see Joe Jackson. "When Joe went out for an auto ride this noon," said the *Plain Dealer*, "he was repeatedly held up by people who wanted to shake his hand and take a snapshot of him."[4] Joe also found that his popularity extended outside of Cleveland and the South. He received the following letter at the ballpark in the first week of the season:

> Kansas City
> April 13, 1912
>
> My Dear Mr. Jackson,
>
> If not asking too much of you, I would like very much to have you give me your complete name, as I have a fat, fine-looking, newly-born twelve-pound baby boy that is somewhat of a ball player and I would like to name him after, in my opinion, the best ball player in the world.
>
> Trusting to receive this information from you at an early date and hoping that you show your superiority over Mr. Tyrus Cobb in the year 1912 on all points that make a perfect ball player,
>
> I am respectfully yours,
>
> C. L. Harding[5]

The *Plain Dealer* commented, "Jackson replied that his full and complete cognomen is Joseph Walker Jackson." Joe always used Wofford as his middle name; obviously, the reporter misinterpreted Joe's southern drawl.

On April 11, the 1912 season began in front of 19,302 fans at League Park, the biggest crowd in Cleveland since the end of the 1908 pennant race. Joe went 3 for 5 as the Naps beat the Tigers 3-2 in 11 innings. The Naps won the next day also against the Tigers, but they committed nine errors in their third game and lost 12-4. Soon the Naps settled to the .500 mark, as the Boston Red Sox, playing in the new Fenway Park, zoomed out of the gate and grabbed the league lead.

The Naps moved to Detroit in mid–April to open the Tigers' new ballpark, then called Navin Field and now known as Tiger Stadium. After

Joe with Detroit stars Ty Cobb (left) and Sam Crawford, 1913 (author's collection).

two days of rain, the Tigers and Naps finally played the opener on April 20. Before the game, Joe revealed another of his superstitions to the press. "Joe is so proud of the new suit [road uniform] handed him yesterday, he keeps it under lock and key," said the *Plain Dealer* on April 20.

"I believe that there are over one hundred hits in that uniform," said Joe.

Jackson played, despite a severe cold, and scored the first run in the new park. He walked in the first inning, stole second, and scored on an error. Ty Cobb tied the score with a steal of home in the bottom of the inning, and the Tigers won the game 6 to 5 in 11 innings on the muddy new field. The next day Detroit pitcher Sleepy Bill Burns hit Jackson in the arm with a fastball. Joe kept playing despite a severe bruise that hurt for several days.

The writers noticed a change in Joe Jackson's hitting. Though Joe was a dead pull hitter in 1910 and 1911, none of his first six hits of the 1912 season went to right field. "Have you noticed any change in my style of batting?" asked Jackson. "No? Well, I have switched a little. They got to playing for me in right and I am going to mix 'em up this year and hit to left field as much as to right. Now and then I will sandwich one in to center."[6]

By this time, Joe's home life in Cleveland had settled into a comfortable routine. The Jacksons rented a bungalow at 3709 Lexington Avenue, mere walking distance from League Park, which stood at East 66th Street and Lexington. Katie came to every home game, cheering the Naps and keeping a detailed scorecard. Joe complained good-naturedly that Katie was tough to please, since she gave errors to the fielders much more often than the official scorers did. If Katie were the official scorer, said Joe, his batting average would take a sharp tumble.

Katie stayed at the game until about the seventh inning, when she would return home to begin cooking dinner for her husband. Joe grew up in a household in which the family ate only one meal, a large one, every day, and Joe liked having dinner on the table when he arrived at home. Katie grew skilled at coordinating the timing of the meal with the end of the game.

She also worked with Joe on the difficult task of signing his name for contracts and for his twice-monthly paychecks. Joe was not familiar with the feel of a pen in his hand, and he worked hard at the painstaking task of scrawling the strange-looking ten-letter signature. Eventually, Joe carried a card with his signature on it in his wallet, and when called upon to sign his name he would bring the card out and do his best to reproduce it.

Lefty George, the pitcher who came from the Browns in exchange for George Stovall, struggled with the Naps. George lost 6-1 to the White Sox on April 24, and in that same game Harry Davis benched first baseman Eddie Hohnhorst and took the position himself. The next day Nap Lajoie played first, with veteran Terry Turner at the second sack. Lajoie, however, lasted only a few weeks at first, until the Frenchman suffered a strained back in May that sidelined him for 37 games. Davis then put minor leaguer Art Griggs, the Naps' fourth first baseman in the young season, at first, but soon Jack Graney suffered a leg injury, and the Naps found themselves short-handed in the outfield.

Joe Jackson kept belting the ball, but with the Red Sox winning nearly 70 percent of their games, the injury-riddled Naps dropped quickly out of contention and into the second division. On June 2 Nap Lajoie returned on the tenth anniversary of his first game for Cleveland, and received a floral horseshoe with 1,009 silver dollars attached to it from the fans. However, by this time the Naps were buried in fifth place, ten games out of first.

Davis, accustomed to winning with the A's, grew increasingly frustrated in Cleveland. His worst mistake came in May, when he publicly blasted his depleted team in the newspapers as "quitters" and told the writers that he would "get new players if the ones ... on the payroll do not act more alive."[7] He also ran players in and out of the lineup with wild abandon, overreacting to the early-season slide. He upset the team by naming Ivy Olson as captain, but in May, Davis assigned the task of positioning the infielders to the veteran Neal Ball, which undercut Olson's position even more. Despite their troubles, the Naps flirted with the .500 mark, but Davis' hysterical lineup juggling turned off any players who may still have been on his side.

However, Harry Davis had no problems at all with Joe Jackson. "Joe is the kind of ballplayer that makes a manager's heart glad," said Davis to the writers. "He hits the ball harder than I ever saw anyone hit it." Joe, as usual, played his game and ignored the turmoil around him. He belted a line drive over center fielder Tris Speaker's head and legged it out for an inside-the-park home run against the Red Sox on June 4. The next day, pitcher Jack Quinn of the Yankees paid Joe the ultimate baseball compliment. He walked Joe intentionally with two men on, preferring to face Lajoie with the bases loaded. The insulted Frenchman quickly drilled a double that scored all three runners.

The Naps rested in fifth place with a 23-21 record when they arrived in Philadelphia for a series against the A's on June 9. Harry Davis made every effort to defeat his old team, putting Lajoie back on second base and Griggs back on first, but an embarrassing 13-2 defeat seemed to take all the starch out of the Naps. The Naps lost the next day by a 6-2 score, despite two doubles and two singles off the bat of Joe Jackson, and then lost the next two games to the A's and three more to Washington. Joe, nursing a sore leg, was reduced to pinch-hitting duty in the Washington series. The Naps finally snapped their eight-game losing streak against the Tigers, after Jackson's return to the lineup.

The American League suspended Ty Cobb in early May for attacking a fan in the stands, and suddenly Joe Jackson seemed ready to annex his first American League batting title. A hot streak in late June pushed Joe's average from .361 to .401 in only 12 days. On June 30 Joe scored four runs and belted three triples in a 15-1 win against the Browns; this tied Nap Lajoie's American League record for triples in a game.[8] The Naps rallied behind Jackson's hot bat to a 39-36 record, their high point of the season, on July 4.

Again, the A's dashed Cleveland's slim hopes of contention. A hard-fought game in Philadelphia on July 16 resulted in Davis' removal from the field by the local police after the manager's altercation with umpire Fred Westervelt got out of hand. This was the same Westervelt who fined

Joe Jackson 50 dollars for leaving the field in Columbus, Georgia, three years earlier. In that same game, Joe suffered a hip injury while sliding into second base and was carried off the field. He recovered enough to belt a homer against the Yankees the next day, but the A's started the Naps on a 2-9 skid which included three straight losses to the last-place Yankees. Lajoie sat out two weeks with shin problems, and the losses mounted as the doubleheaders piled up in the heat of the summer.

In the meantime, Ty Cobb went on another one of his annual midseason hitting tears. Cobb's Tigers fell out of pennant contention, but Cobb roared to a huge lead in the batting race at .423 to .367 for Joe Jackson. Joe's batting average fell 34 points in July without Lajoie's presence behind him in the lineup.

Harry Davis, inevitably, found a way to make things even worse for the Naps. Davis called an unprecedented meeting of three American League managers—himself, the Browns' George Stovall, and Nixey Callahan of the White Sox—and the three filed a joint protest against umpire Westervelt with league president Ban Johnson. Nothing came of the protest, and from that point on the Naps couldn't catch a break with any of the umpires in the league. Davis further angered his players when the papers reported that Somers, at his manager's suggestion, had asked for waivers on more than half of the men on the team.

July and August dragged interminably for the Cleveland fans. After July 4 the Naps won only 15 of their next 50 games. Harry Davis moved Jackson from center field to right, put Joe Birmingham back into center, and juggled his infield almost daily. Ivy Olson moved from second to third to shortstop, where he shared time with rookie Roger Peckinpaugh, while Nap Lajoie shuttled from first to second and back again. The pitching proved inconsistent, and the catchers' lack of experience hurt the team. Lefty George's 0-5 record meant that the Naps traded George Stovall away for virtually nothing. Perhaps the low point of the season came on August 20, when Washington's Jay Cashion threw a six-inning no-hitter against the Naps. Cashion won only 11 other games in the major leagues, and the no-hitter against the Naps was the only shutout he ever pitched.

The club played listlessly as the losses mounted, and it can be fairly said that the Naps gave up on Harry Davis. Almost alone among the Cleveland players, Joe Jackson never let up. On August 11, Joe stole home against the Senators in the first inning, then in the seventh stole second, third, and home in quick succession. Joe also felt secure and bold enough to become more vocal with the umpires. On August 27 in New York, after a close play at first base, umpire Joe O'Brien ejected Jackson from the first game of a doubleheader for arguing. This was the first ejection of Joe's major league career. Joe had to sit out the second game also, the only game he missed in the 1912 campaign.

On August 29, with another season down the drain, the *Plain Dealer* called manager Davis "a driver, not a leader," and offered a list of candidates for his replacement. After a disastrous eastern swing in which the Naps lost 14 of 16 games, Harry Davis reached the end of his patience. On the morning of Labor Day, September 2, Davis submitted his resignation to Charles Somers, and soon rejoined the A's as a coach for the 1913 season. Davis remained as a coach and a scout for Connie Mack until 1927, but never managed again in the major leagues.[9]

Somers quickly named center fielder Joe Birmingham as manager of the Naps. Birmingham joined the Naps in 1906 and by 1912 was the senior member of the starting lineup, except for Napoleon Lajoie.[10] Birmingham wrote the petition that the Naps presented to manager Deacon McGuire on the day of Addie Joss' death in 1911, earning him the respect of the other Naps. He was a fast runner with a strong arm, and though he batted only .255 in 1912, the 28-year-old outfielder was highly regarded by most of his teammates. Unfortunately for the new manager, one of the few players who disliked him was Napoleon Lajoie, and their feud would escalate during the 1913 season.

Cleveland was gaining a reputation as a graveyard of managers. Joe Birmingham was the seventh manager of the club in its 12 years of existence, in contrast to the A's, Pirates, and Giants, who had not changed managers in ten years or more. Charles Somers decided to stop the managerial merry-go-round. He gave the job to Birmingham without the "interim" label and assured the public that Birmingham would be back in 1913.

Birmingham moved quickly to smooth the waters. Ray Chapman, a 21-year-old infielder, came up from Toledo and batted .312 to claim the shortstop job permanently, settling the infield defense. Birmingham moved Chapman into the second spot in the lineup, which pushed Jackson down to fourth and Lajoie to fifth, which greatly improved the Cleveland offense.

The Naps, released from the tension of Davis' strictness, began to win ballgames. They won 21 of the 28 games remaining in the season under Birmingham, including four in a row from the league-leading Red Sox on September 17-19. Connie Mack publicly blasted the Naps for "laying down" to get his friend Harry Davis fired, and the Naps responded by beating the A's three times in a four-game series, damaging the A's hopes of catching the Red Sox. The Naps came close to a first-division finish, but a 13-1 defeat at the hands of the Browns on October 5 clinched fifth place for the Naps. They wound up at 75-78, thirty and a half games behind the Red Sox.

Joe Jackson, too, responded to the change in a positive fashion. His batting average on August 31 stood at .377, but Joe went on an amazing tear in September. He belted 50 hits in 105 trips to the plate in September for a .476 average, which raised his final mark to .395.

Jackson entered the last game of the season with a .393 average. He needed to go six for six to finish at .400, but Joe never had six hits in a game in his career (in fact, he never had five hits in a game either). Joe hit a single, double, and triple in five trips to the plate and ended the season with a .395 mark. He fell three hits short of another .400 season, but his .395 average is still the second best in Cleveland history behind his .408 mark of the year before.

For the second straight year, Joe finished second to Ty Cobb in the batting race. Cobb, despite his suspensions and a series of quarrels with his teammates, batted .410 to win his sixth straight batting title. However, Joe's total of 26 triples not only led the American League, but also set a league record that stands to this day, though Detroit's Sam Crawford tied the record in 1914.[11] Joe had learned to spread his line drives all over the field; the record for triples was the result.

Joe Jackson also led the American League in total bases, despite the fact that he hit only three home runs. Though he finished second in slugging percentage, doubles, batting average, and runs scored, he only finished ninth in the Chalmers Most Valuable Player voting. Cobb, under the award rules of the time, was not eligible for the Chalmers award after winning it in 1911. Boston's young center fielder Tris Speaker, who led the Red Sox to a World Series championship, won the car.

Cleveland's newest star managed to stay healthy all year and played all but one of the 153 games on the schedule for the Naps. He stole 35 bases, finished second in the league with 226 hits and 44 doubles, and picked up 30 outfield assists. He committed 18 errors, three more than the year before, but increased his total of runs batted in to 90. Lajoie also drove in 90 runs, mostly because Joe was on base ahead of him so often, but Lajoie's age was catching up with him. The Frenchman hit only four triples in 1912 and no homers at all. By the end of the 1912 season Joe Jackson, not Nap Lajoie, was the acknowledged hitting star of the Cleveland ballclub.

Still, Joe knew that he would have a hard time winning the batting title as long as Ty Cobb remained in the American League. "What a hell of a league this is," wailed Jackson to a reporter. "I hit .387, .408, and .395 the last three years and I ain't won nothing yet!"[12]

A small item appeared in the sports pages of the *Cleveland Plain Dealer* in late September of 1911. The piece announced that all games of the Cleveland Amateur Baseball Association were canceled until further notice. The problem was that most of the spectators at the games were gamblers, who wagered hundreds of dollars on the outcomes of these amateur games. On September 26, a group of bettors rushed the field in the middle of a game, started a near-riot, and forced the postponement of a game that wasn't going the way they wanted.[13]

Gambling had been a highly destructive force in the earliest days of professional baseball 40 years before. Many old-timers still remembered how four members of the Louisville Grays threw the National League pennant race in 1877 at the behest of gamblers.[14] Now, in 1911, it was obvious that if gamblers had infiltrated even the lowest levels of recreational baseball, then it was reasonable to assume that the minor leagues, and even the majors, were not immune.

The major league club owners didn't want to admit it, but the phenomenon of baseball gambling was growing in all sections of the nation. However, the baseball moguls of the 1910s chose to ignore the painful lessons of the 1870s. Some club owners claimed that gambling and its related activities heightened interest in their ballclubs and resulted in higher ticket sales! They willfully chose to ignore the fact that when gamblers enter a sport, the fixers are never far behind.

Chapter 6

The Greatest
Natural Hitter

> Joe Jackson was another tough one. He hit me one day with a
> line drive off my shin, so hard I couldn't move. You know the
> pitcher isn't very far from the hitter. The ball bounced over to
> Frank Baker who threw him out at first base. Boy, I thought
> my leg was broken, but luckily, it wasn't.
> —*Bob Shawkey* [1]

By the beginning of the 1913 season, Joe Jackson's place as one of
the three or four biggest stars in baseball was secure, and it wasn't difficult
to find those who considered Joe a more valuable player than Ty Cobb.
Joe's .394 lifetime batting average was the highest in baseball at the time,[2]
and Joe didn't cause the turmoil and controversy that Cobb brought to
the Tigers on a yearly basis. Jackson's throwing arm and defensive ability were superior to Cobb's, and though the Tiger star kept winning the
batting title each year, the Naps probably would not have traded Jackson
for Cobb even up at that time. Cleveland manager Joe Birmingham agreed
with that assessment. Comparing Jackson to Cobb, Birmingham stated,
"I consider Joe the greater asset to a club of the two."[3]

The title of "the greatest natural hitter who ever lived," borne for so
long by Napoleon Lajoie, belonged solely to Joe Jackson by 1913. Joe was
not a scientific hitter, like Cobb; Joe never studied the tendencies of
opposing pitchers or kept a mental notebook of their strengths and

weaknesses. Jackson relied solely on his superior strength and his incredible eye-hand coordination to get the fat part of his bat into contact with the ball. If a teammate asked about a pitch Joe hit, Joe would usually not recall if it was high or low, curve or fastball. "It was over," Joe would say, meaning that he could reach it with his long bat. If Joe could reach the ball, that was all he needed to know. He also insisted that it made no difference to him whether the pitcher was a righthander or a lefthander, although he later identified Harry Krause and Reb Russell, both lefties, as the toughest pitchers he ever faced.[4]

No one in baseball swung as hard as Jackson. "I used to wonder why he didn't strike out at least twice a game," remarked Ty Cobb, "taking a full cut at a ball that flopped and ducked from the treatment it got, either by emery or thumbnail or saliva."[5]

Another contemporary of Joe's, Tris Speaker, admired Jackson's swing. "He was not only a natural hitter, but he had a set style, a grooved swing. I can't remember that he was ever in a batting slump. His swing was so perfect there was little chance of its ever getting disorganized."[6] Joe made contact so often that he stunned a crowd in New Orleans in October of 1912, when he struck out twice in an exhibition game against a young pitcher named Edwin Johnson. The unknown Johnson was inundated for weeks thereafter with offers from other minor league teams.

It seems clear, in retrospect, that Joe Jackson was a new kind of hitter. He took a full cut at the ball, rarely struck out, and kept his average stratospherically high, which made him the type of hitter that major league baseball had never seen before. Frank (Home Run) Baker of the A's, the hero of the 1911 World Series, was the closest thing to a modern-day power hitter in baseball at the time. Baker liked to swing hard, too, but he didn't hit for Joe's average and he struck out more often. Gavvy Cravath of the Phillies belted more homers than Joe, but Cravath took advantage of the tiny Phillies ballpark, in which the outfield fence was only 270 feet from home plate. Cravath, like Frank Baker, batted for a lower average and struck out far more often than Joe.

Jackson, unlike Cobb, did not obsess about his statistics. Cobb was the kind of player who would sometimes get a hit his first time up, then sit out the rest of the game to protect his batting average. Early in the 1913 season Joe struck out on three pitches against a Chicago rookie named Reb Russell, a Mississippian in his major league debut. The writers asked Joe how such a thing could happen. "No one was on, so what was the use of getting a hit?" asked Jackson quizzically. "We had the game won, and I didn't want to discourage a kid just breaking in."[7] It may have been a typical tongue-in-cheek answer from the Southern Storyteller, but it's almost impossible to imagine the same words coming out of Ty Cobb's mouth.

Joe also saw his popularity grow off the field. He made money endorsing bats, gloves, tobacco, and even shoes. One of the most famous advertising signs of the era shows a picture of Joe with the caption, "When Shoeless Joe Jackson wears 'em, he wears Selz shoes." He advertised Remington rifles on the back cover of *Baseball Magazine,* and he gave endorsements in magazines for Absorbine Jr. and other such products. In the winter months, he played exhibition games in his native South, sometimes forming a team with his five brothers and two cousins, charging admission and splitting the proceeds. Katie Jackson read and negotiated Joe's contracts, and her shrewd business sense helped Joe supplement his baseball salary, which rose to about $5,000 a year by 1913.

Joe's baseball salary alone was about 20 times greater than the yearly earnings of a Brandon Mill laborer, and Joe thoroughly enjoyed his newfound prosperity. He used his money to buy an interest in a poolroom in downtown Greenville, and he spent some more of it to buy a large house for his mother and father. Early in his Cleveland career Joe purchased some farmland outside of Greenville, and soon after that he bought a larger farm, which he hoped to put on a paying basis in short order. He also developed a fondness for fancy clothes—he owned dozens of pairs of expensive shoes—and, beginning in 1913, Joe bought new cars on a regular basis. The former mill hand was now far removed from his former life of poverty, though some onlookers wondered if Joe Jackson's money was going out faster than it was coming in.

Joe was one of baseball's most popular players, but the kids of Cleveland were his biggest fans. Crowds of children followed Joe from his home on Lexington Avenue to the ballpark every day, and the lucky few would get to carry Joe's glove, bats, or shoes for Joe on the way to the clubhouse. It seemed that every boy on the playgrounds of Cleveland wanted to emulate Joe Jackson. Many of them took to belting the ball rather than slapping at it in their sandlot games, and all over the city kids in the on-deck circle swung three bats, just like their hero. The fans in Cleveland also cheered their favorite player with cries of "Give 'em Black Betsy!" though by 1913 the fans knew the names of some of Joe's other bats. "Give 'em Dixie, Joe!" and "Give 'em Big Jim!" also echoed from the stands at League Park.

However, Joe apparently didn't see his baseball career as something that would last 20 years or more, as other stars such as Cy Young or Napoleon Lajoie did. In an interview that appeared in the highbrow *Literary Digest* in September of 1912, Joe discussed, in his usual slightly exaggerated way, the ups and downs of his career, his early misbehavior, and his newfound maturity as a big leaguer. He also revealed his aspirations for the future. "There is only one thing that I like better than playing ball, and that is farming," said the young slugger, whom the *Literary Digest* identified as "Barefoot Joe" Jackson. "I have owned and managed two different farms, and as soon as I get enough money to buy a good big place, it's me for the South and my farm."[8]

The Cleveland Naps held their 1913 spring training in Pensacola, Florida, and Joe Jackson, who mailed in his contract in February, arrived in camp on March 6 in his usual midseason form. In the first game of the spring, he belted a triple against the Yannigans his first time up. Working on the farm in Greenville and playing exhibition games down south during the winter kept Joe in good physical condition.

Though Joe enjoyed making a nice running catch in the outfield as much as anything, Joe amused himself by fielding grounders at first base whenever he found the chance. Joe liked playing the infield ever since his days with the Greenville Spinners, and he especially enjoyed borrowing a first baseman's glove and taking infield practice. "Joe has a hankering for the first base position," said the *Plain Dealer*.

Many players, in that era and today, liked to try their luck at other spots on the field. Ty Cobb fancied himself a pitcher, and Cobb talked his manager into letting him play second base once during the 1913 season, with disastrous results (Cobb handled five chances and made three errors).[9] Joe Jackson was an excellent outfielder, and already the sportswriters were calling Joe's glove "the place triples go to die." However, Joe also liked playing on the infield, and he made it known that he would be available to play first base if called upon.

As usual, the Naps played a series in New Orleans against the Pelicans at the end of March. However, the Ohio River flood of 1913 disrupted train service all through Ohio and points south, and the Naps canceled games in Mobile, Chattanooga, and Cincinnati. The Naps returned to Cleveland by way of Washington in early April.

The Naps, for once, got off to a good start in 1913. Fred (Cy) Falkenburg, a righthander who won 25 games at Toledo in 1912, joined the starting rotation and made up half of a righty-lefty tandem with Vean Gregg. Catcher Steve O'Neill, whom Connie Mack gave to the Naps to help Harry Davis the year before, blossomed as a hitter. Joe Birmingham broke his leg on May 11, but Jackson, Jack Graney, and Nemo Leibold solidified the outer defense and helped the pitchers with their speed in the outfield.

Nap Lajoie started the season strongly, though his power was almost gone by now, but the Frenchman hurt his back in early May and sat out for two weeks. In his absence, the infield of Johnston, Turner, Chapman, and Olson performed so well that Joe Birmingham didn't want to disrupt a winning combination. When the Frenchman returned he seethed on the bench, but kept silent for the moment. At the beginning of June, the Naps stood alone in second place with a 29-12 record, only one and a half games behind the streaking Athletics.

In the meantime, Joe Jackson grabbed the early-season batting lead, and it appeared that the 1913 season would provide another interesting batting race for the enjoyment of the fans. Ty Cobb, volatile as ever, staged a holdout for the first several weeks of the 1913 season. He de-

Joe Birmingham and Joe Jackson in 1913. This picture was taken not long after Birmingham broke his leg in May of that year (author's collection).

manded an unheard-of $15,000 salary, and for a while it looked like Cobb would play semipro ball in 1913 if he played at all. By the end of April, Cobb softened his position and signed for a prorated $12,000. He played his first game on April 30, and in his first 18 games Cobb belted the ball at a .492 clip before he cooled down to the .400 mark.

Joe, as usual, paid no attention to Cobb's contract dispute. Jackson pounded the ball as hard as ever in the early days of the 1913 season, and he led Cleveland's charge into the pennant race. In early May Joe cleared the bases twice in two days; he hit a bases-loaded triple on May 10 against the Red Sox, and the next day he belted his second career grand slam against the Yankees. In June, Joe Jackson topped the league's batters with a mark of .447, with 71 hits in 159 trips to the plate. The opposing pitchers found, much to Joe's chagrin, that the only way to keep Joe from beating them was to walk him.

"When I go up against an ordinary pitcher," said Jackson, "one I can hit with my eyes shut, he passes me if there is anyone on the bases. So, the only chance I have to get any hits is when no one is on or when one of the star pitchers of the league is in the box. I think the big leagues ought to pass a rule either forbidding the passing of a batter purposely or to let each runner on the sacks advance a base. That would prevent their passing me with a runner on third."[10]

If anyone had failed to acknowledge Joe Jackson's emergence as the most dangerous hitter in the American League, Joe made them all sit up and take notice on June 4, 1913. In that game, Joe golfed a low fastball from the Yankees' Russell Ford over the right-field grandstand at the Polo Grounds and into the street beyond. It was a mammoth blast, estimated at more than 500 feet, and most observers called it the longest home run ever hit in the major leagues up to that time.

The New York writers were impressed. "Jackson's hit was a record," said Sam Crane in the *Evening Journal.* "I have seen famous home runs by Buck Ewing, Dave Orr, Anson, Dan Brouthers, Roger Connor, Sam Thompson, Ed Delahanty, Mike Tiernan, and others at grounds all over the big leagues. I have seen many a historic home run. I could go on for hours and tell you about them, but I take my hat off to Joe Jackson of Cleveland, for making the longest hit I ever saw, and that was yesterday."[11]

Grantland Rice immortalized the blow in the *New York Mail* two days later:

> You know where Wagner's landed,
> We saw where Baker's hit,
> But no one ever found the ball that Joseph Jackson hit.

A mid-season series with the league-leading A's showed that the Naps were not yet ready for World Series contention. On Thursday, June 12, Philadelphia's Eddie Plank beat the Naps 6-1, the only Cleveland run coming from a home run by Jackson in the ninth inning. The Naps lost 2-1 on Friday, won 3-0 on Saturday, and then lost again to Plank on Monday by a 3-2 score. There was no Sunday ball in Philadelphia at the time, so the Naps returned to Cleveland to play Washington and lost 10-5 to the Nationals. After this disastrous weekend, the Naps found themselves five and a half games out of first place.

The season quickly ran downhill from there. Lajoie suffered a hand injury when hit by a pitch thrown by Boston's Joe Wood, and Joe Jackson was beaned in the infield by a ball thrown by Chicago's Morrie Rath on June 20. The blow affected Joe's hearing for several days thereafter. Two days after that accident, a violent argument between Joe and umpire Bob Egan in Detroit resulted in Joe's indefinite suspension by the league.

"I cursed him, but he cursed me first," protested Jackson to no avail. He sat out three games, then paid a $25 fine and rejoined the lineup. In that same game, Ty Cobb ran into Cleveland first baseman Doc Johnston and suffered a wrenched back, knocking the Georgian out of the Tiger lineup.

The worst part of the 1913 season was soon to come, when Joe Birmingham did the unthinkable. He officially benched Napoleon Lajoie on June 28, after which Lajoie cursed the manager in front of his teammates and threatened to quit the team. Birmingham, reluctant to put the slow-footed Frenchman back into the starting lineup, stood firm. "If Lajoie is at all dissatisfied with his treatment by the Cleveland team," said the manager, "he doesn't have to stay with it."[12]

Lajoie, in turn, unloaded his frustrations to the sportswriters. "Birmingham was trying to tell me how to bat, me, who was hitting .300 when he was in primary school," said the Frenchman, "and he was doing the same for Joe Jackson when Joe was hitting over .400. Birmingham never hit .250 in his life, so where does he get the license to pose as teacher?" The manager's gruff manner also irritated Lajoie, who complained, "Birmingham can't tell a man what to do without speaking to him as if he were a dog."[13] The benching lasted only four games, but June ended with the Naps winning only 12 of their 27 games in the month.

The A's pulled away from the rest of the league in July. On July 4 the A's held a nine-game lead over the second-place Naps, and lengthened the lead by beating Cleveland two out of three from July 9 to July 11. The Naps, powered by Joe Jackson's hot bat, chipped away at the lead, and in the last week of July they swept three doubleheaders in a week to pull to within seven and a half games.

Jackson belted the ball at a .400 clip through July, and on August 2 he led the league with a .406 average. Joe then fell into a two-week funk, which ended on August 15 when he borrowed one of Nap Lajoie's bats and hit two singles in a loss to the A's. With Joe's slump over, the Naps beat the A's on August 16 in Cleveland by a 10 to 1 score, as Joe Jackson pounded a homer far over the 40-foot fence in right. The next day, over 25,000 fans saw the Naps beat the A's again, 6-2, as the Naps closed to within seven and a half games of the lead.

Unfortunately, disaster struck the Naps again. A friendly wrestling match on a train between the team's top two pitchers, Cy Falkenburg and Vean Gregg, resulted in arm injuries for both, right before a series with the Senators in Washington. The Naps lost five in a row to the Senators and the Red Sox to drop out of the race for good.

Joe Jackson slumped again in late August, mostly due to a sinus infection that lasted more than two weeks. However, he found an interesting

diversion off the field. Joe became fascinated with the sport of motorcy-
cle racing, and he and several other Naps attended the "chug-bike" races
at Luna Park, a Cleveland amusement park. Joe served as a starter for a
race in late August, and he told the papers that he'd like to race a bike
himself in the near future. The reaction of Charles Somers to this disturbing piece of information was not recorded.

By early September, the Naps struggled back to within seven games
of the A's, but Connie Mack's team pulled away to their third pennant in
four years. The Naps lost two doubleheaders to Washington on September 9 and 10, then lost the next day as Joe Jackson suffered one of the
most unusual injuries ever seen on a ball field. The Senators' park featured a wooden bull on the right field fence, an advertisement for the Bull
Durham tobacco company, and batters could win $50 for hitting the bull.
Joe hit the bull while playing the outfield, knocking himself unconscious
when he slammed into the bull's horns while chasing a fly ball. This injury
sealed the Naps' pennant chances, slim as they were, and on September
22 the A's clinched the flag as the Senators slipped past the Naps into
second place.

Joe's batting average settled into the .380s, and Cleveland fans turned
their attention away from the pennant chase and toward another show-
down between Jackson and Ty Cobb for the batting title. Both Jackson
and Cobb kept their averages above .400 in June and July, and Jackson
led Cobb by ten points in mid–July. However, Cobb again put on a
tremendous rush to the championship, leaving Joe and the rest of the
league in his wake. Cobb sewed up the crown in Cleveland on September 27, when he went six for seven in a doubleheader sweep of the Naps.
At season's end Cobb's average stood at .390, with Joe Jackson in second
place for the third year in a row with a .373 mark.

The Naps finished the season in third place with an 86-66 record,
nine games behind the A's, for their best finish since their near-pennant
in 1908. Most importantly for Charles Somers, the 1913 Naps set an attendance record with 541,000 paid admissions. Despite the injuries and con-
troversies that engulfed the team during the season, the Naps ended the
1913 campaign with high hopes for 1914.

Joe Jackson, despite his failure to wrest the batting title away from
Cobb, enjoyed one of his greatest seasons. Joe finished first in the league
in hits with 197 and doubles with 39, and also in slugging percentage with
a .551 mark, breaking a six-year run by Cobb at the top of the league in
that department. Joe also had 28 outfield assists. The league tracked batters' strikeouts in 1913 for the first time, and Joe, the hardest swinger in
baseball, struck out only 26 times in over 500 trips to the plate.

Most significantly, Joe's total of walks rose from 54 in 1912 to 80 in 1913. Most of those extra walks were of the intentional variety, another indication of Joe's dominance as a hitter. It also proved that the pitchers of the American League were perfectly willing to walk Joe Jackson and take their chances with Nap Lajoie.

Joe's efforts did not go unnoticed. He finished second to Washington's Walter Johnson in the Chalmers Most Valuable Player balloting. If the Naps could have held on to second place, or if Joe hadn't batted only .311 after August 2, Joe might have won the car.

At season's end, the Naps and the Pittsburgh Pirates of the National League agreed to meet in a best-of-seven postseason series. This Pirate team was the remnant of one of the powerhouse teams of the National League in the early 1900s. They had fallen in the standings after defeating the Detroit Tigers in the 1909 World Series, but they still employed several outstanding players on their roster. This series would mark the only time that two of baseball's greatest hitters, Cleveland's Joe Jackson and Pittsburgh's Honus Wagner, would meet on the playing field.

The first two games were played at Cleveland on October 6 and 7, and the Naps won both games in front of 3,735 and 3,971 fans. Joe Jackson won the second game with a run-scoring single in the ninth inning, and he made a rare unassisted double play from the outfield. He caught a sinking liner in League Park's short right field, then ran to first to double up the runner. The scene then shifted to Pittsburgh, where nearly 8,000 fans saw the Pirates defeat the Naps in the third game, 4 to 3.

The Pirates won the next two games, but Vean Gregg tied the series at Pittsburgh's Forbes Field with a 1-0 win in which Gregg struck out 19 Pirates in 13 innings. On October 14 the Naps won the seventh and deciding game in Pittsburgh by a 4-1 score. The victorious Naps took home $232.25 each for their efforts, while the Pirates earned $176.96 per man.

Joe returned to Cleveland and packed his car for the trip down south. Henry Edwards, the baseball writer for the *Plain Dealer*, caught up with the slugger and got his last interview of the 1913 season. "Joe had an automobile, five or six dogs, more or less pedigreed, particularly less," reported Edwards, "and eighteen bats, which he simply could not allow to remain in Cleveland during the winter months."[14]

Joe, the southern storyteller, was in a talkative mood that day. "Climate up in Cleveland is too cold for them bats," said Joe as he picked up each bat, then laid it down again. "Bats are like ball players, you know. They like the warm weather—not too warm—but just warm enough. Wouldn't think of leaving those pets up here." Joe then decided to introduce the reporter to some of the bats. "Now, there's Old Ginril. Not for a moment would I leave him here. Ginril was the one that hit the ball the time I knocked it over the stand at the Polo Grounds. I wish I'd a been in the world's series. I'd turn the trick again.

"Now, here's Old Caroliny. She's one of the sweetest bats I have, but lately she's kind of balked on me. Don't know what's the matter. I could always call on her for a hit in June or July but when the weather got cooler she got cranky and, well, she wouldn't produce. When she got back on me I tried out this baby—Big Jim."

Joe smiled as he picked up Big Jim. "Say now, isn't he a peach? I sure do like to grip him. He'll be a winner next year, but he hasn't got used to the big league yet. You see, it was only a few months ago that he was part of a wagon tongue down in Louisville. Because the weather up here was chilly, we wrapped the handle in cork. Just keep your eye on Big Jim next spring and watch me drive 'em to the bench. But Old Ginril and Old Caroliny will be the pair to get your bets down on next summer. They're my hot weather clubs."[15] With that, Joe waved at Henry Edwards and drove away.

Joe spent most of the winter at home in Greenville, but he and Katie journeyed to New Orleans in late October. Joe and Sam Crawford, the hard-hitting right fielder of the Detroit Tigers, were the star attractions in a series of weekend exhibition games. Joe and Crawford recruited players from other major league teams and from local minor leagues. They made a simple financial arrangement in which the players themselves sold the tickets and the refreshments, then divided the proceeds at the end of the game. There wasn't a lot of money involved; after paying the expenses and splitting the receipts among all the players, Joe's share was usually somewhere between $1 and $7 per game.[16]

However, Joe didn't seem to mind. He loved New Orleans, with its nightclubs and vaudeville shows, and he loved playing ball. His annual vacation in New Orleans allowed him to combine his twin passions, playing baseball by day and attending the shows and bars until late at night. Joe Jackson, at age 25, had never enjoyed himself more. This former millworker was just beginning to discover the glamorous life of a sports celebrity.

Chapter 7

Last Place

The good hitters of that period had to choke the bat or go in for punch hitting. All except Jackson. Joe still took his full swing and he was often up there from .380 to .410. I know I could never have hit above .300 with that type of swing. Only Jackson, old Shoeless Joe, had the eye and the timing and the smoothness to do that.

— *Ty Cobb* [1]

In the winter of 1913-1914, the main baseball news concerned an ill-fated attempt at forming a third major league. The Federal League played as a six-team minor league in 1913 and had even placed a team in Cleveland with Cy Young as manager. That winter, the Federal circuit declared itself "major" and began courting players from the American and National circuits. A Chicago coal millionaire named James Gilmore financed the new league, which immediately began scouting for parks in established major league cities, including Cleveland. They also announced that they intended to ignore baseball's reserve clause, believing it to be unconstitutional.

The reserve clause was the item in each player's contract that assigned the player's services to his club for the current contract year and the next. The owners introduced it in the 1870s to keep players from "revolving"— that is, from jumping from team to team from one year to the next, or even from one week to the next. However, the owners quickly used it to tighten their control over the players. It didn't take long for the owners to regard the reserve clause as perpetual, meaning that the club's hold on the player's services rolled over each year to the next year, forever if the club so chose. The reserve clause, used in this way, restricted the competition between teams for players' services, resulting in lower salaries for players and higher profits for the owners. The Federal League planned to entice players to break these one-sided contracts with the major leagues; they appeared confident that the broken contracts, with the reserve clause, would not hold up in court.

The major leagues feared exactly this kind of legal challenge. As early as 1896 the National League owners paid off Amos Rusie, star pitcher of the New York Giants, to keep him from taking the league to court over the reserve clause. Rusie had endured a nasty series of disagreements with Giants owner Andrew Freedman, and Rusie sat out the 1896 season rather than accept a pay cut. The quarrelsome Freedman refused to give in, and the other league owners feared that Rusie would go to court and have his contract with the Giants declared null and void. This would have voided all other major league contracts as well. The frightened owners paid Rusie his entire 1896 salary to settle the dispute without legal intervention, saving the reserve clause from legal jeopardy.

Shoeless Joe Jackson also felt the effects of the reserve clause. Joe hated playing in Philadelphia in 1908 and 1909, but he couldn't simply return to Greenville and resume playing for the Spinners. According to the rules of organized baseball, the Philadelphia Athletics held the rights to his services in perpetuity, and Joe could either play in Philadelphia or go back to work at the textile mill. In truth, if Joe could have picked his own team to play for, it probably would have been Washington, the closest major league city to Greenville, but Connie Mack sent Joe to Cleveland instead. Mack had the right to do so under the rules of baseball, and Joe's preferences never entered into the decision-making process.

The strategy of the Federal League mirrored that followed by the American League 13 years before. They wanted to sign star players, cause economic hardship to the established majors, and force the majors to settle for peace terms. George Stovall, the former Cleveland first baseman and manager, was the first prominent player to join the Federals. He immediately went to work signing players for the new league, and Stovall was so successful that the papers started calling him "the Jesse James of the Federal League." The Feds also tried to entice players with liberalized free-agency rules and profit sharing in the teams themselves.

However, it seemed obvious to even the most casual observer that the nation would not support 24 major league teams. Baseball attendance fell sharply in 1914, mostly due to the turmoil in Europe and competition from motion pictures and other forms of entertainment. Already, cities like St. Louis and Philadelphia had trouble drawing enough fans to support two clubs, and now the Federals expected them to support three. Most major league observers foresaw the eventual collapse of the Feds but hunkered down for another costly baseball war.

The possible court challenge to the reserve clause concerned the major league owners far more than the competition at the box office worried them. In response, the major leagues began issuing contracts split in a 75-25 arrangement. Seventy-five percent of the contract would be paid for the player's service on the field, while the other 25 percent would be paid for the player's reserve rights for the next season. In this way, the owners sought to head off any threat to the reserve clause.

Soon the Feds had placed teams in Baltimore, Chicago, St. Louis, Pittsburgh, Kansas City, Buffalo, and Indianapolis. The league awarded its eighth team to Toronto temporarily, although the Feds still hoped to invade Cleveland. The greatest damage done to the Naps, however, came on January 27, 1914, when three Cleveland pitchers—Cy Falkenberg, Fred Blanding, and George Kahler—signed contracts with the Federal League. Falkenberg, who had won 23 games in 1913, was Cleveland's ace, and his loss cut the heart out of the pitching staff. The Indianapolis Federal team also claimed that they had agreed to terms with Naps shortstop Ray Chapman, though that report later proved untrue.

Charles Somers, belatedly, got busy. On January 30 the club announced the signings of five key players (Johnston, Olson, Graney, Knight, and James). A few days later, in Greenville, club secretary Bill Blackwood signed Joe Jackson to a three-year deal for $6,000 a year. Federal League agents came to Jackson's farm before Blackwood arrived, but Jackson told the papers that he drove them off his property by threatening to use Black Betsy on them. Joe also said that the Feds offered him $20,000 a year to jump from the Naps.[2]

Soon almost all the Naps were safely under contract, but the loss of Falkenberg hurt the club tremendously in 1914. Their other 20-game winner, Vean Gregg, came up with a sore arm in training camp, and the Naps entered the season without their two key pitchers from 1913.

Jackson's new contract invited a great deal of speculation, most of it false. Henry Edwards wrote in the *Plain Dealer*, "The Feds would have to pay a prohibitive sum to get him, as Joe is now receiving from Somers an amount which puts him right alongside of Speaker and Cobb. The writer is not able to state the exact sum, but it is more than any Cleveland player ever got before and practically the same as is received by those other two distinguished sons of Swat from Dixie."[3] A day later Edwards

Joe Jackson collectible felt "blanket." Cigarette companies issued felt squares, featuring more than 90 major league players, in 1914 as giveaway items. Mothers sewed collections of the squares together as blankets or throws (author's collection).

reported that, "according to rumor," Jackson would receive progressive bonuses for batting .350, .375, and .400.

In truth, Jackson's contract paid him nowhere near the $12,000 or more that Cobb and Speaker were getting at the time, and Jackson's pay was not close to that of the veteran Lajoie. The Naps' top salary was $9,000 a year, which would belong to Lajoie as long as the popular Frenchman remained with the club. It is quite possible that the papers purposely exaggerated Jackson's salary to scare off the Federal League and keep Joe in Cleveland.

Hindsight is always 20-20, but Joe could not have signed a long-

Selz shoes advertising sign, 1914 (author's collection).

term deal at a worse time. Nap Lajoie turned 39 in 1914 and would not last forever in a Cleveland uniform, and when Lajoie was no longer on the club the top salary slot would open up for Jackson. By signing a three-year deal, Jackson tied himself into a $6,000 salary until 1916, when Lajoie would be 41 years old. Joe could have signed a one-year deal and waited to see if the Federal League would sink or swim. Of course, this is exactly what the Cleveland management wanted to avoid.

Lajoie, despite his age, had batted .335 in 1913, and although his relations with Joe Birmingham were frosty at best, the Frenchman wasn't leaving Cleveland any time soon. Joe Jackson apparently saw himself in the $6,000 slot for at least a few more seasons. Also, players at that time always ran the risk of serious injury; many a star player suffered a broken leg or sore throwing arm and found his salary cut in half the next season. That's why Jackson locked himself into a three-year deal instead of a one-year pact.

Joe must have been sorely tempted to cast his lot with the Federal League. The new circuit offered to triple his salary at a time when Joe could have used the extra money. George Jackson, Joe's father, was ill all through the winter of 1913–14, and when George died on February 11 he left a widow and eight children, most of whom were not yet on their own. Gertrude, the youngest, was only eight years old. However, the Federal League's financing looked shaky, and at this point Joe showed no interest in switching leagues. "The Feds got after me when I was in Atlanta," said Jackson to the *Plain Dealer* on March 24, "but there is no use of their bothering me; I am not going to go to them."

First baseman Hal Chase, recently traded from the Yankees to the White Sox, was the most prominent player to jump to the Feds, but most of the other stars stayed put. The Feds offered Ty Cobb a $75,000 five-year contract to jump, but the Tigers quickly agreed to a $15,000 one-year deal with their star outfielder. Walter Johnson signed with the Chicago Federal team, but he soon returned to Washington after the Senators received financial help from the American League to meet Johnson's salary demands. The Senators also had to return the $6,000 bonus that the Feds had given Johnson.

After Johnson's near-defection, the major leagues threatened to permanently ban any players who jumped to the new circuit. Joe Jackson ignored any more overtures, even from his former manager George Stovall, now running the Kansas City Federal team. "If Stovall thinks any of us will jump," said Jackson to the *Plain Dealer*, "he's got another think coming. He might just as well stay away and save himself a lot of time."[4]

In early February 1914 Charles Somers took action to head off a possible Federal League invasion of Cleveland. He moved his American Association team, the Toledo Mud Hens, to Cleveland and renamed them the Scouts. The Scouts would play in League Park when the Naps were on the road, providing baseball every single day for the Cleveland fans. It's not clear whether Somers did this at the suggestion of his friend Ban Johnson, but the ploy worked. On February 7, the Feds officially dropped their plans to place a team in Cleveland. They soon moved the Toronto team to Brooklyn.

In the meantime, the Naps gathered in Athens, Georgia, for spring training. Joe Jackson arrived there on March 3, after driving the 60 miles from Greenville in a shiny new Ford. He hadn't swung a bat since his exhibition series in New Orleans the previous October, and his eyes were watery from the windy drive, but Joe couldn't wait to hit the field. Still in his street clothes, he grabbed a bat and stepped into the batter's box against Nick Cullop. Joe was pleased when he pounded several hard drives to the outfield. "My eyes are all right," Joe announced with relief. "Just watch out for me this year. I just couldn't wait until I had given them a test."[5]

Joe changed into his uniform but elected not to participate in the scheduled practice. Instead, he and Ivy Olson "collected a squad of fifty colored boys and amused themselves for over an hour in knocking grounders and flies ... to the volunteer fielders."[6] Predictably, both Jackson and Olson developed blisters on their hands from this impromptu workout.

The weather that spring was unusually cold and damp all over the South, and the Naps lost a great deal of practice time to the elements. Worse, the "Yannigans" or "Naplets," a team made up of reserves and players destined for the Scouts, began beating the Naps with regularity. Joe Jackson got off to a torrid start with the bat, but Nap Lajoie and most of the other regulars struggled to get into shape in the chilly weather.

In addition, the injury bug bit the Naps with frustrating regularity. Outfielder Jack Graney suffered burns in a freak accident. The trainer gave him a solution to ease the pain of a scraped toe, but Graney applied the solution without diluting it first, then went to bed. He woke up the next morning with severely burned toes, which put him on the sidelines for several days.

The season's most sinister omen occurred on March 11, when Ray Chapman injured his leg sliding into second base at the end of a practice session. The leg turned out to be broken, and Chapman was lost to the Naps for three months. They would have to open the season with Ivy Olson at shortstop. Olson didn't have Chapman's range, and with the slow-footed 39-year-old Lajoie at second base, the infield suddenly became more porous.

Joe Jackson, meanwhile, arranged for the Naps to play two exhibition games in Greenville. According to the *Plain Dealer*, Joe "spent half an hour ... telling [Birmingham] what a great place his town would be for the Naps to train in."[7] Birmingham returned to Cleveland with Chapman and left Joe in charge for two games against Furman College on March 13 and 14.

Joe's family, including his recently widowed mother Martha, attended the games, and his brother Earl donned a uniform and took infield practice with the Naps. The turnout for the first game was disappointingly small; a newspaper headline said that "the crowd [was] busy taking a drink by himself," but the second game, on a Saturday, drew about 400 people in the rain and cold. It was "Joe Jackson Day" in Greenville, and Joe, who served as temporary manager of the Naps, drove in six runs as the Naps bombed the college nine by a 26-4 score. The Naps committed a few intentional fielding miscues in the last two innings to allow the college boys to get on the scoreboard.

The Cleveland writers were disappointed in Greenville, since the red clay infield had no grass and the outfield didn't have much either. Also, the outfield sloped uphill just behind the infield and was rutted from the previous fall's football games. The Greenville park was "everything a well built up baseball plant should not be," groused Henry Edwards in the *Plain Dealer*, and Joe soon dropped the idea of getting the Naps to move their spring training base to his hometown.

A few days later, after the Naps returned to Athens, the team received a visit from an unusual fan. Ty Cobb's mother, the widowed Amanda Cobb, was in Athens to attend a play and found out that the Cleveland team was training in the city. She contacted the team because she wanted to meet her son's two main rivals, Nap Lajoie and Joe Jackson.

Though the other Naps struggled to gain their form, Joe Jackson started hitting right away. By early April Joe's batting average was above .500 for the spring, and his slugging percentage was nearly .900. He pounded two triples and a single against Atlanta on April 1, then followed the next day with the longest home run ever seen at the Atlanta park. That blast flew over a high sign in right field and struck a railroad sign 50 feet beyond, between the words "Round" and "Trip." Joe, usually a slow starter, could not explain his hot bat. "I'd just as soon not hit so well before the season opens," said Jackson. "As a rule when I don't hit well on the training trip I cut loose when the bell starts, but somehow or other I can't help hitting this year."[8]

In one exhibition game in Chattanooga, Joe was called to bat in the ninth inning after he had already taken off his spikes. He went to bat in a pair of street shoes and singled. The only thing that could stop Joe was an attack of ptomaine poisoning, which kept him in bed in Cincinnati for nearly a week just before the start of the season.

When the team played its final southern spring training game in Lexington, Kentucky, on April 4, the weather was cold, and the players wanted to get the game over as quickly as possible. In the sixth inning Joe caught a snake in the outfield, then brought it to the mound and threatened to put it down pitcher Nick Cullop's back if he didn't regain his control. Cullop had walked four men in the inning up to that point, but walked no one else the rest of the game. The last three innings were a farce. Joe went to the plate right-handed and singled. Cullop pitched with one eye on the plate and the other on Joe and the snake. Several Naps hit singles and purposely got thrown out stretching for doubles, as the Lexington outfielders piled up five assists. Cleveland won the game 6-2.

The 1914 season began in disastrous fashion. The Naps lost pitcher

Bill Steen in the second game, when he broke a bone in his hand while trying to lay down a bunt. Fred Blanding returned from the Feds, but Nick Cullop bolted to George Stovall's Kansas City team soon after. The Naps played their first seven games on the road, lost them all, and then returned to Cleveland and lost their home opener as well. They finally broke into the win column at home against the White Sox on April 23. After that game, Joe Jackson's average stood at .406, but Nap Lajoie's was a mere .125. On May 15 Jackson led the American League with a .403 average, but the Naps floundered in last place with a 6-14 record.

Joe then fell into a two-week slump that dropped his average into the .320s, and soon the whole team descended into a mass batting slump. In a five-day period from May 31 to June 4, the Naps were no-hit by Chicago's Joe Benz, and one-hit by St. Louis rookie Wylie Taylor and by Chicago's Jim Scott. The only hit off Scott was a second inning single by Joe Jackson. Nap Lajoie, batting behind Jackson in the Cleveland lineup, struggled to keep his average above .250.

Appearing before small crowds, the Naps played sloppily and listlessly. Joe Jackson crashed a home run against St. Louis on June 1, but he also committed three errors in the outfield, two on one play when he dropped a fly ball and made a wild throw. "The smallest crowd of the year was present," said the *Plain Dealer* the next day. "That is probably one point in favor of the club. The fewer witnesses to such an affair, the better for the financial end of baseball."

The worst calamity to befall the Naps in 1914, besides Chapman's broken leg, was the first serious injury of Joe Jackson's young career. On June 11, he suffered a contusion while sliding against the A's. His knee became seriously infected, badly enough to keep Joe out of the starting lineup. The Naps' rash of injuries forced them to play against the league-leading A's on June 12 without Jackson, Chapman, or Lajoie, though the shorthanded Naps battled hard before losing by a 10 to 8 score. Two days later Joe limped to the plate in the ninth inning against Washington and stroked a pinch-hit double, igniting a rally for a come-from-behind win. His knee soon got worse, and Joe landed in the hospital for nearly a week. He remained in Cleveland when the Naps left for a road trip to Detroit and St. Louis. In all, Joe remained on the sidelines for almost a month; he didn't rejoin the starting lineup until July 8.

By the time Ray Chapman returned to the lineup on June 16, the Naps had fallen too far off the pace to get back into the pennant race. The team rose to seventh place for two days at the beginning of July but quickly reclaimed the basement. On July 9, Jack Graney booted a ball in left field with the bases loaded; all three runners scored, and the frustrated manager Birmingham fined Graney 25 dollars. In the same game, Jackson showed that his knee was sound when he made a tumbling circus catch in right field. Graney was steaming after the fine, and took out his anger on the Yankees the next day with four hits. One Cleveland writer wondered why Birmingham didn't fine the entire team.

The pitching staff had problems too. Vean Gregg, a three-time 20-game winner, battled a sore arm and won only nine games before he was traded to the Red Sox in mid-season. Guy Morton lost 13 decisions in a row, a league record that stands to this day,[9] and finished 1-13. Despite a respectable-sounding team earned-run average of 3.21, the team finished dead last in the American League in that department. They also led the league in hits allowed and walks allowed, as 15 different pitchers started games for the Naps that year.

Off the field, the Federal League sued to keep Fred Blanding from playing for Cleveland. The major league owners also considered plans to start their own third major league to drive the Federals out of business, though that idea quickly died a merciful death.

The Federal League competition caused havoc all over the major leagues. On April 29 the Naps played on a cold, rainy day in St. Louis, because the Browns refused to call off the game. The Federals were playing across town, and the Browns were determined to play their game also, so the Naps and Browns battled to a 12-inning tie before only 289 fans. Attendance suffered in the cities with three teams, St. Louis and Chicago, and many of the clubs resorted to artificially inflating their reported attendance. "The man who guesses the attendance figures at the Brooklyn Feds park should be a census taker," said the *Plain Dealer*. "In case of a double header he takes the attendance of the first game and adds it to the number present at the second game."[10]

In Cleveland, the last-place Naps saw one of the biggest attendance drops in all of baseball. The Cleveland Scouts drew off some of the fans, as well as much of the newspaper coverage that had once belonged solely to the Naps. The fans simply would not come out to see their team, especially when so many of the biggest Cleveland stars were out of the lineup for extended lengths of time. By midsummer, crowds of less than 1,000 were common in League Park on the weekdays.

The ambitious Hal Chase found a weapon for the Federal League to use against the established majors. Chase, like almost all players, had the "ten-day" clause in his contract, which allowed the club to release Chase on ten days notice for any reason at all. The Yankees had traded him to the Chicago White Sox, who promptly cut his salary from $8,000 to $6,000 a year. Therefore, Chase gave ten days notice to the White Sox, then jumped to the Buffalo Federal team. Chase claimed that the players as well as the owners should be allowed to break their contracts on ten days notice.

The Federals argued that if the major leagues allowed only the owners to use this clause to their advantage, then the major leagues qualified as an illegal monopoly in violation of the 1890 Sherman Anti-Trust Act. The major leagues threatened to bring the Federal League into court on a charge of conspiracy for luring players away from their major league contracts. The whole distasteful mess grew worse with each passing week, turning off the fans

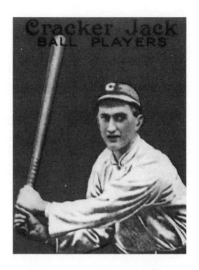

Cracker Jack card featuring Joe, 1915 (author's collection).

in all major league cities and squeezing the games themselves off the sports pages.

The Naps played in a historic game in Boston on July 11, 1914. The Red Sox had signed a big left-handed pitcher named George "Babe" Ruth, a 19-year-old just a few months removed from St. Mary's Industrial School in Baltimore. Ruth took the mound against the Naps in Fenway Park that day for his first appearance in the major leagues. The rookie beat the Naps 4 to 3, though he needed relief help from Dutch Leonard in the late innings. "Manager Joe Birmingham, after the game, appeared to think that Ruth would develop into a sensational twirler," said the *Plain Dealer*. Babe Ruth went 0 for 2 at the plate before Duffy Lewis pinch-hit for him in the seventh.

In the first inning, a play occurred that summarized the entire season for the Naps. With Jack Graney on second and one out, Jackson singled sharply to center. Graney should have scored, but Tris Speaker played a shallow center field, and Graney didn't want to test Speaker's arm. Graney retreated to third as Speaker pegged the ball to Ruth, who threw to first to hold Jackson there. As Ruth's throw went to first, Graney set out for home. The first baseman's throw to catcher Bill Carrigan caught Graney at the plate, and so a single with a runner on second turned into an out with a runner on first. To add insult to injury, Ruth then picked Jackson off first to end the inning. In the fourth inning, Joe singled again with Graney on second, but this time Graney scored without incident, as

Joe Jackson became the first major leaguer to drive in a run against Babe Ruth.

That game cost the Naps dearly. Jackson was hit in the shin with a pitched ball during batting practice before the game and woke up the next morning with a deep, painful bruise. He spent the last three games of the Boston series on the sidelines and watched the Naps lose all three. This losing streak buried the Naps in the cellar for the rest of the season.

Strangely enough, the Naps had no problem beating the best pitcher in baseball at the time, Washington's Walter Johnson. On August 3 the Naps defeated Johnson for the third time in 1914 by a score of 3 to 2, as Joe Jackson belted a double and two singles to lead the Cleveland attack. Johnson explained later that Jackson was the toughest hitter he ever faced. "I could throw my fast one past Cobb, Crawford, Lajoie, and all those fellows," said Johnson years later, "but Jackson was always a puzzle." Jackson hit Johnson so well that Ty Cobb angrily accused Johnson of letting up against Jackson while trying extra hard against Cobb. "But, if anything, I tried harder against Jackson," insisted Washington's Big Train, "because he always seemed tougher."[11]

By the end of the year, only 185,000 fans had paid their way into League Park, a little more than a third of the record turnout of 1913 and the lowest Cleveland attendance since 1901. The Naps held last place all season long, except for a brief peek at seventh place on June 30 and July 1. Nap Lajoie hit only .258 after his .335 of the year before, but most of the Naps performed more poorly than they had in finishing third in 1913. The loss of Falkenberg to the Feds, Chapman's and Jackson's injuries, and the uncertain contract status of Blanding all contributed to the only last-place finish the Cleveland fans would see until 1969. The Naps won 51 games and lost 102, and finished 48 and a half games behind the pennant winning A's. The only interesting thing that happened in the last part of the season was Napoleon Lajoie's 3,000th career hit on September 27.[12] In that same game, Guy Morton won his first game of the season after 13 straight losses.

The end of the 1914 season brought one more humiliation for the Cleveland Naps. A group of independent teams, centered in north central Ohio, held a four-team postseason tournament in early October, and the makeshift league allowed its members to sign players from other circuits to beef up their rosters. The team from Crestline, a small town about 70 miles southwest of Cleveland, signed Joe Jackson and seven other Naps. The Shelby team signed a few major leaguers and dickered with Ty Cobb, but the other teams in the tourney, Mansfield and Bucyrus, contented themselves with players from the high minor leagues.

Everyone expected Crestline to walk away with the title. Bettors could not get anyone to take their action, even at 5 to 1 odds, before Crestline's first game against Mansfield. The Mansfield pitcher, a righthander named Maul, had been raked by Galion and Shelby for 37 hits in his last two starts. The rest of players on the Mansfield team came from the smaller minor leagues in Michigan, Illinois, and Ohio. Crestline decided to start Bill Steen, a second-line Cleveland pitcher, and save the more experienced Willie Mitchell for the title game.

Crestline scored in the first inning when Joe Jackson drove in Elmer Smith with a single, but the Naps got no more runs for the rest of the game. Joe held up his end, with three hits in three trips to the plate, but the rest of the team couldn't figure out how to hit the Mansfield pitcher. Maul held the major leaguers to seven hits, pitching Mansfield to a 2-1 victory and knocking Crestline out of the title chase. "No wonder the Naps finished last!" taunted the Crestline fans as the embarrassed major leaguers left the field. Joe didn't play in the consolation game, in which Crestline defeated Bucyrus 3-0 behind Mitchell. The Shelby team didn't get Cobb into uniform but won the tournament with several players from the A's, White Sox, and Browns in their lineup.[13]

With Ty Cobb on the sidelines for much of the season (he broke his right thumb in a fistfight at a butcher's shop), Joe finally had a chance to win the American League batting title. He led the league in batting as late as August 12 with a .360 mark. On September 10, Joe trailed Philadelphia's Eddie Collins by only two points, .355 to .353, with Cobb at .351. Cobb, however, had batted only 250 times at that point, while both Jackson and Collins had more than 400 trips to the plate. Under modern guidelines, Cobb would not have been eligible for the title, but the rules were much more lenient in 1914. In the following week, Cobb went on a 16 for 28 tear (.518) to raise his season average to .373. At the end of the season, Cobb wound up with his eighth batting championship at .368, 24 points ahead of Collins and 30 ahead of Jackson. Since Cobb played only 97 games, some modern reference works list Eddie Collins as the 1914 batting champ, with Joe Jackson in second place for the fourth year in a row.

Joe batted only .287 in the last six weeks of the season, and he ended the 1914 campaign with a .338 average, his lowest yet in the major leagues. After the hitting explosion of 1911 and 1912 the pitchers had regained the upper hand, as averages fell all over baseball, but there were many other reasons for Joe's fall-off in production. He played only 122 of the 154 games for the Naps because of injuries, and with fewer Naps on base ahead of him, Joe drove in only 53 runs. His slugging average fell below .500 for the first time in his career, and he hit only 22 doubles, less than half of his total from 1911. Despite his problems, Jackson finished fifth in the Chalmers Most Valuable Player voting, which went to Collins, the captain of the pennant-winning A's.

Jackson's fielding improved, however. He committed only seven errors, three of those coming in one game on June 1, and his assist total was down because other teams had stopped testing his arm. He stole only 22 bases and was caught 15 times, most likely a result of his knee and leg problems. For the first time in his career, Joe spent a season battling one injury after another, and this had an effect not only on Joe's statistics, but also on Cleveland's place in the standings.

The most disturbing statistic of Jackson's was the fact that he scored only 61 runs. He had scored over 100 runs in each of the previous three years, but in 1914 Joe was left on base more often because of the weakness of the batters behind him in the Cleveland lineup. The Naps desperately needed a powerful hitter batting behind Jackson, since the 39-year-old Lajoie could no longer handle the job. The Cleveland team would have to rectify that situation if they hoped to contend in 1915.

Joe Jackson found a lucrative diversion in the off-season. His fascination with vaudeville and the money it could bring him led him to sign a contract with a theatrical producer. Together they put together a show called "Joe Jackson's Baseball Girls," which offered the fans a glimpse of Jackson on stage and a bunch of beautiful young women to boot. Joe contributed a monologue to the proceedings ("a sob rendition," one paper said) on his baseball career, from the mill to the major leagues.

The show toured the southern states, and by all accounts, the crowds reacted enthusiastically. *The Sporting News* said of the show, "Just now Joe is elevating the stage at a weekly salary that would make many a college professor sigh. He is doing a monologue telling how he plays ball and how he swings on the ball. He made his debut in Atlanta and has been booked for a tour of Southern cities provided he doesn't grow weary of the footlights. One thing Joe tells them is how he turned down $60,000 to play with the Feds for three years."[14]

Joe, despite his illiteracy, had found what he believed to be a profitable way to supplement his baseball salary of $6,000. His fascination with the footlights had come full circle from the time in Philadelphia when he skipped a game to see a show in the middle of a pennant race. He enjoyed the vaudeville shows in Philadelphia and New Orleans; now, he was the star of his own show.

For the first time in his career, Jackson spent a great deal of the winter on the road instead of working on the farm in Greenville and playing exhibition games in New Orleans. He was out of Katie's watchful gaze, eating in restaurants and gaining weight, falling ever so slightly out of playing shape as the weeks passed. The money came rolling in, but Katie Jackson found herself sitting at home alone for weeks at a time. Her dissatisfaction with this state of affairs would become acute in the first few months of 1915.

Chapter 8

Turmoil and a Trade

> I have had [Jackson] go into a game when I would have pre-
> ferred to let him stay out and get into better shape. Spike cuts,
> however severe, never bothered Joe, and I have seen him line
> in a ball from the deep outfield, though I knew his elbow was
> encased in bandages from injuries at the time. Joe is game,
> there's no mistaking that, and you can't keep him off the field
> when he can possibly play.
> —*Joe Birmingham, 1915*[1]

Once again, the main baseball news in the off-season concerned the Federal League. The Feds filed an antitrust suit against the existing major leagues on January 8, 1915, seeking to overturn the reserve clause. The Feds were overjoyed when the case was assigned to a flamboyant, trust-busting Chicago judge named Kenesaw Mountain Landis.

Judge Landis, appointed to the federal bench in 1905 by President Theodore Roosevelt, had fined Standard Oil a record $29 million in a landmark antitrust case. Although that verdict was overturned on appeal, the case established Landis' credentials as a trust-buster, and the Federal League hoped that Landis would rule that baseball, too, was an illegal monopoly. However, Landis was also an enthusiastic baseball fan and often enjoyed taking in the Cubs games in his leisure hours. "Both sides must understand," said Landis in his courtroom, "that any blows at the thing called baseball would be regarded by this court as a blow at a national institution."

In addition, Landis wasn't sure if he, as a federal district judge, really had jurisdiction in the case, since legal minds differed upon whether baseball qualified as "interstate commerce" or not.[2] Landis feared that a ruling for the Feds, striking down the reserve clause as unconstitutional, would damage baseball irreparably, and that a ruling in favor of the major leagues would be reversed upon appeal on jurisdictional grounds. After hearing testimony from players and owners in January 1915, Judge Landis took no immediate action. He hoped that time and circumstances would force an out-of-court settlement.

The Cleveland franchise released Napoleon Lajoie after the Frenchman batted only .258 in 1914, and Charles Somers appointed a committee of sportswriters to come up with a new nickname for the team. The writers chose the name "Indians," in honor of the popular Native American ballplayer Louis Sockalexis, who played for the National League Cleveland team in the 1890s.[3] The team did not expect the new name to be permanent, since they had used four different nicknames (Blues, Bronchos, Naps, and Indians) in their first 15 seasons. The *Plain Dealer* said in January, "The nickname is but temporarily bestowed, as the club may so conduct itself during the present season as to earn some other cognomen which may be more appropriate. The choice of a name that would be significant just now was rather difficult with the club itself anchored in last place."[4]

The new Indians held their first spring training in San Antonio, Texas, but Joe Jackson did not join the team. His "Baseball Girls" show was touring the South at that time, and Joe was booked for appearances until mid–March. The Indians wanted to get Joe to camp. They may have heard that he was out of shape, but they also wanted to keep him safely away from Federal League agents. The new league had survived the 1914 season, and they needed to sign some big names to make the league a success in 1915.

Joe knew that the Feds were interested in him, despite the fact that his Cleveland contract had two more years to run. To the dismay of Cleveland management, Joe made noises in the newspapers about abandoning baseball entirely for a career on the stage. A theatrical producer named George Greenwood from Atlanta offered Jackson the sum of $25,000 a year to quit the Indians. Greenwood's connection with the Federal League is not known, though the offer almost certainly combined playing ball in the summer and acting in the winter.[5] The amounts of money being talked about must have made Joe's head spin.

Joe startled the Indians when he declared that he had received no notice of when to report for spring training. He said that if he didn't hear from Birmingham in a few days, he would quit the team and sign the theatrical contract. Joe Birmingham quickly wired Jackson to report to the Indians' training camp at San Antonio, and to the team's relief Joe dropped his threat of reneging on the last two years of his contract. Joe's vaudeville tour ended in Durham, North Carolina, the second week of March, and Joe stopped by Greenville only briefly before reporting to San Antonio on March 13.

For the first time in his career, Joe reported to training camp overweight and out of shape. He hadn't touched a bat since the end of the 1914 season, and he surprised the team when he arrived at the camp without any bats. He brought a bull terrier named Tige, but he left all his bats back in Greenville. It wasn't much of a problem, since most of the Cleveland players used Joe's model anyway, and the camp was full of copies of Black Betsy. However, Joe Birmingham and the Indians were troubled by Joe's apparent nonchalance about the upcoming season. He also made an offhand remark to Jack Graney one day that concerned the team management. "I'm through after this season," Joe told Graney. "I've got the stage bug."[6]

Katie Jackson was less than thrilled with Joe's pretensions. Baseball made Joe Jackson a celebrity, and now Joe threatened to throw his baseball career away. It appears that Katie didn't have any input into the decisions that Joe was making; she read about Joe's interest in the Federal League in the papers, like everyone else. Katie also hated sitting home in Greenville while Joe toured the South with young, beautiful females. When Joe suddenly left the Indians camp and traveled to Atlanta to pursue the stage offer, Katie got Joe's attention in the most direct way possible. In March 1915 Katie filed for divorce. Since South Carolina had no divorce statute at that time, she filed in Cuyahoga County, Ohio.

The news hit Joe Jackson hard. The Greenville sheriff journeyed to Atlanta to serve Joe with papers and bring him back to Greenville for a hearing, but their meeting turned into a full-scale brawl in the street when the sheriff attempted to handcuff the reluctant Jackson. Joe landed several hard blows and got away but soon returned to Greenville on his own to post bond. Jackson rejoined the Indians in Chattanooga, but several days later, on April 12, the *Plain Dealer* reported that Joe "has suffered a nervous collapse as a result of his family troubles." The paper said that Joe lost 15 or 20 pounds in a space of ten days while brooding about his situation.

Eventually, Joe and Katie arrived at an understanding and patched up their differences, and Katie soon withdrew the divorce action. "The glare of the footlights blinded Joe temporarily and he lost his balance," said *The Sporting News*. "Advice from those who have his best interests at

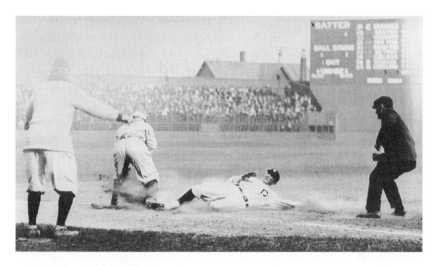

Joe Jackson slides into third against the St. Louis Browns at League Park on April 23, 1915. The third baseman is Jimmy Austin, and the umpire is George Hildebrand. Cleveland won the game 6-2.

heart, and a sensible, forgiving little wife, together with Joe's own native common sense, once it asserted itself, have straightened him out."[7]

Joe recovered quickly enough to open the season in left field on April 14 against the Tigers in Detroit. Joe drove in two runs with a double as the Cleveland team won its first game as the Indians. The *Plain Dealer*, however, couldn't resist sticking the needle in. "Cobb and Jackson conferred for nearly an hour prior to the game," said the paper. "Perhaps Ty was getting pointers on running a burlesque show."[8]

Though Joe soon got his batting average up in the .350 range, the Indians fell to the bottom of the standings, and manager Birmingham found himself in severe danger of losing his job. Somers hoped that the removal of Lajoie would lift the tension from the team and allow them to play better for Birmingham, but the Indians still thrashed around under the .500 mark. As the losses mounted, Somers decided to take a more vocal role in the management of the team.

At least the Philadelphia fans had it worse. Connie Mack's team breezed to the 1914 pennant, but it lost the World Series in an embarrassing four games to the upstart Boston Braves. Mack, stuck with flat attendance, high salaries, and competition from the Federal League, sold or released his stars in the off-season and played rookies, prospects, and over-the-hill veterans in their places. He signed the 40-year-old Napoleon Lajoie, but the Frenchman's time was long past; Lajoie committed a record five errors in a single game in April. Mack also erred in trading two out-standing young pitchers, Bob Shawkey and Herb Pennock, to the Yan-kees and Red Sox respectively, further diluting the talent base on his club.

Rumors abounded about an ulterior motive for the breakup of the A's, since Boston was a notorious hotbed of baseball gamblers (who plied their trade unimpeded in the outfield stands) and the four-game Series sweep shocked the entire baseball world. George M. Cohan, the Broad-way star, won a bundle betting on the Braves, and so did many others. Mack, however, insisted that complacency and high salaries, not wrong-doing, caused the breakup of his team.

The decimated Athletics dropped to last place by midseason and stayed there, so there was no chance that the Indians would finish last for the second season in a row. The Indians didn't play much better than the A's, however, and battled the St. Louis Browns for sixth place.

For two years, first base had been a major problem spot for the Cleve-land team, and Charles Somers thought of a way to fill the hole and get another bat into the lineup. In May, Somers ordered Birmingham to move Joe Jackson to first base to open a spot for Elmer Smith in the outfield. Somers chose to move Jackson because Joe had played around at first base in practice, though the move robbed the Indians of one of the best outfield arms in the American League. Birmingham strongly objected to this move, mostly because he didn't want Joe to get spiked in the infield. He also resented Somers' meddling in the field management of the team.

The move of Joe Jackson to first heightened the tension between Birmingham and Somers, and it set in motion the series of events that led directly to Birmingham's firing. Somers criticized his manager for relying too much on the hit and run and not enough on the bunt, and Birmingham seethed at the interference of the owner. Before long, Somers was dictating lineup changes at other positions as well.

The final straw came on Saturday, May 16. On that day, Birming-ham removed Cleveland's most popular pitcher, Guy Morton, from the lineup without Somers' approval. Birmingham said that he wanted to hold Morton back for Sunday's game, especially when he saw that there were fewer than 2,000 people in the stands for the game. The fans and the newspapers loudly complained to Cleveland management about the switch, and Somers fired Birmingham five days later.

Somers named coach Lee Fohl, a former major league catcher, as interim manager, and initiated a league-wide search for a new skipper, but soon it became apparent that Somers would have trouble filling the position. Many potential candidates, fearing Somers' meddlesome behavior and the lack of talent on the club, shied away from the Cleveland situation. Somers found that it was difficult to find a manager for a troubled, sixth-place club, especially one that had gone through five managers in the last seven years. The owner also admitted what the fans of Cleveland had suspected for three years. "George Stovall ... is the best manager I ever had," said Somers, "and I made a mistake in letting him go."[9]

Joe Jackson played 27 games at first that season, the only time in his major league career he played anywhere besides the outfield, and he found himself making more throws at shorter distances. By early June his arm was sore. He missed a week of action, and Birmingham blamed the switch of positions for Joe's arm problems. "When a team depends so much on one batsman to pull it through," said Birmingham after his firing, "I do not think it is wise to place that player where he runs the daily risk of being hurt."[10]

Fohl also publicly blamed the position switch for Joe's sore arm, but surprisingly, Somers didn't seem to mind the same criticism from Fohl. By mid–June Somers abandoned his futile league-wide search for a new manager and named Fohl to the job full time. Joe returned to action and went three for five against the Red Sox on June 14, but he left the lineup again when Boston's Ernie Shore beaned him two days later. Though Joe was unconscious for several minutes, he pinch-hit the next day and rejoined the lineup the day after that.

Joe Jackson's career, and life, nearly ended one day in the 1915 season.

On July 7, 1915, Joe and his wife Katie were enjoying an off day in their car, driving on the Lake Shore Boulevard east of Cleveland, when the car began balking. Joe had Katie take the wheel while he climbed onto the running board to listen to the engine, and apparently both Joe and Katie were paying more attention to the engine than to the road. Suddenly a horse-drawn lumber wagon sideswiped the Jackson car, knocking Joe off and dragging him some 75 feet before it came to a stop.

Jackson suffered severe cuts and bruises on his left elbow, face, and both legs. He later recalled that "my kneecap came out ... I thought I was through as a ball player," but his elbow turned out to be his most serious injury. He was rushed to Glenville Hospital, where the doctors looked him over and stitched him up. X-rays found no broken bones, but the bruise on his elbow took a long time to heal and caused Joe to miss nearly three weeks of action. He didn't play again until July 26, when he went two for two in an exhibition game in Scranton, Pennsylvania. Joe returned to official action with a pinch-hitting appearance against the Senators on July 27, and he didn't reenter the lineup until July 30 in Philadelphia.

On the day after the accident, the Tigers came to Cleveland for a doubleheader, fully expecting to win both games without Jackson in the lineup. It rained that morning, however, and the Indians quickly called off the twin bill. About 20 minutes after the team made its announcement, the sun came out. The Cleveland club rescheduled the games for mid–August, by which time Jackson would have recovered from his injuries. The Tigers complained bitterly, but the decision to cancel the games stood.

By midseason 1915, Charles Somers found himself in serious financial trouble. Attendance dipped to 185,000 in the disastrous 1914 season, and it fell even lower in 1915 without the popular Lajoie. The papers attacked the team mercilessly. On July 1 the *Plain Dealer*, in a headline, called the Indians "[the] joke of the big leagues" after a 1-9 skid. The paper also criticized manager Lee Fohl and described his players as being "in a rut and don't care much whether Cleveland wins or loses."[11] With the season apparently lost, Somers sold outfielder Nemo Leibold to the Chicago White Sox for a quick infusion of cash. He then reluctantly entertained offers for his two best players, Joe Jackson and Ray Chapman. The White Sox opened the bidding with a reported offer of $20,000 and four players for Chapman on June 28.[12]

Jackson's three-year contract, signed in February 1914, had another year and a half to run, but Joe seemed anxious to move on. For all his professed love of Cleveland, Joe sensed that he might make more money elsewhere. "I think I am in a rut here in Cleveland," Jackson told Henry Edwards of the *Plain Dealer*, "and would play better somewhere else."[13] Somers met with representatives of the Washington Senators, and Jackson's ears perked up at the chance to play in the most southern city in the majors.

The Senators offered several players in exchange for Jackson, but Somers needed cash as well. By August 1915 reports surfaced that Somers stood a whopping $1.75 million in debt, mostly due to real-estate investments gone sour. Jackson may have expected a raise from his 1914–16 salary base with the high-salaried Lajoie gone, but the horrible attendance and Somers' financial problems prevented Jackson from getting a raise to the Ty Cobb level. Joe wanted to play for Washington, the closest major league city to Greenville, but Clark Griffith ran an even tighter operation in Washington than Charles Somers did in Cleveland. Griffith already needed help from the league to pay his ace pitcher, Walter Johnson, and he would have problems paying another star.

As if the Indians didn't have enough problems, the Federal League came calling once again. In early August, Jackson received a visit from

Joe Tinker, the former Cubs shortstop now managing the Chicago Whales in the Federal League. Tinker huddled with Jackson and tried to get the slugger to jump to the Whales. It has been widely reported that Tinker offered Jackson $10,000 a year to make the move, although the Federal League ship was already beginning to sink by this time.

Joe turned down the offer, but not before publicly raising a fuss over his contract. Jackson's contract with Cleveland stipulated that he would be paid on the first and fifteenth of each month. August 15 fell on a Sunday in 1915, and Jackson received his check on Monday as usual. Suddenly Jackson, at Tinker's instigation, demanded his immediate free agency because of a breach of contract![14]

Tinker probably wanted to get Jackson in a Whale uniform for 1916, in hopes that a peace agreement between the Federal League and the majors would leave Jackson in a Whale uniform afterwards. It's difficult to tell how serious Jackson was about gaining his free agency on so trivial a pretext. If he had succeeded in doing so, then almost every major league player could become a free agent anytime that the first or fifteenth of the month fell on a Sunday. However, Joe listened enthusiastically to the Federal League offers, as *Baseball Magazine* writer F. C. Lane discovered when he observed Jackson deeply engrossed in conversation with Federal president James Gilmore in a Chicago hotel lobby.[15]

Charles Somers soon heard, to his great displeasure, that Jackson had given a copy of his contract to Joe Tinker, presumably so Tinker and Gilmore could search it for loopholes. Somers also became concerned when team secretary Bill Blackwood arrived at Joe's Cleveland apartment one day and found Tinker there. These incidents made up Charles Somers' mind. He would keep Ray Chapman and trade Joe Jackson. However, with the Federal League trolling for talented players, no club would trade for Jackson without a signed contract. Since Tinker had followed Jackson back to Cleveland, Somers decided to move quickly.

On the morning of Monday, August 16, 1915, Somers and Jackson began negotiations in Somers' office at League Park. In a matter of moments, Joe Jackson signed a three-year contract, covering 1917, 1918, and 1919, with the Indians for a reported $6,000 a year. The respected baseball historian Lee Allen stated that Katie Jackson, upset with Joe for dallying with the Federal League, marched her husband up to Charles Somers' office that morning and made sure that Joe signed with Cleveland. According to Allen, Somers "made Jackson promise that thereafter he would let his wife make all the decisions for the family." From that day on, said Allen, Katie kept firm control of her husband's business affairs.[16]

Now the Indians could trade Joe, but the Senators' offer still looked unsatisfactory. Joe may have struggled with injuries in the previous two seasons, but he was still the Indians' biggest asset, and Somers didn't want to let a man with a .366 lifetime batting average go for nothing.

On Thursday, August 19, a new bidder entered the Joe Jackson sweepstakes in the person of Charles Comiskey, owner of the White Sox. Comiskey's cleanup hitter, Jack Fournier, broke his arm, leaving a hole in the Chicago lineup, so Comiskey sent his secretary, Harry Grabiner, to Cleveland with a blank check. "Go to Cleveland," ordered Comiskey, "watch the bidding for Jackson, [and] raise the highest one made by any club until they all drop out."[17]

The White Sox at the time ran the most profitable franchise in the American League. They led the league in attendance almost every year after their new Comiskey Park opened in 1910. The White Sox had not won a pennant since the "Hitless Wonders" of 1906, and Comiskey was tired of finishing in the middle of the pack every year. He was more than willing to use his profits to put a winner on the field.

When the Philadelphia A's collapsed after their embarrassing loss in the 1914 Series, Comiskey realized that the league stood wide open for the taking. After the A's hit bottom, Comiskey saw that he could fill a few holes in his lineup with his checkbook and take over the league for several years. The league-leading attendance of the Sox provided Comiskey the wherewithal to buy the 1914 Most Valuable Player Award winner, second baseman Eddie Collins, from Connie Mack for $50,000. Now he needed a power hitter, and Joe Jackson was available.

Grabiner, acting on Comiskey's orders, offered a deal for both Jackson and Ray Chapman, but Somers didn't want to part with the two best players on his club. He had to trade one and rebuild the Indians around the other. The two men batted a few names and figures about before Grabiner offered Somers $31,500 in cash and three players from the White Sox reserve list for Jackson. Somers and Grabiner quickly agreed and completed the deal on the morning of Friday, August 20, 1915. Somers received outfielders Braggo Roth and Larry Chappell and pitcher Ed Klepfer, players who collectively cost the White Sox $34,000 to acquire.[18]

In terms of the total value of cash and players, this was the most expensive deal ever made in baseball up to that time. Grabiner was nervous about telling Charles Comiskey that he had spent $65,500 in cash and players to acquire Jackson, but Comiskey heartily congratulated Grabiner on his return to Chicago and expressed the wish that all of his employees would follow orders so diligently. Jackson arrived in Chicago with Grabiner on the night of August 20 and played left field for the Sox in a doubleheader the next day, going one for seven against the Yankees.

Roth took Jackson's place in left field for the Indians, though he neither hit nor fielded on Jackson's level. Roth was a good hitting outfielder, three years younger than Jackson, and led the league in home runs that year with seven. Chappell, an $18,000 bonus player and the most expensive of the three, lasted only three games with Cleveland. He died in the great influenza epidemic of 1918 after serving with the Army in France. Klepfer won 13 games for the Tribe in 1917, then went into the military and didn't pitch well after that. By 1920, all were gone from Cleveland. The important part of the deal, it appears, was the cash that Somers desperately needed.[19]

Joe's five-year stay in Cleveland ended with some sniping from the sports pages. Henry Edwards of the *Plain Dealer* criticized Jackson on his way out of town. "While he [Jackson] does not admit it," wrote Edwards, "he was becoming ... a purely individual player who sacrificed team work for Joe Jackson ... if he were still the Jackson of 1911, 1912, and 1913, the team would not have let him get away."[20]

Somers, in praising Ray Chapman, delivered a backhanded blow to Jackson also. "Chapman is one player who likes the town and his treatment here, and wants to stay here until his big league career is ended," he said. After Joe's rash of injuries and the difficulties he made for the club in the spring of 1915, it's not surprising that Jackson, not Chapman, was the player dealt away. F. C. Lane speculated that Somers traded Jackson to keep him out of the Federal League and that Charles Comiskey was wealthy enough to keep Jackson from jumping to the Feds.[21]

Jackson's fascination with money, which seemed to have become more pronounced since his early days in Cleveland, stood out starkly on the printed page. One example was a statement to Henry Edwards in which Jackson liked the idea of leaving Cleveland for "some sweet World Series money" coming his way in Chicago, and said of the trade, "I am perfectly satisfied. Why shouldn't I be? I am getting an advance even on the new contract that I signed with Cleveland [on] Monday."[22] Though Joe expressed his appreciation for the treatment that he received in Cleveland, he still looked like one more example of an athlete more interested in his wallet than his performance on the field. The guileless Jackson didn't read the newspapers, so he had no idea how some of his statements looked in print.

Somers rushed to assure the fans that Chapman would not be the next to leave. "Because of a bad financial year, I was forced to let Jackson go," said Somers. "Attendance has fallen off to such an extent that it was up to me to make some radical move to relieve the pressure, and this deal was the result."[23]

Charles Comiskey, owner and president of the Chicago White Sox (author's collection).

Chapman stayed, but in February 1916 Somers sold the club to a group of businessmen headed by James C. Dunn, a construction magnate and good friend of Charles Comiskey, for the reported price of $500,000. The Dunn group scored a coup in heisting star centerfielder Tris Speaker from the Red Sox after Speaker and Red Sox owner Joe Lannin couldn't agree on a contract. The new owners rebuilt the Indians around Chapman and Speaker, and attendance began to pick up again in Cleveland.[24]

The bankers allowed Charles Somers to retain the ownership of the New Orleans Pelicans, but the former Cleveland owner never returned to the league that he helped create. Somers reentered the business world to pay his debts and rebuild his fortune, and within a few years he found new success in coal and real estate ventures. When he died in 1934, he left an estate valued at over three million dollars.

Jackson soon found out that Chicago wasn't the place to make lots of money. The writers and the fans lionized Charles Comiskey, founder and owner of the White Sox, but the players knew the truth. Comiskey took advantage of less educated players. He didn't pay them one penny more than he absolutely had to.

Charles Comiskey began his baseball career in the American Association as a first baseman with the St. Louis Browns in the 1880s. Many admiring sportswriters credited Comiskey with inventing the practice of playing off the bag at first with no runners on base, and with devising plays where the pitcher covered the bag. In the mid–1880s Comiskey took the managerial reins of the Browns and introduced fan violence and umpire intimidation as essential facets of team strategy. The rowdy Browns won four pennants, mostly because visiting teams could never get a fair shake in St. Louis from the frightened umpires.

The Browns collapsed after 1891 along with the rest of the American Association, and Comiskey moved on to the Cincinnati Reds. Aching for respectability, he aspired to own a team himself. In 1895 he bought the St. Paul team in Ban Johnson's Western League, and in 1900 he moved it to Chicago's South Side and named it the White Stockings, which he shortened to White Sox for the convenience of his sportswriter friends. The Western League moved into National League cities, changed its name to the American League, and proclaimed itself major, on a par with the established National Leaguers.

Comiskey's White Sox became one of the powerhouse teams of the new league. They won the first two American League pennants in 1900 and 1901, and the 1906 team, the "Hitless Wonders" managed by Fielder Jones, won the World Series against the crosstown rival Cubs. Charles Comiskey, the former roughneck, now stood on top of the baseball world. "I started out with fifty dollars in 1877," he told the writers with pride, "and look where I am now." The sportswriters of the 1890s, with their enthusiasm for unusual nicknames, called Charles Comiskey "The Noblest Roman of Baseball"; by the early 1900s Comiskey proudly wore the title of "The Old Roman."

In 1910, he built a new stadium, Comiskey Park, which he lent out to the public free of charge for picnics and civic gatherings. His popularity soared in Chicago; he was asked more than once to run for mayor. He always responded to that suggestion by grandly proclaiming, "I'd rather win a pennant than an election!" One can surmise a sense of the Old Roman's pomposity from the original name of Comiskey Park, which was "Comiskey's Base Ball Palace of the World."

The thuggish player and rule-breaking manager of the 1880s loved the limelight of civic respectability. He put together an organization of well-heeled rooters and supporters called the Woodland Bards, who met for hunting and drinking parties at Comiskey's vacation lodge in Wisconsin. Ban Johnson, president and founder of the American League, enjoyed Comiskey's hospitality, but Comiskey couldn't resist needling and playing practical jokes on the flabby Johnson. They patched up one feud after another, but by the late teens, Comiskey and Johnson had become mortal enemies.

Comiskey managed the St. Paul team and the 1900 Chicago pennant winners himself, then turned the field direction over to star pitcher Clark Griffith in 1901. Nevertheless, it was always Comiskey's team no matter who managed it. He released Griffith in 1903 and went through five more managers by 1915. Comiskey's well-developed ego wouldn't allow him to stay in the background, and he developed a penchant for second-guessing his managers in the papers. Comiskey had won five pennants as a field manager himself, but his managers, all of them well-respected major league veterans, didn't appreciate his hands-on style.

In 1915 Comiskey surprised the White Sox faithful by hiring as his manager a career minor leaguer named Clarence "Pants" Rowland, who came from Mrs. Comiskey's hometown of Dubuque, Iowa, and who had managed the Peoria team in 1914. Rowland, a former catcher, had never played in the majors and didn't object to Comiskey's constant stream of advice. Rowland was Comiskey's ideal manager, a loyal retainer widely seen as a puppet following Comiskey's orders. Rowland, whom many opposing players called "the busher from Dubuque," entertained the newspapermen while coach Kid Gleason and captain Eddie Collins ran the team on the field.

To any fair-minded person, it would appear that Charles Comiskey had no reason to underpay his players. In the 1910s, the White Sox were considered the crown jewel franchise of the American League. The New York Yankees at this time played second fiddle in the nation's largest city, mere tenants of the powerful Giants at the Polo Grounds, and had not yet won an American League pennant. This left Comiskey's White Sox as the richest and most prominent team in the league. In the decade from 1910 to 1919, Comiskey's White Sox led the major leagues in attendance, ahead of even John McGraw's New York Giants.

Charles Comiskey's penuriousness showed itself in many ways great and small. All the players deeply resented their $3 a day meal money, when almost all the other teams in the league offered $4. In the late teens, Comiskey began charging 25 cents a day to the players to have their uniforms laundered. The White Sox defiantly refused to pay the fee and took the field in dirt-stained flannels that earned them the name "Black Sox" long before the scandal.

If Comiskey pinched pennies with his players, he spared no expense for the writers. Comiskey knew that the newspapers gave the fans their only window on the team in those days before radio and television, so Comiskey's dining room, always open to the writers as well as his Woodland Bards, oozed magnificence. He treated the writers to fine wine and thick steaks, and he received fawning print coverage in return. The players knew that Comiskey had the local writers wrapped around his little finger. The public had no way of knowing the indignities under which the players operated.

Contract discussions tended to be short, painful affairs. Comiskey gave Harry Grabiner a narrow range of figures from which to choose, and Grabiner would push the contract across the desk at the player with a threatening, "Take it or leave it!" The player had no leverage at all in the relationship, especially after the Federal League folded after the 1915 season. No owner used the reserve clause, which bound player and team together for eternity if the owner so chose, as profitably as Charles Comiskey.

He played favorites, too, with the more educated and refined players. Comiskey admired and respected them, probably because they were the polar opposites of his own unruly self at the same age. He bought Eddie Collins from Philadelphia in December 1914, made him the captain, and continued to pay Collins the same $14,500 salary that Mack paid, more than double anyone else's salary on the team.

Urban (Red) Faber, a young spitball pitcher from a small college in Iowa, came out of nowhere to win 24 games for the Sox in 1915, and Comiskey named a favorite pet moose at his hunting lodge Red Faber in the pitcher's honor. This caused some anxious moments a few years later when the moose startled some hunters, and a headline screamed "RED FABER KILLED IN SELF-DEFENSE." From 1915 on Faber and Collins were Comiskey's pets, to the resentment of the other players.

Charles Comiskey was not a monster. Indeed, Comiskey was a typical purveyor of the business ethics of the era. He made as much money for himself as he could and spent as little of it on his employees as he could possibly get away with spending. He enjoyed a lavish lifestyle and supported it by underpaying the employees who made that lifestyle possible. He certainly noticed that Charles Somers, who handed out $20 gold pieces to his players, went broke. Charles Comiskey was a rich man, and he fully intended to stay that way.

It took awhile for Joe Jackson to get acclimated to Chicago. He batted only .272 in the 45 games he played for the White Sox after hitting .341 with the Indians, and his composite average of .308 was his lowest yet in the major leagues. He also had to move from Cleveland to an apartment in Chicago, and his elbow and knee still bothered him. Joe liked routine and order in his life, and his batting average suffered in the adjustment to new surroundings. By the end of the season, manager Pants Rowland dropped Joe to the fifth spot in the lineup.

Jackson joined a team split into two distinct camps. On one side, the leader was the college-educated Eddie Collins, recently arrived from the Athletics. The nondrinkers and book readers, mostly Northerners, socialized with the Collins faction. The other camp contained the drinking men, mostly from the South and West. When first baseman Chick Gandil joined the Sox in 1917, he became the head of this group.

Eddie Collins was, in many ways, the opposite of Joe Jackson. Collins was a northerner, the son of a wealthy family, a prep school graduate, and a college man, having graduated from Columbia University. Collins played his first year for the A's under the name of Sullivan to protect his college eligibility. Some newspaper reporters discovered the ruse soon enough, and when Collins was not allowed to play his senior season at Columbia, the school hired him as the head coach!

Collins was born only one year before Jackson but made it to the Philadelphia A's as a 19 year old in 1906. By 1909, while Jackson bounced up and down from the majors to the minors, Collins starred as the linchpin of the A's "$100,000 infield." With Eddie Collins at second base, the A's won four pennants and three World Series from 1910 to 1914. His air of confidence could rub people the wrong way, however. His nickname was "Cocky," for one thing. For another, he wrote a ten-part series of magazine columns on "Inside Baseball" in 1912, in which he gave away many of the team's secrets to the fans and also to the other teams. For the most part, however, baseball people considered Eddie Collins a real gentleman, as well as the most intelligent player in the game.

Connie Mack gave up on Joe Jackson, but a reporter once asked Mack which of his players was the easiest to manage in his 53-year career. "All of them, every one," replied Mack, "especially Eddie Collins."[25]

Joe Jackson rarely spoke to Collins; perhaps the unschooled mill hand was intimidated by the college-educated, socially confident Collins. In later years, Joe spoke of the White Sox captain with a respect that bordered on awe. Jackson, though he was only a year younger, always referred to the captain as "Mister Collins." Joe was an established star like Collins, but because Joe liked to drink and because he was underpaid, he had very little in common with the man whom *Baseball Magazine* called "the brainiest player in baseball."

The resentment of Comiskey's penny-pinching ways seemed to center on Eddie Collins, and although Collins served as field captain of the White Sox, many of his charges wanted little or nothing to do with him. In this period, team captains often made defensive changes and sent in pinch-hitters, leaving the pitching staff to the manager. Collins, therefore, represented management to the other players, and his status as Comiskey's favorite rankled many of his teammates. Collins almost never spoke to his shortstop, Buck Weaver, a hard-drinking, tobacco-chewing roughneck from the Pennsylvania coal country. They communicated on the field only when necessary, in a kind of gruff verbal shorthand.

Perhaps Charles Comiskey selected the members of his team as reflections of the competing facets—the rowdy and the respectable—of his own personality. In so doing, he created a poisonous clubhouse atmosphere that would become worse with each passing season. We can now see the White Sox as a lethal mixture of drinkers, roughnecks, illiterate country boys, and educated straight arrows all sharing a locker room and traveling together on trains all summer long. It was a fractured, resentful team, and the fissures would grow wider in the next few years.

There exists one oft-told story about Charles Comiskey that almost certainly is not true. One of the White Sox' star pitchers, veteran Eddie Cicotte, won 28 games in 1917, then didn't pitch for the final two weeks of the season. Supposedly Comiskey had promised Cicotte a $10,000 bonus if he won 30 games that year, the implication being that the Sox held Cicotte out to keep him from winning his thirtieth. This story plays a pivotal role in Eliot Asinof's book on the Black Sox, *Eight Men Out*, which was published in 1963 and made into a movie in 1988.

The story appears to make sense, since Cicotte didn't pitch for the last two weeks, and Comiskey was a notorious tightwad. However, Comiskey wasn't known to put such large incentive clauses in contracts; no other example of any comparable offer can be found in Comiskey's reign as boss of the White Sox.[26] Moreover, why would Comiskey make such an offer to Cicotte, who had never even won 20 games in a season before that time? Ten thousand dollars would have nearly tripled Cicotte's salary for the year. Comiskey tossed nickels around as if they were manhole covers. He wouldn't offer $10,000 so lightly.

In the 1910s, a 30-win season did not carry the importance that it would carry today. No pitcher has won 30 games in a season since 1968, but from 1915 to 1917 Grover Alexander of the Phillies won 30 or more each year. Walter Johnson did so twice in the 1910s, and Joe Wood did it once. In fact, just nine years before Cicotte won 28, Ed Walsh won 40 for the White Sox and Christy Mathewson won 37 for the Giants. If Walter Johnson could win 36 games for the horrible Senators, why should a good pitcher need an incentive to win for the powerful White Sox?

Some versions of the story place the offer in 1919, when Cicotte won 29 games, and gives Comiskey's refusal to pay the bonus as a motive for Cicotte's involvement in the World Series scandal. This offers a simple explanation for a complicated betrayal, but the truth is that the players had discussed the Series fix as early as August 1919, well before Cicotte came close to 30 wins. Also, Cicotte made two starts in September 1919 after getting his 29th win, but was unable to ring up number 30.

If Cicotte had received such an offer in 1917 or 1919, one might expect that Comiskey's favorite, future Hall of Famer Red Faber, would have received a similar offer. He didn't. The story of Cicotte getting cheated out of a substantial bonus played a pivotal role in *Eight Men Out* but probably never happened in real life.

However, let's not let Comiskey off the hook. When the Sox clinched the pennant in 1917, Comiskey made it known to his players that a bonus awaited them if they defeated the Giants in the World Series. The White Sox polished off the New Yorkers in six games. The bonus from Comiskey turned out to be a case of champagne for the victory celebration.

Chapter 9

A New Beginning

Joe Jackson hit the ball harder than any man ever to play baseball. What's more, he would have gone down in history as the
greatest batter of all time had he made a study of the scientific
side of the batting art. Chances are, Joe could have learned to
bunt and beat out slow bounders to the infield ... but he seemed
content to just punch the ball, and I can still see those line
drives whistling to the far precincts.
— *Ty Cobb, 1951*[1]

The Federal League disappeared after the 1915 season. There was no
room for three major leagues at the time, and the sudden death of Robert
Ward, one of the major backers of the new league, cut the financial legs
out from under the new circuit. After mounting losses on both sides, the
Feds and the National Commission brokered a peace agreement. Two
Federal League owners, Phil Ball of St. Louis and Charles Weegham of
Chicago, were allowed to buy the Browns and Cubs respectively, and the
eight Federal teams disbanded. [2] Most of their players never worked in
the majors again, though stars like Benny Kauff and Hal Chase made the
move back into the established circuits.

With the demise of the Federal League came the end of the rise in
player salaries. The Federal League problem resolved itself, just as Judge
Landis hoped it would, and the existing legal structure of baseball emerged
unscathed. This structure included the reserve clause, which was regarded
by the owners as indispensable and by the players as an unconstitutional
infringement on their civil rights. It also included the odious ten-day

clause, by which an owner could cancel a player's contract on ten days' notice for any reason at all. Joe Jackson was fortunate enough to sign his three-year deal before the Federal League closed up shop, since he used his leverage with the Feds to get Charles Somers to strike the offending clause out of his contract. Almost all other players had to live with it, and their resentment grew more pronounced with each passing year.

When the Feds went out of business, the players lost their biggest negotiating weapon. A player could no longer threaten to jump to the Feds if he wasn't paid enough. Neither would the league subsidize a team to meet the salary demands of a star player, as the American League did with the Senators to keep Walter Johnson from jumping ship. The bad old days of low salaries returned with a vengeance. Joe Jackson was the most underpaid star in the game at $6,000 a year, and he was tied into that salary until the end of 1919. If Jackson thought that the profitable Chicago franchise would pay him a higher base salary, he soon found out otherwise, and he had no leverage to change the situation.

In all fairness, it must be stated that Joe Jackson could earn more money in Chicago aside from his base salary than he could in Cleveland. Comiskey spent a great deal of money to turn the White Sox into a winner, and the Sox stood a much better chance at playing in a World Series in the near future than the Cleveland Indians did. The winning Series shares in the 1910s rose from $2,000 per player in 1910 to nearly $5,000 by the end of the decade. In addition, the White Sox played a postseason City Series against the crosstown Cubs in years when neither team appeared in the World Series. These series were well attended and popular with the fans, and though they didn't pay as much as a World Series, they paid a good deal more than the sporadic "All-Ohio Championship" between Cleveland and Cincinnati.

To Charles Comiskey, the answer was simple. If the players wanted more money, many of them could more than double their salaries with a World Series championship. Comiskey spent more than a hundred thousand dollars out of the team's coffers to bring Jackson, Collins, and others to the White Sox. Now it was all up to the players themselves. Comiskey did not intend to renegotiate Jackson's contract, or anyone else's. All they had to do was win, reasoned Comiskey, and the money issue would take care of itself.

Joe Jackson made a few changes in his life in the winter of 1915-16. His farm and his pool room in downtown Greenville were losing money, apparently as a result of mismanagement by those whom Joe left in charge while he played ball up North. Some of the newspapers reported that Joe's monetary losses were substantial, and *Baseball Magazine* stated that Joe had been "mulcted of his savings."[3] Joe also felt uncomfortable in his hometown after his near-divorce and the rancor with the sheriff in the previous spring. Joe and Katie, probably at Katie's insistence, decided to make a fresh start not only in Joe's baseball career, but in their home lives as well.

Joe and Katie usually spent the winter in Greenville, in the home that Joe bought for his parents a few years earlier, but in the winter of 1915-16 the couple stayed in Cleveland. In the meantime, Joe's sister Lula married and moved with her husband to Savannah, Georgia, where Joe had spent the 1909 season. Joe and Katie enjoyed their stay in Savannah seven years before, and the locals still remembered Joe fondly. The Jacksons decided to follow Lula's lead. Joe sold the pool room and the farm and bought a new house for $10,000 near the Savannah waterfront. He moved there with Katie in early 1916, and before long Joe opened another pool room on Congress Street in Savannah.

Joe also began to fit in with his new team. When he joined the White Sox in August 1915, Joe kept to himself as much as possible. Jackson's status as a star entitled him to a room by himself on the road. For home games, Joe dressed at his hotel and walked in full uniform to the ballpark, rather than dress in an unfamiliar locker room. In spring training of 1916 Joe was able to make a few friends, however slowly, and soon he felt comfortable enough to dress with his teammates. Katie, too, did her part. She became Joe's biggest rooter just as she had in Cleveland, attending each home game and keeping score until she left to prepare dinner in the late innings.

Katie also kept Joe abreast of what the newspapers were writing about him. She probably noticed *Baseball Magazine*'s story in its March 1916 issue titled "The Greatest Player That Might Have Been," which took a severely critical look at Joe and his career as it stood in 1916. Joe, according to writer F. C. Lane, possessed "a judgment not always adequate to the task of handling [his talents] to the best purpose, with an wayward temperament and an erratic ambition scarce fitted to develop his wondrous abilities to their fullest measure."[4]

Lane, while professing to admire Joe as a person and an athlete, painted a bleak picture of Joe's future when he quoted an unnamed Brandon Mill textile worker. "Wait five years or so," said the anonymous mill hand. "Then Joe will go through all he has made in baseball and be broke once more." Where would Joe go then? "Why, he will be back in the cotton mill working for $1.25 a day."[5]

It is true that Joe's 1914 and 1915 seasons were not as productive as his first three full seasons in a Cleveland uniform. Lane blamed Joe's decline on "the dissipations which assail the ball player in the big cities," never mentioning the fact that Joe played through injuries, hospital stays, an auto accident, beanings, and a major trade in those two seasons. It also could have been said in Joe's defense that he had no one of stature hitting behind him in the Cleveland lineup after 1913, which was Napoleon Lajoie's last good year.[6] Lane also criticized Joe's "fondness for the life behind the footlights," and he took him to task for his dalliance with the Federal League as well.

The article repeated two oft-quoted criticisms of Joe Jackson that must have irked him and Katie no end. Lane quoted one anonymous fan's assessment of Jackson as "Ty Cobb from the neck down." Another unnamed millworker told Lane his impression of Greenville's favorite son. "Joe's record," said the man, an early acquaintance of Joe's, "is the best example of what a man may accomplish in this world wholly without brains."[7] These statements were made in an article for which the writer had interviewed Joe's mother and four of his five brothers!

Joe was not impervious to criticism; indeed, he was sensitive to the things that were written about him in the newspapers and magazines, especially where speculation about his intelligence was concerned. Whatever Joe felt about the treatment he received from *Baseball Magazine*, he had to admit that he needed to concentrate more on his ballplaying and less on his off-the-field amusements. For the first time in several years, Joe went to spring training in 1916 with something to prove, to his new team and to himself.

Joe Jackson joined a Chicago team that not only placed higher in the standings than the Indians, but also put more people in the seats. The White Sox drew more than 539,000 fans in 1915, tops in the American League, and figured to draw more in 1916 without the Federal League competition. Chicago was a bigger city than Cleveland, and the additional fan interest created electricity in Comiskey Park that was usually not present in Cleveland.

When Joe arrived in Chicago, he was faced with the task of hitting in Comiskey Park, a much different environment than League Park in Cleveland. Comiskey Park depressed batting averages; in the park's 81 years of operation from 1910 to 1990, only one White Sox player (Luke Appling, who did it twice) has managed to win a batting title. This was mostly due to its large foul territory, in which pop fouls were caught before they fell into the seats. It was said that when Charles Comiskey planned his new ballpark, he asked his star pitcher Ed Walsh for advice on the layout of the field. Walsh, as might be expected, talked Comiskey into making the new park as difficult as possible for the hitters of the American League.

The spacious right field area also differed from Cleveland's. The fence in Comiskey Park was 362 feet down the line in right, a full 72 feet longer than Cleveland's. Fly balls that hit the League Park fence were caught in Chicago. All the right fielder had to do was to play deeply enough. Joe's blue darters went more often for singles than for doubles and triples in Chicago, though he still put some triples between the outfielders (enough to lead the league in 1916). However, his batting averages in the first four years with the White Sox never reached the levels of his first three seasons with Cleveland.

Joe reported to the White Sox spring training base at Mineral Wells, Texas, in early March of 1916. Mineral Wells was a small town about 40 miles west of Dallas, in the heart of the vast dry prairie of north-central Texas. The weather in the spring of 1916 was dry and windy, and the sun baked the ground as hard as rock. Joe developed a sore back that bothered him into the season, and the players were happy to get out of the "sand belt," as they called it, in late March.

The White Sox played more exhibition games than most teams, both before the season and during it, mostly to put more money into Charles Comiskey's coffers. Joe soon found out that there was almost no such thing as an "off day" with the Chicago White Sox. The Sox played their way through the dirt fields of Texas, Oklahoma, and Kansas on their way back to Chicago. On April 1 Joe belted a homer, triple, and single in a 15-2 bombing of the Dallas nine, and went three for three in games in Wichita and Topeka, Kansas. The White Sox won their last 15 games in a row against their badly outclassed minor league opponents.

They ended their exhibition campaign on April 11 in Moline, Illinois; Joe pounded a mammoth home run, the longest blast ever seen in Moline, over the roof of the center field clubhouse. That particular game dragged on interminably, because the Sox found it difficult to keep from scoring against Moline. Late in the game, the Chicago batters tried their best to help the Moline players put them out so that the game could end. On defense, Joe and the other outfielders wound up playing almost on the edge of the infield grass, since the overmatched Moline batters couldn't seem to hit the ball any farther. The game was an absolute farce, and the Chicago players grew to resent these seemingly pointless excursions into the heartland.

In the spring of 1916, Charles Comiskey went to the American League meetings in New York intent upon filling the yawning shortstop/

third base gap that had bothered the Sox for several years. He trained his eye on Fritz Maisel of the Yankees, a fine-fielding third sacker who stole 74 bases in 1914 and 53 more in 1915 while batting .281. Apparently, Comiskey was becoming desperate in his search for a third baseman or shortstop to pair with Buck Weaver on the left side of the Chicago infield, and he believed that Maisel was the answer. Strangely enough, the one player whom Comiskey considered sending to New York in exchange for Maisel was Joe Jackson.

Even more astounding, in hindsight, is the fact that the New York papers opined that a Jackson for Maisel trade would be a bad deal for the Yankees! "For all the power in Jackson's bat," said the *New York Tribune*, "there are reasons for believing he is not so valuable a player as Maisel."[8] The *Tribune* also speculated that the other teams of the league would cause an uproar if the Sox managed to obtain so good a player as Maisel in exchange for Jackson. Comiskey paid over $65,000 in cash and players for Jackson, but Joe hit poorly for the Sox in 1915, and there was some speculation in the papers (and in *Baseball Magazine*) that Joe's career might be on the decline at the age of 27. Most observers saw Maisel, one year younger than Joe, as an up-and-coming star.

The trade talk didn't get very far, since Comiskey didn't want to let go of his most expensive acquisition so easily, and the Yankees kept Maisel for one more year before they traded him away. However, the mere suggestion of trading Joe Jackson for Fritz Maisel illustrates how far Joe's value had fallen, especially since Comiskey had paid a record price for Joe only a few months earlier.

Fritz Maisel is almost forgotten today, but his stock was never higher than it was in the spring of 1916. The Yankees turned down a proposed deal with Boston to trade Maisel even up for Tris Speaker in April of that year.[9]

Many observers expected the White Sox to win the pennant as the 1916 season began. The Boston Red Sox were the defending World Series champions, but they suffered a serious blow when the team owner, Joe Lannin, traded star outfielder Tris Speaker to Cleveland after a bitter salary dispute. This self-administered setback brought the Red Sox back to the pack in the American League, and every team except for the hapless Philadelphia Athletics figured to challenge for the 1916 flag.

Comiskey made a few moves to strengthen the pitching staff in the 1915-16 off-season. He signed Claude (Lefty) Williams, a 24-year-old pitcher who had failed to stick with Detroit. Williams threw one of the best curveballs in baseball, and by early 1916 he showed signs of finally being able to get it over the plate. Williams was a southerner, and like Joe Jackson he had a quiet demeanor, though he carried himself in such a way that most people considered him quite intelligent. He and Joe became friends, and Williams, Jackson, and Jack Fournier formed a threesome in the bars and nightclubs on the road.

Perhaps the most important move Comiskey made in 1916 was his acquisition of a left-handed pitcher named Dave Danforth. Danforth, who pursued studies in dentistry in the off-season, was pitching for Louisville of the American Association in 1915 when he made a career-changing discovery. Major and minor league teams then used an oily substance on the infield to keep the dust settled on hot, dry days. Danforth rubbed this oil and some infield dust on half of the ball, then buffed it on his pants to a high shine. This made half the ball shiny and the other half rough, and caused a fastball to sail or dip on its way to the plate. Danforth's invention, the "shine ball," quickly turned him into a winner.

Danforth also taught the pitch to his Chicago teammate, Eddie Cicotte. Cicotte, a righthander, grew up in a French-Canadian immigrant community on the outskirts of Detroit, and pitched briefly for his hometown Tigers in 1905. He then had a few good years for Boston before the Red Sox sold him to the White Sox in the middle of the 1912 season. Financially, Cicotte was one of the unluckiest players in the major leagues. Detroit released him before the Tigers appeared in three consecutive World Series in 1907, 1908, and 1909, and the Red Sox let him go mere months before they won the Series in 1912. Cicotte missed four World Series shares in a space of six years, and by 1916 he was well past 30 and had not yet cashed any checks in postseason play.

Cicotte, whom opposing players called "Froggie" as a slur against his French ancestry, won 18 games for the White Sox in 1913, but fell to 11-16 in 1914 and 13-12 in 1915. Now, at the age of 32, Eddie Cicotte needed to revive his career, and he hoped that the shine ball would be his ticket to a few more years of success in the majors. He also hoped that the White Sox would finally get him into a World Series.

The White Sox began their season on April 12, and 31,000 fans crowded the newly expanded Comiskey Park to see the Detroit Tigers beat the Sox by a 4-0 score. Joe Jackson had only one hit, a single, but he was robbed by a spectacular catch by Tiger leftfielder Bobby Veach in the second inning. Joe, despite his excellent spring hitting, was still batting fifth in the lineup, behind first baseman Jack Fournier.

No team managed to run away from the pack in the early weeks of the 1916 campaign. On May 1 the White Sox occupied sixth place with a 9-9 record, but they were only two games behind the league-leading

Ed Collins

White Sox captain Eddie Collins (author's collection).

Senators. The Chicago fans rallied around the team, and the Chicago Board of Trade decided to keep the fans informed of the daily schedule. A large white flag with the Sox logo outside the Board of Trade building meant that there was a game on that day. A blue flag meant a postponement due to weather, and no flag at all meant that there was no game scheduled.[10]

Still, despite the support of the community and its fans, the White Sox flirted with mediocrity for the first two months of the season. They dipped one game below .500 in a loss to the Indians on May 5, despite two triples by Joe Jackson. When another off-day exhibition game (in which the Sox went to Erie, Pennsylvania, and bombed the locals by a 19-3 score) caused grumbling among the players, Pants Rowland called a team meeting on May 10 to clear the air. The players aired their gripes, but the team stumbled along at a few games under .500 for four more weeks.

The Sox were hampered by the same infield problems that troubled them in 1915. Rowland moved error-prone shortstop Buck Weaver to third base in the early part of the 1916 season and put Zeb Terry at short, but Terry hit only .190 in 94 games. By midseason Rowland was forced to bench Terry and put Weaver back at short. Weaver, bothered by the position shift, played 151 games but batted only .227. At first base, Jack Fournier hit poorly after his serious arm injury in August of 1915. He had batted over .300 in the previous two seasons, but Rowland and Comiskey soon ran out of patience waiting for their cleanup hitter to start hitting.

Despite the uncertainty in the infield, the White Sox began to climb out of their funk in mid–June, shortly after Rowland moved Joe Jackson back to the cleanup spot in the lineup. The White Sox won three of four from the defending champion Red Sox from June 15 to June 18. In the first game, Joe pounded a double and two singles, and then was hit by pitches his last two times up. Joe paid no attention to the brushbacks, and went 10 for 14 in the series to raise his batting average above .370. On July 1 Joe's average stood at .372, only one point behind Cleveland's Tris Speaker for the league lead.

The Sox rose to third place in July, but they lost two doubleheaders to the Red Sox on July 11–12 and fell briefly to fourth. Joe slumped at the plate, but the rest of the club picked up the slack in a four-game sweep of the awful A's on July 14-18. In early August Joe's average settled in the .340s as Ty Cobb and Tris Speaker battled for the batting title, and the White Sox moved into position to challenge the Red Sox and Tigers for the pennant.

The White Sox entered the pennant race on the strength of their starting pitching. Eddie Cicotte, the veteran who went 13-12 in 1915, used the shine ball to fashion a 15-7 mark in 1916. Joe Benz and Jim Scott, long-time mainstays of the pitching staff, fell off in 1916, but a new rotation emerged with Reb Russell, Lefty Williams, Red Faber, and Eddie Cicotte, with Dave Danforth as the relief ace. No team in baseball, with the possible exception of the Red Sox, could match the White Sox' depth of pitching. The White Sox also benefited from the hard hitting of center fielder Happy Felsch, who hit .300 in 1916 after his .248 average of the year before. Eddie Collins, Jackson, and Felsch made a potent 3-4-5 combination in the middle of the Chicago lineup.

On the last day of August the White Sox, still in third place, moved to within four games of the lead by blasting the Philadelphia A's once again. Joe Jackson pounded a home run, triple, and single, missing the cycle by only one hit. This was as close as Joe would ever get to hitting for the cycle in a game. The *Chicago Tribune* reported that Joe broke his favorite black bat in the sixth inning, then grabbed another one and hit the home run with it in the eighth.[11] The White Sox rode a seven-game winning streak to a 76-59 record on September 9, still in third place but only two games out of first.

The Sox finally lost in St. Louis to end the winning streak. Joe slid into third base in that game, and "[his] pants were so badly torn sliding into third in the fourth inning that he had to call for help," said the *Tribune*. Pants Rowland ran out to third with a handful of pins and closed up the tear, allowing Joe to continue until the inning ended and he could have the tear sewn up on the bench. Otherwise, the slugger would have been obliged to leave the game.[12]

The 1916 pennant chase came down to a three-game series between the White Sox and Red Sox in mid–September. Over 40,000 fans saw the White Sox win by a 6-4 score on September 16, boosting the White Sox into second place. Their celebration was short-lived; the Red Sox won 6-2 and 4-3 over the next two days behind Babe Ruth and Ernie Shore to lengthen their lead. Ruth's win was his twentieth of the 1916 season. The White Sox continued to battle, but a stunning 8-0 loss to the A's sealed their fate on September 21. The decimated Athletics had won only 32 of the 142 games they had played up till then. On October 1, the Red Sox officially clinched their second straight flag, with the White Sox in second place.

Joe Jackson redeemed himself in 1916. Despite his midseason slump, Joe finished with a batting average of .341, 37 points higher than his 1915 mark, and finished third in the batting race. Joe also belted 21 triples to lead the league in that department for the second time. Ty Cobb wound up the 1916 campaign with a .371 average, 30 points higher than Jackson's, but for once Cobb did not win the batting title. Tris Speaker, still angry at the Red Sox for letting him go, batted .386 for Cleveland to end Cobb's streak of nine consecutive batting championships.

Joe broke out of his slump in time for the City Series against the Cubs, who finished fifth in the National League that year. Russell, Faber, Williams, and Cicotte all pitched complete games as the Sox defeated the Cubs in four straight contests. Joe was the batting star for the Sox, with three doubles in the third game and a home run in the fourth game. His batting average of .571 in the series, with a slugging average over 1.000, gave Joe a successful end to the 1916 season. The White Sox, with their strong finish, served notice that they would challenge the Red Sox for supremacy in 1917.

Charles Comiskey, buoyed by a new attendance record of 679,923 in the 1916 season, reached further into his pocketbook to build a winning team. The Old Roman wasn't happy with Jack Fournier's play at first base, so he bought Arnold (Chick) Gandil from Cleveland to fill the gap. Gandil, who grew up in Minnesota, ran away from home as a teenager and wound up in the rough-and-tumble mining camps of California and Arizona. He was a charismatic, hard-drinking former boxer, only an average hitter but an excellent fielder. Fournier, one of Joe Jackson's few friends on the team, found himself back in the minor leagues in 1917.

Comiskey also closed the shortstop hole when he bought the strong-armed Charles (Swede) Risberg from Louisville for $10,000. Risberg's arrival allowed Pants Rowland to move Buck Weaver back to his natural position at third base.

The arrival of Gandil and Risberg solved the team's on-the-field problems, but it had negative consequences for the team's chemistry. Gandil had nearly come to blows with Eddie Collins several years earlier when Collins played for the A's and Gandil played for Washington. His hatred of Collins never abated, and Gandil refused to have anything to do with the captain of the White Sox. Risberg was a roughneck from California, and, while playing in the minor leagues, he once knocked out an umpire with one punch. Risberg and Gandil became good friends, while Risberg and Buck Weaver became nearly inseparable. These three men set up their own anti–Collins clique within the team, and from 1917 on the Chicago clubhouse was split into two warring camps.

Chapter 10

The 1917 Season

> When I was up there at the plate my purpose was to get on base any way I could, whether by hitting or getting hit or by a base on balls.... I generally made the pitchers bear down and usually they all looked alike to me. I had no special spots where I could hit some pitchers better than others. I was in there swinging, and if a pitch looked good enough to hit, I went for the ball, low, high, inside or out, if I had the sign from the manager to hit.
>
> —*Joe Jackson, 1942*[1]

The Neanderthal athlete is a widely recognized American character type. Many amusing stories have gained currency through the years, poking fun at the stereotypical "dumb jock." Whether such tales are true is a matter of conjecture, but they remain nonetheless. For example, the story goes that the Pittsburgh team offered its star shortstop, Honus Wagner, $2,000 a year in salary. Wagner hotly objected to the amount. "I won't sign for a penny less than fifteen hundred dollars," proclaimed the rustic Pirate.

The illiterate Joe Jackson, as might be expected, came in for his share of such mythmaking. Joe found that the Chicago writers did not respond to the southern storyteller persona that had worked so well for him in Cleveland. The writers from New York and Chicago saw themselves as more sophisticated than their fellows in smaller cities like Cleveland, and the big-city writers tended to dismiss Joe Jackson as an ignorant country boy. One writer cruelly suggested that the Federal League could have signed Joe if they had shown him the money in pennies. Such insults didn't sit well with the proud ballplayer, and Joe rarely spoke to the writers during his stay in Chicago.

Arthur Daley, who described Jackson in print as a "homesick hillbilly," claimed that one day Joe was scanning the box scores at the newsstand. "What gives with this?" demanded Joe. "I had two hits yesterday, and this paper only gives me one."

"Must be a typographical error, Joe," suggested the newsboy.

"Typographical error, nothin'," growled Shoeless Joe. "Them fielders never touched either one of them balls."[2]

Of course, anyone who knew Joe knew that he wasn't obsessed with his statistics, and he had no interest in reading the newspapers, either, but Daley's anecdote gained wide attention.

Another oft-repeated story concerns the origin of the name "Shoeless Joe." Supposedly, Joe was playing the outfield in his bare feet at Greenville, and he asked to come out of the game in the fourth inning. Joe's Greenville manager, Tom Stouch, asked him why.

"Are the rocks and glass in the outfield cutting up your feet, Joe?"

"Nah," replied the outfielder, "but they're fuzzin' up the ball so I can't throw it."[3] Joe never played in his bare feet in the professional ranks, but the tale has gained a life of its own.

Even worse was an incredibly imaginative scene described in a syndicated column by the respected writer Hugh Fullerton, who wrote "The rumor went around the country that he had been found playing ball in his bare feet, and that it was with difficulty that the scout who hired him to play with a minor league club was forced to hog-tie him to get shoes on him." Joe, the "ignorant idol," liked to bat in his bare feet, wrote Fullerton, because "he wailed that he couldn't hit unless he could get toe holds."[4]

Joe also came in for some not-so-gentle ribbing about his illiteracy. Joe's teammate Happy Felsch once told Eliot Asinof, author of *Eight Men Out*, that Felsch and Jackson were heading into a bar one day when a fan stopped Joe and asked him to autograph a baseball. Felsch went inside, drank four beers, and came back outside to find Joe, who was still struggling to sign his name on the ball.

Joe may have been illiterate, but many of his contemporaries felt that he was mentally sharp. "He had no education, but a surprisingly good head, despite all reports to the contrary," said Chick Gandil in 1956. "He pulls no bones," said Harry Davis in 1912, "and I find, the better I know him, that he has a head for things outside of baseball." After his departure from baseball, Joe made a good living running his various businesses.

Joe resented the aspersions cast upon his intelligence, but his attitude mellowed with his advancing age. "All the big sportswriters seemed to enjoy writing about me as an ignorant cotton-mill boy with nothing but lint where my brains ought to be," said Joe to an Atlanta newspaper reporter in 1949. "That was all right with me. I was able to fool a lot of pitchers and managers and club owners I wouldn't have been able to fool if they'd thought I was smarter."[5]

By early 1917, Joe Jackson's life had settled down in many ways from the turmoil of the previous two years. His marriage to Katie was as solid as ever. He won over the fans in Chicago with a good season in 1916, and for the first time in his career, he played for a team with a chance to win a pennant and a World Series title. He enjoyed living in Savannah, and he had answered the criticisms of F. C. Lane's *Baseball Magazine* article of the year before. Now, at the age of 29, Joe stood on the threshold of what he expected to be the most productive years of his career.

Jackson recognized, however, that he no longer ran as fast as he once did. Although Joe weighed not much more than he weighed in his early days in the American League, he no longer covered as much ground in the outfield or stole as many bases. Joe's foot speed was good, if not spectacular, in his Cleveland days, but age and injuries to his legs and feet took their toll. Joe's stolen base total peaked at 41 in 1911, and dropped every year thereafter until 1915, when Joe stole only 16 sacks and was thrown out 20 times. He rebounded in 1916 with 24 steals, but from then on, Joe paid more attention to driving in runs than to stealing bases. He legged out a league-leading 21 triples in 1916, but that was more a result of Joe belting line drives to the fence in the spacious outfield at Comiskey Park than of Joe's running ability.

Pants Rowland also found it necessary to move Joe around in the outfield in certain situations. Joe's throwing arm was as powerful as ever, and he still made tumbling circus catches in the outfield, but his days of playing center field were now long past. Joe usually played left field, but when the Sox played in New York's Polo Grounds or Cleveland's League Park, Rowland moved Joe to right field on sunny days. The afternoon sun settled above the roof of the grandstand and shone directly into the left fielder's eyes in those two parks, and Shano Collins and Nemo Leibold were much more adept at fighting the sun than Joe was.

Along with the rest of the White Sox, Joe reported to spring training at Mineral Wells, Texas, in early March of 1917. The team's two biggest holes, at shortstop and at first base, were filled, and the White Sox were now established as the pennant favorites in the American League. Most observers agreed with a headline in the *Chicago Tribune*, which stated, "Sox should win flag unless stars are hurt."[6]

Charles Comiskey, too, smelled a pennant, and decided to jettison the sole remaining member of his last championship team, the 1906 "Hitless Wonders." The Old Roman finally gave up on his favorite pitcher, Ed Walsh, who by 1917 was 36 years old and had been trying to regain his form for four long, frustrating years. The White Sox released Walsh in March of 1917, and the old spitballer ended his career with the Boston Braves of the National League that year.

Manager Rowland divided the team into the "Regulars" and the "Goofs," and the Regulars played their way through the sandy fields of Texas and Oklahoma. The club also went to Houston for a week, because they had a grass field there; Comiskey wanted to make sure that the players became used to grass before the season began.

Spring training was not without problems, however. Joe Jackson suffered a severely sprained ankle in Mineral Wells, and when Joe's recovery was slow, the club feared that the injury had damaged some of the tendons in his ankle. When Joe finally got back onto the field, he suffered a spike wound in the same ankle during a play at first base. Joe, who was already slowing noticeably in the field and on the bases, hobbled painfully through the rest of the spring.

The White Sox began their annual exhibition tour from Texas to Chicago in early April. On April 1 Joe belted one of the longest home runs ever seen in Fort Worth, Texas, when his blast flew over the right field fence and into the Trinity River, which ran next to the ballpark. He pounded another homer in Norman, Oklahoma, the next day, then waited with his teammates when sandstorms prevented play in Kansas. In a 15-0 bombing of the local nine at Ottumwa, Iowa, on April 6, Eddie Collins was knocked unconscious by a fastball. He quickly reentered the lineup, but in another game at Des Moines three days later, Collins was beaned a second time. The Sox entered the season with both Jackson and Collins hurting.

In the meantime, overseas developments diverted the nation's attention from the beginning of the baseball season. The American people could no longer ignore the war in Europe, especially after the German government declared unrestricted submarine warfare against all Atlantic ships, including American ones. On February 3, 1917, the United States broke off diplomatic relations with Germany, and on April 6, at the request of President Wilson, Congress declared war on Germany. Since the nation required at least several months to gear up for a war effort, the declaration had little effect on baseball at this early date. A few players, such as the White Sox' Jim Scott and the Braves' Hank Gowdy, enlisted for service, but the rest of the players waited for a military draft to be organized.

Baseball owners seized the opportunity to make a show of their patriotism. The magnates hired drill instructors to teach marching maneuvers to the players, and the fans were treated to the sight of players marching around the field in formation, carrying bats in the place of rifles. Soldiers and sailors were able to buy half-price seats for the games, and stadium ushers collected money for the Red Cross and sold "Liberty Bonds" between innings. On the sleeve of the White Sox uniform Comiskey put an American flag, which remained for the duration of the war.

Comiskey could also claim with pride that the first major league ballplayer to volunteer for service in the war was a member of the Chicago White Sox. Alfred (Fritz) von Kolnitz tried, and failed, to fill the third base position for the Sox in 1916, batting only .227 in 24 games, so he left baseball and joined the Army several months before the 1917 declaration of war. Von Kolnitz, who despite his Teutonic name was a native of South Carolina, eventually rose to the rank of major, the highest rank attained by any ballplayer in the first World War, and became a career officer.

The National Commission, ostensibly in a patriotic spirit, publicly offered to stage a series of Sunday exhibition games in the Eastern cities (Boston, New York, and Philadelphia) to raise money for various war-related charities, such as war relief and the Red Cross. This idea was met with furious disapproval from the mayors of those cities, and cynics suggested that baseball wanted to use such games as a way to "soften up" the East for Sunday ball after the war.[7] The magnates also refrained from complaining too much when Congress passed a bill that slapped a 10 percent tax on entertainment, including baseball tickets. The owners did not want to appear unpatriotic, though the tax certainly was responsible for a drop in baseball attendance in 1917.

The White Sox lost their season opener to St. Louis, but in the second game of the season Eddie Cicotte pitched a no-hitter against the Browns, winning by an 11-0 score. By now Cicotte had mastered the shine ball that Dave Danforth taught him in 1916, and both Danforth and Cicotte profited from the new pitch. The shine ball caused a great deal of controversy, and other players and managers appealed to league president Ban Johnson to outlaw the pitch, as he had done with the emery ball three years earlier.[8]

Johnson, whose decisions seemed to be getting more erratic with each passing year, elected to look into the matter after Washington manager Clark Griffith sent him some baseballs that Danforth had "shined." On May 28, after a thorough investigation of the balls, Johnson revealed his decision. He proclaimed that since infield dust and oil were substances that were found naturally on the baseball field, Danforth could not be found guilty of applying "foreign substances" to the surface of the ball. Therefore, the shine ball was legal, but the emery ball was not. Two years before, using the same logic, Johnson had allowed the league's pitchers to continue throwing the spitball; spit was not "foreign," reasoned Johnson, because it was a natural substance produced by the human body![9]

Other pitchers refined Danforth's invention. Paraffin or talcum powder also produced a high gloss on part of the baseball, so pitchers hid these substances on their uniform pants, and rubbed the ball against their hip or thigh to shine it up. All around the league, hitting took a nosedive in the first half of the 1917 season as pitchers experimented with the new invention. By early June, no American League club had a team batting average higher than .246, and the league as a whole was hitting .234, a full 14 points under the league batting average for the previous several seasons.

In the meantime, the Boston Red Sox jumped out to the league lead, but the White Sox nipped at their heels in the early going. The White Sox went through a slump in early May, which featured two no-hitters thrown at them in two days by the lowly St. Louis Browns. On May 5, Ernie Koob allowed an infield single to Buck Weaver in the first inning, then shut down the Sox without a hit for the rest of the game for a 1-0 shutout. The official scorer changed Weaver's hit to an error after the game, giving Koob a tainted no-hitter. Bob Groom no-hit the Sox the next day, in the second game of a doubleheader.

Charles Comiskey was concerned by the slump, although the season had barely begun, and suddenly Pants Rowland found himself on the hot seat. Rumors swirled around Chicago that the impatient owner was courting Bill Carrigan, the recently retired Red Sox manager, to take over for Rowland. Comiskey denied the report, and the White Sox rallied around Rowland with an eight-game winning streak in mid–May to jump into second place.

Joe Jackson, however, got off to a poor start in 1917. His foot and ankle still bothered him from spring training, and the resulting unnatural running gait made his back act up in earnest. Joe's average in mid–May stood at .265, though Rowland left him in the cleanup spot in the lineup. Punch-and-slap hitters like Ty Cobb were not as adversely affected by the increasing array of shine balls and spitballs tossed by the league's pitchers, but the hard-swinging Joe Jackson found it difficult to adapt, especially with a sore back. By July 1, Joe's average had risen only to .283, more than 70 points below his lifetime average.

If Joe found the going rough in 1917, Eddie Collins found it even more so. Collins thrashed around under .250 in the first two months of the season, possibly due to the aftereffects of his two beanings in three days in April. Fortunately for the White Sox, Happy Felsch kept his average above .300, and led the team in runs batted in. By 1917 the 25-year-old Felsch was already one of the league's most dangerous hitters and was considered the best fielding centerfielder in the circuit after Cleveland's Tris Speaker.

The Red Sox rode the arm and bat of Babe Ruth into first place in the first few months of the 1917 season. The big lefthander not only started the season with ten wins in his first 13 games, but he also kept his batting average well above .300. At age 22, Ruth was the best left-handed pitcher in the American League, but already some sportswriters suggested that the Babe would do the Red Sox more good by playing in the field every day. Ruth's problem, however, was that he had not yet mastered his temper. He punched umpire Brick Owens on June 23 and drew a ten-day suspension, which sent the Red Sox into a tailspin.[10] The White Sox, meanwhile, won 16 games in a 17-game stretch to take the league lead.

It was a two-team race from that point on. On July 1, the White Sox lost to Cleveland when Eddie Cicotte made two bad throws to first base with "shined" baseballs, which sailed over Chick Gandil's head at first base. Despite this loss, and the continuing hitting problems of Joe Jackson and Eddie Collins, the White Sox held first place by one and a half games over Boston. Jackson's back continued to bother him, and after Joe failed twice with the bases loaded in a loss to Detroit on July 5, he took some time off. Joe was "off his feed," said the papers, and Pants Rowland gave Joe some time to rest his aching back and ankle.

Ty Cobb, unlike Joe, was perfectly healthy, and fought to regain the batting title that he lost to Tris Speaker the year before. Now 30 years old and a veteran of 13 major league seasons, Cobb had lost none of his feistiness. In the game on July 5, Cobb reached third in the eighth inning. Chicago's Buck Weaver taunted Cobb by tossing the ball in the air, daring him to break for home. Finally, Weaver rolled the ball about 20 feet behind third, then glared at Cobb. Cobb took the bait and set out for home, but Weaver quickly retrieved the ball, and Cobb dove back into third safely.[11] Detroit beat the Sox again the next day, though Red Faber and Jim Scott ended Cobb's hitting streak at 35 games, the second longest in league history up to that time.[12]

The Red Sox and White Sox traded the lead for the next few weeks.

Joe in 1917 (Chicago Historical Society, ICHi-31132).

Ruth's one-hitter against the Tigers on July 11 moved the Red Sox into a tie with Chicago. Joe stayed out of the lineup until July 15, when he stroked two hits in a loss to Washington. He hit the ball hard all four times up, however, and two days later Joe whacked a rare homer into Washington's faraway right field stands. The White Sox, sparked by Joe's return to action, won four games in two days against the Senators to regain the league lead.

The Red Sox invaded Chicago for a pivotal five-game series on Thursday, July 19, and over 30,000 fans poured into Comiskey Park for each game. The two teams traded wins in the first two contests, then played to a 1-1 tie on Saturday, in a game called because of darkness after 15 innings. They might have been able to finish the game if Buck Weaver had not fouled off 17 pitches in a row in the sixth inning. Thanks to Weaver, the umpires ran out of baseballs, and the game was delayed for half an hour while the umpires rounded up some more balls.[13] The White Sox won the next two, and the Red Sox left town in second place, four and a half games behind.

As the season progressed, the shine ball became more controversial. Some Chicago pitchers, such as Cicotte, Danforth, and Williams, threw it regularly, while others fooled batters by miming the motions of "shining one up." Happy Felsch told a newspaper reporter that the shine ball didn't really exist; it was merely a figment of the imagination. Ban Johnson waffled on whether or not to allow its continued use, as other pitching staffs experimented with the pitch. On August 14, when a shine ball from Dave Danforth hit Cleveland's Tris Speaker in the head, knocking him cold, the controversy flared anew. Johnson formally banned the shine ball a few days later and instructed the American League umpires to diligently enforce the ban. Charles Comiskey and the White Sox protested, thinking that the ban was specifically directed against them, but Johnson held his ground. Soon almost every pitching appearance by Danforth, Cicotte, or Williams became a tiresome series of three-cornered arguments among the Sox, the opponents, and the umpires. In a game in early September, the Indians challenged Cicotte's deliveries in almost every inning. Braggo Roth, one of the players that Cleveland received for Joe Jackson two years earlier, drew an ejection when he took one of Cicotte's baseballs and threw it over the grandstand in frustration.

Boston edged into first for one day on August 17, but the Red Sox stopped hitting, and by September 1 the White Sox had restored their four-game lead. The White Sox virtually clinched the pennant when they won a doubleheader against the Tigers on September 2, while the Red Sox lost twice against the Yankees on the same day. The White Sox beat the Tigers the next day, Labor Day, in both ends of another twin bill, and gained another game on Boston. Chicago now held a seven-game bulge. "Detroit's Play in Field Is Loose," complained a *Detroit Free Press* headline after the Sunday games, though the Tiger fielding had been quite poor all year. After the Labor Day doubleheader, E. A. Batchelor of the *Free Press* wrote, "Only a miracle ... can prevent the White Sox from winning the pennant now."[14]

Shortly thereafter, the White Sox took up a collection to "tip" the Detroit pitchers. The Sox raised a fund of over $1,100, which Chick Gandil delivered to Tiger pitcher Bill James for distribution among his teammates. The stated reason for the "tipping" was to reward the Tigers for bearing down against the Red Sox earlier in the season, though the timing of the gift—immediately after Chicago's four-game sweep of the Tigers—looked suspicious, to say the least.

The practice of paying opposing players for good performances against other teams was prevalent at the time. However, it left open the possibility of misinterpretation, as the White Sox would discover long after the games of September 2–3, 1917, had been forgotten. Ten years later, the White Sox would stand accused of paying the Tigers to lose those four games, in a scandal that threatened to eclipse the Black Sox scandal of 1919.

By September 8, the White Sox lead over Boston stood at seven games, and they gained another game with the help of a forfeit win against Cleveland on September 9. In the tenth inning, with rain falling, the umpire called Cleveland's Jack Graney out at third base for interfering with Chicago's Buck Weaver. This caused a 20-minute argument in which the frustrated Cleveland players threw their gloves in the air and stormed about before finally taking the field for the bottom of the inning. When Chicago's Dave Danforth struck out, the Cleveland catcher pegged the ball down to third baseman Ivon Howard, who let it sail into the outfield untouched. When left fielder Graney refused to retrieve the ball, the flustered umpire forfeited the game to the White Sox.[15] This win came in the middle of a nine-game winning streak that put more distance between Chicago and Boston. The White Sox clinched the pennant on September 21, when Red Faber beat the Red Sox 2-1 in Boston.

Joe Jackson finally began hitting in early September, when a 17 for 30 streak lifted his average from .278 to .294 in one week, and he still had a shot at .300. Joe's average hovered in the .290s all through September, but no one knew his exact average. Each newspaper kept its own set of statistics and published its own box scores at the time. Sometimes, one newspaper might credit a player with a hit, while another paper scored an error on the same play. Only the official league averages counted at the end of the year, and the two leagues did not release their figures until well after the season was over. Joe didn't find out until long after the World Series was completed that he had hit .301 for the 1917 campaign.

Joe suffered through his worst season at the plate, but many of the other Sox players took up the slack. Happy Felsch led the team in batting with a .308 mark, and he became the first member of the White Sox to

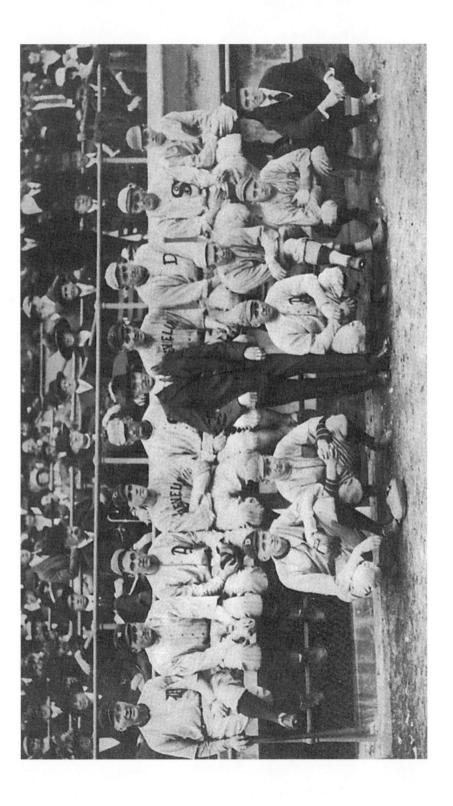

drive in 100 runs in a season. Eddie Cicotte used the shine ball to win 28 games, and he led the league with a sparkling earned run average of 1.53. Dave Danforth led the league in games pitched with 50 and in saves with 11. Eddie Collins, who lifted his final batting mark to .289, stole 53 bases and tied Joe for the team lead in runs scored with 91. Most importantly, the Sox won 100 games in the 1917 season, a total that no other White Sox team in the twentieth century can match. They wound up the season eight games ahead of the second-place Red Sox.

With the pennant safely clinched, the White Sox could afford to play a few rookies and reserves and rest some of their stars for the World Series. The Sox also left two of their players behind in Boston for a charity game. On September 27, the Boston Red Sox hosted an all-star game to benefit the family of Tim Murnane, a popular Boston player-turned-sportswriter who died suddenly in February of 1917. Joe Jackson and Buck Weaver represented the White Sox on the all-star team, which was directed by Joe's first major league manager, Connie Mack. The All-Stars had Cobb, Speaker, and Jackson in the outfield, and Walter Johnson on the mound, making one of the most formidable All-Star aggregations ever assembled. However, the Red Sox defeated the All-Stars 2-0 behind the shutout pitching of Babe Ruth and Dutch Leonard, who held Joe hitless in four trips to the plate.

Before the game, the players competed in fungo hitting, distance throwing, and the like. Joe's fellow All-Stars entered him in the distance throw competition—Joe said that he didn't know he was in it until his name was called—and he heaved the ball 396 feet and eight inches to win the contest. His throw is often described as an all-time record, but several minor leaguers had cleared 400 feet in earlier competitions. However, Joe's heave surpassed the next longest throw that day by more than twelve feet.[16] He took home an inscribed silver bowl as a trophy, and the bowl remained one of Jackson's most treasured possessions for the rest of his life.

Cleveland's Ray Chapman circled the bases in 14 seconds flat to win the footrace competition, and no one was surprised when Babe Ruth won the fungo hitting contest with a belt of 402 feet, only 17 feet short of Ed Walsh's all-time record, set six years earlier.[17]

Opposite: American League All-Star team at Tim Murnane Day, September 27, 1917. *Top row:* Hugh Jennings, Walter Johnson, Stuffy McInnis, Steve O'Neill, Joe Jackson, Ray Chapman, Ty Cobb, Buck Weaver, batboy. *Bottom row:* Howard Ehmke, Rabbit Maranville (of the National League Braves), Connie Mack, Wally Schang, Tris Speaker, Bob Shawkey, unknown man (author's collection).

Chapter 11

World Champions

> You know, before you go into a World Series, you scout the other club mighty careful—and I don't mean just how to pitch to 'em or how to play 'em either. You go over every man on the club and you figure which ones you can ride and which ones you can't. There's no use ridin' a guy if it only makes him play harder and better. So you want to know which ones to get "on" and which ones to lay off of.
>
> —*Buck Weaver*[1]

After a tune-up game against an All-Star team in Cleveland, Joe and the White Sox prepared to face the New York Giants in the World Series. Four years earlier, the White Sox and Giants rode each other mercilessly in their round-the-world trip, and the two teams nearly had a full-scale riot in Egypt, in the shadows of the pyramids. "You're yellow," sneered Buck Weaver at John McGraw and his men in 1913. "I only hope we get you guys in a World Series. Then we'll show you what a real fightin' ball-club is—you and your yellowbellies."[2] Now, in 1917, Weaver and his teammates had their chance to back up their boasts.

The sun shone brightly on the afternoon of Saturday, October 6, and the Chicago fans turned out to see the first World Series game ever held in Comiskey Park. The Sox wore new red, white and blue stockings with their cream-colored uniforms, while the Giants showed up in gray uniforms trimmed with purple. In the stands the Woodland Bards, Charles Comiskey's hand-picked band of supporters, whooped it up long before Eddie Cicotte threw the first pitch of the day. "The Bards are, without a doubt, the most rabid baseball fans in the world," explained the *New York Times*. "They like baseball so well that they even have a clubroom right at the baseball park, so that when the Sox win a game they can sit around and win it all over again."[3]

The White Sox held a meeting before the first game. They knew that the Giants expected a continuation of the needling and riding from the 1913 trip, and to cross them up the Sox decided to ignore the Giants. The New Yorkers piled on the verbal abuse during infield practice, but the Sox kept their mouths shut. "Thought you were a fightin' ballclub!" shouted the Giants, but the Sox refused to respond in kind.

The opposing managers—Pants Rowland and John McGraw—could not have been more different. Rowland never played a game in the major leagues, while McGraw was one of the biggest stars in baseball with the old Baltimore Orioles. McGraw was known as the roughest of the rowdy Orioles, and even in 1917 the 44-year-old McGraw still got into fights in nightclubs and bars. Rowland was a scrappy individual himself, but he didn't drink as much as McGraw and avoided controversy off the field whenever possible. Rowland solicited lineup advice from Comiskey and delegated much of the field leadership of the Sox to Kid Gleason and Eddie Collins; for the Giants, McGraw, the "Little Napoleon," controlled all the action and strategy personally.

Rowland (or Comiskey) made a lineup change before the Series began. The Sox elected to go with Fred McMullin at third base and moved Buck Weaver back to shortstop over the rookie Swede Risberg, who batted only .203 in 1917 and suffered an injury to his throwing hand late in the season. Risberg was a more accomplished fielder than Weaver, but Rowland sacrificed some defense to put a stronger bat in the lineup. The Sox designated their ace, 28-game-winner Eddie Cicotte, to start the first game.

McGraw started his second-best pitcher, lefthander Slim Sallee, who won 18 games in the regular season. Though both Joe Jackson and Eddie Collins had endured sub-par seasons in 1917, McGraw feared their left-handed bats more than any others in the Chicago lineup. The Giants manager certainly noticed that the White Sox in general, and Collins and Jackson in particular, had problems with left-handed pitchers, especially Boston's Babe Ruth. McGraw had two good right-handed starters in Pol Perritt and Jeff Tesreau, but he would start a lefthander in every game of the Series.

Eddie Cicotte floated the first pitch over for a strike to leadoff batter George Burns, who drove the third pitch to center for a single. Buck Herzog then flied out to Jackson in left, and after Burns stole second

Benny Kauff flied to Jackson, who fumbled the ball but managed to hold on for the out. Heinie Zimmerman then belted a liner to center, which Happy Felsch caught for the third out.

The White Sox nearly scored in their half of the first. Shano Collins singled off Giants starter Slim Sallee, and Fred McMullin sacrificed him to second. Eddie Collins hit a grounder to second that moved Shano Collins to third with two outs, and that brought Joe Jackson to the plate. Joe hit a looper into center on the first pitch, but second baseman Buck Herzog made a spectacular over-the-shoulder catch to end the inning.

In the third inning, the White Sox took a 1-0 lead when, with one out, Cicotte and Shano Collins singled. Cicotte tried to take third, but was tagged out by Zimmerman for the second out. Fred McMullin then drilled a double to left to score Collins. The Sox scored again in the fourth when Happy Felsch pounded one of Sallee's deliveries over the left field fence for a home run and a 2-0 lead. The Giants got on the board in the fifth, when Lew McCarty tripled and came home on a single by the pitcher, Sallee.

The White Sox narrowly avoided catastrophe in the sixth inning, when Zimmerman lifted a pop-up between first and second. Eddie Collins called for the ball, but Chick Gandil refused to give way. Gandil, who was several inches taller than Collins, ignored the captain and caught the ball; Collins peeled off a split second before the two players would have crashed into each other. "There were times that it seemed that the White Sox team play lacked harmony,"[4] said the *New York Times*, stating what was only too obvious to the Chicago writers.

Joe Jackson went hitless, but he probably saved the game for Cicotte in the seventh inning. With one out the Giants' Walter Holke singled, and then Lew McCarty belted a sinking liner into short left field. Jackson caught the ball with a spectacular diving, tumbling catch, stealing a sure triple from McCarty and keeping Holke from tying the score. Cicotte retired the Giants the rest of the way, and the White Sox won the game by a 2 to 1 score.

The two teams met the next day for the second game of the Series, which was the first World Series game ever played on a Sunday. The Giants heaped even more abuse on the White Sox before Game 2, but the Sox ignored their taunts once again. McGraw started his 21-game winner, lefthander Ferdie Schupp, while the Sox countered with spitball artist Red Faber.

The Giants struck first in the top of the second. Robertson and Holke singled, and then McCarty singled to left. Jackson's throw to the plate got past Schalk for an error, as both Robertson and Holke scored. Faber then retired Schupp and Burns on grounders, but the Giants led 2-0. The Sox evened things up in the bottom of the inning when Jackson singled on a 3-1 pitch, and then Felsch singled Joe to third. Jackson scored when Gandil bounced a hit off Schupp's glove, with Felsch taking third on the play. Weaver failed twice to set down a sacrifice, but then singled to left to score Felsch, and the score was tied at 2. After Schalk forced Gandil at third and Faber walked to load the bases, McGraw brought in Fred Anderson, a righthander, who retired Leibold and McMullin to end the inning.

The roof fell in on the Giants in the fourth. Weaver and Schalk both singled to right. After Faber popped up for the first out, Leibold singled to bring in Weaver, and McMullin followed with a single to score Schalk and give the Sox a 4-2 lead. McGraw brought in righthander Pol Perritt, who gave up a single to Eddie Collins that scored Leibold. Joe Jackson came up next. He worked Perritt to a 3-1 count, then lashed a single to right that scored McMullin and Collins for a 7-2 lead. Perritt and Jeff Tesreau held the Sox in check for the rest of the game, but Faber spaced out eight hits for a 7-2 Chicago win and a two-game lead in the Series.

Red Faber won the game but also committed one of the most famous gaffes in World Series history. In the fifth inning Faber walked and advanced to second base with two out. Faber then attempted to steal third. Unfortunately, he forgot that the bases were loaded at the time. Faber slid into third and found Buck Weaver, the baserunner, glaring at him. "Where the hell do you think you're going?" snarled Weaver.

Faber thought for a moment. "Back out to pitch," came his embarrassed reply.

The White Sox oozed with confidence as the teams gathered at the Polo Grounds in New York. The Sox made only one minor change to their lineup for Game 3. Joe Jackson didn't play well in the infamous left field area of the Polo Grounds, which was considered to be the most inhospitable sun field of any major league ballpark. Accordingly, Rowland put Joe in right field and moved Shano Collins to left. Many players found left field in New York nearly impossible to play; George Burns, the Giants' left fielder, wore a specially designed long-billed cap and a primitive pair of flip-down sunglasses when he did battle with the sun. "Joe is not an outfielder of the sun persuasion," said the *Chicago Tribune*, and so Rowland switched Collins and Jackson, as he had done many times during the regular season against the Yankees in the same ballpark.

John McGraw, however, had something up his sleeve. He bypassed his best righthander, 17-game winner Pol Perritt, and sent Rube Benton (15-9), a big left-handed curveball specialist, to the hill for the Giants in

Joe and the trophies he won at the Tim Murnane Day game in Boston, September 1917 (Cleveland Public Library).

a bid to neutralize Joe Jackson's power. The Polo Grounds had a short right field line, and McGraw didn't want Jackson to take aim at the right field fence only 257 feet from home plate. He certainly remembered Joe's 500-foot blast at the same ballpark in 1913. Benton's curveball, reasoned McGraw, would break away from Jackson and stay in the middle of the outfield, where the center field fence stood 520 feet away from the plate.

McGraw's ploy worked, as Benton held Joe hitless and shut out the

Sox by a 2-0 score in front of 34,000 fans. The next day brought more of the same, as Ferdie Schupp atoned for his loss in Game 2 by strapping Joe Jackson with another 0 for 4 day. The Giants' Benny Kauff belted a line drive against Red Faber in the fourth, which rolled under the bushes at the base of the center field fence for an inside-the-park homer. Kauff also hit an over-the-fence shot off Dave Danforth in the eighth, as Schupp scattered seven hits and shut out the Sox 5-0. Suddenly, the series was tied at two games apiece.

On the train back to Chicago, recalled Buck Weaver many years later, "We were wild. They had us on the ropes. We'd kept it in so long that we just had to let it out of us."[5] The Sox decided to end the silent treatment. When the series resumed at Comiskey Park on October 13, the Sox came to the park ready for action. They filed their spikes to razor-sharp points before the game. During batting practice, Buck Weaver sliced several sharp line drives into packs of Giants standing on the sidelines. "You want to see a fighting team?" asked the Sox. "Well, now you're gonna see one!"

The fifth game turned out to be one of the nastiest ever seen in any World Series. The Giants scored twice off Chicago's Reb Russell in the first, when Burns and Herzog singled and came home on a double by Kauff. Pants Rowland then brought in Eddie Cicotte to replace Russell, and Cicotte got out of the inning with no further damage. Kauff tried to kick the ball out of Schalk's glove on a force play at home, and the Chicago infielders responded by slamming down their tags with both hands for the rest of the game. The Sox also slid into the bases with their spikes high, and the rancorous chatter turned meaner as the game progressed.

The White Sox scored once in the third when Eddie Collins, Joe Jackson, and Happy Felsch all singled, driving Collins across the plate for the first Chicago run. The Giants answered with two more in the fourth off Cicotte, and the Giants led 4-1. In the fifth inning, Happy Felsch collided with Walter Holke at first base, and the entire Giants infield charged after Felsch. McGraw quickly ran onto the field to pull his players away from Felsch so that the game could continue.

In the sixth, Weaver singled, and when Schalk followed with a base hit, Weaver bowled over both second baseman Buck Herzog and short-stop Art Fletcher on his way to third. The White Sox argued unsuccessfully that Weaver should have been allowed to score on interference, but Weaver scored anyway when Swede Risberg, pinch-hitting for Cicotte, singled Weaver home to cut the Giant lead to 4-2. The Giants made it 5-2 in the seventh on a double by Robertson and a single by catcher Bill Rariden off reliever Lefty Williams.

Now, the constant riding began to pay off for the White Sox. Jackson and Felsch singled with one out in the seventh, and Gandil's double drove them both home to cut the lead to 5-4. Weaver's grounder sent Gandil to third, and Schalk walked. Schalk lit out for second on a double steal, but Rariden, the catcher, threw the ball back to Sallee, who looked Gandil back to third and threw to Herzog at second. Sallee's throw skipped past the rattled Herzog into center field, and Gandil scored to tie the game.

In the eighth, the Sox turned up the pressure once again, and the Giants crumbled under the strain. Shano Collins singled, was sacrificed to second by McMullin, and scored on Eddie Collins' single. Joe Jackson then followed with his third hit of the day, a single that sent Eddie Collins to third. The Sox had been riding third baseman Heinie Zimmerman all day, and when Kauff's throw went to third and Jackson set out for second base, the flustered Zimmerman pegged the ball into the outfield, allowing Collins to cross the plate. Jackson advanced to third, where he scored on Felsch's single as the Sox took an 8-5 lead.

With two out and Perritt replacing Sallee on the mound for the Giants, Felsch attempted to steal second and came into the base with his spikes high. The frustrated Fletcher slammed the ball hard into Felsch's ribs, which brought Rowland charging out onto the field to challenge Fletcher to a fight, but the umpires managed to restore order. Red Faber shut down the Giants in the ninth, and the Sox led the Series three games to two.

Pants Rowland decided to start Faber in the sixth game in New York. Even if the Sox lost, they still had their ace, Eddie Cicotte, available for the seventh game in Chicago, and so the Sox were in the driver's seat. The Giants poured on the abuse before Game 6, but their hearts weren't in it on a cold day at the Polo Grounds. John McGraw sent Rube Benton, the shutout winner of Game 3, to the hill for the Giants. This game turned out to be one of the most memorable in the history of baseball.

Faber and Benton set down the opposition for the first three innings, but the wheels fell off for the Giants in the fourth, in one of the most embarrassing displays of team fielding ever seen in a World Series. Eddie Collins opened the fourth with a grounder to Heinie Zimmerman, who threw the ball over the first baseman's head for a two-base error. Joe Jackson followed with a lazy fly ball to right fielder Dave Robertson, who dropped the ball and put Collins on third and Jackson on first. Felsch then grounded to the pitcher, Benton, and all hell broke loose.

Benton caught Collins off third and threw to Zimmerman, who proceeded to occupy Collins in a rundown with catcher Bill Rariden.

Rariden ran Collins back toward third, and then threw to Zimmerman as Jackson and Felsch motored around the bases behind him. The confused Zimmerman held the ball too long, and Collins set out for home.

Rariden had to let Collins run by him, since he didn't have the ball,[6] and Collins saw to his delight that no one was covering the plate. Zimmerman, still holding the ball, had no choice but to chase the speedy Collins down the third base line with the ball in his outstretched arm. Collins won this comic-opera chase and the Sox took a 1-0 lead, as Jackson and Felsch wound up on third and second respectively.

It wasn't all Zimmerman's fault, since either pitcher Benton or first baseman Holke should have been covering home, but Zimmerman carried the goat's horns for the rest of his life, like Fred Merkle before him and Bill Buckner after him. When a reporter asked Zimmerman why he held onto the ball, the exasperated third baseman replied, "Who the hell was I going to throw the ball to? Klem?"[7] Bill Klem was the home plate umpire.

After the Series, a New York writer immortalized the play with a parody of Rudyard Kipling's poem "Gunga Din," which ended with the line, "I'm a faster man than you are, Heinie Zim."

This play scored only one run, but it knocked the wind out of the Giants. Gandil, the next batter, singled home both Jackson and Felsch and the Sox led 3-0. The Giants scored twice in the fifth when Faber walked two batters and Shano Collins misplayed a line drive by Buck Herzog into a triple, scoring both men. Pants Rowland ordered Eddie Cicotte to warm up, but Faber regained his bearings and allowed only one more run the rest of the way. McCarty's grounder to Eddie Collins ended the game, 4-2, and clinched the 1917 World Series for the White Sox. It was the second, and last, world championship for the White Sox in the twentieth century.

Many years later, Buck Weaver still remembered the scene as the Sox celebrated their first world's championship in 11 years. John McGraw came tearing out of the Giants' dugout, straight at Weaver. The crusty manager offered Weaver his hand. "I want to shake your hand, kid," growled McGraw. "You're the best, and I want to take my hat off to you."[8]

McGraw didn't feel the same way about Pants Rowland, however. Rowland offered his hand to McGraw. "Mr. McGraw, I'm glad we won," said the White Sox skipper, "but I'm sorry you had to be the one to lose."

"Get away from me, you goddamned busher!" snarled the Giant manager.[9]

While the White Sox celebrated far into the night, the New York press roasted McGraw. His decision to start lefthanders in all six games

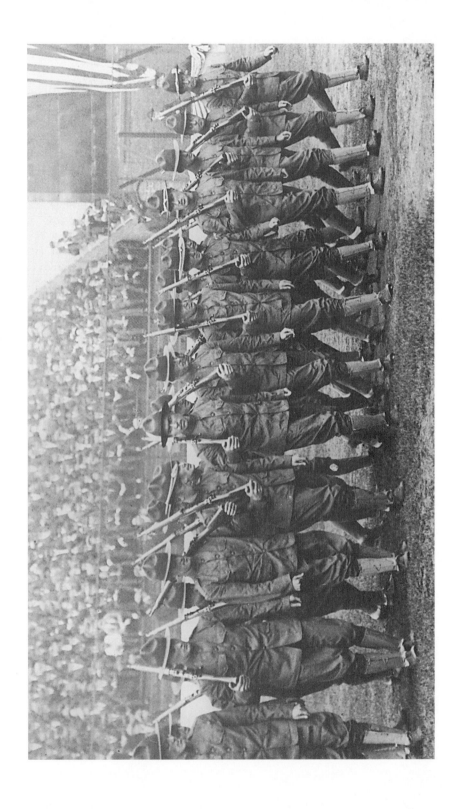

caused him to bypass Pol Perritt (17-7 in 1917) and Jeff Tesreau (13-8) in the rotation. McGraw, complained the writers, was so worried about Joe Jackson that he stayed with his lefties far too long. McGraw's decision to put the poor-fielding Robertson in right field backfired when Robertson dropped Jackson's fly ball in Game 6 and opened the door to Chicago's winning rally.[10] The 1917 World Series was the fourth in a row that the Giants lost, and this was one of the lowest points of the Little Napoleon's 30-year career as manager of the Giants.

Red Faber, with three wins, and Eddie Collins, with a .409 batting average, were the heroes of the Series for Chicago. Joe Jackson gave a good performance, with seven singles in 23 trips to the plate for a .304 average. He drove in only two runs, but he saved Game 1 with a circus catch and moved several runners into scoring position for Felsch and Gandil to drive in. Perhaps his biggest contribution came in getting McGraw to start all lefties, giving the advantage to righthanded batters Gandil, Felsch, and Weaver.

The day after the Series ended, the White Sox and Giants played a charity game for the soldiers at Camp Mills on Long Island. Joe didn't play, but in the ninth inning Chicago's Fred McMullin and well-known player-comedian Herman Schaefer reenacted Eddie Collins' dash for home, much to the delight of the soldiers. This turned out to be the only post–Series exhibition game that the two teams would play. The White Sox and Giants made plans to barnstorm together, but the National Commission turned thumbs down on that idea, fearing that additional games would cheapen the Series itself. The Commission withheld $1,000 of each player's Series share as insurance against the barnstorming trip. Only when each player signed an agreement not to play did the Commission release their money.[11]

The White Sox earned $3,669.32 per man, a new record for winning Series shares, while the Giants took home $2,244.21 each. Joe celebrated the World Series win with a new Oldsmobile Pacemaker that he bought from a Savannah dealership with his Series check. The patriotic Charles Comiskey suggested publicly that the players take their Series money in Liberty Bonds, but the White Sox reacted negatively to that idea, which the Old Roman quickly dropped.

The Sox returned via train to Chicago for a parade in their honor, in which thousands of happy fans carried Pants Rowland on their shoulders around the Loop. The next day, Joe left Chicago for his home in

Opposite: **The White Sox in pre-game military drill, 1917. Joe is the third man from the right (Chicago Historical Society, ICHi-22720).**

Savannah. It had been a difficult year, but Joe Jackson finally had something that Ty Cobb did not. Joe now had a World's Championship to his credit. Ty Cobb retired in 1928 without one.

Buck Herzog, the second baseman of the Giants, had a rough World Series in 1917. He batted only .250, committed two errors, and his misplay of Sallee's throw in Game 5 allowed Chick Gandil to score the tying run and opened the floodgates for the White Sox.

John McGraw, however, noticed something else about Herzog's play. The White Sox hit a lot of singles to right field in the 1917 Series. Many of those singles seemed to skip just out of Herzog's reach. McGraw couldn't prove it, but he always believed that Herzog deliberately played out of position against the White Sox batters.[12]

McGraw never got along well with Herzog anyway—he had suspended the second baseman during the season and only reinstated him in time for the Series—but now he believed that Herzog was deliberately losing games. In accordance with the accepted practice of the era, McGraw did nothing about his suspicions. He merely passed the problem along to another team. He traded Herzog to the Boston Braves after the Series.

All was not well in the champion White Sox camp, either. In 1906, Charles Comiskey was so thrilled that his underdog White Sox won the Series against the crosstown Cubs that he gladly put his own share of the receipts into the players' pot. Some of the 1917 Sox assumed that Comiskey would do the same for them, while others heard through the grapevine that their boss had promised an additional $1,500 per man if they defeated the Giants. However, no extra money came the players' way. Instead, Comiskey sent a case of champagne to the players' victory party.

Apparently, it wasn't the best bubbly on the market. Ring Lardner, a *Chicago Tribune* sportswriter who attended the party, remarked, "It tasted like stale piss." This case of champagne was the only bonus that the players received from Comiskey for winning the World Series.

Chapter 12

War and Controversy

> I take pleasure in stating that I find Absorbine, Jr., to be an
> excellent rubdown after violent exercise and also a good lini-
> ment for loosening up stiff muscles.
>
> —*Joe Jackson, in one of his many*
> *commercial endorsements, about*
> *1916*

World War I had little impact on major league baseball during the
1917 season. The nation took a while to mobilize for the war effort, and
although draft registration began in June, only 40 major league players
entered the military service during the 1917 campaign. As the war effort
intensified, however, all the clubs felt the pinch.

Congress passed the Selective Service Act, the nation's first univer-
sal draft law, on May 18, 1917. This law provided for the registration of
all men between the ages of 21 and 31, including Joe Jackson, who turned
29 in July of that year. This registration took place on June 5; in all, more
than nine million young men were registered.

Draft numbers were chosen by lottery, and in late 1917, after the
World Series, large numbers of young men all over the nation left home
for basic training. The manpower needs of the military forces threatened
to destroy major league baseball, since most ballplayers were in the age
range of the draft-eligible men. The Cleveland Indians saw nine of their
players drafted in October and November 1917, and the club scrambled
to find replacements. In November, Ban Johnson appealed to the Secretary

of War to exempt baseball from the draft, and then suggested an 18-player exemption per team, but both ideas were quickly shot down. The director of the draft, General Enoch Crowder, was loath to offer baseball, or any other industry, special treatment.

Spring of 1918 arrived, and all 16 major league teams waited to see what havoc the war would cause them. The White Sox returned to Mineral Wells for spring training, but the distracted players found it difficult to concentrate on the uncertain season ahead. The Sox postponed the start of training until March 18, due to wartime travel restrictions, and the team had only three weeks to prepare for the season. The White Sox uncharacteristically lost exhibition games against teams that they usually clobbered in the spring.

Two days after the start of camp, Joe Jackson and three other Sox players—Chick Gandil, Eddie Cicotte, and Ray Schalk—caught a ride in a friend's new car and spent the morning at a local golf course. On the return trip, another car ran through a stop sign and plowed into the side of the players' car. Only Eddie Cicotte, who complained of a sore neck, was injured in any way, but Comiskey was furious. "Their place was on the ball field, not out experimenting with golf sticks and looking at scenery," snarled the Old Roman, who banned both golf and automobile rides for the remainder of the spring.

Club owners, as one might expect, did their share of patriotic posturing. Early in the 1918 season the eight American League teams held exercises for the players, in which a drill instructor put the players through military paces. Some teams drilled with the players carrying their bats in place of rifles, but the White Sox drilled in full infantry uniforms, including standard-issue hats, boots, and unloaded carbines. Major league clubs played the "Star Spangled Banner" before games, a practice that began during the war and continues to this day. American League President Ban Johnson, well past 50 and overweight by this time, offered to enlist as a private and go overseas! All this was done for political reasons. The baseball owners and their friends in the press promoted baseball as an indispensable morale builder to a nation at war, hoping to impress the Government into letting baseball continue uninterrupted.

The government was not impressed. On May 18, 1918, Secretary of War Newton D. Baker issued his famous "work or fight" order. Baseball, as an entertainment, was ruled a "nonessential" occupation,[1] and all players from ages 21 to 31 were required to volunteer for the Army or find employment in a shipyard or defense plant by July 1, 1918. In addition, all men from ages 18 to 35 were now required to register for the draft. The Russian collapse was responsible for the necessary increase in manpower. After the Bolshevik revolution in late 1917, Russia dropped out of the war and made a separate peace with the Germans. This made it necessary for the Allies to amass as many troops as possible to defeat Germany before the Kaiser could concentrate all his forces on the Western front.

If all men from ages 18 to 35 were called into service, only the very young, the very old, and the infirm would be available to play major league ball. The Boston Red Sox would lose every one of their players, and the White Sox would be left with only three pitchers and one outfielder on the roster. Many other teams would end up with one or two players. Pants Rowland, the White Sox manager, and Hugh Jennings, the 48-year-old boss of the Tigers, volunteered to return to the active roster themselves if the need arose.

Now came the time for panic. On the day after Secretary Baker's order, Ban Johnson rashly ordered the American League to shut down immediately, but the owners ignored him and kept playing. Almost all of the minor leagues closed down for the year, but the major leagues knew that disaster loomed if they did the same. Though President Wilson, in a letter dated July 27, 1918, allowed the baseball season to continue, the owners recognized that the quality of play would deteriorate as more players left for the service. After much public debate the National Commission, after consultation with the War Department, ordered baseball to end its 1918 season on Labor Day, September 2, and gave permission for the World Series to begin three days later.

Joe Jackson, as a married man, obtained a Class 4 (married) deferment from the draft board in Greenville in 1917. After the government called for more men in early 1918, the local board lifted Jackson's deferment. His wife was ruled to be not dependent on Joe, and Joe was reclassified as 1-A and assigned draft number 846 by the Greenville board.

Joe and the White Sox were stunned by the board's decision. Joe thought that his married status protected him from the draft, and he had given slight consideration to the possibility of going over to Europe to fight in the trenches. Pants Rowland tried feverishly to keep his best hitter from leaving the team. The manager told the writers that the placement of Jackson in Class 1 may have been a mistake; since there were a half-dozen Joe Jacksons in the Greenville phone book, suggested Rowland, maybe the board drafted the wrong Joe.[2]

In May 1918 the Greenville allotment of soldiers passed the 846 mark, and Joe Jackson was ordered to take a physical exam at the nearest draft board. The White Sox were playing in Philadelphia at the time, so Jackson took his physical at the Philadelphia board on May 11, 1918.

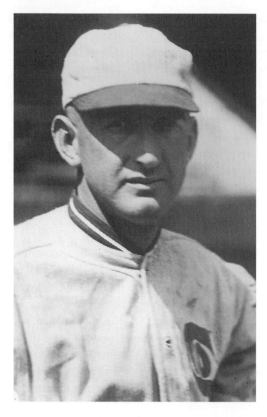

Joe in early 1918 (Cleveland Public Library).

He was pronounced "100 percent sound," and the board notified Jackson that he would be inducted into the Army between May 25 and June 1, 1918. Joe's brother Dave appeared at the Greenville board and asked to be inducted along with Joe, a request which was immediately granted, despite Dave's history of mill injuries.

However, defense-related industries such as steel mills and shipbuilding companies also needed workers, since so many members of their labor force were now serving in the military. The defense industries, like the textile mills in Greenville, decided to put together their own baseball teams, and they sent representatives to offer contracts to major leaguers who wished to stay out of the military draft. They made an offer to Joe Jackson, who informed Pants Rowland on May 13 that he had obtained employment at the Harlan and Hollingsworth Shipbuilding Company, a subsidiary of Bethlehem Steel, in Wilmington, Delaware. The Greenville board protested, but Secretary Baker's work or fight order of May 18 put Jackson beyond the control of the Greenville draft board. The shipyard registered Joe as a "necessary employee," and Joe left the White Sox and began working at the shipyard.

Shipbuilding was probably the single most essential war-related occupation at that time, since the military desperately needed ships to ferry troops and materiel across the Atlantic, and the existing American fleet was tiny and rusting. Still, many baseball men and sportswriters harshly criticized players such as Jackson for accepting war work close to home instead of induction into the Army. Ban Johnson, desperately trying to curry favor with the War Department to keep baseball going, said of Jackson and other players that "I hope ... General Crowder yanks them from the shipyards and steel works by the coat collar and places them in cantonments to prepare for future events on the western front."[3]

The shipyards and steel mills organized their own six-team circuit, called the Bethlehem Steel League, and wooed major league players to stock their teams. Soon the shipyard and defense plants boasted that each would own a full major league roster before long. Reports surfaced that the shipyards and steel mills offered players cash and easy work, and the *Chicago Tribune's* I. E. Sanborn wrote that Joe Jackson and others had, in fact, received cash and favors to join the shipyards. Sanborn stated that players were offered as much as $4,000 or $5,000 a year to play ball in the shipyard league.[4] Other articles claimed that ballplayers were given jobs as "painters' assistants," and that their work consisted solely of carrying two cans of paint to the painters, then playing ball the rest of the day.[5]

Many of these reports were undoubtedly exaggerated by war hysteria, but Jackson and others were tarred as "draft evaders" and "shipyard slackers" by many in the newspapers. The "paint and putty league" or the "Schwab League," so named after Bethlehem Steel chairman Charles Schwab, became the focus of much criticism in the national press. *The Sporting News* published a satiric poem lauding the courageous ballplayer who "swings his trusty paint brush on the foe."

Predictably, Charles Comiskey couldn't resist making himself look patriotic at the expense of Jackson and other players. "There is no room on my club for players who wish to evade the army draft by entering the employ of ship concerns!"[6] fumed the Old Roman.

Since Joe Jackson was the first player to opt for defense work instead of military service, he absorbed the brunt of the criticism. Joe regarded the situation with a special bitterness. He was the only support for his wife in Savannah and his widowed mother in Greenville, and Joe felt that his obligation to them outweighed his obligation to the military. In addition, three of Joe's younger brothers had already been inducted into the service, and Joe believed that the Jackson family had borne more than its share of the national burden. Pants Rowland, who talked to Joe on the telephone on May 15, told the writers that Joe joined the shipyard because he believed that he was "doing the right thing ... to protect his family."[7]

Many of the ballplayers who went into the military didn't fight on the front lines either. Many of them joined "special services" units and played far more baseball than Jackson did. However, because Joe was the first prominent player to decline service in the military at a time when patriotism was running at a fever pitch, Joe was the one who took the greatest amount of criticism from the sportswriters. Joe never forgot this barrage of ill will from the newspapers, and his relationship with the media in Chicago never recovered.

It is quite possible that Joe joined the shipyard instead of the military because he regarded a trip to Europe in much the same way that he regarded his trip to Philadelphia nine years before. No one knew how long the war would last, and if Joe had joined the Army he might have been away from home for several years. He may have chosen to work in a defense plant in Delaware for financial reasons, but perhaps he couldn't bear the thought of going halfway around the world for an indeterminate amount of time.

The frustrated slugger vented his feelings on May 24 from his temporary job in Wilmington. "It makes no difference when the war ends," declared Jackson. "I shall not attempt to go back to ball playing to make a living. I intend to make my home here and follow the trade of shipbuilding."[8] Jackson could not read the papers himself, but Katie Jackson kept her husband apprised of the daily beating that the nation's sportswriters were dishing out. She may have noticed a Robert Ripley cartoon titled "The Sneak," in which a baseball player eludes Uncle Sam by slipping into the safety of a shipyard. She certainly saw that whenever a player joined a defense plant or a shipyard, the papers accused him of taking "the Joe Jackson route" or "pulling a Joe Jackson."

The papers also roasted those athletes who played in semipro games on Sundays to earn extra money while their fellows fought in the trenches in Europe. Joe Jackson spent many Sundays playing in games to raise money for the Red Cross and other war-related charities, but these efforts went largely unnoticed. Joe wound up leading the Bethlehem Steel League with a .393 average, but this was one batting title that he didn't care much about winning.

When Joe's Chicago teammates Lefty Williams and Byrd Lynn jumped to the same shipyard on June 11, Comiskey ordered them to turn in their uniforms and threatened to cancel their contracts. "I don't consider them fit to play on my ball club," snarled Comiskey. "I would gladly lose my whole team if the players wished to do their duty to their country ... but I hate to see any ball players, particularly my own, go to shipyards to escape military service. There can be no other reason for their act, as they as they cannot honestly earn as much building ships as they can playing ball."[9]

The *Boston Record* reported on June 18 that the White Sox raised a service flag of 13 stars, for its 11 players and two club employees already in the service. However, "Manager Rowland wants it understood that no stars were included for Joe Jackson, Williams, or Lynn," the article stated.

The papers blamed Jackson for the defections of Williams and Lynn. "By inducing two of his pals to join him," said the *Tribune*, "Joe Jackson probably thinks he has squared accounts for all the mean things said about him when he jumped to the painters' league."[10] At the same time, the White Sox were playing home games in their road uniforms, since their home whites hadn't returned from the cleaners. The *Tribune* turned this bit of information against Jackson as well. "Comiskey ordered the uniforms disinfected for fear some of the Schwab germs which infected Jackson, Williams, and Lynn might have crept into the other players' suits," jeered the *Tribune*.

Comiskey praised those members of the White Sox who went into the military instead of the defense plants. "I had the greatest respect for Jim Scott when he quit the team last summer to become an officer. When Urban Faber gave up baseball to join the navy I congratulated him and was glad of it, although mighty sorry to lose him. I feel the same about any other players who have or who may quit my team to serve their country."[11] Scott left the team in mid–1917 to join the Army reserve officer training school, but Comiskey made it known that Scott received a full World Series share that fall.

Jackson played only 17 games for the White Sox in 1918, hitting .354. The defending world champions dropped all the way from third place to sixth after Jackson, Williams, Lynn, and Happy Felsch joined the shipyards and Faber and Swede Risberg entered the military. The defection of Williams was the final nail in the coffin of the White Sox in 1918 and virtually handed the pennant to the Boston Red Sox. "The White Sox," rejoiced the *Boston Herald*, "have the best team in the shipyard league."[12]

The White Sox fell apart after the shipyard defections. Pants Rowland took a team with only 16 players on an Eastern trip in August, and the shorthanded White Sox fell well below the .500 mark. Eddie Cicotte, a 28-game winner in 1917, led the league in losses with 19 in 1918, while relief ace Dave Danforth dropped to 6-15. The bickering among the players intensified with the losing; Eddie Collins and Chick Gandil didn't speak a word to each other all year, while Swede Risberg feuded with both Collins and Ray Schalk. Happy Felsch quit the team in a huff and joined a defense plant after he and Collins nearly came to blows on the bench one day. Coach Kid Gleason sat out the season in a contract dispute with Comiskey, and manager Rowland found it difficult to referee the clubhouse arguments without Gleason's steadying presence.

Rowland also had a difficult time holding on to the players who were

Joe Jackson
with his

D & M
Mitt

D & M Old Reliable

Fine tan Cordovon Calfskin. Leather laced all around. Large size and made to stand hard usage. When Joe Jackson is covering the first stop he will use **nothing else.** He says he is "only too glad to recommend it most highly." "It just can't let a ball get by." The D & M goods are recognized as standard and are used by most all of the big league players to-day.

Send for new 1916 Catalogue and Official Rule Books on Baseball and Tennis, free.

THE DRAPER-MAYNARD COMPANY
Dept. A, Plymouth, N. H.

Draper and Maynard glove advertisement featuring Joe Jackson, 1916 (author's collection).

left on his depleted roster. A young player named Dan Cunningham joined the team in July but left after only a few days without appearing in any games. The youngster explained that he wanted to become a preacher of the Gospel, and he didn't approve of the bad language he heard on the bench.[13]

The Boston Red Sox won their third pennant in four years, largely because star pitcher and hitter Babe Ruth joined a reserve unit and was allowed to continue playing. Ruth went 13-7 on the hill and tied for the league lead in homers with 11. Particularly galling to Charles Comiskey was the fact that the crosstown Cubs won the National League flag, though the Red Sox won the World Series in early September. Comiskey did, however, allow the Cubs to use Comiskey Park for their Series games.

The latter part of the war-shortened 1918 season brought the final, fateful parting of the ways for Ban Johnson and Charles Comiskey. In July of 1918 the Pacific Coast League shut down for the duration of the war. Comiskey, with the National Commission's approval, signed Jack Quinn, a 33-year-old spitball pitcher from the Vernon team, to help the depleted White Sox pitching staff. After Quinn went 5-1 for the White Sox, the Yankees bought his contract from the Vernon club and laid claim to Quinn's services. The problem was dumped into the lap of the National Commission, and in late 1918 Johnson and the other two Commissioners awarded Quinn to the Yankees.

This decision completed the rupture between Johnson and Comiskey, both of them hardheaded, strong-willed men. Quinn won 15 games for the Yankees in 1919 and 18 more in 1920, and Comiskey never forgave Johnson. "I made you," screamed Comiskey at one league meeting, "and by God I'll break you!" The Quinn decision helped lay the groundwork for the scandal that was to follow.

At that point, no one knew whether a 1919 season would ever take place. Ban Johnson, acting rashly as usual, ordered the 1919 season canceled, though the club owners ignored him. The shipyard league even offered to stage its own expanded season, replacing the major leagues in the attention of the fans for the war's duration. However, the German offensive stalled in August 1918, and resistance to the Allies quickly crumbled. The two sides declared an armistice on November 11, and the 1919 baseball season was saved. Most teams lost money in 1918, and the White Sox attendance, usually above 600,000 for the season, dropped to under 200,000. The baseball owners cautiously decided to play a 140-game schedule in 1919, not knowing how many of the fans would return.

The war had another, more damaging, effect on the game. Racetracks all over the nation shut down in 1917 for the duration of the war, and gamblers suddenly lost their main betting outlet. Baseball, the only sport allowed to continue, drew new attention from the gambling community. Ban Johnson became concerned, especially with Boston, where new Red Sox owner Harry Frazee saw nothing wrong with bettors operating openly in the right field stands during the games. Bookies and gamblers struck up friendships with players, always plumbing for information about sore arms and clubhouse turmoil, looking for an edge.

Baseball and gambling had always been too close for comfort. Rube Waddell, Connie Mack's eccentric star pitcher, missed the 1905 World Series against the Giants after he injured his arm falling over a suitcase on a train. Many suspicious observers whispered that gamblers had paid Waddell to sit out the Series. In October 1908, the Giants' team physician offered a large bribe to umpire Bill Klem before the pennant-deciding game against the Cubs. After the 1917 World Series, John McGraw told writer Fred Lieb that his second baseman, Buck Herzog, deliberately positioned himself in the wrong spot several times, allowing grounders to go for base hits. The story never broke until years later, but after the Series McGraw sold Herzog to the Braves.[14]

McGraw himself was no paragon of virtue, either. In 1904 he had been arrested at spring training in Texas for running an unlicensed gambling game; specifically, he invited passersby on the street to pitch silver dollars into a bucket, with McGraw scooping up all the misses.[15] No one ever determined who put the Giants' physician, a good friend of McGraw, up to the infamous bribe attempt in 1908. Most disturbingly, McGraw was a good friend of Arnold Rothstein, New York's "King of Gamblers," who also shared an interest in a Manhattan poolroom with the Giants manager. Rothstein, the owner of numerous illegal speakeasies and gambling dens, often sat in a box with Giants owner Charles Stoneham at the Polo Grounds.

Pool betting was another black cloud on the baseball horizon. In the 1910s, working people bet their dollars in baseball pools much as present-day working people play the slot machines in Atlantic City. Pools such as the Keystone in Pennsylvania and the Albany in New York offered prizes in the thousands of dollars, and they raked in tens of thousands each week of the baseball season. In 1920 the *Chicago Tribune* estimated that Chicagoans bought some 400,000 pool tickets a week at a cost of about $150,000.[16] It appeared that baseball betting, not the game itself, was the true national pastime.

The fact that large-scale pool betting was illegal in most communities had very little effect on the practice. The Pennsylvania pools prospered by offering bribes and kickbacks to politicians and police officials. Some of the club owners believed that the pools stimulated interest in baseball, and baseball as a whole ignored the whole gambling scene. Baseball pools represented one more way that shrewd and crooked operators could make a fortune on the labor of the ballplayers, most of whom made only a few thousand dollars a year.

One of those shrewd operators was a Boston Irishman named James "Sport" Sullivan, who struck up a friendship with White Sox first baseman Chick Gandil in the early 1910s, when Gandil played first base for Washington. Sullivan took Gandil to dinner, bought him drinks, introduced him to celebrities like George M. Cohan, and listened closely to tidbits of information about Walter Johnson's arm or who hated who in the clubhouse. Gandil, a poorly educated roughneck from the West, was mightily impressed with Sullivan. He'd always wondered what life on the other side was like, and he watched Sullivan with a mixture of fascination and envy. Sullivan was hobnobbing with people who made a lot more than the miserable $3,500 a year Gandil was pulling down after ten years in the big leagues. Gandil liked what he saw on this side of the street.

Hal Chase had always been intimately involved with the gambling scene. While playing first base for the Cincinnati Reds in 1918, he intercepted relief pitcher Jimmy Ring on his way to the mound and offered the startled pitcher $500 to "lay down" and let the other team win. Ring refused the offer, but lost the game anyway. The next morning Chase, to show his appreciation, handed Ring a $50 bill.

Ring went immediately to his manager, Christy Mathewson, and reported the bribe attempt. Mathewson suspended Chase and reported the incident to league president John Heydler. After a long investigation, Heydler finally held a hearing in January 1919. Ring and Chase testified, but Mathewson, stationed with the Army in France, was unable to attend. To Mathewson's surprise, Heydler cleared Chase of wrongdoing. Oddly enough, Mathewson's friend John McGraw then signed Chase to a contract to play for the Giants. This occurred only about a year after McGraw got rid of Buck Herzog for suspected dishonesty.

The players couldn't help but notice. Chase's machinations were no secret in the baseball world, since opposing players needled Chase with, "Hey, Hal, what are the odds today?" Mathewson caught Chase virtually red-handed, and Chase still wiggled through the net. Did Hal Chase lead a charmed life? Or, more likely, did baseball know it had a serious gambling problem and elect to look the other way? Chase had been suspected of throwing games almost since his entry into the major leagues in 1905. His shady dealings in three leagues—American, National, and Federal— had been talked about for more than a decade. Still, nothing happened.

The baseball owners had painted themselves into a corner. For decades the owners and their friends in the pressbox had promoted baseball as the "national pastime," an integral part of national life next to God, country, and motherhood. *Baseball Magazine* declared that, unlike boxing, wrestling, and horse racing, baseball stood alone on the "top rung of honor." The magnates, reeling from the damage done to their profits by the world war, didn't want to inflict more damage by bringing the integrity of the game itself into question. The owners and league presidents paid no heed to honest players like Jimmy Ring. They looked the other way while gamblers and con men cozied up to the players, hatching schemes and laying plans, virtually unmolested.

The players were quickly losing respect for any decisions made by the owners or the National Commission. The owners, without consulting the players, decided to distribute the receipts of the 1918 World Series among the top four teams of each league. The Red Sox and Cubs, unhappy with their share of the World Series money, threatened to strike before the fifth game of the World Series. Nothing came of the threatened stoppage when Ban Johnson showed up at the park that day too drunk to discuss the issues. Red Sox captain Harry Hooper sensed the futility of negotiating with Johnson, and he talked the players on both sides into starting the game with the issues unresolved. The players, angrily, went forth, and the winner's share of the Series proceeds amounted to less than $1,000 after taxes. Rumors abounded concerning the honesty of the 1918 Series, but when Johnson asked the American League for funds to mount an investigation, the club owners rebuffed him.

The owners blundered again in late 1918. Brooklyn Dodgers owner Charles Ebbets refused to pay his star first baseman Jake Daubert the full value of his contract, claiming that Daubert had no right to expect payment for an uncompleted season. Daubert, a two-time batting champion for the Dodgers, had used the Federal League as leverage to obtain a five-year, no-cut contract from Ebbets in 1915, and Ebbets had never forgiven him. Daubert sued Ebbets for the missing money and forced an out-of-court settlement when it was revealed that Ebbets pushed harder than any other owner for the season to be shortened!

In a fit of anger Ebbets sent Daubert packing to Cincinnati, but now the players had even more reason to distrust the owners. Did the owners shorten the season to help the war effort or to cheat the players out of their salaries in a bad attendance year? A score of Sport Sullivans stepped up their activities after the Chase and Daubert cases.

In addition, the owners found a profitable way to turn the ten-day clause to their advantage. Many of the teams gave their players ten days' notice in late August of 1918 and then released them from their contracts. This not only saved the club owners a few weeks' worth of players' salaries, but they could then attempt to re-sign those same players at a much lower amount. This tactic made many star players (including George Sisler and Ty Cobb) free agents, but the owners agreed among themselves not to sign each other's players.[17] Even the sainted Connie Mack admitted years later, "It was only natural that we should enter into an agreement to protect our interests."[18] Perhaps the owners weren't as badly hurt by the war as they claimed.

Some of the White Sox seethed. What right did Comiskey have to condemn Joe Jackson for joining the shipyard, which was a perfectly legal act of value to the war effort that even General Crowder praised at war's end? Why should Comiskey use Jackson as a whipping boy to make himself look good in the papers? Other players snickered at the aging, diabetic Ban Johnson's useless offer to serve as a doughboy at the front. They stopped laughing when they got their contracts for the 1919 season.

Eddie Collins' $14,500 salary was guaranteed, and Joe Jackson's $6,000 salary was already a bargain for Comiskey. The other White Sox players found their salaries slashed to the bone. Harry Grabiner's "Take it or leave it" seemed more insistent this time around. Grabiner told the players that the attendance fell to under 200,000 in 1918, and Comiskey didn't know how many of the fans would return in 1919. One by one, the Sox signed on the dotted line. They had no choice; the reserve clause and the collusion among the owners mandated that they play for the White Sox or nowhere at all.

Comiskey, however, soon changed his tune. In early 1919—after the players signed their contracts at reduced salaries—Chicago writer G. W. Axelson published a fawning biography of Comiskey, in which the Old Roman grandly proclaimed that 1919 would be "the greatest season of them all!" for the White Sox and for baseball. Axelson's book, which even by the standards of the time was almost embarrassingly laudatory, is best remembered today for its identification of Joe Jackson as "Sockless Joe."

Pants Rowland grew tired of the bickering, the clubhouse tension, and the cliquishness of the White Sox. He managed the best team in baseball, but the daily warfare killed all the enjoyment for him. He had reached the end of his tether, and Comiskey decided that Rowland had lost control of the team. On New Year's Eve, Comiskey appointed coach Kid Gleason as the new manager of the Sox. A few months later, Rowland bought an interest in the Milwaukee Brewers of the American Association and left the employ of the White Sox.

Gleason started his major league career as a pitcher with the Phillies way back in 1888, and he won 129 games before his arm gave out. He then moved to second base and played another 14 seasons, mostly with John McGraw on the old Baltimore Orioles of the 1890s. What Gleason lacked in skill, he more than made up for in his willingness to scratch and claw to win a game, in the roughneck Oriole fashion.

They called him "Kid" because he was enthusiastic, and he liked to have his fun. One day in 1913 Gleason, who was coaching for the White Sox at the time, handed a Chinese laundry list to the umpire in place of the lineup card. "There's no rule that says the lineup card has to be written in English," said Gleason merrily to the sputtering umpire. However, once the game began, Kid Gleason was all business, and he expected his players to follow suit whether they liked each other or not.

Beginning in 1912, Gleason had served the White Sox as a coach for six years, until he had a contract dispute of his own with Comiskey and sat out the 1918 season over a $500 difference in salary. Gleason was tough, and all factions on the team respected him. If anyone could get this team playing harmoniously, Kid Gleason was the man.

Most books and articles about the White Sox of the late 1910s accept the assumption that the Sox grossly underpaid their players, especially Joe Jackson. However, Charles Alexander, in his book *Our Game*, offered a different opinion about Joe's salary. Alexander states that the $6,000 salary of Joe Jackson compared favorably with other stars of the era, such as Hal Chase, George Sisler, and Frank (Home Run) Baker. All three of these contemporary American League stars, says Alexander, were paid approximately the same as Jackson.

This may be true, but Frank Baker left his teams twice in salary disputes and played semipro ball in Pennsylvania in both the 1915 and 1920 seasons. George Sisler's salary may have been about $6,000 in 1919, but Sisler was in only his fourth full year in the majors at the time and was five years younger than Joe Jackson. Sisler also played for the St. Louis Browns, who limped through each season with the worst attendance in the American League.

We can see the extent of the Chicago players' discontent when we compare their salaries to those of the Cincinnati Reds in 1919. Only one of the White Sox, Eddie Collins, earned $8,000 or more in 1919. Three Reds did so—Edd Roush ($10,000), Jake Daubert ($9,000), and Heinie Groh ($8,000). Roush was one of the biggest stars in the National League in that era, and Daubert was a two-time batting champion who got his high salary by finagling a five-year contract during the Federal League years. The Reds managed to pay their salaries, despite the fact that they played in one of the league's smaller ballparks and regularly trailed the rest of the National League in attendance.

With this in mind, there seems to be no reason that Charles Comiskey should pay his players as poorly as he did. Comiskey himself was one of the highest paid players of the 1880s. He was a mediocre hitter with a .259 lifetime batting average when he earned $6,000 a year as first baseman and manager of the St. Louis Browns. Now, 30 years later, he was paying Joe Jackson, the greatest natural hitter in the game, the same amount. The Old Roman certainly could not plead poverty, since the White Sox led the American League in attendance and performed magnificently on the field. In the five years beginning in 1915 the Sox finished third, second, first, sixth (in the war year), and first in the American League standings.

Comiskey formed his attitude toward salaries early in his tenure as club owner. The "Hitless Wonder" White Sox won the pennant in 1906, then shocked the crosstown Cubs in the World Series that fall. Comiskey was aghast when his players added their World Series shares to their salary amounts for 1906 and tried to use the larger figure as a starting point in negotiations for 1907.[19] This led to an unhappy clubhouse atmosphere that helped keep the Sox from repeating as champions. The White Sox came close to the pennant in 1908 when spitball pitcher Ed Walsh won an astounding 40 games, but Walsh had to stage a holdout to get his salary raised for 1909. Once again, the unhappy Sox fell out of contention.

In 1919 the top four salaries in the American League belonged to Ty Cobb ($20,000), Tris Speaker ($16,000), Walter Johnson ($15,000) and Eddie Collins ($14,500). It seems ludicrous that Eddie Cicotte, a 28-game winner in 1917, should receive a base salary of $5,000 for 1918, though he also received a $2,000 bonus. Both Cicotte and Shoeless Joe Jackson should have been paid twice as much as they were making at the time.

Chapter 13

The Fateful Season

> From the very moment I arrived at training camp from service,
> I could see that something was amiss. We may have had our
> troubles in other years, but in 1919 we were a club that pulled
> apart rather than together. There were frequent arguments and
> open hostility. All the things you think—and are taught to
> believe—are vital to the success of any athletic organization
> were missing from it, and yet it was the greatest collection of
> players ever assembled, I would say.
> —*Eddie Collins* [1]

The war ended in November of 1918, and Joe Jackson soon finished
his duties at the shipyard and returned home to Savannah to spend the
winter. His contract with the White Sox was terminated when he went
to the shipyard, and after a bit of haggling Joe signed in February 1919
for the same $6,000 salary that he had been earning since 1914. Joe was
a few pounds overweight when he arrived at camp at Mineral Wells in
March, but he wore a rubber shirt for the first few weeks to get his weight
down to his normal 182 pounds.

Almost all the members of the 1917 World Championship team were
present for the start of 1919 spring training, though Fred McMullin, a
utility infielder and favorite of Kid Gleason, was missing. McMullin asked
the team to put him on the voluntarily retired list, but Gleason prevailed
upon McMullin to return for one more season. The Sox regulars quickly
rounded into shape and pounded the "Goofs," managed by veteran
outfielder John (Shano) Collins, and the local minor league teams. Not

until the last day of spring training in Texas did the Sox lose a game, and that was because they had to hurry to catch a train.

Now that the war was over, the question of Joe's acceptance by the fans remained. He had been roundly pilloried in the papers as a "slacker" and a "deserter," and Charles Comiskey had never publicly apologized for the intemperate remarks he made about Joe in 1918. An article by Hugh Fullerton in the *Chicago Tribune* fanned the flames all over again. He suggested that the fans might boo Joe so lustily that the 31-year-old slugger might be driven from the game. Fullerton did not mention Joe by name, but wrote, "This man is in for a hard summer ... he did the same thing that a score of other ball players did, but he was the most advertised and the dislike of all the paint and putty patriots is likely to be vented upon him."[2]

Four days later, the *Tribune* reported that Fullerton's article caused a rally of support for Jackson. The paper received petitions from fans in Chicago, demanding that the *Tribune* drop the subject of Jackson's war work and allow Joe to concentrate on playing ball. It appeared that the writers took Joe's decision to work in a defense plant far more personally than the fans ever did, though Fullerton insisted that he had no quarrel with Joe. Fullerton said that he was "an admirer of the slugging capabilities of the Sox outfielder," leaving the reader to speculate how Fullerton felt about Jackson personally.[3]

The White Sox, despite their sixth place finish of the year before, were established as the pennant favorites as the 1919 season opened. The Boston Red Sox figured to provide the biggest challenge to the White Sox. Boston had won the World Series over the Cubs in 1918, and they had baseball's biggest and newest star in their lineup. Babe Ruth was a two-time 20-game winner on the hill for the Red Sox, but in 1918 he played the outfield on days he didn't pitch. He appeared in only 95 of the 130 games the Red Sox played in 1918, but he still managed to lead the league in home runs and slugging percentage.

In March of 1919, Babe Ruth served notice that his performance the year before was no fluke. In a spring training game in Tampa, Ruth belted a mammoth home run far over the right field fence. An unofficial measurement gave the distance the ball traveled as 587 feet, much farther than anyone had ever hit a fair ball. This blast surpassed Joe Jackson's wallop at the Polo Grounds in 1913 as the longest home run ever hit.

Writer Grantland Rice asked Babe about his hitting during spring training in 1919. "You swing like no pitcher I ever saw," remarked Rice. "I may be a pitcher," replied Ruth, "but first off I'm a hitter. I copied my swing after Joe Jackson's. His is the perfectest. Joe aims his right shoulder

square at the pitcher, with his feet about twenty inches apart. But I close
my stance to about eight and a half inches or less. I find I pivot better
with it closed … once my swing starts, though, I can't change it or pull
up. It's all or nothing at all."[4]

In later years, Joe Jackson claimed some of the credit for Ruth's phe-
nomenal success. "I was able to help Ruth a little before he began to hit,"
said Jackson in a 1932 interview. "When I first knew him, he was a sprad-
dle-legged hitter and I taught him to change to pivot hitting. He's the
only fellow I ever tried to convert who jumped on to the idea in a minute."[5]
The only difference between the two men was that Ruth uppercut the
ball all the time, while Jackson only did so if he thought he could drive
the pitch over the fence.

Ruth used the swing that he copied from Jackson to its fullest advantage in 1919. The Babe whacked an incredible 29 home runs for the Red
Sox, breaking the major league mark of 27, set in 1884 by Ned Williamson
of the Chicago Colts (now called the Cubs). Ruth's next-to-last homer
of 1919 flew over the grandstand at the Polo Grounds, and onlookers
declared it the longest homer ever hit in a league game, longer than Joe
Jackson's shot over the same grandstand six years before.

Joe always liked black bats, but in early 1919 the Hillerich and
Bradsby batmaking company sent him an all-white bat made to Black
Betsy's specifications. Joe used it in the season-opening series against the
Browns in St. Louis, and he raked the Brown pitchers for ten hits, including three doubles and a homer, in the four-game series.[6] Even the outs
he made were hit sharply, and Joe kept the new "Blond Betsy" in his bat
rotation for the remainder of the campaign.

From the very beginning of the season, it was obvious that the owners miscalculated again. They cut the 1919 campaign to 140 games, not
knowing if the game would regain its prewar popularity. If the owners
had bothered to look at history, they would have noticed that baseball
boomed in popularity after the Civil War and the Spanish-American
War. Record attendance levels greeted almost every team in 1919, as the
nation sought a diversion from the postwar blues and the continuing Euro-
pean turmoil. Cutting the schedule by 14 games merely cheated each club
out of seven more well-attended home dates.

Three teams battled for the flag in the early part of the season. The
Cleveland Indians, led by centerfielder Tris Speaker, made an early charge,
only to fall back by midseason and find themselves passed by the resurgent New York Yankees. On July 18, the Indians held a two-run lead
against the Red Sox, who loaded the bases in the ninth inning with Babe

Ruth coming up to bat. Manager Lee Fohl relied on Speaker for guidance on pitching changes, but he either misunderstood Speaker's signals from the outfield or ignored them, because Fohl brought in the wrong relief pitcher. Ruth belted the second pitch over the fence for a grand slam homer to win the game. That night, the Indians fired Fohl and hired Speaker as their manager.

The Indians played .650 ball after Speaker took over, but the White Sox had too much firepower for the rest of the league. Joe Jackson, batting .420 on May 15, challenged Ty Cobb again for the batting lead, and Eddie Cicotte won 14 games before the Fourth of July. The Sox held first place early in the season, fell to second in early June, then won nine out of ten in early July to climb back into first place. They held off the Indians and Yankees the rest of the way, and the Chicago fans streamed through the turnstiles in record numbers to cheer their first-place team.

It wasn't an easy season for the pitching staff. Reb Russell never regained his form, and in July Comiskey released the former 23-game winner to the Minneapolis Millers. Red Faber made 20 starts early in the season, but he had lost a great deal of weight during his stint in the Navy and struggled to regain his effectiveness. Faber won both games of a doubleheader against the A's on July 9, but soon the soreness in his arm made it difficult for him to pitch more than three or four innings. Joe Benz and Dave Danforth, both pitching mainstays earlier in the decade for the Sox, drew their releases in May. It would have been a much less tumultuous season for the White Sox if they had been allowed to keep Jack Quinn in 1918.

Comiskey brought in a longtime minor league pitcher, Dickie Kerr, and journeyman Grover Lowdermilk to fill the void. Kerr, a 26-year-old righthander from Texas, was only five feet and seven inches tall. He threw a nasty curveball, and by midseason he took Faber's place in the rotation. He battled his way to a 13-8 record for the Sox. Lowdermilk, who arrived in May in a trade with the Browns, filled in as a spot starter, and helped Bill James with the relief duties that Dave Danforth had previously handled. Faber's arm problems worsened by August, but Chicago's three-man rotation of Cicotte, Williams, and Kerr pitched the White Sox into a safe lead on top of the American League.

The Sox, however, took a lot of abuse from the fans in other cities. Because the Chicago writers made such a big issue out of Jackson, Lynn, and Williams joining the defense plants instead of the military, the fans called the White Sox "shipbuilders" and "slackers." Sometimes the opposing fans would chant "Shipyard! Shipyard!" in an attempt to throw the White Sox off their game. The simmering controversy helped the other

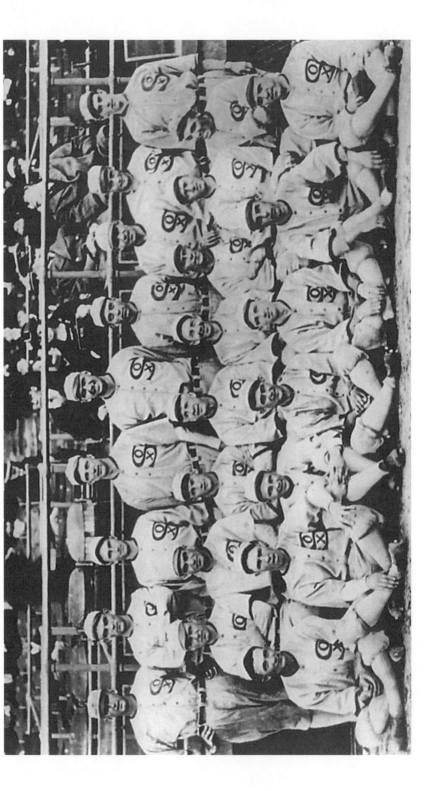

teams draw bigger crowds, though it created more of a siege mentality in the Chicago clubhouse.

The biggest problem facing the White Sox was the same one that had been festering for several years. Eddie Collins, Red Faber, and Ray Schalk made up one clique on the team, while Chick Gandil, Fred McMullin, Swede Risberg and Buck Weaver made up the opposing one. The two groups sniped at each other all season long, and in 1919 the Gandil group carried the hard feelings out onto the playing field. "The wonderful Athletic teams I played for," said Collins many years later, "believed in teamwork and cooperation. I always thought you couldn't win without those virtues until I joined the White Sox. Players would even doublecross each other on the field and yet, despite those things, we still managed to win the pennant."[7]

Buck Weaver, in turn, revealed his feelings about Eddie Collins later in his life when he recalled the 1917 World Series. "[We] sharpened our spikes until they were like razors [before Game 5]," said Weaver. However, Eddie Collins didn't join in the spike-sharpening ritual. "Well, he was a different type of ballplayer," explained Weaver. "He never went in for that sorta stuff because he figured they might come back at him and he'd get hurt playin' there in the infield. He was a great guy to look out for himself. If there was a tough gent comin' down to second, he'd yell at the shortstop to take the play."[8]

A third group stayed out of the controversy, but since they were drinking men, they gravitated toward the Gandil faction. Happy Felsch, the centerfielder from Milwaukee with only a sixth-grade education, sometimes joined Joe Jackson and Lefty Williams in the bars and nightclubs on the road. These three rarely spoke to the college-educated Collins and Faber, less out of animosity than out of a lack of common interests.

The White Sox were a fractured team, but on the field they executed plays with precision. They could hustle when they wanted, as shown by a play in a game on July 13 when Buck Weaver came up with the bases loaded. He punched an unremarkable single into left field; somehow, all three runners scored on the play. Joe Jackson showed his hustle with three spectacular catches against the Red Sox on May 14. On the last one, Joe caught a long fly ball on the dead run and crashed headfirst into the fence, knocking himself dizzy. After a few woozy minutes, Joe opted to remain in the game, which the Sox eventually lost to their nemesis, Babe Ruth.

Opposite: **White Sox team picture, 1919. Joe is standing in the back row on the far left; next to him is Chick Gandil (author's collection).**

The White Sox extended their first-place margin through the summer months, but the turmoil in the clubhouse kept spilling out onto the field, affecting both offense and defense. A simple infield pop-up became an adventure, especially if it came down between Collins and Gandil. Collins complained one day to Kid Gleason that some of his teammates were deliberately ignoring his signs. "When you want them to bunt, tell them to hit straightaway," replied the manager. "When you want them to hit and run, tell them to bunt. Do I have to do all your thinking for you?"[9]

Many teams in the early part of the century divided themselves up into cliques; they still do to this day, and always will. Across town, Johnny Evers and Joe Tinker played side by side in the Cubs' infield for more than ten years without speaking, the result of a spat over a taxicab, or a botched rundown play, or who knows what. However, other teams could not help but notice that when the White Sox infield threw the ball around to warm up between innings, Eddie Collins never touched the ball. He warmed up with catcher Ray Schalk; the other three infielders would not throw Collins the ball.

By early August the 1919 pennant appeared to be safely in the bag for the White Sox, and the players looked forward to their second appearance in a World Series in the past three years. The White Sox wanted to take another shot at the New York Giants in the Series, mostly because the Giants and White Sox owned the two biggest stadiums in baseball at the time. A Chicago–New York series would bring in the biggest crowds and, consequently, yield the largest amount of money for the players. Unfortunately for the Sox, the Giants collapsed in August and the Cincinnati Reds took control of first place in the National League. The Reds played in one of the smallest parks in baseball, with a seating capacity of only 25,000, and their presence in the World Series would cut the players' shares considerably.

Joe Jackson managed to stand apart from the clubhouse turmoil, and he was healthy and productive for the first time since the end of the 1916 season. Joe put together one of his finest seasons at the plate, ending the year in fourth place in the batting race with a .351 mark as Ty Cobb won his twelfth title with a .384 average. Joe also finished second in the league in hits with 202 and in triples with 17, and he only struck out ten times in more than 500 times at bat. He stole only nine bases but drove in 96 runs, a new career high and the highest total on the pennant-winning White Sox. To make it all sweeter, Joe drove in the winning run in the pennant-clinching game against St. Louis on September 24. If there had been a Most Valuable Player award in 1919, Joe Jackson may well have won it.[10]

By the middle of July the seething Chicago clubhouse seemed ready to explode with anger. Comiskey had chopped almost everyone's salary after the 1918 season, pleading poverty after drawing fewer than 200,000 fans through the gates. Now the money was rolling in hand over fist, with the unexpected postwar baseball boom. Attendance for the White Sox in 1919 more than tripled that of the year before, and the players wanted their share. Kid Gleason called a clubhouse meeting, and after listening to the players' complaints, he agreed to take their case to Comiskey.

The Old Roman refused to discuss the matter. A contract is a contract, he stated. No salaries would be changed during the season.

When Gleason reported this to his first-place team the following day, some of the players threatened to strike. Gleason managed to pacify them, holding out the possibility of bonuses after the end of the season, and reminding the team that a fat World Series check lay on the horizon. However, Eddie Cicotte was so angry that Gleason decided to keep him out of that day's ballgame.

Eddie Cicotte was 35 years old in 1919, ancient for a ballplayer of that era, with a wife and four children to support. He didn't have very many baseball contracts left in his future, and in addition he had bought a farm in Michigan and had taken on a $4,000 mortgage. His base salary, after 13 years in the big leagues, did not even approach $6,000.[11] He trusted Comiskey and accepted his salary for the good of the franchise, then assumed the role of staff ace after Red Faber's arm problems. In 1919 Cicotte was Comiskey's number one pitcher, but Comiskey didn't want to pay him accordingly, even though Cicotte was closing in on a 30-win season. A sense of betrayal gripped Eddie Cicotte.

Chick Gandil wasn't any happier with the whole situation. Gandil was making about $3,500 a year after nearly ten years in the major leagues. He hated Eddie Collins for his $14,500 salary, his privileged background, and his popularity. He hated Charles Comiskey for his cheapness. Gandil also resented the fact that his career was winding down and that he would leave baseball with not much more than he had in 1910 when he arrived. He envied a man like his friend, gambler Sport Sullivan, who moved so easily in the night life demimonde and always seemed to have a pocket full of cash. Everyone—club owners, newspapers, gamblers, baseball pool operators—made piles of money off the sweat of the players except the players themselves. Now, with the White Sox ready to advance to the World Series, Chick Gandil plotted the financial killing of a lifetime. The World Series, the biggest annual sporting event in the United States, could be fixed for a price.

While Gandil turned the idea of a fix over in his mind, Eddie

Cicotte's anger made the whole sordid enterprise seem more possible. With Red Faber, the pitching hero of the 1917 Series, on the sidelines, Cicotte and Williams would each be called upon to pitch three games in the best-of-nine Series. If Gandil could get Cicotte and Williams to participate, he could easily convince additional conspirators to make the scheme work. In August, Gandil approached his old friend Sullivan and declared that the World Series could be "put in the bag" for $100,000.

Shortly afterwards Gandil made his pitch to Cicotte, who initially doubted that such a scheme could succeed. For several weeks Cicotte considered the offer; then he suddenly confronted Gandil on a train to Boston. "I'll do it for ten thousand dollars," said Cicotte. "Cash. Before the Series begins."

With the respected Cicotte in the bag, Gandil approached the other members of the anti–Collins faction on the White Sox. Swede Risberg, Gandil's best friend and drinking buddy, was the first to join up. Buck Weaver, competitor that he was, refused to be hurried into a decision, but Fred McMullin overheard Gandil and Risberg discussing the fix in the clubhouse and demanded to be let in as well.[12] Gandil then turned his attention to the three most poorly educated members of the team.

Joe Jackson, Lefty Williams, and Happy Felsch had three things in common. They liked to drink, they didn't speak to the Collins group, and they were all underpaid. Felsch, a .300 hitter and excellent defensive centerfielder, was making only $3,750 a year, while Williams won 23 games for the Sox on a salary of $2,600. Joe Jackson, at $6,000, lagged far behind the other stars of the league, making less than half of the salary of Ty Cobb, Tris Speaker, and Eddie Collins. Joe, one of the greatest hitters in the game's history, had not received a raise in pay since 1914. Many years later, Eddie Collins remarked that Jackson, Williams, and Felsch were "easily led," and that they could just as easily have been led in the right direction as the wrong one, had not Chick Gandil gotten to them first.

Gandil's plan was to involve as few players as possible, not only to lessen the chances of exposure but also to maximize the potential winnings for each member of the fix. Byrd Lynn, the reserve catcher, was Lefty Williams' roommate on the road (and had been for four years) and remained friendly with both cliques on the team, but Lynn was never approached to participate in the scheme. Gandil knew that Lynn and the relief pitchers (Grover Lowdermilk, Bill James, and Roy Wilkinson) would probably play in the Series only briefly, if at all. Though Byrd Lynn was one of Williams' best friends, he would not find out about the fix until September of 1920.

The story of the Black Sox scandal has been told in detail in books and film, but the basic plotline was as follows.

Eddie Cicotte ran into an old friend, Sleepy Bill Burns, a former pitcher turned Texas oilman. Burns wanted to know if the rumors he heard were true; Cicotte, trusting his pal Burns, allowed that they were, and filled Burns in on the sensational details. Burns recognized the plan as the betting opportunity of a lifetime. He realized that he needed a quick infusion of cash to pull it off. As luck would have it, Burns soon ran into another good friend, the ubiquitous Hal Chase, the

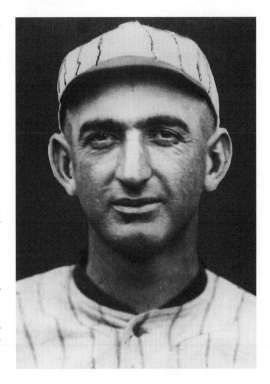

Joe Jackson in 1919 (author's collection).

veteran first baseman and baseball fixer who had recently been cast adrift by the New York Giants. Chase knew just where to go for such an investment. At Chase's suggestion, Burns and his partner, a former boxer and ballplayer named Billy Maharg (Graham spelled backwards) went to New York to put the scheme before the man known as the Big Bankroll.

Arnold Rothstein, the King of Gamblers, was in 1919 the most prominent "sportsman" in the nation. From his base on the upper West Side of Manhattan, Rothstein ruled the world of cards, dice, and liquor. Businessmen and Broadway figures, the famous and the unknown, vied for the chance to drop thousands of dollars at his illicit casinos and speakeasies. All the while Rothstein paid policemen and politicians to look the other way and harass his competitors. At the same time, Rothstein was a popular man-about-town, as well as a friend of New York Giants owner Charles Stoneham and manager John McGraw.

Rothstein listened to these two small-timers, Burns and Maharg, but doubted that the fantastic plan could succeed. He advised the two men that he wasn't interested.

However, Rothstein's second-in-command liked the idea. Abe Attell was the former welterweight boxing champion of the world, a popular and widely recognized athlete in his own right, who served Rothstein as a bodyguard and personal assistant. Attell, as a veteran of the boxing world, was no stranger to corruption, since he was skilled in the art of carrying an opponent for a few extra rounds or arranging a realistic-looking dive for the right amount of money. Abe Attell was the Hal Chase of boxing, and his biggest ambition was to become another Arnold Rothstein—a cool, calculating, fantastically rich operator. The 1919 World Series, thought Attell, was his big chance.

Attell, without Rothstein's knowledge, told Burns that Rothstein had changed his mind and would be all too happy to back the scheme. Attell immediately began recruiting a group of gamblers from St. Louis and Des Moines to provide capital in exchange for a chance at the biggest betting coup of their lives.

Chick Gandil, independently of Cicotte and Burns, contacted Sport Sullivan, who also journeyed to New York to solicit funds from the Big Bankroll. Rothstein, having turned the idea of the fix over in his mind, decided that he trusted Sullivan more than Burns, and the King of Gamblers gave Sullivan the green light. Now the players had two groups of backers, working both together and apart, in a maze of allegiances that would grow more complicated as the days passed.

Gandil called a meeting at the Ansonia Hotel in Manhattan on September 18, when the White Sox were in New York to play the Yankees. Seven of the players were there; Joe Jackson, by all reliable accounts, was not present. Gandil explained to the other players that Sport Sullivan had promised to deliver $80,000 before the first game of the Series, but other than that, no plans had yet been made. Gandil suggested that they wait and see how manager Kid Gleason handled the starting pitchers' assignments before any further strategizing would take place.

With the start of the World Series only a few weeks away, Gandil moved to fill in the last few pieces of the puzzle. Williams and Felsch signed on enthusiastically, but Jackson held back. Gandil hounded Jackson all through the month of September. The two men didn't know each other well, since Jackson preferred to keep his own company and was only close to Lefty Williams on the team. Still, Gandil touted the one thing that always piqued Joe Jackson's interest—the promise of money.

Gandil caught up with Jackson on the way into the Comiskey Park clubhouse one late September day. A few weeks earlier, in Boston, Jackson turned down an offer of $10,000 from Gandil. Jackson later stated that Gandil made the offer of $20,000, while others believe that Jackson demanded that amount to participate in the fix. Gandil's most persuasive argument, that the fix would be carried out anyway whether Jackson participated or not, apparently swayed the reluctant Southerner. On that day, Joe Jackson agreed to help throw the Series, in exchange for a sum of money more than three times the amount of his annual salary.[13]

Joe Jackson had nothing to do with the planning of the fix; unlike Gandil, he had no contacts in the netherworld of gambling and nightlife. In fact, Jackson never met most of the cast of characters that populated the fix and its aftermath. Joe's participation consisted solely of trusting Chick Gandil to deliver $20,000, in return for which Jackson would let up on the field. Joe's acceptance of Gandil's offer at its face value displayed a stunning amount of faith in a man whom he didn't know very well. It was an incredible lapse of judgment, as well as a failure of character, on Joe Jackson's part.

Buck Weaver, however, made a different decision. He listened to Gandil's arguments, and even to Cicotte who tried to convince him to participate. Nevertheless, Weaver, friendly though he was with the seven other crooked players, decided to play all out in the Series. Gandil's assertion that the fix would go ahead anyway swayed Jackson but not Weaver. The third baseman, who attended two of the meetings held by the fixers, decided to pursue a middle course. He accepted no money, but neither would he turn in his errant fellows. Bill Veeck, the future owner of the White Sox, revealed many years later that Eddie Cicotte, not Chick Gandil, offered Weaver $5,000 to join the scheme. "If he [Weaver] had come to a calculated decision not to go along with the fix," wrote Veeck, "he had also come to a calculated decision to keep his mouth shut."[14]

Gandil agreed to Jackson's price, because he needed the silence of the big bats in the middle of the lineup if the fix were to be a success. Where that $20,000 would come from was another matter entirely, because Gandil had trouble rounding up the necessary cash. Gandil had demanded $80,000 before the first game of the Series, but the rules were already changing. Forty thousand dollars, provided by Arnold Rothstein, sat in the safe at the Congress Hotel in Chicago and would be paid after the Series if all went according to plan. Gandil's cut would come out of this money, but he needed the additional 40 grand to keep the other players happy.

Sport Sullivan, like any experienced gambler, possessed an uncanny knack for making himself scarce when people wanted money from him. Gandil needed Sullivan, not only to deliver the promised $40,000, but also to take Gandil's own bets against the Sox. Finally Sullivan appeared, only two days before the beginning of the Series, and gave the dismayed

Gandil only $10,000. An argument ensued, but Sullivan stood firm; he insisted that he couldn't spare any more but promised more cash later. As it turned out, Rothstein had funneled another $40,000 to Sullivan, but Sullivan spent $29,000 of it to finance his own wagers.

At the same time, Attell raised a large amount of cash, about $40,000 or more, from his group of St. Louis and Des Moines backers. Attell scrambled about, laying down as much money as he could on the under-dog Cincinnati Reds. Let Burns and Sullivan worry about the players, thought Attell. He and his friends were too busy placing bets to bother with the players.

Somehow, Gandil had to pacify all the other players with promises, but Eddie Cicotte wouldn't throw Game 1 without his share in hand. Cicotte found the money, ten crisp $1,000 bills, under his pillow on the night of September 29, and sewed it into the lining of his jacket.

Gandil needed much more money than that. He wanted to place his own bets, knowing that he could make a killing if only he had some cash on hand to play with. Nevertheless, he knew that without Cicotte, the fix would never take place at all. Cicotte, because he held out for it, got all of that precious $10,000. Gandil satisfied himself with knowing that he could bet later in the Series. He hoped that the other players would help throw the games and trust that their payments would arrive later.

On September 30, the day before the opening game of the Series, Gandil and six of the other seven conspirators met at the Sinton Hotel in Cincinnati. Joe Jackson was not present at this meeting. Gandil intro-duced Abe Attell as the man who would deliver the promised cash, but Attell, still lying to the players about Rothstein's involvement, changed the rules again. He claimed that he had $100,000 in cash, but he explained that the players would receive $20,000 after each lost game, not $80,000 up front as had been promised. Gandil began sweating, but the gamblers held all the cards now. Gandil had to be content with the promise of $40,000 in the hotel safe. Cicotte already had his $10,000.

The players grumbled, but apparently Cicotte was the only player smart enough to get his money in advance. They agreed to throw the first three games, pitched by Cicotte, Lefty Williams, and Dickie Kerr. They would win Game 4 for Cicotte, so he could use a World Series win to bolster his bargaining position for 1920. Kerr had nothing at all to do with the fix, but the players figured that a mere "busher," as Gandil described him, had no chance of winning with five crooked players behind him.

Jackson's absence from this meeting may be explained by the fact that his wife had come to Cincinnati to stay with him for the first two games. Jackson apparently wanted to hide the fact of his participation in the fix from Katie. It is clear that she had no knowledge at this point, and one can only speculate what might have happened if the sensible Katie had learned of the fix before any games were played. Many couples play the dangerous game of keeping secrets from each other, and Joe Jackson kept a big one, one that would soon wreak havoc on both of their lives.

With so much money changing hands, the odds began to fall precipitously. Bookies lengthen or shorten the odds on sporting events to encourage people to bet; if no one takes the underdog, then they lengthen the odds. The bookie always wins, since the commission (or "vigorish") amounts to 10 percent of the wager, no matter what side the bettor takes. The bookie wants a lot of betting money rolling in and doesn't care which way the money is wagered.

However, in the days leading up to the opening game of the 1919 Series, no lengthening of the odds was needed to encourage bettors to take the underdog Reds. Arnold Rothstein put $270,000 down on the Reds, and so much more money began coming in on Cincinnati that on September 29 the odds dropped from 8-5 to 6-5 in only one day. The "smart money" all was going Cincinnati's way. On September 30, the day before the Series, Sport Sullivan put $29,000 down on the Reds but could get no better odds than even money.

The whole scene smelled, but the club owners were busy fighting their own battles and kept aloof from the situation. Ban Johnson was the only baseball executive who appeared to be concerned about gambling, but by late 1919 the club owners were becoming increasingly disgusted with Johnson's arrogant attitude, especially concerning financial matters. Three American League owners—Boston's Harry Frazee, New York's Jacob Ruppert, and Charles Comiskey of the White Sox—formed a cabal to boot Johnson out of the presidency of the league, but they couldn't get any of the other five owners to go along. The American League magnates were too busy sniping at each other in the papers to concern themselves with the troubling swing in the betting odds.

The writers, however, sensed a fix almost immediately. *Chicago Herald and Examiner* sportswriter Hugh Fullerton, whose accounts of the games would be syndicated across the country, sent a cable to his newspapers: ADVISE ALL NOT TO BET ON THIS SERIES. UGLY RUMORS AFLOAT.

In retrospect, the most intelligent course of action would have been for the players to win the first game for Cicotte. This would have swung the odds back to the White Sox, stilled the ugly fix rumors at least for a while, and opened up a great possibility of more money to be made at better odds later in the Series. Arnold Rothstein, for one, bet most of his cache on the outcome of the whole Series, not on individual games. However, it appeared that Attell and Sullivan, for all their sporting connections and gambling experience, didn't see the obvious. They wanted to make some money, and make it immediately.

The biggest problem with the fix was that too many people knew about it. Lefty Williams nervously warned his friends against betting on the White Sox. Swede Risberg sent a coded telegram to his friend Joe Gedeon, second baseman of the St. Louis Browns, advising him to get in on the action and bet on the Reds. Abe Attell told his friend George M. Cohan, the Broadway star, that the Series was fixed. It didn't take long for the trickle of rumors to turn into a tidal wave. Perhaps Sullivan and Attell, knowing that the circle of the initiated was growing with each passing day, wanted to make their hay as soon as possible and get out before the fix collapsed or was exposed.

Joe Jackson felt the pressure. He thrilled the Cincinnati crowd before the first game of the Series when he belted three batting-practice pitches deep into the right field stands, but he was unusually brooding and morose on the bench before the game. Jackson impulsively bellowed, "I don't wanna play!" to Kid Gleason just minutes before the first pitch. Gleason ignored him. "I don't wanna play, and you can tell the boss that too!" Jackson shouted at Gleason. Gleason merely glared and rumbled, "You'll play, Jackson. You'll play."[15]

For Joe Jackson, playing to lose ran in opposition to all of his values and convictions. Joe was not a highly intelligent man, and he had not succeeded in business ventures off the field to any extent. Playing ball was the one thing that he could do better than almost anybody in the world, and now he had to pretend to give his best efforts while trying his best to lose. Happy Felsch, joker that he was, kidded Gandil about giving extra money to the man who dropped the most fly balls or made the biggest baserunning blunder, but Joe Jackson wasn't laughing.

If Joe had bothered to examine the situation, he would have realized that he had much more to lose than any of the other six players (excepting Weaver, who decided not to go along) involved in the scheme. Jackson was the biggest star by far of the seven, and at age 31 he still had several outstanding years in his future. Jackson hit .351 in 1919, finishing fourth in the batting race behind Ty Cobb, Bobby Veach, and George Sisler, and he could have used a World Series win to get a raise out of Comiskey. Joe's contract ended after the 1919 season, and he could look forward to a more lucrative new deal for 1920.

No one knows if he soon regretted agreeing to participate in the fix, but he couldn't back out on Gandil and his fellow fixers now. It was too late; Cicotte already had his $10,000, and there was no turning back. Joe Jackson's passion for money had trumped his competitive instincts as well as his better judgment, and he already sensed impending disaster. Katie would find out too, since his promised payment of $20,000 would have to be explained eventually.

Kid Gleason, at least initially, didn't suspect a thing. He sent one of the conspirators, the trusted Fred McMullin, to Cincinnati late in the season to scout the Reds. As the Series drew closer, however, Gleason heard the same whispers that were making their way around the hotel lobbies. He didn't know whether to believe the rumors or not, but he realized that if something illegal was in the works, Chick Gandil was probably involved. Gleason started watching the first baseman closely.

On October 1, 1919, a wildly enthusiastic crowd gathered in Cincinnati for the first game of the World Series. The Reds had a checkered history in the National League. They were part of the original lineup of teams in 1876, but four years later the league expelled the Reds for selling beer in their park and playing games on Sunday. The Reds then spent a decade in the rival American Association, where they won a pennant in 1882, before rejoining the National League in 1890. Charles Comiskey managed the Reds for three years in the 1890s, with a notable lack of success, and before 1919 no Cincinnati team had ever finished higher than third in the eight-team National League.

Now the good burghers of the Queen City, excited over their first flag-winners in 37 years, rallied behind their underdog team in its first World Series. More than 30,000 fans jammed the tiny Redland Field (which later would be called Crosley Field), the home of the Reds until 1970. The Reds management erected temporary seats above the left field fence, but they still couldn't handle the huge crowd. More fans sat or stood in left field behind a hastily assembled rope line, mere steps away from left fielders Joe Jackson of the Sox and Pat Duncan of the Reds.

Arnold Rothstein, through Sport Sullivan, issued orders for Cicotte to hit the first batter as a signal that the fix was in place. At a few minutes after three, Cicotte threw his first pitch to Reds leadoff hitter Morrie Rath. The second pitch hit Rath squarely in the back.

Chapter 14

"What the Hell Is Coming Off Here?"

Sure, I heard that the fix was on, but I looked on it as just idle gossip and completely preposterous. I hadn't been close to some of the fellows, but, still, they were my teammates. Why shouldn't I defend them?
—Eddie Collins [1]

The Reds grabbed a 1-0 lead in the first inning. Rath took first after Cicotte's second pitch hit him. Jake Daubert sent Rath to third with a single, and then Heinie Groh flied to Jackson in left, sending Rath home. The Sox tied the score in the second when Jackson reached second on a wild throw by third baseman Larry Kopf. Joe advanced to third on a sacrifice by Felsch and scored on a bloop single by Gandil, who was thrown out trying to stretch it into a double.

It all fell apart for the Sox in the fourth. With the Reds' Pat Duncan on first and one out, Eddie Collins stopped a hard smash by Kopf and threw out Duncan at second, but Risberg's slow throw to first failed to double up Kopf. Greasy Neale, the future Hall of Fame football coach, hit a floater behind second that Risberg knocked down but could not field, and Ivy Wingo followed with a single to right that scored Kopf for a 2-1 Reds lead. Pitcher Dutch Ruether then blasted a triple between Jackson and Felsch in left, scoring Neale and Wingo. Rath's single scored Ruether with Rath taking second, and then Daubert's single sent Rath home. The Reds led 6-1, and a flustered Kid Gleason brought in Roy Wilkinson to relieve Cicotte. Wilkinson got Groh on a fly ball to end the inning.

In the meantime, Dutch Ruether, a good but not great pitcher, was enjoying the game of his life. He held the Sox to only six hits and looked like the second coming of Babe Ruth at the plate, with two triples and a single and three runs batted in. In the seventh, Ruether got three outs with only four pitches as Gandil and Risberg both went out on the first ball pitched. In the ninth inning the Sox trailed by a 9-1 score; Gleason and Eddie Collins still prowled the bench, trying to whip up some fighting spirit from the dejected Sox, but Ruether induced both Jackson and Felsch to fly out, and Gandil's weak grounder ended the game.

Ray Schalk fumed in the clubhouse. Cicotte pitched brilliantly at times, but he threw bad pitches at the very moments when they would do the most damage. Schalk tried to find Cicotte, but the pitcher didn't want to be found. Cicotte showered quickly and left before anyone noticed his absence.

If Schalk was angry, Kid Gleason was angrier still. He had just seen his best pitcher give up six runs in only four innings, and he also had a stack of telegrams in his room. The telegrams came from all over the country, warning Gleason that the Series was fixed. Some of them named specific players who were alleged to be involved. Gleason didn't know what to believe at this point. At the Hotel Sinton that evening, dozens of surprised onlookers saw a red-faced Gleason screaming at Risberg, Cicotte, and several other players on the sidewalk outside. Gleason finally realized the futility of it all and stormed back to his room.

The seven players weren't happy either. The $20,000 that the gamblers promised Gandil did not materialize. Jackson confronted Gandil after the game, but Gandil didn't have an answer for him or the other players, because neither Abe Attell nor Bill Burns delivered the cash that they promised.

Attell gave no thought to the players who followed orders and lost the first game. He had stacks of money, thousands and thousands of dollars, in his hotel room at the Sinton, but he didn't want to share it. All Attell could think about was how to make more money in Game 2. He didn't seem to care that the players themselves, the ones who actually carried out the fix, had not gotten their promised payoff. Bill Burns tried to convince Attell to give something, anything, to the players, but the former boxer wouldn't listen. "It's all out on bets," he explained.

However, Attell realized that he had to promise something to keep the fix on track. The next morning Attell, Burns, and Maharg met with

Joe in front of the White Sox dugout (author's collection).

Gandil and Lefty Williams, the starting pitcher for Game 2, and promised to deliver the money the next day. Attell, like most gamblers, was a master at putting off his creditors. He left the meeting confident that Williams would deliver another loss in Game 2 and that the stacks of cash in Room 708 would grow even higher.

Burns knew better. Attell was a liar, and he had no intention of paying the players. Burns had to get some money somewhere, and quick, or else the whole fix would collapse.

Lefty Williams didn't have any money yet, but he wasn't worried. He trusted Gandil to deliver the promised $10,000 in due time. Gandil delivered for Cicotte, didn't he? The promise of $10,000 put stars in the eyes of a 23-game winner making only $2,600 a year. His manager, however, had plenty to worry about. Kid Gleason drew Ray Schalk over to a corner of the dugout, away from the other players, and nodded toward Williams. "Watch him," said Gleason.

The Cincinnati pitcher, lefthander Slim Sallee, had faced the Sox before. The White Sox pounded him all over the lot two years before in the World Series against the Giants. Most observers expected the same result today. Williams would have to lose while making himself look good against a journeyman pitching opponent. After the 9-1 debacle of the day before, Williams knew he'd have to do a better job than Cicotte did.

Williams started Game 2 like a pitcher possessed. In the first three innings he faced the minimum nine batters. The only baserunner was Cincinnati captain (and National League batting champ) Edd Roush, who walked in the second and was promptly erased by a double play from Collins to Gandil. In the meantime, Sallee allowed only two hits, by Jackson in the second and by Williams in the third. Jackson made it to third, but Gandil and Risberg failed to bring him home. The two teams headed to the fourth inning with no score.

Weaver and Jackson started the fourth with singles, and Felsch sacrificed them to second and third. But Gandil forced Weaver at the plate, and Risberg popped out to Daubert to end the threat. Now the wheels fell off for the White Sox. Williams walked Rath, then walked Groh after Daubert's sacrifice. Roush then singled for the first Cincinnati hit, scoring Rath. Roush tried to steal, but the ball squirted through Collins' glove straight to Risberg, who tagged out Roush with Groh holding third. Williams then walked Pat Duncan, his fourth walk of the game, while Ray Schalk shouted and cursed at him from behind the plate. Kopf followed with a triple to left center, scoring two more runs. The Reds ended the inning with a 3-0 lead.

The Reds scored again in the sixth when Roush drew a walk, Williams' fifth of the game, and came around on a sacrifice by Duncan and a single by Neale. The Sox scored twice in the seventh when Risberg singled and Schalk doubled, and a bad throw by Neale allowed them both to score. The game ended when McMullin, batting for Williams in the ninth, grounded to Rath. The Reds left the field with a 4-2 victory.

Williams pitched well, aside from the six walks. He allowed only four hits. Nevertheless, Schalk wasn't fooled. "He crossed me three times!" Schalk screamed at Gleason. "He wouldn't throw the curve!"

Gleason boiled with impotent rage. He had nothing more to go on than he had the day before, but he sensed that two of the three members of his Series pitching rotation were crooks. He spied Gandil contentedly puffing on a cigar in the clubhouse, seemingly unconcerned. "You had a great day today, Gandil," sneered Gleason.

"So did you, Kid," chirped the first baseman.

Suddenly, Gleason lunged for Gandil's throat. He got hold of Gandil only briefly before the other players stepped in. Gleason retreated, almost daring Gandil to say something else, but Gandil kept quiet. Later, Gleason collected himself well enough to speak to the writers. "We made some mistakes in our defense," said the manager, diplomatically. "Of course, Williams' wildness hurt. Every one of their four runs was passed to first base. But Williams was good. He was always trying to do something, but his control wasn't quite good enough."[2] Off the record, though, the manager unloaded his suspicions to the writers, who could only nod their heads sympathetically.

Outside, Schalk spotted Williams emerging from the clubhouse and motioned him to come over. Schalk pulled Williams away from the others and started punching the surprised pitcher, landing several solid blows before the other White Sox arrived to break it up.[3]

That evening, in a tavern outside of Cincinnati, an inebriated *Chicago Tribune* columnist Ring Lardner sang an off-key rendition of "I'm Forever Blowing Bubbles" with lyrics of his own devising. "I'm forever blowing ballgames," Lardner sang to the startled patrons. "I come from Chi, I barely try, just go to bat and fade and die...." Lardner reported later that "three of the Cincinnati players were in our party and seemed to enjoy the song."[4]

Charles Comiskey couldn't believe his eyes. At 11 o'clock that night Comiskey called Gleason to his room. "Do you think they're throwing the Series?" Comiskey demanded. "Answer me!" Gleason admitted to Comiskey that something smelled fishy, but he had no evidence, nothing solid to go on. Maybe they just had a bad game. Maybe the boys were overconfident.

Comiskey tried to sleep, but at 2:30 A.M. he bounded out of bed and called John Heydler. Comiskey admitted to Heydler that he had no proof, but something was amiss. Heydler then went down the hall and knocked on Ban Johnson's door. Johnson, reportedly groggy after a night of drinking, listened as Heydler explained the situation, but Johnson was in no mood to hear complaints from Comiskey, the man who was trying to force him out of the league presidency. Johnson sneered, "That is the yelp of a beaten cur!" and ordered the National League president out of his room.

The crooked players had followed orders and lost the first two games, but still no money arrived. Jackson confronted Gandil again that evening. "What are you going to do?" demanded Jackson.

Gandil didn't have any answers. "Everything is all right," he said impatiently, though he knew it wasn't. Abe Attell's piles of money were even larger than the day before, and still Attell wouldn't give any of it to the players. In fact, Attell could leave right now with a healthy profit, without giving the players another dime. Attell, not Gandil, was in the driver's seat.

Burns arrived at Attell's room to plead the players' case. After much arguing and pleading, Attell handed Burns $10,000. "That's all they can have," said Attell.

"To hell with the players," chimed in one of Attell's cronies. "What do we need them for?"

Joe Jackson waited for his $20,000, though he had no idea where the money would come from. All he knew was that he hadn't seen any of it. He also hadn't been told how the third game should proceed. He didn't know if the Sox should try to lose a third game in a row, or go all out and count on the Reds to beat the rookie Dickie Kerr. Sleepy Bill Burns and the other gamblers confidently put down their money on another Chicago loss, but Joe Jackson arrived at Comiskey Park with no idea of how to proceed.

More than 34,000 fans jammed into Comiskey Park for the third game of the World Series. Several thousand of them had made their way in from Cincinnati, cheering their unexpected good fortune in the first two games, but the White Sox faithful weren't yet ready to give up on their team. Their faith was rewarded in the second inning, when Joe Jackson singled and Reds pitcher Ray Fisher misplayed a bunt by Felsch and put runners on second and third. Chick Gandil then lashed a single to right field that scored both runners and gave the Sox a 2-0 lead. Gandil, however, loafed on a perfect sacrifice bunt by Schalk and got himself thrown out at third.

Perhaps Gandil and the other fixers decided to win Game 3 to double-cross the gamblers; perhaps they intended to lose all along, but expected the Reds to score more than two runs against the "busher" Dickie Kerr. After another perfect bunt by Schalk drove in an additional run in the fourth inning, the players reverted to their old tricks. Jackson and Felsch both reached first base in the sixth, but both were thrown out trying to steal second. Jackson even fell down once while swinging at a high

Joe warming up in 1919 (author's collection).

pitch. Nevertheless, the Reds could not touch Dickie Kerr on this day. The little Texan pitched the Sox to a 3-0 victory that took less than 90 minutes to complete.[5]

Bill Burns started the day with more than $12,000. Now he and Maharg were broke, after betting all their money on a White Sox loss. They left Chicago and pulled out of the fix, and Maharg had to pawn his diamond stickpin to get enough money for his train ticket back home to Philadelphia. "Somebody is getting a nice little jazz," said Jackson to Gandil that night. "Everybody is crossed."[6] Gandil explained that Attell and Burns had crossed him. Gandil's only hope was that Sport Sullivan, missing the last three days, would pop up again and put the fix back on track.

Sullivan spent the day of the third game in New York, explaining his machinations to Arnold Rothstein. The King of Gamblers was pleased, but Sullivan's problem now concerned getting additional funds to the players. Attell had his pile, but now it fell to Sullivan to deliver the goods. Rothstein could deal with Attell later if he wanted, but Rothstein had nearly $300,000 worth of bets at stake, and Sullivan knew better than to let him down.

Sullivan made another series of promises to Gandil on the phone. Twenty thousand dollars after Game 4 and another twenty thousand after Game 5. I'll get it, said Sullivan. Don't worry. You'll get your money if you lose Games 4 and 5. He then spent the morning on the telephone. It took several hours, but by noon, Sullivan had $20,000 in hand. It didn't take long for Sullivan to realize that he could get two losses, not one, with a single $20,000 payment. By the time the fourth game began, Sullivan had already made the decision to cheat the players out of their promised second payoff.

Game 4 on Saturday, October 4 opened with Cicotte his usual masterful self. He allowed only two hits in the first four innings. In the meantime, Jackson made it to third with one out in the second, but Gandil popped up and Cicotte grounded out to keep the game scoreless. Collins made it to third in the third inning, but Felsch grounded out to end the threat.

The game turned in the fifth inning. With one out Duncan grounded to Cicotte, who threw wildly to Gandil at first. Duncan wound up at second on the play. Kopf then singled sharply to left. Jackson's throw home was right on target and had Duncan beaten by ten feet, but Cicotte deflected the ball with his glove and allowed Duncan to score.[7] Cicotte's clumsy cutoff play made jaws drop all over the ballpark. "There wasn't any occasion for Cicotte to intercept that throw," said an angry Gleason after the game. "He did it to prevent Kopf from going to second, but Kopf had no more intention of going to second than I have of jumping into a lake."[8]

"That's when we knew for sure there was some horseshit going on," said the Reds' Jimmy Ring years later. "I'll never forget Schalk standing there in front of home plate staring at Cicotte. Eddie went back to the mound and was standing there with his back to the plate, staring out to center field and rubbing the ball up very slowly, like he didn't want to turn around and face Schalk."[9]

Greasy Neale was the next batter. Joe Jackson decided to play close to the line in left field, despite the fact that Neale was a left-handed hitter, and Neale lifted a pop fly that fell for a double. Joe "had time to catch the ball," wrote Henry Edwards in the *Cleveland Plain Dealer* the next day. "He ran in circles before getting one mitt under it, only to let it drop."[10] Kopf scored, and the Reds left the inning with a 2-0 lead. Jimmy Ring, the Cincinnati pitcher, struck out both Jackson and Felsch in the eighth inning. He breezed to a 2-0 win, a three-hit shutout.

Hugh Fullerton, covering the Series for the *Chicago Herald-Examiner*, found it impossible to control his disgust. Before the Series, he and Christy Mathewson, the former Reds manager reporting for the *New York Evening World*, agreed to circle any suspicious-looking plays on their scorecards. When Cicotte deflected Jackson's throw, both men reached immediately for their red pens. For the first time in the Series, the dismayed reporter decided to air his suspicions, however carefully. "There is more ugly talk and more suspicion among the fans than there ever has been in any World's Series," wrote Fullerton. "The rumors of crookedness, of fixed games and plots, are thick. It is not necessary to dignify them by telling what they are, but the sad part is that such suspicions of baseball is so widespread."[11]

Kid Gleason was an enthusiastic horseplayer, and he knew gamblers and confidence men when he saw them. He saw lots of them, especially Sleepy Bill Burns, Billy Maharg, and Abe Attell, skulking about the hotel and talking furtively with the players. Gleason noticed the suspicious activity, and after the fourth game he called a team meeting in which he ripped into his players and accused them of "throwing down" the White Sox and Charles Comiskey. Only Gandil and McMullin argued with the manager. "You'd think we wasn't trying," complained Gandil defensively, while McMullin offered to punch anyone who questioned his honesty.[12] The other White Sox, who were either not involved or, except for Cicotte, hadn't yet been paid, kept their silence.

After the meeting adjourned, Gandil counted the $20,000 from

Sullivan into four different envelopes of $5,000 each. He gave one to Felsch, one to Risberg, and two to Williams, with instructions to give one to Jackson.

Williams went to Jackson's room and knocked on the door. When Joe answered, Williams offered him the envelope, and whether Jackson counted it or Williams told him that it only contained five thousand dollars, Jackson became angry. "What the hell is coming off here?" Jackson shouted. Williams explained that Gandil told him that Attell had double-crossed the players, that Attell hadn't kept his end of the bargain. A loud argument ensued, after which Williams threw the envelope on the floor and left the room.[13]

Jackson then went out to find Gandil. The first baseman told Jackson the same thing he told Williams—that Attell had "given us a jazzing" and kept most of the money for himself. "Take that [the five thousand]," said Gandil to Jackson, "or leave it alone." He may have promised Jackson that another wad of cash would arrive after Game 5.

Jackson returned to his room. Katie was in the bathroom when Williams came to the room, and now she knew the truth, since she heard her husband's argument with Williams and saw an envelope full of cash on the floor. The rumors were all true after all. She "thought it was an awful thing to do ... she felt awful bad about it, cried about it for a while," as Jackson said in his testimony a year later, but there was no way out now. They were both stuck in this mess, and Joe would have to see it through to the end. Joe stuffed the cash, mostly hundreds and fifties, in his pocket.

It rained the next morning, and the players gathered in the clubhouse to wait for the inevitable postponement of the day's game. While some of the relief pitchers played cards, Gleason fussed and fumed with the writers. "It's the best team that ever went into a world's series," said the manager about his White Sox, now down three games to one, "but, it isn't playing the baseball that won the pennant for me. I don't know what's the matter, the players don't know what's the matter, but the team has not shown itself thus far. But we'll be there tomorrow."

A writer asked Gleason if Williams would still pitch Game 5. "No," remarked Gleason. "I think I'll go in myself."[14] The manager was joking through his pain, but he toyed with the idea of sending Kerr to the hill in the crucial fifth game. In the original plan, each pitcher would work on two days' rest, since there were three pitchers, nine games, and no off days in the Series schedule. However, the Sunday rainout pushed the schedule back one day and gave Kerr an extra day to recover from his shutout victory.

Gleason weighed the pros and cons of such a move carefully before he arrived at a decision. Kerr, though he pitched courageously in Game 3, was still a mere rookie, and if he lost in Game 5, the White Sox would be behind by four games to one, and the honest Kerr wouldn't be available again for three days. Gleason reluctantly sent Williams to the mound the next day and kept his fingers crossed.

Lefty Williams started Game 5 for the White Sox, and for the first four innings he didn't allow a single hit. In the meantime, Cincinnati's Hod Eller struck out Gandil, Risberg, and Schalk in the second inning, then struck out Williams, Leibold, and Collins in the third. His six strikeouts in a row set a new Series record. In the fourth, Weaver and Jackson tapped meekly to Eller, then Felsch struck out for Eller's seventh whiff of the game. Kopf got the Reds' first hit in the fifth, but Williams got out of the inning with a scoreless tie.

Eller, the pitcher, led off the Cincinnati sixth with a fly ball between Jackson and Felsch in left. Joe got a late start on the ball; according to the summary of the Series in the 1920 *Reach Guide*, "Jackson seemed to be daydreaming when Eller's fly was hit in his direction." Felsch picked up the ball and threw wildly to the infield, and Eller wound up on third with a triple. Rath singled to score Eller, and after Daubert sacrificed Rath to second, Groh walked on four straight pitches. Roush hit a fly to center that Felsch should have put away easily, but Felsch muffed it so badly that two more runs scored. The generous scorer gave Roush a triple on that one. Felsch claimed later that he lost the fly ball legitimately, but this play, along with Cicotte's deflected throw in the fourth game and the misplay of Eller's fly ball, raised eyebrows all over the baseball world.

Ray Schalk, who had worked hard to control his anger all through the Series, finally boiled over. Schalk, who had been barking at umpire Cy Rigler all day, thought he tagged Groh out at the plate, and argued so vehemently that Rigler tossed him out of the game. Byrd Lynn finished up behind the plate. A sacrifice fly from Duncan to Jackson in left scored Roush with the fourth run of the inning.

Weaver belted a triple in the ninth, but Jackson ended the game with a grounder to Kopf as the Reds left the field with a 4-0 win. Eller matched Ring's performance in Game 4 with a three-hit shutout of his own.

In the clubhouse Kid Gleason didn't even bother looking for Williams. His Sox had not scored a single run in 23 innings, and had suffered back-to-back shutouts from Jimmy Ring and Hod Eller, two pitchers not to be mistaken for Cy Young and Walter Johnson. "The bunch I had in August fighting for the pennant," snarled Gleason to the writers, "would have trimmed this Cincinnati bunch without a struggle. The bunch I have now couldn't beat a high school team."[15]

A reporter asked Gleason about Game 6. "I'll send Dickie Kerr to the slab tomorrow," promised the Kid, "and maybe if he wins I'll send him back the next day, and if he wins that one I'll send him back again."[16] Gleason already knew the cause was hopeless, even if Kerr won again the next day. Even a great team like the White Sox would be hard-pressed to win four games in a row in the World Series. If the Series were still a best-of-seven affair, the Reds would be the world champions already.

Joe Jackson kept his perfect record intact. In the first five games of the Series, he had not driven in a single run.

Chick Gandil and Swede Risberg sat morosely in Gandil's room on the morning of Game 6. Sport Sullivan's second installment of $20,000 was due, and as usual Sullivan was nowhere to be found. After waiting for several hours, the two players drove to the park and discussed their strategy. Cicotte wanted a win to help his negotiating position for 1920, but a loss with Kerr in Game 6 would end the Series. They had to win Game 6 for Kerr, then win Game 7 for Cicotte before blowing either Game 8 or 9. Or, perhaps the Sox could double-cross the gamblers and win the Series, which would mean an extra $2,000 per man. Since Sullivan never materialized with the $20,000, Gandil would call the shots now. The word passed discreetly to go out and win.

The sixth game turned out to be a wild, tense affair. The Reds scored twice in the third on a double by Duncan, and scored two more in the fourth on a double by the pitcher, Ruether, and a grounder that Risberg misplayed. The Sox got one back in the fifth when two walks and an infield hit by Kerr loaded the bases and Eddie Collins hit a fly ball to score a run. Schalk, on second, did not try to advance to third, but Kerr ran down to second and was caught by Groh, who ran across the infield to tag him out.

In the sixth inning, the Sox tied the score. Jackson drove in Weaver from second with a single, for his first run batted in of the Series. Felsch's double scored Jackson, and Schalk's single scored Felsch. Kerr wobbled in the late innings and sustained a bruise on his pitching hand by a liner off Kopf's bat, but he stayed in the game while Ring came in to pitch for the Reds.

The Sox finally won the game in the tenth. Weaver doubled, and Jackson's sacrifice bunt went for a base hit with Weaver taking third. Felsch struck out, but Gandil, of all people, singled to drive Weaver home with the go-ahead run. Kerr made it stand up in the bottom of the tenth for a 5-4 win. That evening, Eddie Cicotte went to Kid Gleason and begged for the chance to pitch Game 7.

The next day, before a surprisingly small crowd of only 13,000 in Cincinnati, the Sox scored first for a change. Shano Collins singled to lead off the game, and Eddie Collins sacrificed him to second. After a fly ball by Weaver, Jackson rapped a single to left to bring Shano Collins home. In the third, Jackson's single drove Shano Collins home again for a 2-0 Chicago lead. They went ahead 4-0 in the fifth when Felsch's bases-loaded single brought home two more runs. Through it all Eddie Cicotte pitched like a 29-game winner for the first time in the Series, and the Sox left the park with a 4-1 victory. Suddenly the White Sox found themselves two wins away from a world championship.

Arnold Rothstein had other ideas. He calmly ordered Sport Sullivan to make sure that the Series ended in Game 8. That evening a beefy stranger, known to history only as "Harry F.," accosted Lefty Williams and strongly suggested that he lose the next day's game. It would be better for Williams if he followed orders, the man said. It would be better for Mrs. Williams, too.

Thursday, October 9, 1919, was a typically cold, overcast fall day in Chicago, a day more suited for football than for the deciding game of the World Series. All morning and into the early afternoon, Kid Gleason paced in the clubhouse like a hungry tiger. He considered not starting Lefty Williams, but who would start if Williams didn't? Kerr? No, he had just pitched ten innings two days before, and he would be needed in Game 9. Lowdermilk, James, Wilkinson? No, they're just mop-up guys at best. Gleason had to send Williams out and hope for the best. Besides, how could a 23-game winner lose three times in eight games? Deep down, Gleason knew the answer. "I'd use an iron on any son of a bitch who'd sell out this ball club!" shouted Gleason to his team before the game. In 1919, an "iron" was a gun.[17]

Gleason moved Felsch to right field and installed Nemo Leibold in center, but no amount of lineup juggling could prevent the coming disaster. Williams retired Rath to start the game, but Daubert and Groh singled and Roush doubled to score Daubert. Duncan then singled home Groh and Roush, and the Reds led 3-0 before the Chicago fans settled into their seats. After one pitch, a fastball strike, to Kopf, Gleason brought in Bill James to relieve Williams. Once again, Williams had refused to throw his curveball. In only 15 pitches, the lefthander had given up four hits and three runs.

James allowed one more run before the inning ended. The Reds scored again in the second when Groh singled and Roush's drive cleared Jackson's head in left for a double and a 5-0 lead.

In the third, down by five runs, the White Sox finally showed some signs of life. With the bases empty, Joe Jackson stepped into a pitch from Hod Eller and drove it into the bleachers in right field for a home run, the only one hit by either team in the Series. Nevertheless, the Reds scored once more in the fifth and three more times in the sixth for a 9-1 lead. Jackson drove in two more runs in the eighth, but it was too little too late. In the ninth, Joe grounded to Rath, who threw to Daubert to end the game and the Series. The Reds won the game by a score of 10 to 5 and clinched their first world championship.

The White Sox clubhouse was as quiet as a morgue, except for the furious Kid Gleason. "The Reds beat the greatest ball team that ever went into a world's series!" shouted the dejected manager. "… I don't know yet what was the matter. Something was wrong. I didn't like the betting odds. I wish that no one had ever bet a dollar on the team."[18]

In the next day's papers, some of the writers complained that Gleason should have started Kerr instead of Williams and worried about the ninth game later. Gleason disagreed but acknowledged that Roy Wilkinson, who relieved Bill James in the sixth inning, pitched well. "Wilkinson would have won that game for me yesterday if I had started him," remarked the manager. "I wish now that I had."[19]

On the morning after the last game, Sport Sullivan knocked on Gandil's door. He gave Gandil and Risberg the $40,000 from the Congress Hotel safe and bade the players good-bye. Gandil gave $15,000 to Risberg, with instructions to give $5,000 to McMullin and keep the other $10,000 for himself. Gandil kept the rest; in all, Gandil went home to California with a cool $35,000 in hand. Why play any more baseball with nearly ten years' worth of salary in my pocket, Gandil asked himself. The final game of the Series was Gandil's last in the major leagues.

Jackson spotted Gandil that morning on his way to Comiskey Park to clean out his locker. Gandil looked drunk to Jackson, but Joe confronted him anyway. "I told him there was a hell of a lot of scandal going around for what had happened," recalled Jackson a year later.

Gandil sneered, "To hell with it." Gandil then got into a taxi and rode off. He was anxious to get back to California and leave baseball behind.[20]

Jackson went to Comiskey's office in the ballpark and waited to see the Old Roman. He stayed for several hours, but Comiskey didn't want to see him. Comiskey holed up in his office while Jackson cooled his heels outside. Finally Jackson gave up and left the park. He left that night for Savannah with Lefty Williams.

Joe Jackson led all Chicago batters in the Series with a .375 average, and also led the team with five runs scored and six runs batted in. Still, all six of his runs batted in came in the last three games, and half of them came in the last game when all was already lost. For all his gaudy statistics, Jackson utterly failed to hit in the clutch, especially in the first five games of the Series.

Joe returned home to Savannah, happy to leave the stress and betrayal of the 1919 World Series behind him. He arrived the next day to tend to his Savannah businesses. The poolroom on Congress Street needed his attention, and so did a new dry-cleaning service he had started. The dry-cleaning establishment soon employed more than 20 people, and Joe would be busier than ever in the winter of 1919-20. He also was occupied with the illness of his sister Gertrude, who was undergoing treatment at the hospital in Savannah. Katie deposited the $5,000 in cash in the Jackson's bank account; some, if not most, of the money was used to pay Gertrude's medical bills.

The day after the series ended, Hugh Fullerton wrote his final column of the Series. He knew what had happened, but he also knew that he couldn't prove his suspicions. Fullerton wrote the following dispatch from deep in the well of his own frustration: "Yesterday's in all probability, is the last game that will be played in any World Series. If the club owners and those who have the interest of the game at heart, have listened during the series, they will call off the annual inter-league contest. Yesterday's game also means the disruption of the Chicago White Sox ballclub. There are seven men on the team who will not be there when the gong sounds next Spring."[21] Fullerton received a lot of criticism for that last sentence, and only later did the writer reveal that he was merely quoting Charles Comiskey.[22]

As the 1919 World Series scandal unfolded, the idea that the Reds victory was actually a deliberate White Sox loss must have been hard for the Reds to bear. Some team members were still protesting in interviews years later:

> We could have beat them [the White Sox] no matter what the circumstances. Sure, the 1919 White Sox were good. But the 1919 Cincinnati Reds were better. I'll believe that to my dying day.[23]

So said Edd Roush, the star centerfielder of the Reds, to Lawrence Ritter in *The Glory of Their Times*. Many other Reds believed the same.

The question is, how good were the 1919 Reds? Could they have beaten the White Sox in an honestly played World Series?

The answer: certainly not.

The entire scandal was based on one important assumption: that the White Sox could win or lose as they saw fit. The players, led by Gandil, seemed to accept this assumption with absolutely no reservations. In the pre–Series meeting of the crooked players, the Sox decided to lose Games 1, 2, and 3 for Cicotte, Williams, and Kerr respectively, then win Game 4 to help Cicotte in his contract negotiations for 1920. At no time, it appears, did anyone suggest that the Reds might have anything to do with the outcomes of the games.

The Reds won 96 games in 1919, eight more than the White Sox, but the National League in 1919 was by far the weaker of the two leagues. The Boston Braves dropped to the second division again after their surprising World Series triumph of 1914, and the Philadelphia Phillies never recovered from their panic sale of Grover Cleveland Alexander to the Cubs in 1918. The Dodgers ruined their shot at a pennant when they exiled their star first baseman Jake Daubert to the Reds after a contract dispute in 1918. The Giants destroyed their team chemistry when they hired Hal Chase to play first base. The Reds won their first pennant in 1919 by climbing on top of the wreckage of the other clubs.

In 1919, most of baseball's biggest stars belonged to the American League. Ty Cobb, Walter Johnson, Tris Speaker, Joe Jackson, and Eddie Collins all played in the American League. The biggest gate attraction of all, Babe Ruth, belted 29 home runs for the Red Sox to set a new major league record, while the up-and-coming George Sisler batted .352 for the Browns. The National League featured performers like Roush, Rogers Hornsby, Grover Alexander, and Zack Wheat, but most of the newspaper space went to the American League stars. No wonder the so-called "junior circuit" won eight of nine World Series from 1910 to 1918.

The Reds had some good players on their team. Edd Roush won his second batting title in 1919, and Jake Daubert had won two of them earlier in the decade for the Dodgers. If the All-Star game had existed in 1919, Heinie Groh would have been the starting third baseman for the National League. The Reds' pitching, though not spectacular, was deep. They started five different pitchers in the first five games of the Series (Ruether, Sallee, Fisher, Ring, and Eller) and they had a hard-throwing young Cuban, Dolf Luque, in the bullpen. Luque would win 193 games in his long career.

Still, the Reds had no pitchers to equal the caliber of Cicotte (29-7) or Williams (23-13). Their hitters, other than Roush and Daubert, could not hope to match the Sox lineup of Collins, Felsch, Jackson, Gandil, and Weaver. The Reds' catchers, Bill Rariden and Ivy Wingo, were serviceable, but Ray Schalk was considered at the time to be the best catcher in the game.

The real strength of the two teams can be seen in Game 3. Some writers felt that the Sox tried to win the game to cross up the gamblers. However, Gandil loafed on a ground ball, and Jackson's later admission that "the eight of us did our best to kick it" indicates that the Sox were trying their best to blow the game. Despite their best (or worst) efforts, the White Sox won the game by a score of 3 to 0 behind a rookie pitcher. The players were right; they could win at will in this Series.

Only one of the Cincinnati players, Edd Roush, landed in the Baseball Hall of Fame. Three White Sox (Collins, Schalk, and Faber) gained election, and Jackson and Cicotte would have if the scandal had never happened. Weaver and Williams would also have had a good chance at a plaque on the wall in Cooperstown. If Red Faber was healthy, the White Sox would have won the Series anyway, crooked players or none. Even without Faber, an honest White Sox team should have wiped out the Reds in five or six games.

Chapter 15

The Winter of 1919-20

Any man who insinuates that the 1919 World's Series was not honorably played by every participant therein not only does not know what he is talking about, but is a menace to the game quite as much as the gamblers would be if they had the ghost of a chance to get in their nefarious work.
—Francis C. Richter, 1920[1]

The losers' share of the 1919 World Series receipts amounted to $3,154.27 per man. Joe waited patiently in Savannah for his share to arrive, but several weeks went by with no word about the checks. Joe and Katie waited until the end of October, then composed a letter to Charles Comiskey. It reads as follows with misspellings uncorrected:

> Savannah, Georgia, October 27, 1919
>
> Mr. Charles A. Comiskey,
>
> As I haven't heard anything from the club in Regards to my Saries check and would like to know why you are Holding it as I kneed the money Would like to have something as earley as possiable. And if possiable send it to me this week.
>
> Joe Jackson
> 621 W. 39th Street,
> Savannah, Georgia[2]

Comiskey had held onto the checks of all eight suspected players and had received similar letters from at least two of them. Comiskey replied to Jackson about two weeks later, in a letter that he sent to Joe's billiard parlor:

> November 11, 1919
>
> Mr. Joe Jackson
> 17 Congress St.,
> Savannah, Georgia
>
> Dear Friend,
>
> In answer to your recent communication, wish to state that there has been a great deal of adverse talk in which your name has been mentioned, along with several others, referring to and reflecting on your integrity in the recent World's Series. One or two players took the stand and they would gladly return to Chicago at any time to uphold any reflection cast on them.
>
> I wish to advise you that I have nothing whatever to do with the handling or issuing of same, as the National Commission turned over to Manager Gleason the players' share for distribution so would suggest you take up the matter with him direct.
>
> Would gladly pay your expenses to Chicago and return if you wish to come on in reference to the matter pertaining to the talk emenating from the World Series.
>
> With kindest regards, I remain,
> Yours very truly,
> Charles A. Comiskey

The "one or two players" who "took the stand" apparently was only one, St. Louis Browns second baseman Joe Gedeon. On October 15, a mere six days after the end of the Series, Comiskey made a public offer of $20,000 for information that the Series had been fixed. Gedeon, who had been advised by Swede Risberg to bet on the Reds before the Series began, hoped to collect the reward. Gedeon gave his story to Comiskey and team attorney Alfred Austrian, who politely thanked him and then refused to pay the reward.

They also talked to a St. Louis theater operator named Harry Redmon, who identified Abe Attell and gave details of the meeting at the Sinton Hotel in Cincinnati. Redmon named the eight players and gave the names of the St. Louis and Des Moines gamblers in the Attell cabal. Once again Comiskey did nothing with this information.[3] It appears that Comiskey wanted to gain only enough information to use as leverage at contract time, but not enough to blow the whole scandal onto the front pages.

Jackson received Comiskey's letter and immediately sent another of his own. Again, misspellings are uncorrected:

Savannah, Georgia
Nov. 15, 1919

Mr. Charles A. Comiskey,

Your letter just came, and I sure am surprised to hear that my name has been connected with any scandle in the recent World Series, as I think my playing proved that I did all I could to win, and I wrote Mr. Gleason yesterday and as soon as I hear from him I will be onley to glad to come to Chicago or any place you may say and clear my name and whoever started this will have to prove his statements, and that has nothing whatever to do with holding our checks, and as soon as I hear from Mr. Gleason as to why he is holding the checks I will come to Chicago if you say. But in the first place the National Commission is responsible for our money and why is Gleason holding it as I am under no contract to him, I am not looking to him for the money, and I don't see why they make a lot of fus because we Lost as it isent the first time a Series was lost and I am sure I did all I could to win and I think my record for the Series Will Show if you Look at it, I diden know Gleason's address in Philly, so I had to write the Club there and hope it will be forwarded to him at his home adress.

And let me hear from you as to when you want me to come to Chicago as I expect to hear from Gleason in a few days.

Joe Jackson
621 W. 39th St.,
Savannah, Ga.[4]

Comiskey, predictably, declined to follow up on Jackson's offer to return to Chicago and tell what he knew. The Old Roman recognized that the scandal (and his own knowledge of it after the fact) was a powder keg that would destroy his team, possibly forever, if the fuse were lit. By mid–October 1919 Comiskey knew the outlines of the entire fix and had already decided to tough it out and wait for the stench to dissipate. The club sent the belated Series checks to the eight players, and nothing further was said about the Series. By late November 1919 the controversy about the suspicious Series had evaporated, just as Comiskey had hoped.

Still, Ban Johnson lay in wait, like a vulture, ready for the right opportunity to pounce on Comiskey. Johnson was also investigating the Series, using his own personal funds when necessary to supplement the available money from the league budget. Since Johnson's detectives were talking to the same people that Comiskey's dicks had interviewed, Johnson knew now that Comiskey's cover-up was already under way. This piece of information, Johnson hoped, would be useful in the future.

Hugh Fullerton, meanwhile, had pieced together almost all the facts by this time. He wrote the whole story, naming names, dates, and places, but his editors in Chicago wanted nothing to do with it. Fullerton took the story to the *New York Evening World*, and though the paper forced Fullerton to water down his strongest allegations, the story created a national controversy when it hit Page One on December 15, 1919. Fullerton's story named no ballplayers, but it identified Attell, Rothstein, and most of the other gamblers involved. The writer revealed that he knew beforehand that the White Sox would lose the decisive eighth game, because a gambler told Fullerton just before the first pitch was thrown, "It'll be the biggest first inning you ever saw!"[5]

He skillfully avoided saying that the Series was fixed, though he recounted that he himself had heard fix rumors before the first game was played, and that such rumors were common knowledge within baseball itself. Fullerton decried the fact that, with all the gossip swirling around, the bosses of baseball did nothing to assure the public of the honesty of the sport. "The time has come for open talk!" declared Fullerton.[6]

Of course, there would be no open talk. Controversy raged for a few weeks, then died down again. Comiskey, Ban Johnson, and others made indignant denials, all the while holding their own knowledge close to the vest. Comiskey grandly repeated his offer of a reward for proof that the Series of 1919 had been played dishonestly, though the amount of the reward had dropped to $10,000, without explanation.

Most of the other writers ignored the allegations and ripped Fullerton, though most of them knew the same facts that he did. *Baseball Magazine* condemned Fullerton as a writer of "sensational stories, usually with the vaguest foundation," and called Fullerton's conclusions "wholesale vicious charges" which were "all the more inexcusable."[7]

The Sporting News, too, refused to believe that anything was wrong with the 1919 Series. Only seven days after the Series ended, the Bible of Baseball thundered its dismay at the rumors. "There is no such evidence" of wrongdoing, cried *The Sporting News* in an editorial, "except in the mucky minds of the stinkers who—because they are crooked—think all the rest of the world can't play straight."[8] The editors suggested that Comiskey should offer his reward to anyone who would be willing to accuse one of the players face-to-face. "There wouldn't have been any takers, unless some of the scandalmongers are a good deal better with their fists than they are with their brains."[9]

It seemed like everyone involved in baseball, from the National Commission to the lowest beat writer, simply wanted the stench of the Series to go away. The sale of Babe Ruth from the Red Sox to the Yankees on January 5, 1920, knocked the 1919 World Series off the front pages once again. A few days later, Cincinnati Reds owner Garry Herrmann resigned from his seat on the National Commission. The leagues could not agree on a replacement, and baseball entered the season of 1920 with an impotent, deadlocked Commission.

Charles Comiskey sent a letter to Joe Jackson in January of 1920. "I am formulating plans for the season of 1920 pertaining to the personnel of the White Sox," Comiskey wrote, "and would like to hear from you at your earliest convenience as to your playing terms for the coming season." Jackson wrote back a few days later:

> Savannah, Ga.
> January 24, 1920
>
> Mr. Charles A. Comiskey,
>
> Your received in Regards to my contract. First I Diden get the Nine days pay for the Series that i understand the other Boys got, and also a pare of Shoes and new Glove that was stolen in the Club House when Bill James trunk was stolen. Mr. Gleason had the club House Boy to make a list of things that was stolen and send to the office. But I never heard anything from it, and unless I get this and a three year ironclad contract for ten thousand a year I cant signe as living expenses are going up all the time and I dont rate myself the class of player Eddie Collins or Buck Weaver, I think that if Eddie is worth fifteen thousand and Buck ten that I am also worth ten thousand a year. I can't live in Chicago at what I am getting pay a Hundred for a flat. Besides, other living expenses there, as I am going to open a nother Billiard parlor in Birmingham and can make more by Beeing with the Business all the time than I can at my present Salrie there.
>
> Yours Respectfuley,
>
> Joe Jackson
> 621 W. 39th St.,
> Savannah, Ga.

No one knows where Jackson got his information on the salaries of his teammates. Collins was indeed earning around $15,000 a year, but Buck Weaver's salary was nowhere near ten thousand. In fact, Weaver's pay was certainly no more than Jackson's $6,000 in 1919.

Comiskey decided to low-ball Jackson. He fired a return salvo in the salary war:

> Jan. 29, 1920
>
> Mr. Joe Jackson
> 17 Congress St.,
> Savannah, Ga.
>
> Dear Friend,
>
> Your letter of recent date received, and contents noted. I wish, to advise you that your last season's contract was filled to the letter. You received the amount that was agreed upon in full, namely, $6000.00.
>
> Herewith enclosed please find contract for the season of 1920 for $7000.00. which is a very liberal increase over that of the past season.
>
> I am completing all my plans for the personnel of the club for 1920, and of course no one will be taken on the spring training trip who has not signed a contract.
>
> In reference to the part of your letter pertaining to something being taken from the Club House, I have heard nothing regarding that up to this time and that matter can be adjusted with Manager Gleason after your arrival here in Chicago.
>
> Trusting you have been spending a very pleasant winter, I remain,
>
> Yours very truly,
> Charles A. Comiskey

Jackson responded as follows:

> Savannah, Ga.
> February 1, 1920
>
> Mr. Chas. A. Comiskey,
>
> Your letter and also contract Received and am returning the contract. You may think a thousand dollars is a liberal encreas. But I don't as I know what other players are getting that isent any Better player than I am, as I consider myself as good a Ballplayer as you have on the club, and as I stated to you Before I can make more money in the Billiard Buisness then you offer me, as Mr. Sullivan and I just checked up and Did make more the past year with one place, and will open up another one soon. So if I Don't get ten thousand and a three year ironclad contract I will not signe.
>
> Joe Jackson
> Congress Billiard Parlor
> 17 Congress St.,
> Savannah, Ga.

An "ironclad" contract was one without the ten-day clause, which the players found so repellent and the owners found so necessary. Comiskey sent the contract back to Jackson on February 9, along with an offer to extend the $7,000 contract for both 1920 and 1921. Comiskey's letter made no mention of the ten-day clause.

Jackson's reply:

> February 13, 1920
> Savannah, Ga.
>
> Mr. Charles A. Comiskey,
>
> Please find enclosed contract as I can't signe a contract for what you offer, and you must remember By the time I pay encome tax and live out of the Salrie you offer I dont have anything Left and as far as the Billiard Buisness I have been in it for the Past two years and have Played for you for less money than any player on your club of my class of player, and I think I was very fair with you Last year, and if you dont think you can pay me what I am worth as a player I think it Best you trade or sell me as there ar other clubs that will.
>
> And I will not signe a contract unless the ten Day clause is cut out and a three year contract.
>
> Joe Jackson
> 17 Congress St.
> Savannah, Ga.

The Old Roman's teeth must have been gnashing by this time. He knew most, if not all, of the facts of the World Series scandal, and he also knew that Jackson had received $5,000 of crooked money. Now, Jackson had the temerity to stage a holdout! Worse, Comiskey had no way of using his knowledge of Jackson's participation in the fix against him, since public exposure of the scandal was the last thing Comiskey wanted. He had worked for months to cover up the evidence and smooth over the traces. The controversy had finally died down, and Comiskey saw no need to disturb it.

Comiskey also realized that Jackson and his fellow fixers, accomplished players though they may be, had no trade value at all. The other club owners heard all the whispers about the 1919 Series, and a fire sale by the White Sox would only ratify the worst of the rumors. No other club would take on the contract of a player under suspicion, as John McGraw learned the hard way in 1919 with Hal Chase. Like it or not, Comiskey and the Black Sox were stuck with each other for the 1920 season.

Weaver, Risberg, Gandil, Cicotte, Jackson—all sent their contracts back to Chicago, unsigned. Babe Ruth had signed with his new team, the Yankees, for the incredible sum of $20,000 a year. The holdout Sox hoped that the rising salary trend would put pressure on Comiskey to raise their salaries also.

The Associated Press reported on February 14 that Jackson had returned his contract and would not play in 1920 unless the White Sox met his salary demands. Comiskey sent a letter to Jackson that same day:

> February 14, 1920
>
> Mr. Joe Jackson
> 17 Congress St.,
> Savannah, Ga.
>
> My dear Sir,
>
> Your letter of Feb. 13 received, together with returned contract.
>
> I note in your statement that your billiard business will not interfere with your playing baseball. Up to the present time, have not received any offer to trade or buy your services from any club, and if we did receive such an offer, I have not the slightest idea of trading or selling. Neither do I intend to enter into a contract with the ten-day clause eliminated.
>
> The matter of the length of the contract is one for decision after the salary terms have been agreed upon. Kindly advise me your lowest playing terms for the season of 1920 and upon hearing from you will advise you immediately whether or not we can get together.
>
> I note by the papers this morning that you are a hold out according to your own statement, even after you were asked to keep the matters of terms confidential.
>
> With kindest regards, I remain,
>
> Yours very truly,
> Charles A. Comiskey

Jackson stood his ground:

> Savannah, Ga.
> Feb. 18, 1920
>
> Mr. Charles A. Comiskey:
>
> Your Letter received and note the contents. I wrote you before that I would play Ball for ten thousand and nothing Less, and I will not play for Less. I understand you have Raised some of the players

Joe batting with Blond Betsy (author's collection).

without asking. I know of one you offered $2300 Hundred raise that Didn't make any showing in the Series and I think my Past Record entitles me to what I ask and I don't think I am asking any more than I am worth as a player so will not sign for less.

Joe Jackson

The player to whom Joe referred who was offered a $2,300 raise was probably Happy Felsch, who hit only .192 in the Series against the Reds.

Finally, Comiskey decided to take action. He traveled West to get Risberg, Gandil, and Weaver to sign their contracts for 1920, and he dispatched Harry Grabiner to Savannah to obtain Joe Jackson's signature.

Joe Jackson in May 1920 (Cleveland Public Library).

When Grabiner arrived at the Savannah railroad station, he found a pay phone and called the Jackson home.

Joe was surprised to hear from the club secretary, since Comiskey had never sent before to get his signature on a contract. Joe's mind was occupied with the illness of his teenaged sister Gertrude, and Joe was, in fact, leaving for the hospital to visit her at the very moment that Grabiner phoned. The ballplayer asked if the negotiations could wait, but Grabiner was a man in a hurry, and he asked Joe to pick him up at the railroad station on his way to the hospital. Grabiner waited while Joe visited his sister, then brought up the contract in the car. The secretary delivered Comiskey's final offer—$8,000 a year for three years.[10]

Joe took the contract in hand and flipped through the pages. He couldn't read the words, but he could pick out the numbers, and although it wasn't the $10,000 that Joe wanted, he was pleased with the $2,000 per year raise. Still, Joe hesitated. He didn't want to tie himself down to one salary for three years, as he had when he signed his deal with the Indians in August 1915. Besides, Jackson had a great year in 1919 and figured to do as well or better in 1920. Grabiner noted Jackson's age—Joe would be 32 in July—and suggested that the security that Jackson would receive would afford him a measure of protection against injury. When the car pulled back in at the Jackson home, Grabiner handed Joe the contract and a pen.

This is where the stories diverge. Grabiner later insisted that the Jacksons knew that the ten-day clause was included in the contract and that Joe signed it in the house in Katie's presence. Joe claimed that Katie was not home at the time and that he signed the contract on the hood of the car only after Grabiner assured him that the ten-day clause was not included. That evening, Harry Grabiner headed back to Chicago with Jackson's signed contract. The ten-day clause appeared in Article 10 on the third of the contract's four pages.[11]

Chapter 16

The Most
Difficult Season

We [the Yankees] would play them [the White Sox] in one
series and they would look terrible; we'd play them the next
time and they'd look like the best club in the world ... you just
never knew when they were going to go out there and beat
your brains out or roll over and play dead. Somebody was betting on those games, that's a cinch.
— *Roger Peckinpaugh, 1977*[1]

American League president Ban Johnson had campaigned for years
to get rid of "freak deliveries," especially the spitball, and in February of
1920 Johnson finally had his way. The two league presidents, Johnson
and the National League's John Heydler, formally banned the spitball on
February 9. In the interest of fairness, they inserted a grandfather clause
under which two pitchers from each team would be allowed to continue
throwing the pitch.[2] The White Sox designated Red Faber and Eddie
Cicotte as their spitball pitchers, and Faber used the pitch successfully
for 14 more seasons. When Faber retired in 1933, he was the last legal
spitball pitcher in the American League.

The clause helped Faber but harmed another White Sox hurler.
Frank Shellenback was a 21-year-old righthander who tasted brief action
for the Sox in 1918 and 1919, and by 1920 he seemed ready to crack the
Sox bullpen, if not the starting rotation. However, Shellenback was on

the Minneapolis roster in the spring of 1920 and was not eligible for the spitball exemption. Suddenly Shellenback found himself stripped of his bread-and-butter pitch. He never pitched in the major leagues again, though he returned to the Pacific Coast League (where the spitball remained legal) and won more than 300 games in a long minor league career.[3]

Comiskey moved the White Sox spring training camp to Waco, Texas, after five seasons at Mineral Wells. Waco had grass fields, and Comiskey believed that the Sox traditionally got off to a slow start because the players needed time to get used to grass after playing on the baked dirt at Mineral Wells. Waco was also a much larger city, serviced by major highways and railroads, and it was easier to travel from Waco to Houston, San Antonio, and Dallas–Fort Worth for exhibition games.

In a cost-cutting move, Comiskey began spring training in the third week of March, a full two or three weeks later than most other teams. He believed that he could do this with a veteran team, which would not require as much time to prepare for the season. The problem was that the White Sox had so many holdouts that Kid Gleason found it difficult to hold practice. Joe Jackson reported to Waco on time, but Gandil, Risberg, Weaver, Cicotte, and Felsch were among the missing.

Many of the suspected players were unusually combative about their 1920 contracts. Buck Weaver demanded a trade to New York, though his contract with the White Sox still had two more years to run. Weaver explained to the writers that Babe Ruth and Carl Mays had broken their agreements with the Red Sox, and why shouldn't he be allowed to do the same thing?[4] Eddie Cicotte haggled with Comiskey and Harry Grabiner all winter, and arrived at Waco unsigned. Swede Risberg did not even report, opting instead to stay home until Comiskey met his price.

Chick Gandil, predictably, had no intention of returning to the White Sox. Comiskey's detectives reported that, after the 1919 World Series, Gandil deposited thirty $1,000 bills in his hometown bank, and that he bought diamonds and other luxuries for himself and his wife that winter. In March of 1920 Gandil turned down a reported $2,000 raise, and elected to remain at home in California and play semipro ball for $75 a game. With Gandil, Risberg, and Weaver all threatening to sit out the season, the White Sox faced the prospect of replacing three-quarters of their infield.

Comiskey had never had so many holdouts on his team, not even after his 1906 world champions created so much rancor about their 1907 salaries. To Comiskey's great annoyance, these holdouts were the very players who pocketed thousands of dollars in crooked money mere months before (with

Joe's signature as it appeared on his disputed 1920 contract (National Baseball Library).

the exception of Weaver). Comiskey was especially upset at Risberg, who hit .080 in the World Series, and Felsch, who batted only .192 against the Reds. However, Comiskey realized that if he took a hard line against his reluctant athletes, the scandal might explode and destroy the White Sox. It seems apparent, with the benefit of hindsight, that at least some of the conspirators realized that they had Comiskey in an awkward position.

In the end, the Old Roman finally decided to pay his players what they were worth. Cicotte got a raise to $10,000, and Felsch's salary nearly doubled from $3,750 to $7,000. Williams received an increase from $2,600 to $6,000, with a promised bonus of $1,000 for another 20-win season, and even the reserve McMullin got a healthy raise. Weaver's pay rose to over $7,000 and, amazingly, Comiskey cut the ten-day clause out of Weaver's contract.[5] Did Comiskey finally have a change of heart? Or, more likely, did he raise salaries across the board to buy the players' silence and keep them happy?

Again, Joe Jackson underestimated himself. If Felsch and Weaver were getting $7,000 each, shouldn't Jackson have been getting more than $8,000? Perhaps Joe should have stood firm for the $10,000 he demanded (and that Cicotte got) and the removal of the ten-day clause. The last thing Comiskey needed was another holdout, and Jackson could have benefited from the owner's belated largesse. Once more, Joe Jackson tied himself into a low salary for three years, just as he had done in 1914 and again in 1915. Bill Veeck, after reading Harry Grabiner's diaries in the 1960s, called Jackson "the world's worst negotiator."[6]

Charles Comiskey found himself in a vulnerable position. He could not risk the public exposure of the 1919 Series fix, since his enemies could use his own early awareness of the details against him. Also, with Red Faber healthy, the 1920 White Sox could pick up where the 1919 team left off and win the team's third pennant in the last four years. The temptation to cover up the scandal proved irresistible, so Comiskey and Grabiner soon got all the crooked players, except for Gandil, back in the fold with healthy raises. Comiskey, like Richard Nixon 50 years later, chose to hide the World Series mess and hope that the whole problem would simply fade away.

However, Comiskey wasn't going to provide those large raises solely out of his own pocket. The White Sox raised ticket prices across the board for the 1920 season. The 25-cent seats increased in price to 50 cents, and the 75-cent box seats went up to one dollar. Even with the dramatic increase in the team's payroll, Charles Comiskey was certain to reap a handsome profit for the 1920 campaign.

Joe Jackson arrived in Waco in mid–March, but he was not able to get on the field for two days. His trunks, containing all his baseball clothes and equipment, were lost somewhere between Savannah and Waco. Fortunately, the trunks arrived and Joe began working out in earnest.

Only one of the eight suspected players was not in a Chicago uniform for the start of the 1920 season. Chick Gandil was working as a plumber and playing semipro ball in Bakersfield, California, and no amount of cajoling from the White Sox could get him to sign a contract and join the team. This led to a great deal of newspaper speculation on who would replace Gandil at first base. Some writers suggested that Gleason move Swede Risberg to first, Buck Weaver to short, and Fred McMullin from the bench to third. Comiskey and Gleason knew this wouldn't work; McMullin was a valuable bench player but didn't hit well enough to play every day. Comiskey tried to pry the veteran first baseman Stuffy McInnis away from the Red Sox, but the Boston team turned down his offer.

In Gandil's place, Kid Gleason decided to try Ted Jourdan, a 25 year old from Louisiana who had hit well at Milwaukee. If Jourdan failed, figured Gleason, perhaps the veteran Shano Collins could fill the hole at first. Either way, at least Eddie Collins would have someone in the infield who would talk to him.

Even after the holdout players reported to camp, the writers couldn't help but notice a chill in the air. The seven remaining suspected players rarely spoke to anyone but each other. They rode together on the trains, ate together in the restaurants, and went to the movies or the bars together in the evenings. In previous years, the Gandil-Risberg-Weaver group sniped and argued with the Collins-Schalk-Faber group, but now there seemed to be no overt animosity between the seven suspected players and the rest of the team. In its place was a stony silence, an unbreachable wall of quiet.

Joe's guilt about the 1919 Series scandal gnawed at his conscience, and he and the other players fell into secretive conversations about the thrown ballgames. Joe told Eddie Cicotte that he only received $5,000 from Gandil, and Cicotte called Joe a "God-damned fool" for not getting the money in advance, as Cicotte had done.[7] During a preseason trip to Memphis, Joe asked Swede Risberg how much he had received. Risberg claimed that he only received $5,000, which Joe believed—accurately—was a "damned lie." Fred McMullin, however, refused to discuss the crooked Series. When Joe brought the matter up, McMullin turned on his heel and stalked away without a word.

The White Sox opened their 1920 season on April 14 against the Detroit Tigers, despite the snow which covered many of the seats in Comiskey Park. More than 31,000 fans braved the chill and saw Lefty Williams defeat the Tigers by a 3-2 score in 11 innings. Joe went hitless, but Buck Weaver pounded out four hits and drove in the game-winning run. Rain and snow kept the teams from playing for the next two days, but on April 17 Eddie Cicotte beat the Tigers again, 4-0. The crowds at Comiskey Park remained large through April and May, and it soon became apparent that 1920 would be the best attendance year for the White Sox by far, even with the steep rise in ticket prices.

Despite the euphoria of the fans, the writers seethed with disillusionment. They knew what had happened in the World Series six months before, and they were fully aware that the Sox were capable of winning another pennant and throwing the Series again. The writers also knew that there wasn't a thing they could say about it. They had no proof of wrongdoing by the players, and they could not air their suspicions without inviting a libel suit.

In response, the writers did their best to tiptoe around the matter, while dropping subtle hints in their columns. Jim Crusinberry, in the *Tribune*, alluded to Gleason's "bales of trouble with eccentric and mercenary players."[8] Robert Maxwell, in a syndicated column, wrote that "the hose appear to be run down at the heels and out at the toes, and it will take considerable darning to make them presentable ... [Kid Gleason] has been darning the Sox all spring, but in much stronger language." The success of the White Sox in 1920, wrote Maxwell, "is largely up to the contract jumpers, and there is no telling what they will do."[9]

Many of the writers picked the White Sox for fourth or fifth place, but the Sox won their first six games before they lost to Cleveland on April 27. In that game, Red Faber led 2-1 in the eighth inning when a fly ball by Cleveland's Larry Gardner sailed over Jackson's head in left field and rolled all the way to the fence. Jackson retrieved the ball and threw to Risberg, who made such a poor throw home that Gardner scored to tie the game. The Indians won the game in the ninth on a sacrifice fly by Charlie Jamieson. The next day, Tris Speaker made what the papers called "the greatest catch in League Park history" when he caught a long drive by Joe Jackson over his shoulder, then slammed headfirst into the center field fence. Joe belted a homer over League Park's 40-foot right field wall and into Lexington Avenue two innings earlier, but Speaker's catch saved the game for the Indians, who beat Eddie Cicotte by a 7-4 score.

On May 1, the White Sox stood alone in second place, one and a half games behind the surprising Boston Red Sox. Most people expected Boston to drop to the bottom of the league after they sold almost all of their good players (Babe Ruth, Carl Mays, and others) to the Yankees. The biggest surprise of the early season, however, was the poor performance of the Detroit team. The Tigers were expected to challenge Cleveland for the pennant, but they lost a league record 13 games in a row to begin the season. By May 1, the Tigers were already ten games out of first place and out of the pennant race.

Joe Jackson got off to a superb start in the 1920 season. He battled Cleveland's Doc Johnston for the batting lead with a .469 mark for the month of April. On May 1, Joe hit a single, double and triple in an 8-5 win against the Browns, missing the cycle by one hit. Ty Cobb, bothered by knee and ankle problems, entered May with a .284 mark, and it appeared that Jackson would defeat Cobb in the batting race for the first time in his career.

The Indians jumped out to an early lead, and the Red Sox and White Sox held second and third through the month of May. Felsch, Eddie Collins, Weaver, and Jackson all belted the ball at a .300 clip or better in the early going. On May 20 the White Sox hit five triples against Walter Johnson, defeating Washington by a 13-5 score. The next day, Joe Jackson's double in the eleventh inning beat the Nats 11-9.

Joe was perfectly healthy in the 1920 season until he went to Philadelphia in late May. "Joe Jackson ate some crab meat in Philadelphia Thursday," said the Cleveland paper on May 29. "He forgot to ask how long said crab had been dead. The sequel was an attack of ptomaine poisoning which kept Joe out of the lineup yesterday."[10] This illness put Joe on the sidelines for an important weekend series against the league-leading Indians, in which Tris Speaker's Cleveland team won three of four from the defending league champions. This minislump dropped the White Sox into fourth place, five and a half games behind the Indians. Joe, still weakened from his illness, rejoined the lineup on Memorial Day in St. Louis, going one for nine in a doubleheader.

The Red Sox cooled off and fell off the pace in early June, but the resurgent New York Yankees climbed the standings and entered the pennant chase. Their newest acquisition, Babe Ruth, started the season slowly, with no home runs in April, but Ruth soon found his groove. He belted an unprecedented 12 homers in the month of May, and on June 2 he hit three more in a doubleheader against the Nationals. Joe Jackson was so impressed that he asked the Babe for one of his bats to keep as a souvenir. Ruth handed Joe one of his favorite clubs with the admonition, "Just don't use it against us, okay, kid?" Joe kept his word; he used it against other teams, but not against the Yankees, who passed Chicago in the standings and battled the Indians for first place.

The Sox fell six games behind the Yankees and Indians by mid–June. First baseman Ted Jourdan stopped hitting, and Gleason moved Shano Collins from the outfield to first base to replace him. Collins and Nemo Leibold had shared right field in a platoon arrangement until then, but now Leibold became the permanent right fielder, against left- and right-handed pitching. Red Faber regained his effectiveness and again emerged as the ace of the pitching staff, while Dickie Kerr picked up where he left off in the World Series and pitched brilliantly ("little pitchers have big years," said the writers). Faber, Cicotte, Williams, and Kerr gave the Sox the best pitching rotation in the league, but the bullpen was frightfully weak, and Gleason came to rely on complete games from his starters.

Joe Jackson, in third place behind George Sisler and Tris Speaker in the batting race, led the Sox into a three-game series against Cleveland on July 5–6. The Sox beat the Tribe in a doubleheader behind Williams and Kerr, then won again the next day to move to within three and a half games of the lead. In the July 6 game, Joe saved the game in the eleventh inning with a diving, tumbling catch of a sure triple by Cleveland's Larry Gardner. Joe's catch kept the score tied until Felsch pounded a game-winning homer in the bottom of the eleventh. Ten days later, Joe belted the fourth grand slam of his career, an inside-the-park shot off Eric Ericksen, to provide the winning margin in a 8-5 win over Washington.

Most people expected the Sox to challenge the Indians, but the Sox played mediocre ball in late July and fell six games out of first place by the end of the month. The White Sox hit well, but their fielding was inconsistent, and rumors soon swept the league that the Sox were not giving 100 percent of their effort on the field. On July 14, Lefty Williams took a 4-3 lead into the eighth inning against the Nationals, but a walk and three triples in succession scored three Washington runs and gave the White Sox a 6-4 loss. Joe's grand slam carried the day on the 16th, but the next day, Eddie Cicotte fell behind 8-2 in the first five innings against the Yankees, who won the game by a 20-5 score. The Yankees scored four runs against Lefty Williams in the first inning on the 18th, as the New Yorkers took an 8-5 win, dropping the White Sox further down in the standings.

The Yankees and White Sox then split two doubleheaders in the next two days. In the second game on the 19th, Babe Ruth belted two homers off Dickie Kerr, but Joe Jackson saved the day with a home run of his own to end the three game losing streak. On the 20th, Red Faber won the first game of the twin bill, but Eddie Cicotte pitched poorly again and lost the second. The Sox left town with only two wins in the crucial six-game series.

On July 25 the Indians defeated the Sox by a 7-2 score, and even the Cleveland writers smelled a rat. "Risberg did not look like a world's championship shortstop," said the *Plain Dealer*. "He had one bad throw to second when an easy double play was in front of him, let Wood's pop fly fall safely in front of him, and then went to sleep with the ball in his hand and allowed Chapman to stretch a single into a double."[11] The public didn't know it yet, but the White Sox were still throwing games.

There is no way of knowing how many of the seven suspected players took part in the shenanigans, but apparently some of the World Series conspirators found a way to pick up a few hundred extra dollars a game. A bad throw here, a dropped fly ball or a botched rundown there—it wasn't difficult to do, and it wasn't easy to detect. Buck Weaver told investigators after the season that Fred McMullin offered him $500 to "lay down" in a game in August.[12] Weaver reportedly turned down the offer, but the team's maddening inconsistency turned the spotlight of suspicion their way during the long, hot summer of 1920.

However, this time there was more at work besides greed. The ballplayers now paid the price for the easy money they made in October 1919, because the gamblers who profited from the Series scandal now held the threat of exposure over the tainted White Sox. The gamblers used threats to get the players to lose certain games, and the players complied, unwilling as they were to disappoint those gamblers with connections to organized crime.

Red Faber had no doubt that some of his teammates were not giving their best efforts. Forty years later, he told Eliot Asinof, author of *Eight Men Out*, that in 1920 he never knew when some disaster might strike during the course of a game.[13] Nemo Leibold, the Sox right fielder, also knew that something strange was happening. He talked to his friend and former teammate Roger Peckinpaugh, now the shortstop for the Yankees, before an important New York–Chicago series in the 1920 season. Peckinpaugh recalled, many years later, that Leibold was upset. "Something screwy is going on here," said Leibold to Peckinpaugh. "I don't know what it is, but it's something screwy, all right. You guys bear down and you ought to take all four games."[14]

In addition, some of the White Sox players were doing some informal financial planning. They knew that if the Yankees won the pennant, the World Series might set a record for attendance, especially if the New York Giants won the flag in the National League. This would make a greater pool of receipts, and more second-, third-, and fourth-place money to be divided among the first-division finishers of each league. Also, if the White Sox lost the 1920 flag, they would be available to play a profitable, well-attended City Series against the crosstown Cubs.[15] Some of the players believed that they could make more money by throwing games, losing the pennant, and winning the City Series than they would make in winning the World Series.

Joe Jackson felt alienated from most of the other Series conspirators, especially Risberg and McMullin, who appeared to be the ringleaders of the fixers. Joe never talked much to anyone on the team except Williams and Byrd Lynn anyway, but in 1920 his emotional distance from his teammates was complete. His evenings on the road consisted of going to the movies or bars with Lefty Williams, his best friend on the team. Byrd Lynn, Williams' roommate, found himself frozen out of Jackson's and Williams' conversations. Lynn was not a part of the Series conspiracy, and perhaps Joe was afraid of letting the secret of the thrown Series slip in an unguarded moment.

Joe also believed that Gandil and Risberg had taken far more money from the scandal than they had admitted to him. Eventually, Joe came to suspect Williams also. When the whole mess exploded in late September, Joe was asked in court about the division of money. "I think that those fellers cut it up to suit themselves," Joe replied.

Lee Magee, whose real name was Leopold Hoernschemeyer, was an infielder in the National League in the late 1910s and a good friend of the crooked Hal Chase. Magee seems to have been one of the most incompetent game-fixers in the league. In late 1918 he and Chase, both members of the Reds at the time, arranged to throw a game, betting heavily on it beforehand. Magee was foolish enough to give Chase a check for $500 for his part of the wager. With the Reds behind by one run in the bottom of the eleventh inning, Magee found himself on base when Reds slugger Edd Roush whacked an inside-the-park homer to win the game. "Run, you son of a bitch, run!" screamed Roush at Magee, who reluctantly scored the tying run in the game that he was supposed to have fixed!

To make matters worse, Magee then stopped payment on his check to Chase. National League president John Heydler found the check in the course of his investigation of Chase in 1919, and Magee was dropped by the Cubs, with whom he had signed. The league hoped that Magee would go quietly, but he still had a year to go on his contract, and he sued the Cubs for the balance of his salary. Magee's suit made national headlines in July of 1920. He lost, but the Magee case gave the public a peek into the sordid world of baseball gambling.

John McGraw, manager of the New York Giants, also raised eyebrows across the nation when he released his star centerfielder, Benny Kauff, to the minor leagues in early July. Kauff, the former "Ty Cobb of the Federal League," was one of the Giants' best players, but his indifferent play and his friendship with Hal Chase drew suspicion his way. Any one of the other major league teams could have claimed Kauff, but all 15 clubs passed on the opportunity.

More disturbing headlines soon came to the attention of the fans. In August of 1920, the Pacific Coast League suspended several players and investigated reports that their 1919 pennant race had been thrown. It appeared that the team in Vernon, a suburb of Los Angeles, raised a slush fund to pay off players in Salt Lake City and Portland to lose the pennant race on purpose. The league not only suspended the players, but also found it necessary to physically ban them from the league's ballparks. The name of Hal Chase surfaced here too. In early 1920 Chase, who drew his release from the New York Giants in 1919 and returned to his home state of California, was banned from the league and its parks for gambling-related activities. Inevitably, with new revelations about baseball gambling making the headlines almost daily, rumors about the 1919 World Series gained more currency.

Chicago Tribune writer Jim Crusinberry obtained a much more disturbing look into the truth of the crooked Series. In July of 1920, Kid Gleason called Crusinberry and invited him to listen to a conversation that the Kid was having in a local bar. Crusinberry and fellow writer Ring Lardner arrived and found Gleason deep in conversation with, of all people, Abe Attell. The two writers sat at a table behind Gleason and Attell and listened to the incredible details of the Series fix. "You know, Kid," explained Attell, "I hated to do that to you, but I thought I was going to make a lot of money and I needed it, and then the big guy [Rothstein] double-crossed me."[16] The writers couldn't reveal this conversation to the public, since Attell would undoubtedly deny it all, but now the writers knew for certain what Gleason had known since the previous October.

In the meantime, the White Sox entered the month of August in third place, four and a half games behind the Indians, when the Yankees came into Chicago for a four-game series. A crowd of over 40,000, a new major league attendance record, jammed Comiskey Park on a Sunday to see Eddie Cicotte beat the Yankees 3-0. The most spectacular play of the game occurred in the fourth inning, when Joe Jackson robbed Babe Ruth of a homer with a tumbling catch into the outfield overflow. Joe didn't have the ball when he emerged from the crowd, but he convinced the umpires that he had caught it and then lost it to a fan. The umpires called Ruth out and precipitated a ten-minute argument on the part of the Yankees, who argued loud and long that Joe dropped the ball. They continued the game under protest only after the umpires threw manager Miller Huggins out of the game.

The Yankees bombed Lefty Williams 7-0 on Monday—the game featured Ruth's 38th homer—but the Sox won the next day, as Red Faber walked Ruth three times and Joe Jackson drove in all the Chicago runs in a 3-1 win. On August 4, Joe drove in four runs with two singles and a triple as the Sox beat the Yankees 10-3 behind Dickie Kerr.[17] The four-game set with the Yankees drew a total attendance of 126,000, a new major league record for a non-holiday series, as the White Sox pulled to within half a game of the second place New Yorkers and within four and a half games of the first-place Indians.

Jackson's average rose to .400 on August 4, the latest he had been at that mark in any season since 1913, but the whispers soon started again. Joe fell into a slump that dropped his average back into the .380s, and the Sox lost to Boston on August 5 in a game that featured a poor throw from the outfield and two baserunning mistakes by Jackson. In the third inning, Joe was on first when Amos Strunk hit a blooper into right field; Joe misjudged the ball and was forced out at second. In the sixth inning, Joe belted a line drive to the wall in left center, but he slammed into Boston first baseman Stuffy McInnis and gained only two bases instead of a triple or inside-the-park homer.[18] Two days later, Swede Risberg committed three errors in another loss to the Red Sox. However, the White Sox then swept a four-game set against Washington and moved within a game of the lead.

The Indians nearly unraveled in August of 1920. On August 16 in New York, Yankee pitcher Carl Mays hit Joe's ex-teammate Ray Chapman in the head with a pitched ball. Chapman, perhaps the most popular member of the Indians among the fans and the players, never regained consciousness and died the next morning at the age of 29. The grief-stricken Indians wobbled; manager Tris Speaker suffered a nervous collapse at the funeral home and was ordered to bed by his physician, and outfielder Jack Graney became so hysterical at Chapman's funeral that he had to be restrained.[19] Graney recovered quickly, but Speaker did not return to the Cleveland lineup for five days as the Tribe lost their hold on first place. The stunned Indians defeated the Yankees on the 19th, but on the 21st they lost a doubleheader to Boston by scores of 12-0 and 4-0.

In the meantime, Joe Jackson belted a homer in each game of a doubleheader sweep of the A's in Philadelphia, putting the White Sox in first place. Three days later, the White Sox owned a lead of three and a half games over the reeling Indians, who appeared to be more interested in getting revenge on Carl Mays than they were in winning games. They started a petition to have Mays banned from baseball and encouraged the other American League teams to join in. The Red Sox, who hated Mays for running out on their team the previous year, happily joined Cleveland's effort, but other teams balked, and soon the protest against Mays fizzled out. The White Sox showed no interest in joining the Cleveland protest, possibly because a club as badly divided as the Sox could hardly agree on much of anything.

On August 26 the Sox defeated the Yankees in New York by a 16-4 count, though Babe Ruth hit his 44th homer of the season, and the Chicagoans appeared to be in control of the pennant race. Then the roof fell in on Gleason's crew. The Sox lost two to the Yankees and three in a row in Boston to fall back into second place. The Sox then lost two to St. Louis before they finally broke their seven-game losing streak against the Browns on September 4, in the second game of a doubleheader.

The stench of crooked baseball was overpowering. On August 30 in Boston, the hard-hitting White Sox managed only five singles, three by Eddie Collins, as Lefty Williams lost a 4-0 decision. On August 31, Joe Jackson let a fly ball get over his head for a crucial error in Cicotte's 7-3 loss to the Red Sox. Cicotte and Williams seemed to let up at the worst possible moments, and catcher Ray Schalk shouted himself hoarse, screaming at both pitchers for crossing up his signals. The next day, the Sox were behind 6-2 when they hit four singles in the ninth inning and couldn't manage to tally a single run.

In the game on September 1, a Boston batter hit a lazy fly to left field that dropped between Joe Jackson and Happy Felsch, neither of whom seemed to make much effort to catch it. It fell for a double. The next batter bunted to the pitcher, Dickie Kerr, who threw a perfect peg to third base. Buck Weaver, however, dropped the ball, and the runner was safe. The Red Sox scored three runs in that inning, after which Kerr threw his glove across the infield in disgust.

Kerr then confronted Risberg and Weaver, who were standing together. "If you'd told me you wanted to lose this game," snarled the angry pitcher, "I could have done it a lot easier." Risberg answered with a punch, and a near-riot erupted on the Chicago bench. Eddie Collins and Kid Gleason dragged Risberg and Kerr apart as the Boston players looked on in amazement.[20]

Eddie Collins had seen enough. His White Sox fell from first place all the way to third in only seven days, and he could no longer keep silent about what he had witnessed. When the Sox returned to Chicago, the frustrated captain paid a visit to Charles Comiskey and vented his suspicions. The owner merely thanked Collins for his concern and sent him on his way. The Old Roman knew that his carefully orchestrated cover-up would collapse soon enough. All Comiskey could do was wait for the other shoe to drop.

It dropped that very week.

Chapter 17

The Grand Jury

> Taking him by and large, Jackson was as nice a fellow as I ever knew in sports, and the disclosure that he had sold out to the Rothstein-Attell combination came to me as a small personal tragedy. I didn't believe it then, and there are times, even now, I don't like to believe it...
>
> —*Joe Williams, 1946*[1]

On the morning of August 31, 1920, William Veeck, president of the Chicago Cubs, received a series of ominous telegrams from Detroit. The telegrams warned Veeck that the Cubs-Phillies game to be played that afternoon was fixed. Gamblers were storming the speakeasies in Detroit, desperately trying to get their money down on a sure thing, and the odds shifted wildly—all for an unimportant late-season game with no impact on the standings. Detroit was an American League city, no less.

Veeck moved quickly, removing his scheduled pitcher Claude Hendrix and inserting his ace, the great Grover Alexander. Veeck also offered Alexander a $500 bonus to win the game. Nonetheless, the Phillies beat Alexander 3-0.

Veeck hired a detective agency to investigate the matter quietly, but on September 4 the *Chicago Herald and Examiner* exposed the story. The details, which included descriptions of gamblers waving thousand-dollar bills in the air, excitedly poring over pitch-by-pitch accounts of a meaningless game in the other league, filled the public with disgust.

The rival *Tribune*, not to be outdone, gauged that the public was fed up with baseball's foot-dragging. *Tribune* sportswriter Jim Crusinberry figured that the truth of the 1919 World Series was ready to be exposed. He arranged for a prominent Chicagoan named Fred Loomis to write a letter to the editor demanding a thorough investigation of major league baseball.

The letter, which Loomis signed but was actually written by Crusinberry, was published on the front page of the sports section on September 5. In it, Loomis (and Crusinberry) demanded the one thing that baseball had successfully avoided for a year—a grand jury investigation of the 1919 Series. "There is a perfectly good Grand Jury located in this county," the letter stated. "The citizens and taxpayers of Illinois are maintaining such an institution for the purpose of investigating any alleged infraction of the law. Those who possess evidence of any gambling last Fall in the World Series must come forward so that justice will be done in this case where public confidence seems to have been so flagrantly violated."[2]

The public outcry forced State's Attorney Maclay Hoyne and Circuit Court Judge Charles McDonald to impanel a grand jury. It met for the first time on September 7, eight days before the local Democratic primary election. For those eight days, Hoyne moved too slowly for the public's taste; he was not only busy campaigning for reelection but was widely known to be a close friend of Charles Comiskey, and Hoyne lost his job in the balloting on September 15. He then left Chicago for a vacation, and Ban Johnson stepped up to the plate.

Johnson saw his chance to play the role of the white knight of baseball and to destroy his enemy Charles Comiskey. He had not been idle. For a year, Johnson, motivated by his hatred of Comiskey, had diligently pieced together the story of the scandal, and by September 1920 he had all of his facts in order. On September 20, Johnson unveiled his findings to Judge McDonald, providing the judge with a virtual road map for the investigation. The delighted judge, no stranger to ambition himself, and Assistant State's Attorney Hartley Replogle attacked the investigation with renewed vigor. The Cubs-Phillies affair faded into the background as the public's attention returned to the 1919 World Series.

Many sources insist that Johnson knew the whole story by early 1920 and waited until September to reveal his evidence in order to destroy Comiskey's White Sox at the height of the pennant race. Johnson, these sources state, found out about the Cubs-Phillies game of August 31 and tipped off the *Herald and Examiner* personally. Bill Veeck, son of Cubs president William Veeck and the future owner of the White Sox, took that line even farther. Veeck, who read the diaries of Comiskey's secretary

Harry Grabiner, claimed that a cabal headed by Johnson wished to destroy the White Sox, drive Comiskey out of baseball, and then buy the team at a fire-sale price. The younger Veeck also made the astonishing charge that the telegrams his father received on August 31, 1920, came not from gamblers, but from Ban Johnson himself.[3]

Others say that Johnson waited for Charles McDonald to be appointed to the circuit court, so that Johnson could control the investigation through a friendly judge. Johnson and McDonald were good friends from their days as guests at Comiskey's hunting lodge before the Johnson-Comiskey feud heated up in earnest. Already baseball men were discussing the creation of a single, all-powerful Commissioner of Baseball, and Johnson was grooming his friend McDonald for the job. In any case, the guiding hand behind the investigation belonged to Comiskey's mortal enemy Ban Johnson, and the Grand Jury subpoenaed, as one of its first witnesses, Charles Comiskey himself.

Comiskey's testimony was predictably self-serving. He claimed that he had made an investigation of the 1919 Series but found nothing of substance with which to formally accuse any one of his players. If Johnson had any evidence, said Comiskey, the rest of the American League knew nothing about it. The Old Roman blamed Johnson for the whole mess, insisting that the league president had not given him even the slightest amount of assistance in tracking down the truth behind the rumors. Johnson, in turn, told the writers that he had heard that "the White Sox would not dare win the 1920 pennant because the managers of a gambling syndicate, alleged to have certain players in their power, had forbidden it!"[4]

Comiskey reminded the public of an embarrassing disclosure that came to light in the fall of 1919, when the Old Roman's campaign to oust Johnson from the league presidency heated up in earnest. In 1916, Johnson loaned $100,000 of his own money to James Dunn so that Dunn could buy the Cleveland Indians. Dunn had only repaid half of the amount, so that made the American League president, in effect, the part owner of the Cleveland team, the very team that was battling the White Sox for the pennant. Some of the Chicago players complained that Johnson had favored the Indians for years, ever since he engineered the trade of Tris Speaker from Boston to Cleveland in 1916, and that the league president wanted to wreck the White Sox in order to protect his own financial interest in the Indians. As the days of testimony dragged on, the investigation went nowhere, bogged down in a public rehashing of the Johnson-Comiskey feud.

In the meantime, the Sox continued the pennant scramble. They pulled into virtual tie for first place on September 10, but they fell back

to second when they committed seven errors the next day in a 9-7 loss to
Boston, in a game which featured a three-run homer by Joe Jackson. They
dropped to third place when Lefty Williams lost, 5-0, to the Nationals
on the twelfth. Two days later, the Sox lost a 7-0 decision to Washington; some of the papers decried the Nationals' runs as "outright gifts" of
poor fielding and bad baserunning.[5] The White Sox knocked the Yankees out of the race with three wins in a row the following week (after
some of the honest players physically threatened Eddie Cicotte if he didn't
win his game[6]), but Cleveland maintained its hold on first place.

Through it all, the seven White Sox players waited, day by day, for
the finger of accusation to be pointed their way. They understood little
about the boardroom machinations playing out around them, but they
knew that their names would eventually come to the public's attention.
The pressure seemed to wear on Cicotte the most. When Giants pitcher
Rube Benton, a former teammate of Hal Chase, appeared before the
Grand Jury and spilled the names of Cicotte, Gandil, Williams, and
Felsch, Eddie Cicotte knew that his long nightmare was finally drawing
to an close.

Joe Jackson, too, knew that the end was near. Jackson and Happy
Felsch discussed the matter one day while walking in the outfield before
a game. They agreed that they would soon be called before the Grand
Jury, probably in a few days. There was nothing that either man could do
about it now.

The White Sox invaded Cleveland for a crucial three-game series
against the Indians in late September. They needed to win at least two
to stay in the pennant chase, and on September 23, a Thursday, the Sox
played like the defending league champs with a 10-3 win. The Sox suffered
a setback when Cleveland's rookie pitcher Duster Mails beat Dickie Kerr
on Friday, allowing only three singles by Collins, Jackson, and Felsch, but
they regrouped behind Lefty Williams with a 5-1 win on Saturday. Joe
Jackson belted two doubles and a home run to pace the win before 31,000
screaming fans in Cleveland.

It was a difficult performance under pressure, since the morning
papers were full of the newest revelations from the hearings in Chicago.
Grand Jury foreman Henry Brigham revealed that on the previous day,
the jury received the names of the eight Chicago players whose checks
were held up by Comiskey after the 1919 World Series. Joe and the other
players knew that their day of reckoning was not far off, because the papers
printed the names of the eight players that morning, and for the first time
Joe heard jeers and taunts from the stands in Cleveland. He didn't like it
one bit, and when Joe homered in the fifth inning, he thumbed his nose

at the Cleveland fans as he rounded third. The fans seemed stunned by the insulting gesture, and when the embattled slugger repeated the insult, the fans loudly booed their former hero.[7]

The White Sox then went to Detroit and beat the Tigers on Sunday and Monday, but the Indians beat St. Louis twice to stay half a game ahead of the Sox.

On Monday, September 27, the *Philadelphia North American* published an interview with Billy Maharg that, for the first time, laid out the inner workings of the scheme, especially the $10,000 payoff to Eddie Cicotte. Maharg, who lost all his money in the fix the year before and was now working on the assembly line of an auto plant, stated that the first, second, and eighth games were thrown by the White Sox. More importantly, he identified Cicotte as the man who came to Maharg and Bill Burns with the offer to fix the Series.

By this time, Cicotte had reached the end of his emotional tether. He could no longer live with his guilty secret, and the pressure weighed more heavily on his conscience with each passing day. Kid Gleason, for his part, knew that the whole truth would never emerge unless one of the players confessed. Gleason told Comiskey that Eddie Cicotte would be the first of the eight men to crack under the strain. "I've been working on him all summer," said the manager. "Do you want me to bring him in?"

Comiskey, who now realized that his attempted cover-up was a complete failure, resigned himself to the inevitable. The Old Roman hoped to salvage some credibility by bringing the players in to confess, before Ban Johnson could get hold of them and claim the credit for himself.

The next morning, on an off day for the White Sox, Gleason went to Cicotte's hotel room and convinced the pitcher to tell Comiskey the whole story. Cicotte went to the office of the club attorney, Alfred Austrian, and, after a nerve-racking wait, an attendant ushered him into a room with Comiskey, Gleason, and Austrian. Cicotte slumped heavily into a chair and broke down. "I'm a crook, Mr. Comiskey," sobbed Cicotte. "I'm a crook, and I got $10,000 for being a crook."

"Don't tell me," said Comiskey to the pitcher, "tell it to the grand jury!" Austrian then escorted Cicotte to the courthouse.

For more than two hours, Eddie Cicotte told the Grand Jury of his involvement in the fix. He told how he'd gotten ten thousand-dollar bills and sewn them into the lining of his jacket. He described how he deflected Jackson's throw from the outfield to let a Cincinnati runner score. He described his anguish when his friends bet huge sums on the White Sox, and how he betrayed them by keeping his silence. Cicotte did not even tell his wife about the scheme. "I'm through with baseball," said

Cicotte sadly. "I'm going to lose myself if I can and start life all over again."[8]

Cicotte said little about the organization of the scheme itself, despite the judge's prodding. Cicotte named only the small-timers Burns and Maharg as the plotters behind the fix. He told the grand jury nothing at all about Attell and Rothstein, although he attended the meeting in Cincinnati with Attell on September 30, 1919. Cicotte found it prudent to serve up the small fry and let the big fish swim away. He had a wife and children to think about.

Joe Jackson reacted to the growing turmoil by getting drunk on Monday night.

Jackson woke up on Tuesday, September 28, with a painful hangover. He knew he was in trouble, but Katie wasn't there to advise him. Jackson needed a clear head to decide on his next course of action, and his wasn't. Impulsively, he called the Circuit Court building and asked for Judge McDonald. "Judge, you've got to control this thing. I'm an honest man..." pleaded Jackson.

"I know, Jackson, that you are not!" thundered the judge, and slammed down the phone.

Jackson then went out for a walk and met up with Risberg and Felsch. The worst had happened; Cicotte was testifying at that very moment, spilling the beans. Risberg desperately attempted to stop the flow of information. "Just keep your mouth shut, Joe, that's all," said Risberg menacingly. "I swear I'll kill you if you squawk!" Risberg was the master of the one-punch knockout, and Jackson knew better than to tangle with the hard-living shortstop.

Thoroughly confused, Jackson called Judge McDonald again. This time the judge was more conciliatory. He advised Jackson to come to the Grand Jury room and tell his story. Jackson had a few more drinks, put on a suit and bow tie, then left the hotel. When Jackson arrived at the courthouse, Charles Comiskey's lawyer Alfred Austrian was waiting for him.

Alfred Austrian was a Harvard graduate, a senior partner in one of the most prestigious law firms in Chicago. He spoke in confident and self-assured tones, as had Chick Gandil when the first baseman roped Joe into the scheme in the first place. Austrian politely, but firmly, advised Jackson to tell what he knew about the fix. Joe at first claimed that he had nothing to confess, but Austrian shook his head. That would do no good, said the lawyer. Tell everything and you'll stay out of trouble, advised Austrian, because the Grand Jury wants to indict the gamblers, not the ballplayers. Austrian's words, like Gandil's 12 months before, made sense to the uncertain, intimidated Southerner.

Jackson, like Cicotte, had not thought to call a lawyer of his own. He trusted Austrian's promise that he would not be indicted. This was a huge mistake, since Austrian was representing Comiskey's interests, not Jackson's. An attorney looking out for Joe Jackson would have recognized that Comiskey's interests in the matter were at odds with those of Jackson and would never have allowed the ballplayer to confess.

Austrian pulled a piece of paper from his briefcase and told Jackson to sign it. The confused and half-drunk Jackson scratched his signature on the dotted line. He had no way of knowing that he had signed a waiver of immunity. Austrian then took Jackson to Judge McDonald's chambers, where the judge warned Jackson to tell the truth or face charges of perjury. Joe promised to tell what he knew.

Hartley Replogle then appeared to lead Jackson down the hall to the Grand Jury room. Dozens of reporters and photographers blocked the way, and Jackson bulled through the crowd like a football player, cursing and sweating, shielding his bloodshot eyes from the painful flashbulbs. According to the Associated Press, Jackson muttered, "I am going to reform," before he entered the Grand Jury room, though the scene was so tumultuous that it would have been difficult to make out anything Joe may have said. Finally, Joe made it through the chaos, and he sat down to testify. Jackson's testimony, for the most part, supported Cicotte's. Joe explained that Chick Gandil approached him about the fix, and that Gandil promised him $20,000 and delivered only $5,000 through Lefty Williams:

Q. How much did he (Gandil) promise you?

A. $20,000 if I would take part.

Q. And you said you would?

A. Yes, sir.

Q. When did he promise you the $20,000?

A. It was to be paid after each game.

Q. How much?

A. Split up in some way. I don't know just how much it amounts to, but during it would amount to $20,000. Finally Williams brought me this $5,000, and threw it down.

Q. What did you say to Williams when he threw down the
   $5,000?

A. I asked him what the hell had come off here.

Q. What did he say?

A. He said Gandil said we all got a screw through Abe Attell.
   Gandil said that we got double-crossed through Abe
   Attell, he got the money and refused to turn it over to him.
   I don't think Gandil was crossed as much as he crossed us.[9]

Replogle and Brigham, the jury foreman, probed Jackson about the
inner workings of the fix, but Jackson knew very little about it, and he
revealed even less than Cicotte did. Jackson never met Abe Attell, and
all reliable accounts agree that Jackson was not present at either of the
two meetings called by Gandil before the Series began. All Joe knew is
that he got his $5,000 from Lefty Williams, who got it from Chick
Gandil. He had no idea where Gandil got it.

According to the story that appeared in the *New York Times* the next
day, "Jackson testified … that throughout the series he either struck out
or hit easy balls when hits would mean runs."[10] Unfortunately, this oft-
quoted passage, which is usually reported at face value since it came from
the highly respected *Times*, was patently untrue. Joe never said any such
thing, and testified that he always played all out:

Q. Did you make any intentional errors yourself that day (in
   Game 4)?

A. No, sir, not during the whole series.

Q. Did you bat to win?

A. Yes.

Q. And run the bases to win?

A. Yes, sir.

Q. And fielded the balls at the outfield to win?

A. I did.

Still, Jackson left room for doubt about his own intentions during
the Series. In response to a question about the second game, Jackson
replied, "We went ahead and threw the second game … I said to him
[Gandil] 'What are you going to do?'" Jackson also stated that he wanted
to win the Series in 1920, "above all times."

Q. Why?

A. Because I wanted to get in there and beat some National League club to death, that's what I wanted to do.

Q. You didn't want to do that so bad last year, did you?

A. Well, down in my heart I did, yes.

Jackson testified for more than two hours, but the most telling moment came about halfway through. Replogle asked, "Weren't you very much peeved that you only got $5,000 and you expected to get twenty?"

Jackson looked at the floor. "No," he said quietly. "I was ashamed of myself."

Joe Jackson finished his testimony at about 3:30 in the afternoon. He was placed in protective custody, though he was not arrested, and although some newspaper accounts say that Joe exited the courthouse with his face hidden behind his hat, Joe came out of the Grand Jury room with a smile on his face. "I got a big load off my chest!" said Jackson in the hall outside. "I'm feeling better."

"Don't ask Joe any questions," said Replogle to the assembled newspapermen. "He's gone through beautifully, and we don't want him bothered." A car appeared, and Jackson got in with two bailiffs, who drove Jackson back to his South Side hotel.[11]

That afternoon, a telegram arrived from Charles Comiskey. It said:

> To: Charles Risberg, Fred McMullin, Joe Jackson, Oscar Felsch, George Weaver, C. P. Williams, and Eddie Cicotte:
>
> You and each of you are hereby notified of your indefinite suspension as a member of the Chicago American League Baseball Club.
>
> Your suspension is brought about by information which has just come to me directly involving you and each of you in the baseball scandal resulting from the world's series of 1919.
>
> If you are innocent of any wrongdoing you and each of you will be reinstated; if you are guilty you will be retired from baseball for the rest of your lives if I can accomplish it.
>
> Until there is a finality to this investigation it is due to the public that I take this action, even though it costs Chicago the pennant.
>
> Chicago American Baseball Club
> by Charles A. Comiskey[12]

Since Joe had no need to take care of himself for the next day's game, he "went out and got polluted," in Jackson's own words.

Outside the Grand Jury room, Alfred Austrian preened for the news-men. "Mr. Comiskey and myself, as his counsel, have been working on this for a year," said Austrian. "We have spent a great deal of Mr. Comiskey's money to ferret it out. It is because of our investigation that the lid has been blown off this scandal."[13] Just six days before, Comiskey testified that he had found nothing in his investigation of the 1919 Series rumors. Now the White Sox owner insisted that he, not Ban Johnson, had cracked the case. Comiskey, after all, was the one who delivered Eddie Cicotte and Joe Jackson to the grand jury. If anyone could pose as the White Knight of Baseball, it would be Charles Comiskey.

It worked, at least for a while. For several days, newspapers across the country lionized Comiskey for his sacrifice in suspending his players, though it would certainly cost the White Sox the pennant. Colonel Jacob Ruppert, the beer baron and part owner of the Yankees, sent a telegram to Comiskey that said:

> Your action in suspending the players not only challenges our admiration but excites our sympathy and demands our immediate assistance. You are making a terrible sacrifice to preserve the integrity of the game. Therefore, in order for you to play out your schedule, and, if necessary, the World Series, our entire club is at your disposal.[14]

That evening, some reporters found Joe Jackson at the hotel, where the ballplayer was in a talkative mood. "I figured that somebody had squawked," said Jackson, "and that the place for me was the ground floor … I told [the judge], 'I got $5,000 and they promised me $20,000.'" Joe said that Judge McDonald "didn't care what I got [for throwing the Series], that if I got what I ought to get … I wouldn't be telling him my story. I don't think the judge likes me." Joe was feeling sorry for himself. "I never got that $15,000 that was coming to me," he complained.[15]

Joe also told the reporters that Risberg, Gandil, and Williams told him after the Series, "You poor simp, go ahead and squawk. Where do you get off if you do? We'll all say you're a liar, and every honest ballplayer in the world will say you're a liar. You're out of luck. Some of the boys were promised a lot more than you, and got a lot less."[16]

"And that's why I went down and told Judge McDonald and told the grand jury what I knew about the frame-up," said Jackson. It is not known how much alcohol Joe had ingested by that time, but there was no stopping the flow of words now. "And I'm giving you a tip. A lot of these sporting writers who have been roasting me have been talking about the third game of the World's Series being square. Let me tell you something. The eight of us did our best to kick it and little Dick Kerr won the game by his pitching. And because he won it these gamblers double-crossed us for double-crossing them."

Still, Jackson knew that he had played his last game in the major leagues, and he lashed out at the writers. "They've hung it on me. They ruined me when I went to the shipyards. But I don't care what happens now. I guess I'm through with baseball. I wasn't wise enough, like Chick, to beat them to it. But some of them will sweat before the show is over ... Now Risberg threatens to bump me off if I squawk. That's why I had all the bailiffs with me when I left the grand jury room this afternoon."

"I'm not under arrest yet and I've got the idea that after what I told them old Joe Jackson isn't going to jail. But I'm not going to get far from my protectors until this blows over. Swede is a hard guy."[17]

Joe told the writers that Lefty Williams gave him the $5,000 in a dirty envelope after the fourth game of the Series. The writers then sought out Williams, but the pitcher remained defiant under the pressure. "If I've got anything to say, I'll say it to the grand jury, if they want to call me," snarled the pitcher to a gaggle of reporters. "Nobody's got anything on me. My word is as good as Jackson's. They're not stampeding me. I've got no yellow streak. Did I give Jackson five thousand dollars? Ask the policemen on the corner. He may tell you something."[18]

However, after the pitcher had an evening to think it over, he decided to testify. His testimony mirrored both Cicotte's and Jackson's, and to the judge's annoyance Williams was unable to cast much light on the inner workings of the fix either. The only man who could do that was Chick Gandil, safely retired from baseball half a continent away.

Happy Felsch gave an interview to a newspaperman, Harry Reutlinger of the *Chicago American*, in which he summed up the fix. "Well, the beans are all spilled and I think that I am through with baseball," said Felsch. "I got my five thousand and I suppose the others got theirs too ... Don't make it appear like I'm trying to put up an alibi. I'm not. I'm as guilty as any of them. We all were in it alike."

"I got five thousand dollars," said Felsch sadly. "I could have got just about that much by being on the level if the Sox had won the Series. And now I'm out of baseball—the only profession I know anything about, and a lot of gamblers have gotten rich. The joke seems to be on us."[19]

The confessions of Cicotte, Jackson, and Williams finally exposed the scandal and the massive cover-up that kept it hidden from public view for almost a whole year. However, it was not readily apparent what the next step would be. The prosecutors found that the state of Illinois had no statute on its books specifically outlawing the fixing of a sporting event. The eight ballplayers, in the mere act of withholding their best efforts in the 1919 World Series, did not commit a crime. The state's attorney would have to prosecute the players and gamblers on the more nebulous charges of fraud and conspiracy, which made their task all the more difficult.

Captain Eddie Collins, by all reports, was devastated by the news of the scandal, but he also felt a great relief that the truth was finally known. "Hardly any of us have talked with any of those fellows except on the field since the season opened," said one unidentified player to the *Chicago Tribune*, though some writers credit the statement to Collins. "Even during the batting practice our gang stood in one group waiting our turn to hit and the other gang had their own group. We went along and gritted our teeth and played ball. We had to trail along with those fellows all summer, and all the time felt that they had thrown us down. It was tough. Now the load has been lifted. No wonder you feel like celebrating."[20]

Comiskey gave the honest players a good reason to celebrate. He called ten of them into his office, one at a time, and handed each man a check for $1,500. This, the Old Roman told them, would make up the difference between the loser's and winner's shares of the 1919 World Series money.

The untainted White Sox, who publicly thanked Comiskey in a statement to the press, felt as though a huge weight had been lifted from their backs. They went out to find Kid Gleason, but he wasn't at home, so they threw a party at Eddie Collins' apartment that evening. Ray Schalk spent the day in Gary, Indiana, but hurried back to Chicago to join the celebration, which lasted far into the night. The next day, rain prevented the Sox from working out at Comiskey Park; some of the "Clean Sox," as the papers were calling them, suggested that Kid Gleason should burn the uniforms of the eight suspended players.[21]

Some of Collins' teammates reflected on the difficult 1920 season. Byrd Lynn told the Associated Press that the suspected players watched the scoreboard all season long. "They always made errors which lost us the game when Cleveland and New York were losing. If Cleveland won, we won. If Cleveland lost, we lost. The idea was to keep up the betting odds, but not let us win the pennant."[22]

One player, who "refused to allow his name to be used," according to the *Cleveland Plain Dealer*, recalled the seven-game losing streak at the end of August. "Williams and Cicotte seemed to go bad without any reason. Some of us talked it over and agreed it looked like they were grooving the ball. Then Jackson, Felsch, and Risberg began dumping the ball to the infield every time they came to bat when we had a chance to get runs.... We all hope the grand jury will look into this end of the affair. If it fails to act, we may take some action ourselves—if we can get hold of some of the players we feel sure did the cheating."[23]

Perhaps the most interesting comment on the 1919 World Series came from umpire Billy Evans, who called balls and strikes in two games of the Series and worked the bases in the other six games. "Well, I guess I'm just a big dope," remarked the umpire. "That Series looked all right to me."[24]

The remainder of the White Sox team went to St. Louis to close the 1920 season with a three-game set against the Browns. They lost two of the three games and finished two games behind the pennant-winning Indians. Reports from the World Series cities, Cleveland and Brooklyn, said that there was little or no betting activity on the outcome of the Series. However, Cleveland manager Tris Speaker didn't want to leave anything to chance. He kept the identity of his starting pitcher secret before each game of the 1920 Series, which the Indians won in seven games.

In the meantime, Joe Jackson returned to Greenville for a visit, but the people of his hometown seemed to be as stunned and dismayed as all the other baseball fans around the country. Joe and Eddie Cicotte arranged for a series of exhibition games with hand-picked all-star teams of minor leaguers and mill league stars, but the Greenville Spinners refused to allow Joe and Cicotte to play the games in their ballpark. A few days later, a report in the *Chicago Tribune* stated that a Greenville apartment complex owner had refused to rent a room to the disgraced Cicotte.

While Joe hunted for a place to play, the local all-stars found themselves under pressure to pull out of the scheduled exhibition games. Local minor league teams took a dim view of their players competing against the recently-suspended Black Sox, and *The Sporting News* harshly criticized Pittsburgh shortstop Walter Barbare, a native of Greenville who signed an agreement to play for Joe's team. Barbare and others soon rescinded their agreements, and there is no record that the games were ever played.

In his last major league season, Joe Jackson hit .382 and set personal highs in home runs with 12 and runs batted in with 121. He pounded out more than 200 hits for the third time in his career, he led the league in triples for the third time with 20, and his slugging percentage of .589 was his highest since 1912. In many ways, 1920 was Joe's best season in the major leagues. He only struck out 14 times all year, and his 336 total bases stood as the team record for the White Sox for nearly 80 years.[25]

However, Jackson's 1920 season actually ended on October 22. On that day, the eight Chicago ballplayers, including Joe Jackson, were indicted by the Cook County Grand Jury on nine counts of fraud and conspiracy. Specifically, Joe and the others stood accused of engaging in a conspiracy to injure the business of their boss, Charles Comiskey, and of perpetrating a fraud on the ticket-buying public.

Joe Jackson's appearance before the Chicago Grand Jury on September 28, 1920, was responsible for one of the most enduring legends in the history of sports. As Joe exited the court building and ducked into a waiting car, a small child is said to have looked at the disgraced slugger and begged, "Say it ain't so, Joe." This tearful plea, reported by Charley Owens of the *Chicago Daily News* the next day, instantly crisscrossed the nation. It neatly summed up a nation's sadness and disbelief that its revered sports heroes had sold their integrity for a few thousand dollars.

In fact, the story was so poignant that it sounded too good to be true. Warren Brown, the veteran writer of the *Chicago Tribune*, recorded the incident in his book on the history of the White Sox, but later said that he doubted that it ever happened. "It's like most good stories," Brown told writer Dick Schaap in 1960. "It was made up."[26]

Several people on the scene remembered that a man stepped out of the crowd, looked down at Jackson's feet, and walked off without a word to the slugger. The man was heard telling his companions, "I told you the big son of a bitch wore shoes!"

Another who denied that the incident ever happened was Joe Jackson. "There wasn't a bit of truth in it," said Jackson to reporter Furman Bisher in 1949. "…There weren't any words passed between anybody except me and a deputy sheriff. When I came out of the building this deputy asked me where I was going, and I told him to the Southside. He asked me for a ride and we got in the car together and left. There was a big crowd hanging around the front of the building, but nobody else said anything to me. It just didn't happen, that's all. Charley Owens just made up a good story and wrote it."[27]

However, Jim Crusinberry of the *Chicago Tribune* claimed that he heard the child's words that day. Crusinberry, interviewed by Dick Schaap for *Coronet* magazine in 1960, said that a kid grabbed Jackson's hand as the ballplayer left the courthouse and said, "Say it isn't so, Joe. Say it isn't so." Crusinberry said that the ballplayer jumped into the car without a word and sped off.

Another man who waited outside the courthouse that day in 1920 was Donald Ewing, a 24-year-old night editor for the Associated Press. Forty years later, Ewing told Schaap that a group of children called out, "It isn't so, is it, Joe?"

The ballplayer turned around, according to Ewing, and said, "Yes, boys, I'm afraid it is."[28] Ewing then returned to his office and put the story on the Associated Press wire that evening.

Did Charley Owens make up this poignant tale, or did it really happen? We'll never know, but true or not, the story has earned an indelible place in American folklore. Eighty years later, it remains as perhaps the most enduring legacy of the Black Sox scandal.

Chapter 18

The Trial

For a good many years, I held a deep resentment against Cicotte for his initial confession. I felt I would never forgive the guy, but I think I have by now. Still, I don't believe we would have ever been caught if he hadn't gabbed.
— *Chick Gandil, 1956*[1]

The court ordered Joe Jackson and the other indicted players not to leave the state of Illinois until the trial could begin, so Joe returned from his visit to Greenville and spent an uncomfortable winter in chilly Chicago, far away from Savannah, his poolroom, and his valet service. As the months dragged on, Joe looked for a new outlet for his energies. He found it when he bought an interest in a poolroom across the street from the University of Chicago. If Joe couldn't play for the White Sox or return to his home in Georgia, at least he could make some money.

While Joe and the others spent their days consulting with their lawyers, the 16 baseball owners planned to change the very structure of the game itself. The National Commission, consisting of the presidents of the two leagues and a mutually acceptable club owner, had ruled the game since the American-National League merger in 1903. Ban Johnson, by engineering the selection of an owner friendly to his aims, controlled the Commission and, through it, baseball itself for nearly two decades. By 1920 many of the owners grew to resent his erratic dictatorship. The eight National League owners, frightened by the 1919 Series scandal and disgusted by the commission's consistent bias toward the

Judge Kenesaw Mountain Landis, first Commissioner of Baseball (author's collection).

American League, formed a plan to create a new National Commission to restore the public's shaken confidence in the sport.

The owners considered such luminaries as former President Taft and generals John J. Pershing and Leonard Wood to head the new Commission. Soon Judge Kenesaw Mountain Landis, the jurist who handled the Federal League case in 1915, emerged as the leading candidate. He was the man who faced down Standard Oil in 1907, fining the giant corporation a record amount of $29,000,000 for violating the anti-trust laws. Though the fine was overturned on appeal, the case made Judge Landis the most famous jurist in America.

Landis was a publicity-seeker (his enemies called him a dangerous demagogue), and twice during his tenure on the federal bench he was the object of impeachment resolutions. His demand that the German Kaiser stand trial in the United States for the deaths of American soldiers in World War I brought the Judge national headlines. There was no more publicly patriotic judge in America than Kenesaw Mountain Landis; the prison sentences he handed down to socialist agitators and draft evaders were almost medieval in their harshness.

However, the public approved of Landis' courtroom theatrics, and the trust-busting Judge gained a national reputation for honesty and integrity. Baseball's club owners, in turn, appreciated his hands-off posture when he presided over the Federal League case in 1915. The public demanded that baseball clean its house, and Judge Landis was just the man to do it.

Over Ban Johnson's strenuous objections, 11 of the 16 owners declared the 1903 National Agreement null and void and on November 11, 1920, appointed Landis as sole Commissioner at a salary of $50,000 a year. Johnson retained the presidency of the American League, but Judge Landis was now the virtual dictator of baseball. Johnson would serve as league president for another seven years, but he spent the rest of his term of office desperately trying to hold on to his last shreds of influence.

In the meantime, the investigation into the crooked World Series ground almost to a complete halt. The Grand Jury filed its final report on November 6, 1920, but Robert Crowe, the new state's attorney, found that the whole backbone of his case was missing. His predecessor, Maclay Hoyne, had left him with virtually nothing upon which to build a case against the Black Sox, because the signed confessions of Cicotte, Jackson, and Williams, along with their waivers of immunity, were missing from the files.

Crowe assigned the prosecution of the Black Sox to Assistant State's Attorney George Gorman, but Gorman soon realized that he had little, if anything, with which to work. Gorman stalled all through the winter of 1920-21, then, at the prodding of Ban Johnson, finally decided to get the process under way before the baseball season started. The prosecutors also faced an important deadline, since, under Illinois law, they were required to file charges within 18 months of the alleged crime. On February 14, 1921, the eight players were arraigned before Judge William Dever, but Cicotte, Williams, and Jackson repudiated their now-missing confessions, denying that they had conspired to fix the 1919 World Series. Judge Dever dismissed the original indictments; the prosecutors would have to rebuild the case from scratch.

Judge Landis, oddly enough, didn't take much interest in prosecuting the Black Sox. Perhaps the new commissioner realized that convictions would be difficult to obtain and that the whole exercise was a waste of time, especially with the confessions missing. Landis also knew that he could expel the eight men from baseball unilaterally, with or without a trial. "There is absolutely no chance for any of them to creep back into organized baseball. They are, and will remain, outlaws,"[2] declared the Judge in late 1920, though the eight players had only been suspended by the White Sox, not by baseball itself. On March 12, 1921, when it became obvious that the trial would not take place for another several months, Landis moved to prevent the return of the eight players. "I deeply regret the postponement of these cases," Landis announced. "However, baseball is not powerless to protect itself. All of the indicted players have today been placed on the ineligible list."

Judge Landis probably would have been content to let the Black Sox scandal fade into the background at that point, but Ban Johnson refused to drop the matter. The Black Sox had embarrassed his beloved American League, and Johnson took the scandal as a personal insult. Landis may have become the most powerful man in baseball, but Ban Johnson decided to perform one last act of service to the game. If the prosecutors needed evidence to rebuild their case, Johnson would get it for them.

Johnson was, by 1921, nearly 60 years old, overweight and diabetic, but he roused himself to action. He went to Philadelphia to find Billy Maharg, and offered the ex-prizefighter immunity from prosecution if he would lead Johnson to Sleepy Bill Burns. Maharg found Burns in the Texas border town of Del Rio, and Johnson quickly boarded a train for Texas to strike a deal with the former pitcher. Johnson offered immunity to Burns in exchange for his testimony, and Burns decided that he would rather face a courtroom and tell his story as a witness, not as a defendant. Burns returned to Chicago with his friend Maharg, and together they helped the prosecutors piece together the case against the Black Sox.

On March 26, 1921, mere days before the expiration of the 18-month time limit, seven of the eight players were re-indicted. Fred McMullin, who batted only twice in the Series, was off the hook. Also indicted with the seven players were Hal Chase, Sport Sullivan, Abe Attell, and several of Attell's gambling cronies from St. Louis and Des Moines.

Joe Jackson grew fidgety as the weather warmed up. For the first time since he was a teenager, Joe would not be going to spring training. The decimated White Sox began their season in April and quickly fell to the bottom of the standings, ahead of only the hapless Philadelphia A's, and Joe Jackson couldn't do anything to help them. In Joe's place was a

21-year-old outfielder from Texas, Bibb Falk, who became a steady .300 hitter and forevermore would be known as "the man who replaced Joe Jackson."

Joe could, however, play some ball. A Chicago promoter put together a semipro team called the Major Stars, with all of the defendants except for Eddie Cicotte and Buck Weaver, who stoutly maintained his innocence and kept his distance from the other indicted players. The Major Stars found it difficult to schedule other teams in the Chicago area, since the members of other teams feared reprisals from organized baseball and its new Commissioner, Judge Landis, if they played against the accused. Despite these obstacles, the Major Stars played a few games and made some money for the six indicted players on their roster.

Joe also slipped out of Illinois to play semipro ball in Wisconsin and Indiana every now and then, returning to the state before the authorities knew he had gone. Joe's funds may have been running low by this time—he had $5,000 tied up in bail—and he plied the only trade he knew to keep body and soul together in these difficult months.

The trial finally got under way on June 27, 1921, in the courtroom of Judge Hugo Friend. All seven of the indicted ballplayers showed up, but the gamblers proved more elusive. Abe Attell slipped through the net in New York after he claimed not to be the same Abe Attell that the cops were looking for. Hal Chase bluffed his way out of arrest in California, and Sport Sullivan fled to Canada. Arnold Rothstein was not indicted. Bill Burns and Billy Maharg turned state's evidence and gained immunity from prosecution in exchange for their testimony. The major fixers got away, leaving the players and a few minor gamblers to sweat it out at the defendants' table.

Joe and the other players had testified before the Grand Jury nine months earlier without benefit of counsel, but now they were represented by some of the leading defense lawyers in Chicago. Benedict Short, a former state's attorney, defended Jackson, Williams, and Cicotte, while James (Ropes) O'Brien, who started the case as one of Ban Johnson's special prosecutors, represented Gandil. Thomas Nash, a powerful figure in the local Democratic party, and Michael Ahearn, a colorful mob lawyer, defended Weaver, Risberg, and Felsch. George Gorman, the chief prosecutor, was a respected former congressman and courtroom veteran, but even he was stunned by the formidable array of legal talent on the defendants' side of the courtroom.

Onlookers wondered—who was paying for this high-priced legal talent? The players made a few payments early on, but no one was pressing

The Black Sox in court, 1921. Seated from right: attorney Thomas Nash, Jackson, Weaver, Cicotte, Risberg, Williams, Gandil (Chicago Historical Society, ICHi-28764; photograph by *Chicago Daily News* [SDN-62959]).

them for more. O'Brien, Nash, Ahearn, and Short were four of the most expensive lawyers in Chicago. Did they offer their services, virtually for free, to get themselves publicity on the front page of every paper in America? Or, did Charles Comiskey pay them, hoping to get his players acquitted so they could come back to play for the White Sox? It certainly looked suspicious that several members of the prosecution team switched sides and joined the defense just before the beginning of the trial.

Under pressure from the commissioner's office, Comiskey had released all eight players from their contracts a few months before. However, Comiskey left himself an out. In the suspension telegram that he sent to the eight players on September 28, 1920, Comiskey stated, "If you are innocent of any wrongdoing, you and each of you will be reinstated." If the trial ended in acquittals, this assemblage of talent, more than $230,000 worth by Comiskey's estimation, could be in uniform again in a matter of days.

Ben Short, Jackson's attorney, came out swinging. Short called the state's case "lame" and demanded to know why the "men who made millions" walked free while the players, "who made practically nothing," sat in the dock. Days of legal maneuvers and motions followed in the hot courtroom.

Joe Jackson was impressed by the proceedings. He liked watching the legal eagles argue their points and may have envied them their mental agility. "Those are certainly smart men, and that lawyer of mine is one lawyerin' bird," said Jackson. "They'd better not get him riled up."[3]

Six of the seven indicted players faced another legal challenge. Shortly after the Black Sox were suspended, the fledgling Internal Revenue Bureau, forerunner to the present-day IRS, announced that it would conduct an investigation of its own. If the six players (excepting Weaver, who received no crooked money) failed to declare their ill-gotten gains as income in 1919, they would be liable to prosecution for income tax evasion.[4]

It took two weeks to seat a jury, and the nervous excitement of the trial soon turned to sheer boredom for Joe and the other defendants. They sat, in unfamiliar suits and ties, sweating in the stifling courtroom, day after day, while the lawyers quizzed the jury candidates. After eight days the court managed to impanel only four jurors out of more than 200 candidates. Finally, Judge Friend threatened to start night sessions if the pace did not pick up soon. By July 15, a Friday, the jury was complete. The state began presenting its case the following Monday.

Charles Comiskey was the first prosecution witness, and Ben Short tried to throw Comiskey off his game by accusing him of jumping a contract in 1890, when the Old Roman joined the short-lived Players' League. "Don't you dare say I ever jumped a contract! I never did that in my life! You can't belittle me!" shouted Comiskey, shaking with rage. Short then tried to pry into Comiskey's profits for the years 1919 and 1920, but the prosecution objected and Friend sustained. Later in the trial, it was revealed that the White Sox made over $500,000 in 1919 gate receipts and over $900,000 in 1920. This revelation made the claim that the players had injured Comiskey's business ring hollow.

Sleepy Bill Burns, the state's star witness, testified over the next few days. Burns described the scene at the Sinton Hotel in Cincinnati the day before the World Series (and reiterated the fact that Joe Jackson was not present at that meeting) and detailed Abe Attell's string of promises to the players. At this point, Judge Friend ruled that there was enough evidence that a conspiracy had indeed existed. He would allow the prosecution to carry the questioning into matters that happened out of state; specifically, they could now discuss what happened at the meeting at the Ansonia in New York on September 18, 1919. Burns did so, revealing the fact that on that date, Gandil approached him with the offer to throw the World Series for $100,000. The prosecution hammered home its point that the ballplayers, not the gamblers, initiated the whole sordid enterprise.

When Burns' testimony ended, the prosecution attempted to enter the confessions of Cicotte, Jackson, and Williams into evidence. The prosecution had unsigned copies of the confessions at hand, made from the stenographers' notes, but without the waivers, they had no solid proof that the players had signed the confessions voluntarily. Judge Friend wanted to investigate the matter further. He sent the jury out of the room.

Judge Friend called Eddie Cicotte to the stand. Cicotte admitted that he signed the waiver of immunity, but that he really didn't understand what it meant. Besides, Alfred Austrian had assured him that he would be "taken care of," which he had taken to mean that he wouldn't be indicted. The judge excused Cicotte and called Joe Jackson to the stand.

Joe nervously took his seat. He told Ben Short that Austrian had promised him that he would not be prosecuted. "He [Austrian] said that after confessing I could go anywhere," said Jackson, "all the way to the Portuguese Islands, the Judge said. Then they gave me two bailiffs to protect me, and I went out and got polluted."

"Were you drunk when you went before the grand jury?" asked Short.

"About half, I guess," replied Jackson. "I'd been boozing."[5]

Jackson further stated that assistant state's attorney Hartley Replogle "read a bunch of stuff to me. I didn't know what it was." Short asked the ballplayer if he read the waiver of immunity before he signed it. "No, they'd given me their promise," replied Jackson, neatly deflecting the question of his illiteracy. "I'd have signed my death warrant if they'd asked me to."[6]

After a complicated legal argument, Judge Friend ruled that the three players had signed the waivers of immunity voluntarily. The unsigned copies of the confessions would be admissible, but only as evidence against Cicotte, Jackson, and Williams. These three players remained legally vulnerable, but the judge's decision blew a huge hole in the cases against all the other defendants. A few days later the judge declared that there was so little evidence against Felsch, Weaver, and gambler Carl Zork that he would not even let a conviction stand against those three.

The strangest moment in the trial came on July 12. Kid Gleason took the stand, and Short asked him if he suspected that the players were not giving their best efforts. Surprisingly, prosecutor George Gorman leapt to his feet and shouted "Objection!" Judge Friend quickly sustained the objection. The same scene played out a little later with Ray Schalk on the stand. Gorman objected, and Friend again sustained. These exchanges puzzled observers. If anyone would know if the players were laying down, manager Gleason and catcher Schalk would. Wouldn't the prosecution want to know this?

Harry Grabiner's diary, found in the bowels of Comiskey Park in the early 1960s, reveals the answer. An entry in the diary states that Gleason and Grabiner interviewed Harry Redmon, a St. Louis gambler and friend of some of Attell's circle, on October 12, 1919, only three days after the end of the World Series.[7] Within a few days of the final Series game Grabiner and Comiskey knew the full story and decided to cover it up, an act that could be interpreted as obstruction of justice on Comiskey's part. The prosecution didn't want Gleason to reveal this fact in open court, especially if Comiskey paid Redmon for his silence. The prosecution preferred to leave this hornet's nest alone.

The final arguments were held on August 2. Jackson fidgeted in his seat. He, Cicotte, and Williams were still on the hook, though the rest of the players seemed to be out of danger, especially Weaver and Felsch. Joe listened to prosecutor George Gorman's demand for a $2,000 fine and five years in prison for Jackson and his teammates. In return, Ben Short claimed that the state was "trying to make goats out of some underpaid ballplayers and penny-ante gamblers,"[8] and reminded the jury that the major figures (Attell, Sullivan, and Rothstein) were absent from the courtroom.

Short also played on the jury's sympathies for the poorly paid players. "The magnates led the public to believe that the ball players got about $10,000 a year," said Short, "and here we find out they got as little as $2,600. At the end of the season, they have nothing left but a chew of tobacco, a glove, and a few pairs of worn out socks..."[9]

In his instructions to the jury, Judge Friend handed the defendants their biggest victory of the trial. He ruled that the fact that the players threw games for money was not sufficient to convict them. The jury had to find that they had done so with the intent to injure their employer's business and defraud the public. Since baseball fans all over the country streamed through the turnstiles in record numbers in 1920, especially in Chicago, it seemed ludicrous to suggest that Comiskey's business had suffered or that the public felt defrauded. As far as intent went, it was clear from the testimony that the object of the whole enterprise was not to harm Comiskey or the fans, but was nothing more than sheer greed.

The jury retired to their deliberations in the early evening, though most knowledgeable observers felt that the outcome was a foregone conclusion. Less than three hours later, the jury foreman read the verdict. The jury found the ballplayers and gamblers not guilty on all counts.

Bedlam erupted in the courtroom. The players slapped each other's backs and the backs of their lawyers. Spectators threw papers into the air in a wild celebration, which ended with the jurors carrying several of the players around the courtroom on their shoulders. Chick Gandil offered a "sailor's farewell" to the absent Ban Johnson. "Goodbye, good luck, and to hell with you," shouted Gandil. "That'll show Ban Johnson he can't frame an honest bunch of ballplayers!"[10] The celebration resumed at a local Italian restaurant, where jurors and defendants drank and caroused together, far into the night.

Joe shook hands with the jurors, but he was remarkably subdued in the aftermath of the verdict. "I'm through with organized baseball," said the 33-year-old outfielder. "I'm going to play ball with Williams in Oklahoma for a while this summer. At present I'm contemplating taking a position with a university team in Japan. I've also had an offer to go before the footlights."[11] Heaven only knows how Joe could have gone to Japan, when a trip to Philadelphia in 1908 was too much for him to handle. Joe may have lapsed into his "southern storyteller" mode for the interview, in the midst of all the shouting and excitement.

The other acquitted players put their faith in the telegram they received from Charles Comiskey on September 28, 1920, and in the sentence that said, "If you are innocent of any wrongdoing, you and each of you will be reinstated...." The court found them not guilty, and most people fully expected them to return to action as soon as possible. Buck Weaver was already investigating the possibility of joining John McGraw's New York Giants. However, Judge Landis was making the decisions now. The 16 major league owners, panicked about the effect of the scandal on their investments, granted the crusty Judge dictatorial power over the game and its players, and the Judge had no reservations about using it.

That very evening, the new Commissioner made his feelings known. "Regardless of the outcome of juries," said the Judge, "no player that throws a ball game, no player that entertains proposals or promises to throw a game, no player that sits in a conference with a bunch of crooked players where the ways and means of throwing games are discussed, and does not promptly tell his club about it, will ever again play professional baseball."[12] With that, the major league careers of Joe Jackson and the other Black Sox were over.

Joe Jackson's decision to participate in the scheme to lose the 1919 Series was easily the worst decision he could have made. He trusted Chick Gandil for the $20,000 he had been promised, but Jackson came out of the fix with only $5,000 and his career and life in tatters. Jackson would have earned more than that in the next few seasons. A winner's share of the Series in 1919 totaled nearly $5,000, and if the Sox won the pennant again in 1920, they would have faced the mediocre Dodgers in the World Series, almost insuring another winner's share. The World Series checks would have stopped in 1921 when Babe Ruth's Yankees took over the league, but when Ruth's hitting brought a new wave of prosperity to baseball, salaries rose to new levels. In fact, Ruth's teammate Waite Hoyt once suggested that ballplayers' children should thank Babe Ruth in their prayers at night, "because Daddy's paycheck has risen by 15 to 40 percent."

Jackson's annual salary rose from $6,000 to $8,000 with the contract that Harry Grabiner had him sign in Savannah in February of 1920. Jackson still was underpaid, but a 33 percent raise is nothing to sneeze at. If the White Sox could have held their team together, the huge attendance increases would have continued into the early 1920s and provided Comiskey, cheap as he was, with more money for salaries. Even Comiskey had to realize eventually that his low payroll was killing the team from within. By 1922, when the three-year contract ran out, Jackson could have commanded much more than $8,000 a year. Jackson could have played several more seasons at a higher pay level, Comiskey or no Comiskey.

Could Joe have batted .400 again? Perhaps he could have. Jackson hit .382 in 1920, after batting at the .400 mark as late in the season as August 6. After Cleveland shortstop Ray Chapman was killed by a pitched ball in August 1920, an effort was made to keep a new white ball in play at all times. This would have made it even easier for Jackson to see, and hit, the ball. In addition, beginning in 1921 the use of the spitball was more severely limited than it had been in 1920, being restricted to only eight pitchers in the American League and nine in the National. Batting averages soared in the early 1920s for these reasons. George Sisler and Rogers Hornsby cleared the .400 mark five times between them, and even the 35-year-old Ty Cobb hit .401 in 1922. Jackson, though aging as a ballplayer, might well have joined the parade.

Eddie Cicotte, too, was a major loser in the scandal, and his participation haunted him his death in 1969. His $10,000 payment represented two years' worth of salary, and at age 35 Cicotte's career was mostly behind him. It stands to reason, however, that he could have made up the money with a few more seasons of good play and a 1920 Series appearance. Crafty control pitchers like Cicotte often last into their forties, and Cicotte, after winning 50 games in 1919 and 1920, could expect at least four or five more good years, in an era of higher salaries. If Cicotte had pitched until 1924 or 1925, his career win total would have landed at 260 or so, more than enough to put Cicotte into the Baseball Hall of Fame. As it is, his win-loss record of 210-149 is better than those of several pitchers who have plaques on the wall in Cooperstown.[13]

Some writers have expressed sympathy with Cicotte's desire to throw the Series "for the wife and kiddies," in Cicotte's own words. Some, like Victor Luhrs in *The Great Baseball Mystery*, criticized Judge Landis for banning Cicotte at all! However, the truth remains that the fix would never have happened without two essential ingredients—Red Faber's injury, which opened up three or more games to the gamblers' machinations, and Cicotte's agreement to participate. No Cicotte, no fix.

If Faber had been healthy, he would have started three or four games, and he could have won at least three, as he did in 1917 against a superior Giants team. Faber was an ironman, and Kid Gleason could have pitched Faber in more games if he lost confidence in Cicotte or Williams. Dickie Kerr pitched admirably, winning two games, but Kerr was a rookie and Faber a future Hall of Famer. There was no way that Gleason could start Kerr ahead of Cicotte or Williams. Faber's injury robbed Gleason of the flexibility he needed to overcome the poor pitching of Cicotte and Williams.[14]

Eddie Cicotte played semipro ball for a few years after his suspension, then farmed in Michigan and worked as a game warden. Later in life, he took a job on the Ford assembly line. He used an assumed name to protect his family. In 1966 he told a *Detroit Free Press* reporter, "I admit I did wrong, but I've paid for it…. I don't know of anyone who ever went through life without making a mistake. Everyone who has ever lived has committed sins of his own. I've tried to make up for it by living as clean a life as I could. I'm proud of the way I've lived, and I think my family is, too."[15]

The other players scattered to the four winds. Buck Weaver met with Judge Landis in December of 1921 to plead for reinstatement, and Landis promised to give the matter due consideration. Weaver had barely left the commissioner's office when Landis issued a statement denying Weaver's request with a terse, "Birds of a feather flock together. Men associating with gamblers and crooks could expect no leniency."[16] Weaver, still protesting his innocence, died of a heart attack in Chicago in 1956. By 1975 they were all gone; Swede Risberg, at age 81, was the last of the Black Sox to die.

The biggest winner in the scandal, besides the gamblers, was Chick Gandil. Comiskey's investigators reported that Gandil, who got nearly ten years' worth of salary for fixing the World Series, spent the winter of 1919 buying diamonds and flashy clothes. Gandil never publicly mentioned the crooked Series again until 1956, when he and writer Melvin Durslag wrote

a half-hearted *mea culpa* for *Sports Illustrated*, which did nothing but add
to the confusion of the scandal.

In retrospect, one can only guess what course Charles Comiskey
should have pursued. If Comiskey had investigated and made the truth
public in late 1919, the news would have shaken his club, and Ban Johnson may have salivated at the thought of wrecking his enemy's team. Nevertheless, the complete disintegration of the White Sox might not have
happened, and Comiskey's friends in the pressbox may have hailed him
as the white knight of the scandal. By the time the story broke in September 1920, after a year-long cover-up, it was too late for Comiskey to
save his team or his reputation.

From 1917 to 1920 Charles Comiskey owned the most powerful team
in baseball. His attempt to preserve his team's dominance of the American League led to disaster, and it's difficult to guess how he could have
managed the situation any worse. Comiskey, blinded by the record attendance and hands-over-fists profits in 1920, hushed up the scandal with all
the fervor of a Richard Nixon, and failed just as miserably.

The White Sox tumbled all the way to seventh place in 1921, ahead
of the rebuilding Philadelphia A's. With many of their stars suspended,
the Black Sox trial in session all summer, and public revulsion at the
White Sox and their owner, attendance at Comiskey Park dipped nearly
300,000 from the record 833,000 of 1920. Only the presence in the lineup
of four future Hall of Famers (Collins, Schalk, Faber, and newly acquired
Harry Hooper) kept the Sox from falling all the way to last place. Johnny
Evers took over as manager from Kid Gleason in 1924, but finished dead
last in the American League. Eddie Collins then managed for two seasons, followed by Ray Schalk for the next two, as the Sox made a habit
of finishing in the second division. The Yankees won six pennants in the
1920s as the predominance of the American League passed from Chicago
to New York, where it resides to this day.

The heady days of 1917 to 1920 never returned to the South Side,
and within a few years the Depression and a series of bad White Sox
teams dropped the attendance at Comiskey Park to pre–1910 levels. In
October 1931 Charles Comiskey died at the age of 72; one source claimed
that the 1919 scandal cost Comiskey ten years of his life, as well as his
reputation. Comiskey was elected to the Baseball Hall of Fame posthu-
mously in 1939,[17] but his White Sox never managed to finish higher than
third place until the 1957 and 1958 seasons, after which the Comiskey
family sold the Sox to Bill Veeck. The Sox responded by winning the
pennant in 1959, their first flag in 40 years, but they won no others in the
remaining years of the twentieth century, as Comiskey Park and its South

Side environment slowly decayed. Only a last-minute bailout from the Illinois state legislature in 1988 kept the White Sox from pulling up stakes and moving to Florida.

Another victim of the fix was Kid Gleason. Gleason chose to ignore his suspicions about Cicotte and Williams in the first two games of the 1919 Series, and his failure to act haunted him for the rest of his career. In retrospect it became clear to Gleason that he should have started Kerr in Faber's place, but how could a 13-game winning rookie like Kerr take his turns ahead of a 29-game winning veteran like Cicotte? Should Gleason have sent Kerr, not Williams, to the hill in Game 8? Gleason possessed no solid information; he had no way of knowing that the rookie would mow down the Reds a third time. Maybe he should have started Roy Wilkinson that day, but you go with your best, don't you? Don't you?

Gleason chased the team to fifth in 1922, but another seventh place showing in 1923 spelled the end for Gleason in Chicago. He rallied the Sox to a City Series win over the Cubs in October of 1923, then resigned and went home to Philadelphia. He stayed there for two years, hardly going out, paying little attention to the world of baseball, seemingly lost and tired. By 1925, Eddie Collins managed the White Sox and Gleason, nearing 60, took a coaching job with Connie Mack.

Gleason, by all accounts, was a changed man after the scandal; no longer "Kid," people called him "Pop" now. He went through the motions for his friend Mack, but the old enthusiasm, even with a rising team, had long disappeared. Kid Gleason was 66 years old when he died on the day after New Year's in 1933.

Chapter 19

"Regardless of the Verdict of Juries..."

There is such a thing as condemning the acts of these men and still forgiving the individuals. I don't think Kid Gleason and the rest of the White Sox wanted to see their former comrades sent to the penitentiary for violating the trust placed in them by the fans. They would not have been human if they did.
— *Christy Mathewson* [1]

Now that Joe was out of legal jeopardy, he was free to make a living in any business other than organized baseball. This was more difficult than it sounds, since the term "organized" included all levels of professional ball, from the major leagues all the way down to Class D. Joe and the other Black Sox could play semiprofessional or "outlaw" ball, which was not controlled by Judge Landis, but it was difficult to find employment here also. The crusty Judge threatened to suspend, or even ban, any player who took the field against Joe and his former teammates.

Dickie Kerr found this out the hard way. Kerr was one of the honest White Sox in the 1919 Series, and he won 21 games for the Sox in 1920 and 19 more for the decimated team in 1921. Comiskey rewarded Kerr with a $4,500 salary offer for 1922, the same salary that Kerr had been getting for the previous two years. Kerr found that he could earn more in outlaw ball than he could with the White Sox, so he signed a contract with a semipro outfit in Texas. When Kerr pitched against a team that contained several members of the Black Sox, Judge Landis suspended him from organized baseball for two years.

Joe Jackson played in the thriving Eastern Seaboard semipro circuit in 1922, making a few hundred dollars a game, changing his name every now and again to hide his identity. On June 25, 1922, Joe played for a semipro team in Westwood, New Jersey, under the name of Joe Josephs. After Joe pounded out four hits, including a tremendous home run, and threw a runner out at the plate from deepest center field, the opposing team figured out that Joe Josephs was really Joe Jackson. He played only two more games for Westwood before he moved on to another team and another alias.

Wherever Jackson went, his cannon arm and effortless swing usually gave him away after a game or two, and the controversy would inevitably begin anew. Some opposing players, knowing what happened to Dickie Kerr, refused to play against Joe, but a New York promoter hired Joe and some of the other Black Sox for a team that he called the "Big League Martyrs," and he organized a campaign to reinstate Joe. However, the attendant publicity seemed to irritate Judge Landis, who refused to reconsider Joe's lifetime suspension.

Joe opened the 1923 season with a semipro team in Bastrop, Louisiana, with Eddie Cicotte and Swede Risberg. Joe played under the name of Johnson, and Cicotte called himself Moore, but most everyone knew that the three men were former Black Sox. Joe batted nearly .500 for the season, but his presence in the league prompted controversy once again. Some teams refused to play against the Black Sox, and tensions between Risberg and Cicotte, caused by money disputes, escalated as the weeks passed. Risberg finally settled the matter with one of his trademark one-punch knockouts.

Joe decided to leave Louisiana and settle closer to home. To this end, in July of 1923 he signed with a team in Americus, Georgia, in the "outlaw" South Georgia League. There was some controversy when the Americus team signed Joe, since the league did not want its younger players to be penalized or banned from organized ball in the future. Morgan Blake, sports editor of the *Atlanta Journal*, blasted the South Georgia League, comparing Joe Jackson to Benedict Arnold; Joe responded that Blake was "making a tempest in a teapot" and that the other reluctant teams were afraid of "the long bat I swing."[2]

However, Thomas Bell, president of the Americus team, convinced the other club owners that the fans would come out to see Shoeless Joe Jackson, increasing attendance and putting more money in all their pockets. The team paid Joe $75 a week, and in Georgia no one cared about the crooked World Series or the dirty envelope with $5,000 in it. Joe batted well over .400, made incredible catches and throws, and drew large crowds wherever he played. Americus was in last place when Joe arrived, but they won the second half of the split season with Joe in right field and batting cleanup. In the South Georgia League's "Little World Series" of 1923, Joe pounded out 11 hits in 22 trips to the plate for a .500 average and led Americus to the championship. Joe also belted two homers in the second game of the six-game series.

For all the controversy surrounding his arrival in Americus, Joe stayed with the team for less than two months. In early September, shortly after the Little World Series, Joe left Americus and signed a contract with a team in Waycross. The South Georgia League was already in deep trouble—two of its six teams failed to finish the season—and when its biggest gate attraction left for greener pastures, the rest of the league closed up shop. The town of Americus would not have another professional team until 1935.

Joe Jackson, now 35 years old, enjoyed playing in his familiar Southern surroundings, but he still felt cheated by the end of his major league career. He signed a three-year contract with the White Sox in February of 1920, but Comiskey released him, using the ten-day clause, after only one year. Joe insisted that the ten-day clause was not in the contract when he signed it, and if it was, then Harry Grabiner lied to him about its presence. Joe believed that Grabiner took advantage of his illiteracy in obtaining his signature on that contract. If the ten-day clause had not been in the contract, Comiskey could not legally have released him, and so Joe believed that the White Sox cheated him out of $16,000 of salary for the 1921 and 1922 seasons.

One other issue irked Joe Jackson. He and the other banned players never received their share of the 1920 second-place money, a sum totaling slightly less than $700 per man. It wasn't much, but Joe pursued the matter, more for his wounded pride than for anything else. In March of 1922 Joe and Katie composed a letter to Ban Johnson, inquiring about the second-place money. Johnson replied that he had turned the matter over to Judge Landis for consideration.

Landis wrote back to Joe in April of 1922, stating that, in light of the "crime" that Joe and his teammates committed in 1919, the second-place money would not be forthcoming. Joe was angry, since he had been acquitted of the alleged crime, and it appeared that a lawsuit was the only avenue open to him in his quest to recover the money that he felt was rightfully his. It was around this time that Joe received a letter from an attorney named Raymond Cannon.

Joe batting in the mid–1930s (Greenville County Historical Society/The Coxe Collection).

Cannon, a former minor league pitcher who gave up the game to study law, was engaged at the time in the formation of a new baseball players' union. Ray Cannon was thoroughly disgusted with baseball and its monopolistic practices, especially the reserve clause and the ten-day clause. However, a Supreme Court decision of the previous year had granted baseball an exemption from the anti-trust laws, which saved the magnates' most objectionable practices from legal challenge in the near future. Cannon's response was to embarrass the magnates by exposing their practices in court. He had already represented Happy Felsch in a suit against Comiskey, and now he offered his services to Jackson as well.

By early 1923, Cannon claimed to have over 200 major leaguers in his organization, which he called the National Baseball Players Association. Cannon offered to help Joe Jackson recover his money, because he wanted a forum in which to further the cause of the active players and gain public support for his union. The Jackson and Felsch cases provided an opportunity for Cannon not only to gain fair treatment for the Black Sox, but also to publicize the indignities under which the active players operated.

Ray Cannon was exactly the kind of aggressive, confident operator who appealed to Joe Jackson, especially if the promise of money was involved. Joe hired Cannon to represent him, and in early 1923 Joe filed suit against Comiskey for the sum of $119,000. One hundred thousand of the total was for slander, and the rest was for the remaining two years of salary on Joe's terminated contract and for the 1920 second-place money that Joe never received. Joe also claimed, as Felsch had, that Comiskey promised each member of the White Sox a $1,500 bonus for winning the 1917 World Series; Comiskey never paid it, and Joe included that amount in his suit.

In April of 1923, Joe and Katie gave depositions in Savannah; then Joe busied himself with his ballplaying and left the details of the case to Cannon, who kept in contact with Joe through the mail. In one letter, Cannon reported that Comiskey deposed Lefty Williams, but the pitcher said nothing damaging about Joe. In another, Cannon told Joe that Buck Weaver had signed an affadavit declaring that Joe had nothing to do with the fix, and that Joe was free to sign one for Weaver if he was so inclined. Cannon assured the ballplayer that since he hit .375 and led the team in runs driven in and runs scored in the Series, the case was winnable. He warned Joe not to discuss the case with anyone, since Comiskey undoubtedly had detectives investigating Joe at that very moment.

The case focused upon the contention that the White Sox cheated Jackson out of $16,000 worth of salary for 1921 and 1922. This assertion was founded on the claim that Joe would not have signed the three-year contract in early 1920 if he had known that the ten-day clause was in it. Joe stated that Grabiner read him the contract and purposely skipped over the offending clause, knowing that Joe couldn't read it for himself, and Katie wasn't there to decipher it for him. Cannon found it "suspicious" that Grabiner did not give Joe a copy of the contract, and he insisted that the White Sox had obtained Joe's signature through fraud and deception.

If Cannon could get the court to declare the ten-day clause in Joe's contract null and void, then Comiskey's refusal to pay Joe for the last two years of that contract would hinge solely on Joe's actions during the Series. Cannon's next task was to convince a jury that Joe had no knowledge of the crooked goings-on and did not participate in throwing games. To do so, Cannon had to surmount one obstacle—the fact that Joe received a $5,000 payoff from Lefty Williams during the Series.

Four years earlier, both Jackson and Williams told the Chicago grand jury (and the newspapers) that Joe received the envelope of money after the fourth game of the Series. This would indicate that Joe was well aware of what was happening in Games 5 through 8, two of which were thrown by the crooked White Sox players. However, Joe and his lawyer now claimed that Joe received the money after the last game of the Series. Joe was as surprised as anyone that he received any money at all, said Raymond Cannon. Joe knew nothing about the fix, hadn't talked to Chick Gandil before the Series began, and certainly never agreed on a payment of $20,000 to help throw the Series. In fact, he was shocked beyond belief when Williams handed him an envelope with $5,000 in it!

The story, as constructed by Cannon, was that Williams used Joe's name, without his permission, to make the sordid enterprise look good for the moneymen. Joe didn't find out about the fix until the night of the last game, when Williams handed him the envelope full of hundreds and fifties. Joe was angry that anyone would think he was crooked and stormed off to Comiskey's office the next morning to expose the whole evil plot. However, Harry Grabiner slammed a window in Joe's face and shouted, "Go home, we know what you want!" when Joe tried to tell them about the Series fix.

Joe could back up this version of the story with the letter that he wrote to Comiskey in November of 1919, in which Joe offered to tell the owner what he knew of the scandal. Comiskey, of course, turned down the offer, which indicated that Comiskey didn't want to have the fix exposed, by Joe or by anyone else.

This version of events stood in direct contradiction to the story Joe told to the Chicago grand jury in September of 1920, but Joe and Cannon were not concerned. The Chicago testimony had been missing for three years, and Jackson's prior statements could not refute his new explanation of the events of 1919. Besides, Joe was not present at either of the two meetings that the players held before the Series began. Jackson's claim that he knew nothing about the crooked scheme would sound perfectly logical to a jury of his peers.

Ray Cannon and his client hoped for much more than a monetary settlement. They also believed that a victory in court would pave the way for Joe Jackson's return to organized baseball.

On August 2, 1921, after the conclusion of the Black Sox trial, Judge Landis told the press, "No player that throws a ball game, no player that entertains proposals or promises to throw a game, no player that sits in a conference with a bunch of crooked players where the ways and means of throwing games are discussed, and does not promptly tell his club about it, will ever again play professional baseball." If Joe could establish that he didn't throw any games, didn't know about the scheme until after the Series was over, and did not attend any of the meetings in which the plot was hatched, then he did not qualify for banishment under Landis' edict. In fact, Joe's case for reinstatement would be much stronger than that of

Buck Weaver, who took no money but did "sit in a conference" with the other conspirators.

After several delays—and a settlement offer by Comiskey, which Cannon rejected[3]—the trial finally got under way in Milwaukee on January 28, 1924, in front of Judge John J. Gregory. The slander part of the suit was dropped, and the total amount of money that Joe demanded from Comiskey was now set at $18,200.[4] The suit was heard in Wisconsin because Comiskey had registered the White Sox as a corporation in that state, probably for tax purposes. The court quickly impaneled a jury, and arguments began the next day. A group of sportswriters began the proceedings by testifying that Joe had given his best efforts in the Series. Then it was Joe's turn on the stand.

The ballplayer told his new version of events to the court. He explained that Williams used his name without his permission and that he had no knowledge of the fix until after the last game was played. He also told how Comiskey and Grabiner blocked all his efforts to tell what he knew. In the middle of Joe's testimony, one of Comiskey's lawyers, George Hudnall, asked Joe if he had testified before the Chicago grand jury in 1920. When Joe answered "Yes," Hudnall, to the astonishment of all present, produced Joe's missing grand jury testimony from his briefcase!

Cannon was dumbfounded. "Where did you get those papers?" Cannon demanded.

Hudnall looked at Comiskey, who turned pale. "I don't know," the Old Roman murmured. "I don't know."

It was obvious what had happened. Comiskey's lawyer, Alfred Austrian, also represented Arnold Rothstein. Austrian, or agents acting on his behalf, arranged for the theft of the confessions, as well as all information about Rothstein, from the prosecutor's office before the investigation of the Series could begin in earnest. Comiskey wished to derail the investigation to hide his early knowledge of the scandal, while Rothstein wished to conceal his financial backing of the scheme. The Old Roman, therefore, aligned himself with the Big Bankroll as early as October of 1920, all the while mouthing platitudes about the integrity of the sport. Now George Hudnall, in an effort to save his employer from paying $18,000 to Joe Jackson, brandished the stolen papers for all to see.

Cannon demanded that the court refuse to allow Joe's 1920 testimony to be used, but the judge ruled that the confession was admissible under Wisconsin law. This ruling was disastrous to Joe's case, since his testimony in 1924 contradicted what he told the Chicago grand jury four years before. The ballplayer, completely flustered by this turn of events, tried his best to contain the damage. When Hudnall read passages from Jackson's 1920 testimony, Joe admitted making some statements and denied others. However, Joe could not rectify the differences.

As soon as the jury retired to their deliberations on the evening of February 14, the judge rapped his gavel and called Joe to the bench. "Mr. Jackson," intoned the judge, "you are guilty of perjury, rank perjury, and I order you placed under arrest and fix your bail at five thousand dollars."[5] Joe wasn't the only one. Happy Felsch, who lived in Milwaukee, testified on Joe's behalf, and also made some statements that differed from the story he told in 1920. The judge ordered the arrest of Felsch as well, fixing his bail at $3,000. Both players posted bail, though Joe spent several hours in jail before he could manage to do so.

When the jury returned the next day with a judgment for $16,711.04 in Joe's favor, George Hudnall leaped to his feet to protest the verdict, but he need not have bothered. The visibly angry Judge Gregory announced that "the court will act on its own motion," set the verdict aside, and dismissed the case. The judge understood, even if the jury did not, that Joe must have perjured himself in one of the two trials, and the judge could not accept a finding in favor of someone whom he considered a liar. "He [Jackson] is just as guilty as if he had the blood of a victim that he is accused of killing on his hands," sputtered the enraged judge. "I can't understand it. I can't understand it!"[6]

Raymond Cannon, stunned by the sudden reversal, did his best to put a positive face on the outcome. "We view the victory obtained by Jackson from a jury of twelve men and women to be so far-reaching as to bring about Jackson's return to organized baseball," said Cannon hopefully to the reporters after the trial.[7] Nevertheless, Ray Cannon knew as well as anyone that the judge's decision was the only one that mattered. He also found out too late that the active major leaguers strongly disapproved of his defense of the Black Sox, whose crooked behavior in the 1919 World Series cast suspicion on all players. By the end of 1924 most of the major leaguers withdrew their support of the union, and the National Baseball Players Association collapsed.

Comiskey offered a settlement, which Joe accepted, to forestall an appeal (and, most likely, to avoid any questions about the stolen testimony). Still, despite Cannon's optimistic spin doctoring of the verdict, the Milwaukee case ended in disaster, not only for Cannon's union, but also for Joe's reputation. Joe returned home with a small amount of money from Comiskey, and for the next several years, Joe Jackson remained mum in public about the Black Sox scandal.

The Milwaukee trial showed Joe in the worst possible light, and he was more than happy to leave the jailhouse and return home to Georgia. Charles Comiskey's reputation, however, may have suffered more damage than Jackson's. Comiskey, who by 1924 was 65 years old and in poor health, never explained how the stolen grand jury testimony from 1920 wound up in his possession. Seven years later, he took the secret to his grave.

For the next several years, Joe Jackson played ball in the South, where folks regarded him with kindness and still stood in awe of his ability. Joe was nearly 40 years old by now and sported a sizable paunch around his midsection, but he could still knock the stuffing out of a baseball. His dry cleaning service prospered, and by the late 1920s Joe employed 22 people and owned two delivery vans. Joe was doing well and showed little interest in the affairs of major league baseball.

He was, however, peripherally involved in one more baseball scandal. In December of 1926 Ban Johnson, still president of the American League, forced Ty Cobb and Tris Speaker out of their managerial positions at Detroit and Cleveland respectively. There was some evidence that the two had conspired to fix a game between their two teams in September of 1919, after the White Sox had already clinched the pennant. Swede Risberg, now working as a dairy farmer in Minnesota, made an even more astounding accusation shortly afterward. Risberg stated in a newspaper interview that the Tigers threw two doubleheaders to the White Sox on September 2 and 3, 1917, and that the Sox had paid the Tigers a total of $1,100 to do so.[8] Chick Gandil, said the former shortstop, collected $45 each from the Chicago players and journeyed to Philadelphia to present the cash to Detroit pitcher Bill James, with the approval of manager Pants Rowland.

Risberg further asserted that the White Sox returned the favor two years later. In September of 1919, according to Risberg, the Sox threw two games to Detroit to help the Tigers clinch third place after the Sox had already won the pennant. The former shortstop was perfectly willing to incriminate himself in the matter. "I know I played out of position," said Risberg to Judge Landis, "and Jackson, Gandil, and Felsch also played out of position."[9]

Risberg implicated Eddie Collins, whom he still hated, and former White Sox manager Rowland, now a respected umpire, as key participants in the scandal. "They pushed Ty Cobb and Tris Speaker out on a piker bet," said the angry shortstop. "I think it's only fair that the 'white lilies' get the same treatment."[10]

Judge Landis thought that he had cleaned up the game several years before, and he fairly exploded with rage when he saw Risberg's charges in the *Chicago Tribune*. "Won't these God-damned things that happened before I got into baseball ever stop coming up?"[11] thundered the Judge at no one in particular. Landis, despite his anger, should not have been surprised by the allegations. Rumors about the honesty of those particular games had been floating around for a decade. The Chicago prosecutor's office had heard about the affair during the Black Sox investigation in October of 1920, and Ray Schalk had told Landis the details of the matter in 1921.[12] Landis quickly arranged for a hearing to be held in his Chicago offices on January 5, 1927.

The Commissioner invited Jackson to the hearing, but Joe told the Associated Press that "because of the press of business interests," he was unable to make the journey to Chicago in the dead of winter.[13] In truth, Joe was simply not interested in testifying anywhere after his experience in Milwaukee three years earlier. Joe was comfortable down south among his friends and family, and he saw no need to go to Chicago and expose himself to more ridicule and accusations. Eddie Cicotte felt the same way. He lived near Detroit, which was only a short train ride from Chicago, but he didn't even respond to Landis' invitation.

Landis held a two-day hearing without Joe's participation. Chick Gandil traveled all the way from Arizona, where he was managing a semi-pro team, to back up Risberg's story, but he was the shortstop's only supporter. More than 30 other Detroit and Chicago players insisted that all the games in 1917 and 1919 were played on the level, though they admitted that the White Sox paid the Tigers $1,100 in 1917. Collins and others claimed that they raised the money to reward the Tigers for beating the Red Sox earlier in the season. It was a noisy and often contentious hearing, in which a former Tiger player hissed, "You're still a pig" to Risberg. Buck Weaver, who stated on the stand that the Sox played the four games honestly, seized the opportunity to ask Landis for reinstatement, which the judge denied soon after.

In the end, Landis found no cause for punishment in the case and let the matter drop. However, Landis condemned the practice of tipping opposing players, as the White Sox had done for the Tigers in 1917. It was "an act of impropriety, reprehensible and censurable, but not corrupt,"[14] said the Commissioner, and he issued new orders that specifically prohibited the practice.

He also introduced new rules, adopted by the club owners, which fixed the punishments for betting on baseball games. A player who bet on a game in which he was not involved would be suspended for one year, and a player who bet on a game in which he was involved would be banned for life.[15] Landis also overruled Johnson and reinstated Cobb and Speaker, though they both moved to other teams, and neither man ever managed in the major leagues again.

If anyone needed an insight into the personality of Chick Gandil, the architect of the 1919 World Series scandal, they got one during the trial. Pants Rowland testified that he allowed Gandil to go to Philadelphia in September of 1917, but denied that he knew Gandil was going to deliver money to the Detroit team. Rowland claimed that Gandil went to Philadelphia "to visit friends."

"Rowland lied," snarled the former first baseman, now making his living as a plumber. "I never had any friends."[16] This was the man to whom Joe Jackson had given his full measure of trust, with disastrous results.

There was an epilogue to this latest controversy. In late 1925, Commissioner Landis finally decided to disperse the 1920 second-place money that the American League had withheld from the Black Sox. Landis' office had held this money, a sum of $4,800.53, for five years. It was, by order of the Commissioner, to be divided equally among the honest members of the 1920 Chicago White Sox.[17]

Chapter 20

"I Gave Baseball All I Had..."

Almost any day of the week, if you drive down East Wilborn Street on the South side of Greenville, South Carolina, you'll find an aging man with sparse white hair sitting in the shade of a sapling oak at No. 119. He will be Joe Jackson—Shoeless Joe Jackson, sometimes known as the greatest natural hitter in baseball history.... In his South Carolina textile country, where he lives comfortably, he is revered as an idol and as a persecuted man. They will always believe Joe innocent.

—*Sport (magazine), October 1949*[1]

Joe Jackson heard about the reports that he lived in poverty and despair, scraping out a living. Perhaps the sportswriters up north thought that Shoeless Joe should be living in dire straits, tortured with regret, drowning his sorrows. Poor Shoeless Joe, they wrote, barely making ends meet, earning a meager living as a mere "pants presser." They never mentioned the fact that Jackson pressed the pants in the dry-cleaning business that he owned. Some well-meaning baseball fans sent checks for small amounts "to help you out"; the proud Jackson sent them back.

Joe played outlaw and semipro baseball until age 44, not because of a pathetic need to be connected to the game, but because the money was good and because he could still hit. One widely quoted story has a fat, decrepit Jackson swinging and missing two curveballs, then smashing a fastball over the fence; as Joe circled the bases, he called to the pitcher,

259

"You never could sneak a fastball by old Joe Jackson." Jackson did gain weight after he left the major leagues, but he could still astound people with the beautiful left-handed swing that never left him. Joe was past 40 when he belted a 500-foot home run in Waycross, Georgia, for the longest home run ever hit in that city.

He could still show off his throwing arm, too. It was reported that at a field day in Brunswick, Georgia, Joe threw a ball from behind home plate all the way on a straight line over the center field fence. Some versions of the story claim that Joe threw the ball from behind the backstop!

Other writers assumed that since Jackson, later in his life, owned a liquor store, he must have spent a lot of time drinking the profits in the back room. Again, such reports were misguided. Jackson drank, but he was not a drunk, and his liquor store was a profitable enterprise.

Despite his illiteracy, Joe Jackson became a successful businessman. Perhaps the poolroom and the farm in Greenville failed because Joe was too busy playing ball up north to pay enough attention to them. After he stopped playing, his dry-cleaning establishment and his liquor store provided a comfortable living for the Jacksons. Katie Jackson handled the family finances. "Giving her the money," said Joe in 1949, "was as good as putting it in the bank."[2]

Joe's mother Martha became ill in 1929, and Joe and Katie sold the dry-cleaning establishment and moved back to Greenville to care for her. They bought a small brick house at 119 East Wilborn Street, in the old Brandon Mill neighborhood, and Joe opened a barbecue restaurant that he called "Joe Jackson's Barbecue Cabin." It prospered, and a few years later he opened a liquor store on Pendleton Street in Greenville, which also did well. Martha Jackson died in the summer of 1932, but Joe and Katie stayed in Greenville for the rest of their lives.

For the next few years, Joe traveled with a barnstorming team in the summer months, playing ball as far north as Minnesota and Saskatchewan, but he missed the South and eventually tired of the road. In August of 1932, Joe signed a contract to play right field for Greenville's semipro team, the Spinners, at a salary of $100 per game, which was not a bad paycheck during the Depression. Joe still terrorized every pitcher he faced, but he was about 40 pounds overweight, and he could no longer cover much ground in the outfield. "When I have to run, I can do it, I guess," admitted Joe. "But I just sort of trot out my singles and doubles and walk out my home runs."[3]

Joe enjoyed his return to Greenville, but he allowed himself to express some bitterness about his banishment from organized baseball 12 years before. "I didn't throw that series," said Joe in a column that appeared across the nation in late August of 1932. "I hit nearly .400, didn't I? I had the record for most hits in a series until Pepper Martin tied it last year, didn't I? I threw out men at the plate and led both teams at bat. If you ask me, I got the dirtiest deal any man in organized baseball ever got."[4]

Joe once remarked that the fact that he never had children was the greatest disappointment of his life, greater even than his banishment from baseball. However, Joe's brothers and sisters had families of their own, and Joe and Katie enjoyed the company of their nieces and nephews. They became especially close to their nephew McDavid Jackson, the son of Joe's brother Dave. McDavid went to work in Joe's restaurant as a teenager, and although he showed more interest in football than in baseball, he became so close to the former ballplayer that Joe and Katie offered to adopt the young man. That never came to pass, but the Jacksons treated McDavid as one of their own.

In 1933, when Joe was 45 years old, organized baseball beckoned one last time. In late 1933 a group of Greenville businessmen applied for a franchise in a new Class D league, at one of the lowest levels of minor league baseball. They petitioned Commissioner Landis to allow Joe Jackson to serve as playing manager, a move that would almost certainly ensure the success of the franchise. Joe, 13 years removed from organized baseball, was enthusiastic. "The people of my town want me to put professional baseball back," said Joe to the Associated Press, "and they want me to manage the club. At my age of 45 years, I do not think I can play big league baseball, but I think I can do a lot for minor league ball."[5]

However, many of the nation's sportswriters were not yet ready to forgive the Black Sox, and Joe's plea for reinstatement caused a great deal of controversy. Westbrook Pegler spoke for many of them when he wrote in the *New York World-Telegram* that Joe and the other Black Sox "should be made horrible examples ... [they] marred the brightest illusion and shook the innocent confidence of American youth." Pegler dramatically ended his piece with the assertion that Joe's reinstatement might "set an example which might lead to grafting in public office, contempt for the public intelligence and the degradation of government."[6]

On January 19, 1934, Judge Landis released his decision. To the surprise of no one, Landis turned Joe down. "Of course there are not, and cannot be, two standards of eligibility" for the major and minor leagues, said Landis. "The game played in a small town in a Class D league is no less important to the spectators and players than is the game played in the large city in a high class league.... This application must be denied."[7] Landis also revealed that some of the other Black Sox had recently applied for reinstatement, and he had rejected their applications as well.

The Commissioner of Baseball was unwilling to do any favors for Joe Jackson, but the people of Greenville still admired and respected their local hero. He served as the supervisor of umpires for the Western Carolina Semi-Pro League, outside of Judge Landis' jurisdiction. Joe ruled on appeals and evaluated the performances of the umpires in the league, and his decisions bore a good deal of weight with the locals. Joe also became involved with coaching in the mill leagues. His cousin William (Pink) Jackson was managing the Southern Worsted Mill team in Greenville County at this time, and Joe often appeared at the team's practices, demonstrating his swing for the eager mill hands with an ever-present replica of Black Betsy.[8]

Joe also spent a great deal of time teaching baseball to the local youngsters. The neighborhood kids weren't even born when Joe played in two World Series up north, but they enthusiastically absorbed the lessons taught by the man they called "Uncle Joe." The former ballplayer would close his liquor store in the evening, roll up his sleeves, and organize an impromptu game in the old Brandon Mill neighborhood, pitching for both sides and offering advice until Katie called him in to dinner. Sometimes, at the end of a game, Joe would march the whole crowd downtown and treat them all to ice cream cones.

Joe ended his baseball career in 1937. In May of that year he signed on as manager of the Woodside Mills factory team in Winnsboro, South Carolina. Woodside Mills played on dusty dirt fields in the semipro King Cotton League, which some called the "Linthead League," and one of the pitchers on the team was Joe's brother, Jerry. It was a long way from Comiskey Park in Chicago, but it seemed somehow fitting that Joe Jackson, the most famous graduate of textile baseball, should end his active career where it began some 40 years before.

He still swung the bat every now and then, however. On August 1, 1939, Joe was invited to participate in the annual Western Carolina League All-Star Game. Joe batted once for each team and pounded two blue darters deep into the outfield. If he were a younger man he would have legged them both out for inside-the-park homers, but at age 51 Joe's speed was only a memory. He wound up with two doubles, to the cheers of the 3,000 fans in attendance.[9]

On a hot, sunny summer day in June of 1939, the baseball world turned its attention to the sleepy community of Cooperstown, New York. On that day, thousands of people from all over the country jammed the tiny town for the dedication of the National Baseball Hall of Fame and Museum. As part of the festivities, Commissioner Kenesaw Mountain

Joe Jackson in the mid–1930s. He was still playing ball in his late forties (Greenville County Historical Society/The Coxe Collection).

Landis introduced a group of 25 men, honored players and founders of the game of baseball, as the first members of the Hall of Fame.

Ten of the eleven living honorees gathered for a group portrait. Seventy-seven-year-old Connie Mack, who signed Joe Jackson in 1908 and offered to teach him to read and write, was the oldest man in the group. Joe's old Cleveland teammate Napoleon Lajoie smiled broadly in the back row, behind the pipe-puffing Ohio farmer Cy Young and the former White Sox captain Eddie Collins, now employed as general manager of the Boston club. Walter Johnson, who called Joe Jackson "the toughest batter I ever faced," left his farm in Maryland to attend the ceremony and renew acquaintances with George Sisler, Grover Alexander, and Honus Wagner. Tris Speaker, who succeeded Jackson as the star of the Cleveland Indians, was there, and the 44-year-old Babe Ruth stood out from all the older men around him with his jet-black hair and shiny two-toned shoes. "I copied my swing after Joe Jackson's," Ruth liked to say. "His is the perfectest."

The only man missing was the irascible Ty Cobb, who channeled his ruthless energy into the business world after he left the game and became a millionaire. Cobb, who battled Joe Jackson for the batting title in almost every season of Joe's career, was still bitter about the way Judge Landis handled the 1926 game-fixing controversy. Cobb didn't want to speak to the Commissioner, so he stayed away from the ceremony until it was nearly over.

The Hall of Fame also honored 14 men who were no longer living, whose relatives and friends accepted their accolades in their stead. Most of them were the old-time stars of the 1880s and 1890s, men like Cap Anson and Wee Willie Keeler, and founders of the game like Alexander Cartwright, who set the bases 90 feet apart nearly 100 years before. Christy Mathewson, who built the Cincinnati team that beat the White Sox in the 1919 World Series, was also one of their number, as was John McGraw, the "Little Napoleon" who juggled his pitching staff in the 1917 Series in an attempt to neutralize Joe Jackson's powerful bat.

The Hall of Fame also inducted the two men whose friendship turned into a bitter animosity that destroyed them both—Byron Bancroft Johnson, founder of the American League, and Charles Albert Comiskey, the man who spent a record amount to bring Joe to the Chicago White Sox.

Joe Jackson was not among the players honored in Cooperstown that day. The Black Sox scandal had taken place only 20 years before, and baseball's darkest hour was still fresh in the minds of the nation's sportswriters. The directors of the Hall of Fame, at the suggestion of Judge Landis, entrusted the writers with the responsibility of voting for the first members of baseball's shrine; three years before, they elected Cobb, Ruth, Mathewson, Johnson, and Wagner as the first five honorees. Joe Jackson, the greatest natural hitter who ever lived, received only two votes from the 226 participating writers.

However, if the Black Sox scandal had never happened, Joe Jackson would have appeared in that famous photograph with Mack, Lajoie, Ruth, and all the rest. Of the twentieth-century players honored by the Hall of Fame on that day in 1939, only one, Ty Cobb, compiled a higher career batting average than Joe Jackson did. Only three—Cobb, Sisler,

Joe behind the counter in his Greenville liquor store, October 1938 (©Bettmann/Corbis).

and Lajoie—belted the ball for a higher average in a season than Joe did in 1911, when he hit .408. None of the three batted .400 as a rookie like Joe did. Only Ruth, Speaker, Collins, and Mathewson played on more World Championship teams than Joe; Jackson's teams won the Series only once, but Cobb, Lajoie, and Sisler never did, and the latter two never appeared in a World Series.

If Joe's absence from the big ceremony bothered him, or if he even noticed it, he didn't mention it to anyone. Joe spent the day in Greenville, operating his store and trading pleasantries with his customers, just as he spent every Monday down home. Joe Jackson was now 50 years old, almost two decades removed from his last big league game, and his days in the major leagues seemed like another lifetime ago.

In the early 1940s, Joe Jackson's health took a turn for the worse. At one point, his weight ballooned to 254 pounds, some 70 pounds over his playing weight in the major leagues. He was diagnosed as a diabetic, and his heart was weak. He began to experience regular chest pains, and in early 1942 Joe spent a month in bed, on doctor's orders, to rest his fragile heart. The doctors also put Joe on a strict diet, eliminating sweets, fatty foods, and alcohol. Joe's family and friends remarked that Joe was the only liquor store owner they knew who was not allowed to touch a drop.

Carter (Scoop) Latimer was the sports editor of the *Greenville News* at this time, and in the summer of 1942 he visited Joe on the occasion of the ballplayer's 54th birthday. The neighborhood children presented their "Uncle Joe" with a replica of Black Betsy. Joe and Katie, in turn, provided ice cream and cake for all, although Joe's dietary restrictions prevented him from joining in.

Joe gave Latimer the most extensive interview that the ballplayer had given to anyone since the end of the Black Sox trial 21 years earlier. "The world couldn't treat me any better," said Jackson. "I have no regrets, and I love to look back upon the diamond and the fellows I knew."[10] He told stories about his old Cleveland teammate Napoleon Lajoie, who dropped by that day for a visit, and Connie Mack, for whom Joe said he wished he could have played for his entire career. Joe also picked his all-time All-Star team, with Ty Cobb, Tris Speaker, and Babe Ruth in the outfield.

Lajoie, who at this time was 67 years old and living in Florida, suggested to Latimer that Joe would have been the greatest hitter of all time if he had played in the post–1920 "lively ball" era. Joe modestly disagreed. "Let Ruth have the honors," said Joe. "The fact that Babe was quoted as saying he copied his swing and stride from me is praise enough, don't you think?"[11]

Joe touched upon the 1919 World Series only briefly, but his residual bitterness about his banishment from the game had hardened into denial by this time. "Regardless of what anybody says, I'm innocent of any wrongdoing," said Joe defiantly. "I gave baseball all I had. The Supreme Being is the only one to whom I've got to answer. If I had been out there booting balls and looking foolish at bat against the Reds, there might have been some grounds for suspicion. I think my record in the 1919 World's Series will stand up against that of any man in that Series or any other World's Series in all history."[12]

Latimer sold the story to *The Sporting News*, which ran it as a front-page feature in its issue of September 24, 1942. The story was accompanied by pictures of Joe behind the counter in his liquor store, cooking eggs in his kitchen at home, and swinging a bat in his later playing days. The photos showed a stout, bald, middle-aged man, missing a few of his teeth, but with a smile on his face and a twinkle in his eye. Joe had some health problems, but the nation could see that Joe Jackson, after two decades out of the spotlight, was doing well for himself down home in South Carolina.

Judge Landis, however, was not pleased. The aging Commissioner "hit the ceiling," according to the editor of *The Sporting News*, J. G. Taylor Spink, after Landis saw Jackson on the cover of the so-called "Bible of Baseball." Landis, from what Spink heard, deemed the use of the article "deplorable."[13]

Perhaps Landis thought that *The Sporting News* was angling for Jackson's return to baseball, but the 76-year-old Commissioner needn't have worried. Joe Jackson was content with life as a local celebrity in Greenville, running his store and helping the neighborhood kids learn how to swing a bat. As Joe stated in the article, "I've had requests to go to New York for broadcasts, but I'm content to live here in a house by the side of the road." Joe didn't even hold any hard feelings for Latimer, who stuck him with the moniker "Shoeless Joe" back in 1908 as a cub reporter in Greenville. Joe never liked the nickname, but by 1942 he had grown to accept it.

However, Joe never came to terms with his illiteracy. Many times a stranger would come into the liquor store with a baseball and ask Joe for an autograph. Joe would smile and allow that he was mighty busy now, "but if you'll come back tomorrow morning, I'll have the ball signed for you." The fan would return the next day for his baseball, not knowing that Katie was the one who signed "Joe Jackson" on it.

Jackson also never came to terms with the scandal that caused his banishment from baseball. His friends and family in Greenville accepted the explanation that Joe had been caught in a web not of his own making, that he had somehow been suckered into the scheme and left holding the bag by fast-talking Yankees. Some people even suggested that Joe had put one over on the Northern "city slickers," because he played to win in the Series and kept the $5,000!

The people down home in Greenville never pressured Joe too much about the facts of the case. They were his friends, not his prosecutors, and Joe's fans were content to let the crooked Series fade into memory. However, one of Joe's acquaintances asked him one day where the money went. "I gave it to a hospital," replied Joe. This was not entirely a lie, since at least some of the money was used to pay his sister's hospital bills in the winter of 1919-20. It wasn't entirely the truth, either, but Joe said no more about the situation, and Joe's questioner dropped the matter.

Ty Cobb, in his autobiography, told about his final meeting with his old rival Joe Jackson. Cobb wrote that in 1946, he and writer Grantland Rice found themselves passing through Greenville, and they decided to seek out Jackson. They stopped at Jackson's liquor store on Pendleton Street and shared small talk with the former slugger, who busied himself with his stock and pretended not to recognize his former opponent. Cobb played along for a while before blurting out, "Don't you know me, you old so-and-so?"

Jackson whirled around with a grin on his face. "Sure I do, Ty," replied Jackson, "but I didn't think you knew me after all these years. I didn't want to embarrass you or nothin'."

"Joe," said Cobb to the smiling Jackson, "I'll tell you how well I remember you. Whenever I got the idea I was a good hitter, I'd stop and take a good look at you. Then I knew I could stand some improvement."[14]

However, over the years, other writers have twisted Cobb's story into another tale about poor, pathetic Joe. Some writers say that when Cobb asked Joe if he knew who he was talking to, Joe sadly replied, "Sure I do, Ty, but I didn't think anyone up there would want to know me after all these years." Some versions of the tale have Jackson bursting into tears at this point. However, Joe Jackson didn't wallow in self-pity in his later years, though he steadfastly continued to deny his guilt in the 1919 scandal. Joe was a proud man, a celebrity in his hometown, and would never have felt the need to hide his identity from Ty Cobb or anyone else. There are people living in Greenville today who remember the day that Joe Jackson showed his friend Ty Cobb around town.

Joe suffered a blow in late 1947 when his favorite nephew, McDavid Jackson, died suddenly. McDavid had married several years before, but his new wife died in childbirth (the baby was stillborn as well) and the young man joined the naval air corps to put the tragedy behind him. McDavid returned from the war and remarried, but "he was killed accidentally … when a gun he was cleaning went off," Joe told a magazine writer. "Katie and me felt like we'd lost our own boy." The sad truth of the matter was that McDavid, still depressed over the death of his first wife, killed himself with a shotgun on Christmas Eve. Many Jackson family members believe that Joe's health problems, which flared anew in 1948, were a direct result of the death of his beloved nephew.

Commissioner Landis died in 1944, and Senator Albert B. (Happy) Chandler, like Jackson a southerner, took office as commissioner in May 1945. Chandler, like Landis, refused all overtures on behalf of both Joe Jackson and Buck Weaver. In early 1951 Ford Frick, a former sportswriter and president of the National League, took Chandler's place, and he also declined to consider Jackson's case.

Furman Bisher, an Atlanta sportswriter, visited Jackson twice and interviewed him in the summer of 1949. He found the 61-year-old Joe Jackson at home on East Wilborn Street in Greenville, South Carolina, gray-haired but still active. Jackson explained that he had battled heart and liver trouble the previous year but had regained his health and returned to the management of his liquor store, which he had leased out during his illness. "I've been doing about $50,000 to $100,000 a year business," said Jackson proudly.

The retired ballplayer gave his side of the story because "it seems that 30 years after the World Series, the world may want to hear what I have to say." Jackson recounted his childhood, the origin of his nickname "Shoeless Joe," and his days in the major leagues. He also described the scandal, leaving out the fact that he agreed to throw the World Series for $20,000 and later received $5,000. Incredibly, Jackson said that Landis banned him "because of the company I kept," because Lefty Williams was his roommate on the road. "I had to take whoever they assigned to room with me on the road. I had no power over that," said Jackson, somewhat disingenuously.[15]

Jackson blamed his expulsion from baseball on Ban Johnson, Charles Comiskey's archenemy. "When Mr. Johnson got a chance to get even with Mr. Comiskey, he did it. He was the man who ruled us ineligible. He was the man who caused the thing to go into the courts. He did everything he could against Mr. Comiskey."[16] Jackson, in his full southern storyteller mode, also made the surprising claim that he visited Charles Comiskey, in the presence of Hugh Fullerton, to warn him of the fix on the morning of the first game!

Joe also allowed that by the end of the 1920 season, his career was mostly over anyway. "I guess one of the reasons I never fought my suspension any harder than I did," said Jackson, "was that I thought I had spent a pretty full life in the big leagues. I was 32 years old at the time, and I had been in the majors 13 years; I had a lifetime batting average of .356; I held the all-time throwing record for distance; and I had made pretty good salaries for those days. There wasn't much left for me in the big leagues."[17] This after a 1920 season in which Jackson hit .382 with a career high 12 home runs and 121 runs batted in.

Indeed, despite reports to the contrary, Joe Jackson insisted to Bisher that he never applied for reinstatement to baseball. Other people made overtures on his behalf many times, but Jackson himself stood aloof from the effort. "I gave baseball my best," said Jackson, "and if the game didn't care enough to see me get me a square deal, then I wouldn't go out of my way to get back in it."[18]

We all write our autobiographies in our minds; our memories wipe out the bad things and embellish the good, leaving each of us as either hero or victim. In his old age, Joe Jackson chose to remember the good times and to forget that dirty envelope that Lefty Williams handed to him on the evening of October 4, 1919. His playing career ended too soon, but he didn't mind. He was finished with it anyway. Moreover, if Joe Jackson said that he warned Comiskey before the first game, well, Comiskey was dead and so was Hugh Fullerton. Who could prove otherwise?

Bisher's article appeared in *Sport* magazine in October 1949 and immediately focused attention again on Shoeless Joe Jackson. In early 1951 both houses of the South Carolina legislature appealed to Commissioner Ford Frick to reinstate Jackson, but Frick, like Landis and Chandler before him, refused to reopen the case.

Joe Jackson recovered from his 1948 liver troubles and resumed the operation of his liquor store, but then his heart started to fail. He suffered two heart attacks early in 1951, and knew the end was coming. On March 23, 1951, Joe Jackson made out his will, which reads as follows with misspellings uncorrected:

> STATE OF SOUTH CAROLINA
> COUNTY OF GREENVILLE
>
> WILL
>
> IN THE NAME OF GOD, AMEN:
>
> I, Joe Jackson, of the County and state aforesaid, being of sound and disposeing mind and memory, do make, publish and declare this as and for my last will and testament, hereby revokeing all letters or instruments of a testamentary character by me heretofore executed.
>
> ITEM ONE: It is my will that as soon after my death as possable my Executor, hereinafter named, shall pay all my just debts and expences of burial.
>
> ITEM TWO: I give, devise and bequeath all of my property of which I die possessed, both real and personal, wheresoever it may be, unto my beloved wife, Katie Jackson, for her to have and to use as she may see fit for her best interest.
>
> ITEM THREE: I hereby nominate, constitute and apoint my wife Katie Jackson as Executor of this my last will and testament, IN WITNESS WHEREOF, I have hereunto set my hand and seal this 23rd day of March 1951 A.D.

/s/ Joe Jackson

Signed, sealed, published and declared as and for his last will and testament, by Joe Jackson in the presence of us, present at the same time, who, at his request, in his presence and in the presence and in the presence of each other, have hereunto subscribed our names as witnesses the day and year last above set forth.

/s/ W.A. Turner ADDRESS 411 Ansel St.
/s/ W. Eugene Ertes ADDRESS 148 Pleasant Ridge Ave.
/s/ Mrs. Gene A. Sine ADDRESS 216 Frank St.

The Cleveland Indians made plans to open their own Hall of Fame in 1951. The club decided to honor ten players—two pitchers, three outfielders, and one at each other position—chosen in a newspaper poll of the fans of Cleveland. A screening committee made up a ballot of eligible players, which was published in the local papers, and after much discussion the committee members decided to include Joe Jackson's name on the ballot. The Cleveland fans didn't forget their last .400 hitter. Joe Jackson finished third in the outfield balloting, earning election to the Cleveland Hall of Fame with nine other stars from bygone days, including Joe's former teammates Steve O'Neill, Cy Young, and Napoleon Lajoie.

The ten players, all of whom were still living,[19] were invited to attend the ceremonies on September 2 at club expense, but Joe Jackson was absent from the proceedings. Joe told the Indians that his doctor would not permit him to travel to Cleveland, so the club kept his gift—an inscribed gold mantel clock—for presentation at a later date.

The nationwide notice paid to the Cleveland Hall of Fame voting brought Joe Jackson to the attention of the producers of a popular television show hosted by gossip columnist Ed Sullivan. The show, which was then called *Toast of the Town* and would later be called *The Ed Sullivan Show*, was a live variety program that aired on Sunday evenings, and the producers asked Joe Jackson to come to New York for an appearance. Perhaps, suggested the producers, Joe's fellow Cleveland Hall of Fame electee Tris Speaker could present Joe with his gold clock on the broadcast.

Jackson, always wary and uncomfortable in the big city, had to be persuaded to accept. He resented looking like a charity case, but his family prevailed upon him to accept the Sullivan appearance, and Joe finally agreed to appear on the show of December 16, 1951.

Sadly, his heart failed him one last time. Joe, now 63 years old, wasn't feeling well on the first weekend of December, but by the following Tuesday he had recovered enough to spend the entire day at his liquor store.

The exhausted ballplayer spent all of the next day in bed, but woke up about 9:30 that evening complaining of chest pains. Katie quickly called for a doctor, but Joe was having another heart attack. Joe's brother Dave sped to his brother's bedside. Joe gripped Dave's hand and said, "Goodbye, good buddy. This is it," then fell unconscious. By the time the doctor arrived, at a few minutes after ten o'clock on the night of December 5, 1951, Joe Jackson was dead. He was the first of the eight banned Black Sox, and the first of George and Martha Jackson's eight children, to die.

Joe Jackson was buried in Woodlawn Memorial Park in Greenville. Hundreds of people attended his funeral, and a huge pile of flowers covered the grave after it was filled in. A flat stone slab labeled "Jackson," with a bronze plate that contains the inscription, "Joseph W. July 16, 1888 December 5, 1951," marks his grave. Katie Jackson lived for eight more years. She died in April of 1959 and was buried next to her husband.

Chapter 21

Epilogue

[Eddie Collins] liked to talk about Babe Ruth, the big monkey, and Lou Gehrig, the Iron Horse, and other great players, but not with the same dreamlike vision that he spoke of Jackson. Finally one day, I was sitting in my mother's living room and he was sitting right in front of me, and I said tell me about Joe Jackson. He was looking at me and his head dropped. This wasn't an act. Then he looked at the ceiling, and said, "Boy, what a player." He said it with reverence, and he said it with sadness.

— Ted Williams, 1999[1]

God knows I gave my best in baseball at all times and no man on earth can truthfully judge me otherwise.

— Joe Jackson[2]

What place does Shoeless Joe Jackson occupy in baseball history?

Jackson, for most of his baseball career, was in the wrong place at the wrong time. When he arrived in the major leagues in 1908 with the Philadelphia Athletics, he encountered hostile teammates and a big-city environment for which the young slugger was woefully ill prepared. He moved on to Cleveland, to a city and team that seemed to fit him perfectly; however, within a few years, the cash-strapped Cleveland management traded him to a club with greater financial resources. He joined the Chicago White Sox, the most profitable team in baseball, but his expected monetary windfall didn't happen, and Joe played for six years

Joe, Ty Cobb, and Nap Lajoie, three of the Junior circuit's all-time great hitters.

without a raise in pay. Gamblers and fixers found this bitterly divided team ripe for the picking, and Joe became involved in the scandal that ended his major league career.

Joe Jackson also had the bad luck to play in the American League as a contemporary of a fellow southerner, Ty Cobb. In the nine full seasons of Joe's career, Cobb bested him in the batting race in every season but one (the last one, 1920). Joe finished second in this rivalry on three occasions, third twice, and fourth twice in those nine seasons. However, Joe almost always out-hit the National League batting champ. If Joe had played in the National League and posted the same averages, he would have won seven batting titles from 1911 to 1920.[3]

Still, Jackson left a lasting impression on the game. His career batting average of .356 is the third best of all time, behind Cobb's .366 mark and Rogers Hornsby's .358 average. He shares the American League record for triples in a season with 26, and he led the league in triples three times. Joe pounded out over 200 hits in a season three times, and in another year, led the league with 197 hits. Only Joe and Hall of Famer

Rod Carew hold the career batting average records for two different teams; Joe is the all-time average leader of both the Cleveland Indians and the Chicago White Sox.

Most importantly, Joe was a power hitter before power hitters came into vogue in baseball. Before Joe came along, baseball was a station-to-station kind of game, in which runs were scored one at a time by bunting and stealing bases. Joe Jackson swung hard and hit the ball a long way, which delighted the fans and paved the way for Babe Ruth, who copied Joe's swing and changed the face of the game. All home run hitters, from Lou Gehrig to Mickey Mantle, to Henry Aaron and Mark McGwire, are spiritually descended from Babe Ruth, who learned his swing from Shoeless Joe Jackson. Joe was baseball's first true power hitter.

Joe Jackson's career was a bridge between the old style of play, epitomized by Ty Cobb, and the new game which was introduced by Ruth in the early 1920s. Joe cleared the path for the Babe and other power hitters to follow; this, not his ill-advised participation in the 1919 World Series scandal, is Joe Jackson's legacy to the game of baseball.

If Joe had been honest, he would have been inducted into the Baseball Hall of Fame when it opened in 1939. As it is, we must content ourselves to say that Joe Jackson, the greatest natural hitter who ever lived, is the best player in the history of baseball who is not a member of the Hall, with apologies to Pete Rose.

As far as anyone knows, the Baseball Hall of Fame in Cooperstown, New York, rarely, if ever, entered Joe Jackson's thoughts. He didn't mention the Hall of Fame to Furman Bisher in 1949,[4] and though some of Joe's friends in Greenville watched the voting results with interest each year, there is no evidence that Joe ever spoke of Cooperstown to anyone. How ironic it is that Joe's name is at the center of a still-raging controversy—should Joe Jackson be elected to the Hall of Fame after all?

Ted Williams and Bob Feller think so. In 1998 Williams and Feller, both members of the Hall, publicly announced their conviction that the Hall should enshrine Shoeless Joe.

"He's served his sentence and it's time for baseball to acknowledge his debt is paid and the Hall of Fame Committee on Veterans to list him as a nominee," said Williams, the former Red Sox slugger. "It's time, and it's the right thing to do. Joe Jackson was one of the finest hitters of all time, and he could field too.... I wished I could have talked hitting with that man. It's too late, but it's not too late for him to come and join me— and all the other Hall of Famers—in Cooperstown."[5]

Jackson, although he was placed on baseball's ineligible list in 1921, was fully eligible for election for the Hall of Fame until 1991, when the Pete Rose case intervened. In 1989, Commissioner A. Bartlett Giamatti suspended Rose from baseball for life for gambling, and the Hall of Fame faced the dilemma of Rose's probable election to the Hall upon his eligibility in 1992. The Hall of Fame ruled in February 1991 that those players on baseball's ineligible list would not be considered for election. This decision put both Pete Rose and Joe Jackson in the same category, and merged their campaigns together in the minds of the public.

Since Jackson played prior to 1945, the Baseball Writers' Association of America (BBWAA) can no longer elect him to the Hall of Fame even if he gains reinstatement. The Committee on Veterans, a 15-member body that includes Ted Williams, considers pre–1945 players, as well as managers, umpires, and executives. Twelve of the 15 members must agree for a nominee to be elected from the Committee on Veterans. For now, however, Jackson's candidacy depends on the present commissioner, Bud Selig, lifting the lifetime ban imposed upon Jackson in 1921.

There had been some intermittent interest in reinstating Joe to baseball's good graces in the decades after his death, but the campaign to put Jackson in the Hall of Fame started in earnest in 1989 with the release of the movie *Field of Dreams*. Based on the novel *Shoeless Joe* by W. P. Kinsella, *Field of Dreams* concerns an Iowa farmer whose late father was Joe Jackson's biggest fan. The farmer hears a voice that says, "If you build it, he will come," and so he converts part of his cornfield into a baseball diamond. Sure enough, the ghost of Shoeless Joe Jackson walks out of the cornfield one day to play a game of catch with the farmer; soon, all the rest of the Black Sox do likewise, in their 1919 uniforms and fold-up fielding gloves.

This nostalgic movie, the most successful baseball film of all time, showed Joe Jackson in a sympathetic light and brought him to the forefront of the nation's attention once again.[6] One year earlier, Eliot Asinof's book *Eight Men Out* reached the screen in a film by director John Sayles, portraying Jackson and his teammates as victims of Charles Comiskey's greed and creating more public sympathy for the disgraced slugger. By the early 1990s a full-fledged national campaign, fanned by the popularity of *Field of Dreams*, took shape with the aim of reinstating Joe Jackson and electing him to the Hall of Fame.

Those who support Joe's reinstatement most vehemently, in South Carolina and elsewhere, do not base their activities on the idea that Joe should be forgiven for his role in the Black Sox scandal. They insist that Joe was innocent, and many of Joe's most vocal supporters claim that he was framed by Charles Comiskey, Alfred Austrian, and Commissioner

Landis. They say that since Joe hit .375 in the Series, played errorless ball in the field, and was tried and acquitted of scandal-related charges in 1921, his subsequent banishment from the game was an injustice that can only be righted with a plaque on the wall in Cooperstown.

Was Joe Jackson guilty of throwing the 1919 World Series? Let's look at a few of the arguments in his favor.

Jackson played errorless ball in the 1919 Series.

Triples are almost never hit to left field. The left fielder is much closer to third base than the center or right fielders, and a left fielder with Jackson's arm would almost never play a ball into a triple unless he fell down. The Reds hit three triples into left in the 1919 World Series, although the writers called Jackson's glove "the place triples go to die." Pitchers hit two of those triples! In all, the Reds hit seven triples in the 1919 Series, three of them by pitchers. In some World Series since, no triples at all were struck.

In addition, contemporary accounts suggest that Jackson played out of position at crucial moments in the Series. In Game 4, Cincinnati's Earle (Greasy) Neale hit a fly ball that dropped for a run-scoring double. Joe couldn't reach the ball, since he was playing all the way over near the left field line, despite the fact that Neale was a left-handed batter. The *Cleveland Plain Dealer* reported that Joe "played ... Neale's fly to left like an old lady."[7] In the first inning of Game 1, Heinie Groh hit a fly ball to Joe with a runner on third, and some felt that Joe's weak throw home allowed the runner (Morrie Rath) to score. Jackson also got a bad jump on Hod Eller's lazy fly in Game 5 that fell for three bases and started Cincinnati's winning rally in that game.

Dickie Kerr, the winning pitcher in Games 3 and 6 of the 1919 Series, shared that view. "Our outfielders fielded base hits slow, allowing the Reds to take extra bases," said Kerr. "And, there were times when the fielders played the Reds just opposite of what they were supposed to do. In that way they left gaps for the ball to fall safely."[8]

Jackson hit .375 in the Series and hit the only home run by either team. His 12 hits stood as a Series record until 1960.

"How dishonest could Jackson have been in that 1919 Series?" asked Ted Williams in 1998. "How much a fixer? He hit .375, slugged .563, got 12 hits—that was a record—and even homered, homered into the right field bleachers in Cincinnati. Homers didn't come easy then. It was a dead ball. Hell, it was the only homer of the Series—by either team. And to top it off he led the Sox in RBI and runs scored."[9]

Jackson won Game 7 with a run-scoring single, after the players finally decided to try to win the game for Cicotte. He hit a home run in Game 8—with the bases empty and the White Sox down 5-0. He hit a run-scoring double late in Game 8, but the Sox trailed 10-1 at the time. Besides, with Felsch, Gandil, and Risberg hitting behind him, Jackson knew he would die on base most of the time. Jackson set a record with 12 hits in the Series, but the 1919 Series lasted eight games, not seven as they do now. Two years earlier, the Giants' Dave Robertson banged out 11 hits in only six games.

Joe led the White Sox in runs batted in in the Series, though he only drove in six runs in the eight games, and three of those came late in Game 8 when it didn't matter anymore. Two Reds drove in more, and Reds pitcher Dutch Ruether drove in four runs in only six times at bat. In the first five games, four of which the Sox lost, Jackson drove in no runs at all. Except for the Game 7 winner, Jackson utterly failed to hit in the clutch at any time in the Series.

Alfred Austrian and Charles Comiskey coerced Joe's confession to the Chicago Grand Jury in 1920. The story that Joe told in his civil suit in Milwaukee four years later is the true one.

On September 28, 1920, Joe admitted to the Chicago Grand Jury that he agreed to help lose the Series for $20,000, and received $5,000 in cash from Lefty Williams after the fourth game. Three and a half years later, Joe told a completely different story to the court in Milwaukee, in his suit against Charles Comiskey for back pay. Joe claimed that he never agreed to throw the Series and had no knowledge of the Series fix until after the Series was over. He stated that Lefty Williams used his name, without his permission, to make the scheme attractive to the mobsters who financed the shady deal, and that the fixers gave Joe $5,000 because they thought—falsely—that he was involved.

Obviously, Joe was either lying in Chicago in 1920 or he was lying in Milwaukee in 1924. Joe's defenders insist that he told the truth in 1924 and lied in 1920, but to what end? If Joe was innocent, why would he incriminate himself in front of the Chicago Grand Jury and get himself thrown out of baseball?

Some of Joe's defenders claim that Joe's 1920 testimony was meticulously rehearsed, but Joe had been drinking heavily before he testified that day. How could he possibly keep all the lies straight in his nervous, addled condition? Moreover, why would he continue to tell the same story to the newspapermen that evening, especially if it falsely incriminated him?

It makes more sense to assume that Joe, believing that his 1920 confession was lost forever, lied in the Milwaukee trial in an effort to clear himself. He also had strong motives to lie in Milwaukee — namely, an $18,500 judgment and a possible reinstatement to major league baseball.

One major pillar of Joe's 1924 suit was the assertion that Joe received his $5,000 payment after the last game of the Series. However, Joe stated in 1920, both in the Grand Jury room and to the newspapers afterward, that he received the payment after Game 4 of the Series. Williams also said in 1920 that he paid Joe after the fourth game, both to the Grand Jury and to the reporters afterward. Did Cicotte, Jackson, and Williams all rehearse their 1920 testimony beforehand in an effort to make themselves look as guilty as possible?[10] Or, did Joe Jackson tell the truth in 1920 and lie in 1924? The second scenario makes far more sense.

There is another huge hole in Jackson's 1924 story. Why would Chick Gandil give Joe $5,000 if Joe was not involved in the fix? Lefty Williams testified in Milwaukee that Gandil and the mobsters thought Joe was in on the fix, only because Williams falsely told them that he was. Of course, the players could tell who was going all out and who was lying down. Gandil, an experienced fixer, didn't need to be told whether or not Joe was in on the scheme. Gandil could see that clearly enough for himself.

Some of Joe's apologists suggest that Williams felt badly about using Joe's name with the mobsters and offered the money to make amends. Others say that Jackson might have found out about Williams' machinations in the future, and if Williams had kept all the money, Joe would want to know where his share was. However, none of these scenarios can explain why Gandil, who had trouble stretching out the available money to make all the players happy, still held out $5,000 for Joe Jackson. Buck Weaver didn't receive any money, because he played to win. If Joe had done the same, Joe would not have received any money either, or else a crook like Gandil would have no reason to cut him in on the take.

Jackson was found innocent in a court of law.

No, he wasn't. He was found not guilty. "Innocent" and "not guilty" are not the same thing.

When Judge Hugo Friend instructed the jury that they must find the ballplayers guilty of intending to defraud the public, not merely of throwing ball games, a verdict of not guilty became a foregone conclusion. The act of throwing a baseball game was not a crime in the state of Illinois, just as the act of rigging a television quiz-show in the 1950s was not specifically a crime.

Charles Van Doren, the key figure of the quiz show scandals, bears more than a few similarities to the Black Sox. Like Joe Jackson in 1919, Van Doren participated in a scheme, kept his mouth shut, and profited from the arrangement. Van Doren's mistake was to lie about it under oath, and so Van Doren was convicted of perjury, as was Jackson in 1924 in his suit against Comiskey.

Van Doren wasn't found guilty of participating in a rigged quiz show, because a television program, like a baseball game, is considered to be "entertainment." Did Charles Van Doren—or Shoeless Joe Jackson—defraud the public? How much can a ballplayer or a game show contestant defraud a public that seeks to be entertained?

The question that bedeviled the Black Sox trial in 1921 was the same one that arose in the quiz show investigation three decades later. The question is, what can the public legally expect and demand from a television show or a sporting event? If the public's right is merely to be entertained, both the quiz shows and the 1919 World Series were highly entertaining, to say the least. Does the public have a right to demand that the proceedings unfold without premeditation? Wrestling matches, watched by millions, do not meet this standard. Neither do variety programs in which performers "lip-synch" their performance while a tape machine plays off-camera. Such arrangements are in no way illegal, and, as the Chicago prosecutors discovered in 1920, the activities of the Black Sox were not specifically illegal either.

However, what is legally allowable is not always morally acceptable. Judge Landis suspended the eight players, despite the fact that they were acquitted in court, because he held the reasonable position that team sports must be held to a higher standard of conduct than what the law allows. Failure to do so would eventually destroy baseball, because baseball survives only as long as the public has confidence in its honesty. That confidence was severely shaken in 1920; it took four years for the major leagues to match the attendance record set in 1920, and the Chicago White Sox did not surpass their 1920 attendance record until 1946. Judge Landis used harsh medicine in banning the eight Black Sox, but merciless as it was, it restored the public's faith in the game.

In the early part of the century, wrestling as a sport held every bit as much public respect and esteem as boxing, perhaps even more. Champions like Frank Gotch, George Hackenschmidt, and Stanislaus Zbysko were as well known as baseball stars like Ty Cobb and Christy Mathewson. Individual sports like wrestling and boxing were easier to manipulate than team sports, and both went through their share of scandals after World War I, just as baseball did. However, wrestling didn't clean its house, mostly because sporting contests between individuals are highly resistant to structured operation. Baseball and football teams must, by sheer necessity, organize themselves into leagues, while wrestling promoters cut their own deals and set their own schedules independently. The opportunities for shady dealing and outright dishonesty proved too difficult to resist.

Today, wrestling doesn't even acknowledge itself as a sport. The World Wrestling Federation, the largest wrestling organization in the United States, bills its matches as "exhibitions" in order to evade regulation (such as drug testing) by state and federal agencies. Wrestling lost the confidence of the public and can now only survive as a soap opera, a pageant of good versus evil, where any pretense to sport was forgotten long ago. True wrestling, the kind that existed eight decades ago, survives today only at the amateur level, in college and the Olympics. Corruption destroyed wrestling as a professional sport, and Judge Landis wanted to make sure that baseball didn't stumble down the same path.

Jackson's case is often compared to that of Pete Rose, baseball's all-time hits leader. Rose was not accused of throwing games as Jackson was, but of betting heavily on the outcomes of baseball games, including those involving his own team. Commissioner Bart Giamatti suspended Rose in 1989 because the influence of the gambler in baseball almost destroyed the game in 1920, and Giamatti wanted to stamp out any smoldering flames.

In Giamatti's view, Pete Rose's gambling activities had a strong possibility of influencing his managerial decisions. All good managers know that the baseball season is a marathon, not a 100-meter dash, but Rose was often criticized for overworking his bullpen and treating each game like the seventh game of the World Series. Did Pete Rose manage in this fashion because this is the all-out, hell-bent way he played the game? Or, did he do so to win his bets? Some, including the late Commissioner, were convinced that this actually did happen, that gambling concerns insinuated their way into the actual field management of the Cincinnati Reds, and that Rose's direction of the team was compromised by his betting.

To be sure, Giamatti erred several times during the Rose affair. His investigator, John Dowd, gave Giamatti a report that was almost comically biased in some of its assumptions and conclusions. Giamatti complicated matters by sending a letter to the judge hearing an unrelated case against one of Rose's chief accusers, praising the hapless defendant's "truthful cooperation" in testifying against Rose, before the Rose investigation had even been completed. Rose, understandably, accused Giamatti of prejudice and bias. In the end, Rose accepted a lifetime ban in exchange for an understanding that there would be no finding that he bet on baseball games. Rose and Giamatti signed the agreement, and then Giamatti blew it out of the water at the press conference of August 24, 1989, in which he stated his belief that Rose had bet on baseball no matter what the agreement said.

In any case, Rose deserved a long suspension from the sport, certainly more than the one year banishment handed to Brooklyn Dodgers manager Leo Durocher in 1947 for "conduct detrimental to the game." A lifetime ban seems too harsh, especially after Giamatti cynically violated the spirit of the agreement on the very day that it was announced to the public. Rose insists to this day that he did not gamble on baseball, but whether he did or not, Rose's misdeeds caused injury to himself, while the Black Sox scandal damaged the very fabric of the game.

On August 2, 1921, when Chick Gandil shouted in the Chicago courtroom after the verdict, "That'll teach Ban Johnson that he can't frame an honest bunch of ballplayers!" his hubris would have been funny if it weren't so disgusting. Gandil not only cheated the public but swindled his own teammates as well. Joe Jackson is not as guilty as Gandil, but he is guiltier than Pete Rose. Rose may have bet on games; Jackson threw them.

Though he took the $5,000, Jackson always played the game honestly.

There is ample evidence that this is not the truth, and the evidence is not limited to the 1919 World Series.

The White Sox, by several accounts, picked up extra money from gamblers by booting games here and there all through the 1920 campaign in order to keep the pennant race close. In the first important series of the season, in which the undefeated White Sox challenged the eventual pennant-winning Indians, Jackson misplayed a fly ball to lose the game for Red Faber. On August 5, Joe lost a game almost single-handedly with a bad throw from the outfield and two baserunning blunders. On August 31, Jackson let a fly ball get over his head while two runs scored. Eddie Cicotte took the loss in that game, which was the third game of a seven-game losing streak. They lost the next day as well, when a lazy fly ball that dropped between Joe and Happy Felsch triggered a fistfight on the Chicago bench. The White Sox didn't stop losing until they fell into third place after being in front by three and a half games.

All through the summer of 1920, the Indians, Yankees, and White Sox battled for the league lead, though the White Sox looked even stronger than they had in 1919. Partly through greed, partly through fear, the suspected Sox threw games to keep from running away with the pennant, playing with one eye on the scoreboard to see how the Indians and Yankees were doing. Somehow, Lefty Williams and Eddie Cicotte always managed to throw the wrong pitch at the worst possible moment, and the hitters would go for days unable to drive in a runner from third if their lives depended on it. The gamblers raked in the cash while the players settled for small amounts here and there, fearing exposure all the while.

The 1920 White Sox should have been a stronger team than the 1919 edition, with Red Faber's return to health and Dickie Kerr's maturity into a reliable fourth starter. All four starting pitchers won 20 games, and perhaps no team in baseball history ever had a rotation as good as the White Sox had that year. However, the Sox spent the entire season getting close to the top and then falling back to the pack, up and down like a seesaw all summer. Eddie Collins visited Charles Comiskey in early September to vent his suspicions, but Comiskey merely shrugged his shoulders. He knew what was happening on the field as well as Collins did, but both men found themselves powerless to stop it.

Even murderers get paroled, for heaven's sake.

"Joe served his sentence," says Ted Williams, one of Jackson's biggest and most public supporters, "and paid his debt to baseball. Baseball can't impose a sentence longer than Judge Landis did. Joe Jackson's not alive any more. He's served his sentence. It's time for Baseball to acknowledge his debt is paid; and for the Hall of Fame Committee on Veterans to list him as a nominee."[11]

This may be the most persuasive argument of all.

When the quiz show scandals erupted in the 1950s, the show *Twenty One* bore the brunt of the criticism. Producer Dan Enright and host Jack Barry, who virtually invented the quiz show format on television, disappeared from the nation's screens. They were disgraced, but they came back in the early 1970s with a popular syndicated game show called *The Joker's Wild*. If Barry and Enright could get a second chance, why not Shoeless Joe Jackson?

Jackson, after all, wasn't a Chick Gandil or a Hal Chase. He didn't plan the fix. Even Buck Weaver attended more meetings than Joe did. "Not that he didn't do it," says Eliot Asinof, author of *Eight Men Out*, "but he was an innocent."[12] To Jackson, the fix was a merely a way to make a little extra cash, to support his family and his lifestyle. The fix would be carried out anyway, whether or not Jackson participated. Why not pick up a few thousand extra bucks?

That dirty envelope with $5,000 inside separates Joe Jackson and Buck Weaver. Money was tight, since the gamblers never delivered all the promised cash, and Gandil was having problems stretching out the money enough to satisfy everybody. Nevertheless, Gandil still held 5,000 of these precious dollars out for Jackson. Joe was deeply involved, or else Gandil would have had no reason to pay him anything.

In Jackson's grand jury testimony on September 28, 1920, he was asked what he did after none of the promised payoff money appeared after the first game of the Series. Jackson answered, "I asked Gandil what was the trouble. He says, 'Everything is all right,' he had it." Then, in response to the next question, he said "We went ahead and threw the second game, we went after him [Gandil] again. I said to him, 'What are you going to do?' … After the third game I says, 'Somebody is getting a nice little jazz, everybody is crossed.'"[13]

Jackson's concern about the promised windfall belies his later insistence that he played to win and paid no attention to the shenanigans around him. After he testified to the Grand Jury, according to *The New York Times*, Jackson stated, "Let me tell you something [about the third game of the Series]. The eight of us did our best to kick it and little Dick Kerr won the game with his pitching. And because he won it the gamblers double-crossed us for double-crossing them."[14]

Gandil knew that Jackson was helping throw the games, and Gandil wanted him to keep doing so. Gandil delivered the $5,000 to keep Jackson happy and to keep the fix on track.

Joe Jackson profited from the fix, nearly doubling his admittedly meager salary, and actively participated in the throwing of games in 1919 and (possibly) 1920. This should be enough to bar his entry to the Hall of Fame.

There were many contributing factors to the Black Sox scandal. Red Faber's injury, Chick Gandil's greed, the head-in-the-sand attitude of baseball owners confronted by evidence of gambling, and Charles Comiskey's stinginess all contributed to the tragedy that destroyed the careers of Shoeless Joe Jackson and seven of his teammates.

However, the bulk of the blame for the tragedy of Joe Jackson rests with Jackson himself. He was a great ballplayer and, in many ways, an admirable individual. Those people now living in Greenville who knew him in his later years, especially the children who learned how to play baseball from him, still regard Joe Jackson with a respect that borders on reverence. Nevertheless, Joe agreed to help throw the World Series for $20,000 because he had a weakness for money, and, at that point in his life, his athletic talent far outstripped his judgment and maturity. Joe Jackson's fascination with money led him into the scheme that ended his baseball career. One could hardly imagine Eddie Collins, or Napoleon Lajoie, or Walter Johnson, making such a deal with the devil.

If any member of the Black Sox deserves sympathy, it is Buck Weaver, who didn't receive any of the gamblers' cash and played all out in the Series. Commissioner Landis banned Weaver for having "guilty knowledge," suggesting that Weaver should have told what he knew of the fix. However, whom would Weaver tell? Charles Comiskey, who hid from Joe Jackson the day after the Series ended? Kid Gleason, who told Comiskey what he suspected and got nowhere? The Chicago sportswriters, who drank Comiskey's wine and ate his steaks and had no incentive to cause discomfort to their benefactor? Hugh Fullerton, who had the courage to speak up and found himself the target of a vicious mudslinging campaign for his efforts? Maybe Weaver should have told Christy Mathewson, who caught Hal Chase almost red-handed fixing a game and saw him exonerated and hired by Matty's old friend John McGraw?

Weaver could have saved his career by telling either Comiskey or Kid Gleason of his knowledge of the fix before the Series began, but how could he do this in September of 1919? If nothing came of it, as nothing had come of Hal Chase's machinations, Weaver would become a rat, a snitch, a traitor. Chase stayed in baseball after trying to bribe Jimmy Ring in 1918, didn't he? Weaver had knowledge of wrongdoing, but so did many players at the time.[15]

The appointment of Judge Landis as commissioner did not take place until November 1920. Before that time, baseball's ruling body, the National Commission, had three members: Comiskey's mortal enemy Ban Johnson, who had already brushed off the fix rumors; National League president John Heydler, who had reinstated Hal Chase; and Garry Herrmann, owner of the victorious Cincinnati Reds. Landis never told Weaver how he should have made his story known to a baseball hierarchy that desperately wished not to hear it.

Still, Weaver's expulsion served an important purpose. Before 1920, honest players would help cover up wrongdoing by their teammates. After 1920, they didn't dare. No one wanted to be the next Buck Weaver.

In the meantime, as the Hall of Fame debate continues, the rehabilitation of Shoeless Joe Jackson proceeds apace. The state legislature of South Carolina passed a resolution in 1998 that reads as follows:

A CONCURRENT RESOLUTION TO MEMORIALIZE THE COMMISSIONER
OF BASEBALL TO REINSTATE "SHOELESS JOE" JACKSON AS A MEMBER
IN GOOD STANDING IN PROFESSIONAL BASEBALL.

Whereas, nearly eighty years have elapsed since the scandal of the
1919 World Series; and

Whereas, although the story has frequently seen print, fact, and fancy
have been so confused that today it still is not known what actually
took place; and

Whereas, Joe Jackson was acquitted of all charges of conspiracy by a
jury of "twelve good men and true"; and

Whereas, although set aside by the judge, a jury verdict against the
Chicago White Sox was awarded him for the balance of his contract;
and

Whereas, the fact that his fielding average for the Series of 1919 was
perfect and the fact that in that Series he set a record of twelve hits
for a World Series offer strong evidence that he was no party to a
conspiracy to "throw" the Series; and

Whereas, he suffered lifelong ignominy as a result of the scandal of
1919 and his subsequent banishment from organized baseball; and

Whereas, eighty years is far too long for any man or the memory of
him to be tainted for an act as to which strong evidence exists that it
was never committed by him; and

Whereas, Joe Jackson was active in civic matters, particularly in programs for the benefit of young boys, after his return to private life;
and

Whereas, the General Assembly of South Carolina recognizes the
desire of the family, friends, and baseball fans, who have loyally supported "Shoeless Joe," that he be exonerated; and

Whereas, the General Assembly of South Carolina believes him to
have been innocent of any conspiracy to "throw" the World Series of
1919; and

Whereas, although he is now deceased, the General Assembly feels
that he should be exonerated by baseball as he was exonerated in both
criminal and civil courts. Now, therefore,

Be it resolved by the Senate, the House of Representatives concurring:

That the General Assembly of the State of South Carolina, by this
resolution, recognizes that "Shoeless Joe" Jackson was exonerated of
any wrong doing in the 1919 World Series in both criminal and civil
courts and, therefore, the Commissioner of Baseball is memorialized
to reinstate "Shoeless Joe" Jackson as a member in good standing in
organized baseball.

Be it further resolved that copies of this resolution be forwarded to the Commissioner of Baseball, the President of the American Baseball League, the President of the National Baseball League, and the family of Joe Jackson.

The resolution passed unanimously on May 23, 1998. That same year, more than 90,000 people from Jackson's hometown of Greenville signed a petition asking baseball officials to give Joe Jackson a plaque in Cooperstown.

The Internet also plays a role in the rehabilitation of Shoeless Joe Jackson. A number of Web sites devoted to Jackson can be found through any reliable search engine. Most of these sites are more dedicated to Jackson's memory than to the truth, accepting Jackson's declarations of innocence at face value and demonizing Charles Comiskey, Judge Landis, and even Eddie Collins ("as fine a man as there is in baseball," said Jackson himself in 1949). Some Web authors have set up their own "Virtual Hall of Fame" for Jackson, while others offer links to the Hall of Fame itself and urge their readers to send electronic mail on Jackson's behalf to the directors of the Hall and the office of the Commissioner of Baseball. Some Web sites tie their campaigns to Pete Rose's continuing quest for reinstatement, and others run concurrent campaigns to put Joe Jackson in and push Charles Comiskey out of the Hall.

Shoeless Joe memorabilia is also much in demand. In 1990 one of the six known signatures of Joe Jackson sold at auction for $23,500, a record for a nineteenth or twentieth century autograph. One is on the bottom of Jackson's will, on file since 1951 in the Greenville County Probate Court in South Carolina. A Greenville lawyer named Leo Hill, representing the estate of Katie Jackson, who died in 1959, asked for possession of Jackson's original will so that Katie Jackson's estate could profit from its sale. The two charities named as Katie Jackson's beneficiaries hoped to sell Joe's will with its valuable signature for as much as $100,000. The Probate Court refused to turn the will over to the charities, insisting that the law requires the original itself, not a copy, to remain on file. On September 2, 1997, the state Supreme Court of South Carolina sided with the Probate Court, and Jackson's original will remains in the Court's possession.

The campaign to elect Joe Jackson to the Hall of Fame continues to gather steam at the dawn of a new century. In November 1999, the United States Congress passed a resolution urging Commissioner Bud Selig to consider Jackson's reinstatement, and the issue has surfaced in the 2000 presidential primaries, especially in South Carolina and in Iowa, where

Field of Dreams was set. Joe's hometown of Greenville, South Carolina, celebrated the month of July 1999 as "Shoeless Joe Jackson Month" and repeated the event in July 2000 with the slogan, "Greenville's Goin' Shoeless!" Local politicians promise to hold a similar celebration every July until Joe enters the Hall of Fame.

     Joseph Jackson died in 1951 but lives on as Shoeless Joe, more a myth than a man, a ghostly figure walking out of a cornfield wanting nothing more than to play the game he loved. The real Joe Jackson, the South Carolina mill hand and small-town businessman, would smile and shake his head at the legend that surrounds Shoeless Joe today. Strangers leaving flowers at his grave, paying tens of thousands of dollars for his autograph, writing emotional letters to the Commissioner of Baseball. For what, really? Joe Jackson played baseball, that's all. Played the game, made some money, got into a little scrape up north, and came back home to South Carolina. That's all. He'd wonder what got into all those people in Greenville, with their flyers and banners celebrating this "Shoeless Joe" character and proclaiming "Greenville's Goin' Shoeless!"
     The real Joe Jackson never liked the name "Shoeless Joe" anyway.

Chapter Notes

Chapter 1

1. Eliot Asinof, *Eight Men Out*, page 61.

2. Jackson's date of birth has been recorded as 1887, 1888, and 1889 in different places. The family Bible was lost in a fire many years ago, but although Joe's official death certificate listed his birth year as 1889, his tombstone lists his year of birth as 1888.

3. F. C. Lane, "The Man Who Might Have Been the Greatest Player in the Game," *Baseball Magazine*, March 1916, page 59.

4. Asinof, page 61.

5. Lane, page 61.

6. Furman Bisher, "This Is the Truth," *Sport*, October 1949.

7. *Cleveland Plain Dealer*, April 8, 1914.

8. The Sampson game was played on April 11, 1908, and the Wake Forest game was played on April 25. Apparently, Joe returned to help out Brandon Mill before the Greenville Spinners started their season in earnest.

9. *Greenville News*, July 2, 1908, page 2.

10. This line is usually reported as "You shoeless son-of-a-gun" or "You shoeless so-and-so."

11. *Sport*, October 1949.

12. The Washington team was popularly called the Senators, though from 1905 to 1955 they were officially nicknamed the Nationals. Both names will appear in this book.

13. Harvey Frommer, *Shoeless Joe and Ragtime Baseball*, page 13.

14. *Cleveland Plain Dealer*, March 12, 1912.

15. These figures were reported in the *Greenville News* on August 17,

1908. Other sources state that the A's paid the Spinners $1,175 for Barr and only $325 for Jackson, though by all accounts it would seem that Joe was the more valuable of the two.

16. Lane, page 61.

17. *Greenville News*, August 22, 1908.

Chapter 2

1. Harvey Frommer, *Shoeless Joe and Ragtime Baseball*, page 20.

2. F. C. Lane, "The Man That Might Have Been the Greatest Player in the Game," *Baseball Magazine*, March 1916, page 61.

3. *Philadelphia Evening Telegraph*, August 25, 1908.

4. *Philadelphia Evening Times*, August 25, 1908.

5. Lane, page 63.

6. Furman Bisher, "This Is the Truth," *Sport*, October 1949.

7. David Cataneo, *Peanuts and Crackerjack: A Treasury of Baseball Legends and Lore*, page 117.

8. *Washington Post*, September 15, 1908, page 8; also reprinted in the *Greenville News*, September 20, 1908, page 4.

9. *Ibid.*

10. Harvey Frommer, *Shoeless Joe and Ragtime Baseball*, page 15.

11. *Detroit Free Press*, August 28, 1908, page 6. The writer's name was Joe S. Jackson, no relation to the ballplayer.

12. This story was related by Jackson to the *Cleveland Plain Dealer* on March 8, 1911.

13. *The Sporting News*, September 29, 1910.

14. "Joe Jackson's Ups and Downs," *Literary Digest*, September 14, 1912, pages 443–447.

Chapter 3

1. "Joe Jackson's Ups and Downs," *Literary Digest*, September 14, 1912, pages 443–447.

2. Many sources, including Asinof's *Eight Men Out*, say that Jackson stood on third base after hitting a triple. However, all of Jackson's hits in a Philadelphia uniform were singles.

3. Paul Dickson, *Baseball's Greatest Quotations*, page 204.

4. Some sources state that Jackson had five hits in 1909, but this researcher could only find three.

5. "Joe Jackson's Ups and Downs," pages 443–447.

6. *Ibid.*

7. *Cleveland Plain Dealer*, March 21, 1913.

8. "Joe Jackson's Ups and Downs," pages 443–447.

9. The *Cleveland Plain Dealer* of July 31, 1910, reported the amount of cash as $6,000.

10. *Cleveland Plain Dealer*, July 31, 1910.

11. Fred Lieb, *Connie Mack: Grand Old Man of Baseball*, pages 131–132.

12. Furman Bisher, "This Is the Truth," *Sport*, October 1949.

13. *Cleveland Plain Dealer*, September 17, 1910.

14. *Cleveland Plain Dealer*, September 20, 1910.

15. In 1981 the *Sporting News* found that Cobb was credited with an extra two hits by mistake in the final averages. Lajoie actually hit .383 to Cobb's .382, but Commissioner Bowie Kuhn refused to take the 1910 batting title away from Cobb. Some references now list Lajoie as the rightful winner.

16. Harold Seymour, *Baseball: The Golden Age*, page 289.

17. *Chicago Tribune*, October 12, 1910, page 21.

Chapter 4

1. *New York World-Telegram and Sun*, February 5, 1946..

2. *Cleveland Plain Dealer*, April 11, 1911.

3. *The Sporting News*, September 26, 1910.

4. *New York World-Telegram and Sun*, February 5, 1946.

5. *Ibid.*

6. *New York World-Telegram and Sun*, December 12, 1951.

7. Furman Bisher, "This Is the Truth," *Sport*, October 1949. The Naps, struggling financially as they were, wouldn't have had $10,000 to give Jackson at that time.

8. *Cleveland Plain Dealer*, March 24, 1911. The whereabouts of the original Black Betsy is still a mystery, though some say it is still the property of the Jackson family. Other reports say that Joe gave the bat to the mayor of Greenville after his playing days were over.

9. Scott Longert, *Addie Joss: King of the Pitchers*, page 131.

10. When Joe left baseball in 1920 he was tied for the American League career lead in grand slams. Nap Lajoie and Babe Ruth had also hit four grand slams at that time. The current record holder is Lou Gehrig with 23.

11. The Cleveland team moved their game from League Park to the suburb of Collinwood, on the outskirts of Cleveland, that day, but the authorities invaded the field and arrested the players anyway.

12. *The Sporting News*, April 13, 1911.

13. *The Sporting News*, September 24, 1942.

14. *Toledo Blade*, July 25, 1911.

15. Under modern rules, which consider a player with less than 130 at

bats in the majors a rookie, Joe Jackson would be eligible for the rookie of the year award. When the award began in 1947 the rules allowed for only 75 at bats, and Jackson would not have been eligible.

16. The National League Rookie of the Year award, had there been one in 1911, would have gone to Phillies pitcher Grover Cleveland Alexander, who set a rookie record with 28 wins.

17. *Cleveland Plain Dealer,* October 4, 1911.

18. The agreement to hire Davis as manager may, or may not, have been a side agreement to the Jackson-Rath-Lord trade between the A's and Naps in July 1910.

19. Ty Cobb with Al Stump, *My Life in Baseball: The True Record,* page 132.

20. *The Sporting News,* September 24, 1942, page 1.

Chapter 5

1. *Cleveland Plain Dealer,* March 3, 1912.

2. *Cleveland Plain Dealer,* March 7, 1912.

3. F. C. Lane, "The Man Who Might Have Been the Greatest Player in the Game," *Baseball Magazine,* March 1916, page 55.

4. *Cleveland Plain Dealer,* April 6, 1912.

5. *Cleveland Plain Dealer,* April 16, 1912.

6. *Cleveland Plain Dealer,* April 14, 1912.

7. *Cleveland Plain Dealer,* July 16, 1912.

8. More than twenty players in both leagues now share the modern record of three triples in a game. The all-time record is four, by Bill Joyce of the New York Giants in 1897.

9. Davis, always popular with the Philadelphia fans, went into politics after his Cleveland sojourn ended. He served two terms as a Philadelphia city councilman in the late teens.

10. Terry Turner joined the club in 1904, but by 1912 was reduced to a part-time role.

11. 1912 was a good year for triples. Owen Wilson of the Pittsburgh Pirates set the major league record of 36 that same year.

12. Harvey Frommer, *Shoeless Joe and Ragtime Baseball,* page 41.

13. *Cleveland Plain Dealer,* September 27, 1911.

14. Those four players were expelled from the National League for life.

Chapter 6

1. Eugene C. Murdock, *Baseball Players in Their Times: Oral Histories of the Game, 1920-1940,* page 37.

2. It was the highest in the history of baseball for anyone who had played two or more seasons.

3. F. C. Lane, "The Man Who Might Have Been the Greatest Player in the Game," *Baseball Magazine*, March 1916, page 55.

4. *The Sporting News*, September 24, 1942, page 8.

5. Allan Danzig and Joe Reichler, *The History of Baseball*, page 222.

6. *New York World-Telegram and Sun*, February 5, 1946.

7. *Cleveland Plain Dealer*, April 19, 1913.

8. "Joe Jackson's Ups and Downs," *Literary Digest*, September 14, 1912, page 447.

9. Charles C. Alexander, *Ty Cobb*, page 114. One Detroit writer called Cobb "the worst second baseman living or dead" in the paper the next day.

10. *Cleveland Plain Dealer*, June 7, 1913.

11. *Cleveland Plain Dealer*, June 6, 1913.

12. *Cleveland Plain Dealer*, June 29, 1913.

13. *The Sporting News*, May 27, 1915.

14. *Cleveland Plain Dealer*, October 16, 1913.

15. *Ibid.*

16. Harvey Frommer, *Shoeless Joe and Ragtime Baseball*, page 44.

Chapter 7

1. Allan Danzig and Joe Reichler, *The History of Baseball*, page 222.

2. Harvey Frommer, *Shoeless Joe and Ragtime Baseball*, page 52.

3. *Cleveland Plain Dealer*, March 23, 1914.

4. *Cleveland Plain Dealer*, March 24, 1914.

5. *Cleveland Plain Dealer*, March 9, 1914.

6. *Cleveland Plain Dealer*, March 4, 1914.

7. *Ibid.*

8. *Cleveland Plain Dealer*, April 8, 1914.

9. The record was tied by the Twins' Terry Felton in 1982.

10. *Cleveland Plain Dealer*, July 12, 1914.

11. Allan Danzig and Joe Reichler, page 222.

12. Years later it was found that nine hits made by Lajoie in 1901 had been misplaced in the records. Lajoie's 3,000th hit actually came on September 17 against the Red Sox.

13. The league held another tournament a week later. Cobb played for Shelby and went 5 for 6 in two games, helping Shelby to win the title once again.

14. *The Sporting News*, February 11, 1915.

Chapter 8

1. F. C. Lane, "The Greatest Player That Might Have Been," *Baseball Magazine*, March 1916, page 65.

2. The onset of television in the 1940s removed all doubt about baseball's qualification as "interstate" commerce.

3. *Cleveland Plain Dealer*, January 16 and 18, 1915. Many sources say that the name "Indians" was decided by a vote of the fans, but the newspaper accounts of the period do not support this assumption.

4. *Cleveland Plain Dealer*, January 16, 1915.

5. *Cleveland Plain Dealer*, March 5, 1915.

6. *Cleveland Press*, March 27, 1915.

7. *The Sporting News*, April 15, 1915.

8. *Cleveland Plain Dealer*, April 15, 1915.

9. *The Sporting News*, May 27, 1915.

10. *Cleveland Plain Dealer*, June 8, 1915.

11. *Cleveland Plain Dealer*, July 1, 1915.

12. *Cleveland Plain Dealer*, June 29, 1915. On the same day Joe Birmingham sued Somers for back pay.

13. *Cleveland Plain Dealer*, August 21, 1915.

14. *Ibid.*

15. Lane, page 66.

16. Lee Allen, *The American League Story*, page 82.

17. *The Sporting News*, August 26, 1915.

18. Roth cost $11,000, Chappell $18,000, and Klepfer $5,000.

19. The deal worked out for Cleveland in the long run. In 1919 the Indians sent Roth to the A's for three players, two of whom (Larry Gardner and Charlie Jamieson) contributed to the Indians' first pennant in 1920.

20. *Cleveland Plain Dealer,* August 21, 1915.

21. Lane, page 66.

22. *Cleveland Plain Dealer,* August 21, 1915.

23. *Ibid.*

24. Sadly, by September 1920 both Jackson and Chapman's careers had ended. Chapman was killed by a pitched ball on August 16, 1920. If Chapman, not Jackson, had gone to the White Sox they both might be in the Hall of Fame.

25. Daniel Okrent and Harris Lewine, ed., *The Ultimate Baseball Book*, page 89.

26. In 1920 pitcher Lefty Williams' contract offered a $500 bonus for 15 wins and $1,000 for 20.

Chapter 9

1. *Cleveland News*, December 7, 1951.

2. The remaining legacy of the Federal League is Wrigley Field, the home park of the Federal League Whales and since 1916 the home of the Cubs.

3. F. C. Lane, "The Greatest Player That Might Have Been," *Baseball Magazine*, March 1916, page 65.

4. Lane, page 66.

5. Lane, page 67.

6. Ty Cobb had the dangerous Sam Crawford protecting him in Detroit's lineup.

7. Lane, page 56.

8. Lyle Spatz, "Fritz Maisel for Joe Jackson?" *The National Pastime* #17 (1997), pp. 108–110.

9. *Ibid.*

10. *Chicago Tribune*, May 1, 1916, page 20.

11. *Chicago Tribune*, September 1, 1916, page 23.

12. *Chicago Tribune*, September 10, 1916, page 3-A.

Chapter 10

1. *The Sporting News*, September 24, 1942, page 8.

2. Arthur Daley, *Inside Baseball*, page 25.

3. Daley, page 26. Apparently, this story originated with Grantland Rice.

4. *New York Evening World*, September 30, 1920.

5. Furman Bisher, "This Is the Truth," *Sport*, October 1949.

6. *Chicago Tribune*, April 8, 1917, page 2-A.

7. Harold Seymour, *Baseball: The Golden Age*, page 245.

8. The "emery ball" was the result of a pitcher applying an emery board or a piece of sandpaper to the surface of the baseball, making part of the ball rough and leaving the rest smooth. Russell Ford of the Yankees was the acknowledged master of the emery ball until Johnson banned it in September 1914.

9. Eugene C. Murdock, *Ban Johnson: Czar of Baseball*, pages 95–96.

10. This was the game in which reliever Ernie Shore picked a runner off first, then retired the next 26 Senators in a row to complete a "perfect" game. Ruth's ten-day suspension was another strange decision by Ban Johnson; other players have been suspended for as much as a year for assaulting an umpire. Pete Rose was suspended for a month in 1988 for merely bumping one.

11. *Chicago Tribune*, July 6, 1917.

12. The longest at the time was Cobb's 40-game streak in 1911.

13. *Chicago Tribune*, July 22, 1917.

14. *Detroit Free Press*, September 4, 1917, page 11.

15. *Chicago Tribune*, September 10, 1917. This was Cleveland's last forfeit loss until the infamous "Ten Cent Beer Night" fiasco of 1974.

16. The current record throw is 445 feet and 10 inches, by minor leaguer Glen Gorbous in 1957. The major league record at the time was held by Tony Mullane, a pitcher who threw a ball 416 feet and seven and three-fourths inches in 1881.

17. On July 31, 1929, Ruth hit a fungo 447 feet, which stands as the record to this day.

Chapter 11

1. Charles Einstein, *The Third Fireside Book of Baseball*, page 489.

2. *Ibid.*

3. *New York Times*, October 7, 1917, page 20.

4. *Ibid.*

5. Einstein, page 490.

6. If Rariden had blocked Collins on the baseline without the ball, Collins would have been awarded home on interference.

7. Frank Graham, *The New York Giants*, page 102.

8. Einstein, page 491.

9. Noel Hynd, *The Giants of the Polo Grounds*, page 208.

10. Robertson, however, hit .500 in the Series and set a new record with 11 base hits.

11. The practice of barnstorming remained a bone of contention between players and owners for several years thereafter. Babe Ruth and two of his teammates were suspended for the first part of the 1922 season after they defied an order not to play exhibitions after the World Series in 1921.

12. Fred Lieb, *Baseball as I Have Known It*, page 105.

Chapter 12

1. Stage and movie actors had been ruled "essential" and exempt from the draft, but ballplayers did not rate that same status. Later in 1918 the exemption for actors was removed.

2. *Chicago Daily News*, May 3, 1918, page 3.

3. *Chicago Tribune*, May 17, 1918, page 13.

4. *Chicago Tribune*, May 19, 1918, page 14.

5. Harold Seymour, *Baseball: The Golden Age*, page 251.

6. *The Sporting News*, June 20, 1918.

7. *Chicago Tribune*, May 19, 1918, page 14.

8. *Cleveland Press*, May 24, 1918.

9. *Chicago Tribune*, June 13, 1918, page 11.

10. *Ibid.*

11. *Ibid.*

12. *Boston Herald*, June 18, 1918.

13. Joseph P. Murphy, "The Busher from Dubuque," *Baseball Research Journal #24* (1995), page 118.

14. Charles C. Alexander, *Our Game: An American Baseball History*, page 118.

15. Charles C. Alexander, *John McGraw*, page 105.

16. Seymour, page 250.

17. Seymour, page 253.

18. *Ibid.*

19. Warren Brown, *The Chicago White Sox*, page 28.

Chapter 13

1. Bob Broeg, *Super Stars of Baseball*, page 38.

2. *Chicago Tribune*, April 9, 1919, page 20.

3. *Chicago Tribune*, April 13, 1919, page 2-2.

4. Peter Golenbock, *Fenway: An Unexpurgated History of the Boston Red Sox*, page 56.

5. *Savannah Morning News*, July 20, 1998.

6. *The Sporting News*, May 1, 1919.

7. Broeg, page 38.

8. Charles Einstein, *The Third Fireside Book of Baseball*, page 490.

9. Warren Brown, *The Chicago White Sox*, page 117.

10. The Chalmers car company discontinued its Most Valuable Player awards in 1914. *Total Baseball*, a reference work published annually by John Thorn and Pete Palmer, awarded "mythical" MVP Awards for the years when no real award was given. They named Joe Jackson the winner of the mythical 1919 MVP.

11. Cicotte had signed for $5,000 with a $2,000 bonus for 1918. This kept his base salary, the starting point of future negotiations, at $5,000 instead of $7,000. Bill Veeck, *The Hustler's Handbook*, page 256.

12. Another explanation of McMullin's participation appeared in the *Chicago Herald and Examiner* after the scandal broke. The newspaper stated that Risberg refused to take part in the scheme unless his friend McMullin was included. McMullin, the story goes, didn't know about the

fix until Risberg told him about it. *Chicago Herald and Examiner*, September 29, 1920.

13. This is the explanation that Joe gave in his testimony to the Chicago Grand Jury on September 28, 1920.

14. Bill Veeck, *The Hustler's Handbook*, page 284. Harry Grabiner's diary reveals that Cicotte, not Gandil, offered Weaver $5,000 to join the fixers.

15. Eliot Asinof, *Eight Men Out*, page 64.

Chapter 14

1. Bob Broeg, *Super Stars of Baseball*, page 40.

2. *Chicago Tribune*, October 3, 1919, page 22.

3. In later years, Schalk denied that this incident ever happened.

4. John Wheeler, "Ring Lardner," *Collier's*, March 1928. Lardner may have sung the same song on the train carrying the White Sox party back to Chicago that night, as reported in Eliot Asinof's *Eight Men Out* and other sources.

5. One of the greatest mysteries of the Series is whether the players tried to lose Game 3. Gandil, of all people, drove in what proved to be the winning run. Jackson stated in his testimony that the Sox tried to lose the game, while others were not so sure.

6. This quote came from Jackson's grand jury testimony on September 28, 1920.

7. The official scorer gave Jackson an error on the play, but quickly reversed his decision and gave the error to Cicotte.

8. *Chicago Tribune*, October 5, 1919, page 2-A.

9. Donald Honig, *Baseball America*, pages 109–110.

10. *Cleveland Plain Dealer*, October 5, 1919, page 2-A.

11. Ken Burns and Geoffrey C. Ward, *Baseball: An Illustrated History*, page 139.

12. Warren Brown, *The Chicago White Sox*, page 99.

13. This description of events comes from Jackson's grand jury testimony of September 28, 1920. Joe told a much different story four years later in his suit against Comiskey for back pay.

14. *Chicago Tribune*, October 6, 1919, page 23.

15. *Chicago Tribune*, October 7, 1919, page 20.

16. Eliot Asinof, *Eight Men Out*, page 121.

17. Asinof, page 130.

18. *Chicago Tribune*, October 10, 1919, page 19.

19. *Ibid.*

20. Jackson's grand jury testimony on September 28, 1920.

21. *Chicago Herald and Examiner*, October 10, 1919. Harvey Woodruff in the *Chicago Tribune* echoed the same sentiment that same day.

22. Harold Seymour, *Baseball: The Golden Age*, page 335.
23. Lawrence Ritter, *The Glory of Their Times*, page 243.

Chapter 15

1. *1920 Reach Baseball Guide.*
2. These letters were introduced as exhibits in Jackson's 1924 suit against Charles Comiskey for back pay.
3. Bill Veeck, who bought the White Sox from Comiskey's heirs in 1958 and whose father was president of the Cubs in 1919, always believed that Comiskey paid Redmon secretly. Bill Veeck, *The Hustler's Handbook*, page 286.
4. When most sources say that Jackson wrote a letter to Comiskey and offered to tell what he knew about the scandal, this is the letter to which they refer.
5. *New York Evening World*, December 15, 1919.
6. *Ibid.*
7. *Baseball Magazine*, February 1920.
8. *The Sporting News*, October 16, 1919.
9. *Ibid.*
10. The contract specified that $7,000 of the total was for his playing services, and the other $1,000 was for Joe's reserve rights for the following year.
11. Most of this description came from Joe's testimony at his Milwaukee lawsuit against Comiskey in 1924.

Chapter 16

1. Donald Honig, *The Man in the Dugout*, page 216.
2. In 1921 the rule was amended to allow nine American League and eight National League hurlers to continue throwing the pitch.
3. Shellenback returned to the majors many years later as Leo Durocher's pitching coach. His nephew Jim pitched in the majors in 1966–77.
4. Mays had forced the Red Sox to trade him to the Yankees when he quit the Boston team in early 1919, but it is unclear how Weaver felt that Ruth had broken a contract.
5. Bill Veeck, *The Hustler's Handbook*, page 266.
6. *Ibid.*
7. Joe's grand jury testimony of September 28, 1920.
8. *Chicago Tribune*, April 11, 1920, page 2-A.
9. *Cleveland Plain Dealer*, April 1, 1920, page 18.

10. *Cleveland Plain Dealer*, May 29, 1920, page 16.

11. *Cleveland Plain Dealer*, July 26, 1920, page 12.

12. Veeck, page 284.

13. Author's conversation with Eliot Asinof, March 16, 2000.

14. Honig, page 216.

15. There was no City Series in 1917 or 1919 because the White Sox were in the World Series. There was no City Series in 1918 because the Cubs were in the fall classic.

16. Jim Crusinberry, "A Newsman's Biggest Story," *Sports Illustrated*, September 17, 1956, page 70.

17. Some reference works, most notably Joseph Reichler's *The Great All-Time Baseball Record Book*, credit Joe Jackson with eight RBI on this day and claim that he tied the American League record for RBI in a game set in 1911 by Roy Hartzell. Those sources are incorrect. Joe drove in only four of the ten Chicago runs on that day, as Felsch drove in two and Kerr, Eddie Collins, Shano Collins, and Schalk drove in one each.

18. *Chicago Tribune*, August 6, 1920, page 17.

19. *Cleveland Plain Dealer*, August 21, 1920. The papers reported that Napoleon Lajoie loaded the weeping Graney into his car and drove him away from the church before the funeral began.

20. *Baseball Digest*, June 1949.

Chapter 17

1. *New York World-Telegram and Sun*, February 5, 1946.

2. *Chicago Tribune*, September 5, 1920, page 2-A. Crusinberry did not reveal until 1956 that he, not Loomis, wrote the letter.

3. Bill Veeck, *The Hustler's Handbook*, page 269.

4. *Cleveland Plain Dealer*, September 24, 1920, page 22.

5. *Cleveland Plain Dealer*, September 15, 1920, page 19.

6. *Cleveland Press*, September 29, 1920. A United Press reporter innocently asked one of the honest Sox who would pitch the third game against the Yankees. "Cicotte," the player answered, "and if he doesn't win, we will mob him on the field." The intimidated Cicotte staggered to a 15-9 win.

7. *Cleveland Press*, September 27, 1920.

8. *New York Times*, September 29, 1920.

9. Joe Jackson's grand jury testimony, September 28, 1920.

10. *New York Times*, September 29, 1920.

11. *Ibid.*

12. *Ibid.*

13. *Ibid.*

14. *Ibid.*

15. *Chicago Tribune*, September 29, 1920, page 2.

16. *New York Times*, September 29, 1920.

17. *Ibid.*

18. *Chicago Tribune*, September 29, 1920, page 1.

19. Eliot Asinof, *Eight Men Out*, pages 217–18.

20. *Chicago Tribune*, September 29, 1920, page 3.

21. *Chicago Tribune*, September 30, 1920, page 2.

22. *Cleveland Plain Dealer*, October 4, 1920, page 18.

23. *Cleveland Plain Dealer*, September 30, 1920, page 5.

24. Harvey Frommer, *Shoeless Joe and Ragtime Baseball*, page 116.

25. In 1998, Albert Belle amassed 399 total bases for the Sox to break Jackson's team mark.

26. Dick Schaap, "Say It Ain't So, Joe," *Coronet*, September 1960.

27. Furman Bisher, "This Is the Truth," *Sport*, October 1949.

28. Schaap.

Chapter 18

1. Arnold (Chick) Gandil and Melvin Durslag, "This Is My Story of the Black Sox Series," *Sports Illustrated*, September 17, 1956, page 68.

2. David Pietrusza, *Judge and Jury: The Life and Times of Judge Kenesaw Mountain Landis*, page 173.

3. Harold Seymour, *Baseball: The Golden Age*, page 326.

4. *Chicago Tribune*, September 30, 1920, page 1.

5. Eliot Asinof, *Eight Men Out*, page 294.

6. *Ibid.*

7. Bill Veeck, *The Hustler's Handbook*, page 286.

8. Seymour, page 329.

9. J. G. Taylor Spink, *Judge Landis and Twenty-Five Years of Baseball*, page 9.

10. *New York Times*, August 3, 1921, page 1.

11. *Chicago Tribune*, August 3, 1921, page 2.

12. *Ibid.*

13. Rube Marquard, who pitched from 1908 to 1925, had a record of 201-177. He was elected to the Hall in 1971. Other Hall members with similar records to Cicotte's are Jesse Haines (210–158), Rube Waddell (191–145), Hal Newhouser (207–150), and Don Drysdale (209–166).

14. The loss of Jack Quinn to the Yankees in 1918 also served as a minor factor in the scandal. Quinn could have taken Faber's place at the head of the rotation in the 1919 Series.

15. Joe Falls, "I Did Wrong, but I Paid for It," *Baseball Digest*, February 1966.

16. Pietrusza, page 192.

17. Comiskey's mortal enemy, Ban Johnson, who also died in 1931, was elected to the Hall of Fame two years before Comiskey. Eddie Collins also gained election to the Hall in 1939.

Chapter 19

1. Ray Robinson, *Matty: An American Hero*, pp. 201–202.

2. *Atlanta Journal-Constitution*, July 25, 1999, page 2-G.

3. Many sources state the amount of Comiskey's settlement offer as $2,500.

4. Joe demanded $16,000 for the two years remaining on his three year contract, $1,500 for Comiskey's alleged 1917 bonus offer, and $700 for the 1920 second place money.

5. *Cleveland Plain Dealer*, February 15, 1924, page 18.

6. *Chicago Herald-Examiner*, February 16, 1924, page 16.

7. *Cleveland Plain Dealer*, February 16, 1924.

8. *Chicago Tribune*, December 30, 1926.

9. J.G. Taylor Spink, *Judge Landis and Twenty-Five Years of Baseball*, page 143.

10. David Pietrusza, *Judge and Jury: The Life and Times of Judge Kenesaw Mountain Landis*, page 297.

11. Spink, page 144.

12. Pietrusza, page 297.

13. *New York Times*, January 4, 1927.

14. Spink, page 148.

15. These rules were still in effect in 1989, when Cincinnati Reds manager Pete Rose was banned for life for gambling activities. The rules make no distinction between betting on one's team to win or to lose.

16. Pietrusza, page 297.

17. Spink, page 132.

Chapter 20

1. Editor's introduction to "This Is the Truth," *Sport*, October 1949.

2. Furman Bisher, "This Is the Truth," *Sport*, October 1949.

3. *New York Sun*, August 29, 1932.

4. *Ibid.*

5. *Cleveland Plain Dealer*, January 20, 1934, page 18.

6. *New York World-Telegram*, December 28, 1933.

7. *Cleveland Plain Dealer*, January 20, 1934, page 18.

8. Letter to the author from Pink Jackson's daughter, Ethel Jackson Copeland, March 14, 2000.

9. Thomas Perry, *Textile League Baseball*, page 55.

10. *The Sporting News*, September 24, 1942, page 1.

11. *Ibid.*

12. *Ibid.*

13. J. G. Taylor Spink, *Judge Landis and Twenty-Five Years of Baseball*, page 83.

14. Ty Cobb and Al Stump, *My Life in Baseball: The True Record*, page 266.

15. Furman Bisher, "This Is the Truth," *Sport*, October 1949.

16. *Ibid.*

17. *Ibid.*

18. *Ibid.*

19. The ten players were: catcher Steve O'Neill, first baseman Hal Trosky, second baseman Nap Lajoie, third baseman Ken Keltner, shortstop Joe Sewell, outfielders Tris Speaker, Earl Averill, and Joe Jackson, and pitchers Cy Young and Mel Harder. Active players, like pitcher Bob Feller and shortstop Lou Boudreau, were not eligible for election.

Chapter 21

1. "The Splinter Sounds Off," *The Sporting News* web site, July 13, 1999.

2. *Greenville News*, December 6, 1951, page 1.

3. The averages of Joe Jackson and the National League batting champs of each year:

1911   Joe Jackson .408, Honus Wagner (Pittsburgh) .334
1912   Joe Jackson .395, Heinie Zimmerman (New York) .372
1913   Joe Jackson .373, Jake Daubert (Brooklyn) .350
1914   Joe Jackson .338, Jake Daubert (Brooklyn) .329
1916   Joe Jackson .341, Hal Chase (Cincinnati) .338
1919   Joe Jackson .351, Edd Roush (Cincinnati) .321
1920   Joe Jackson .382, Rogers Hornsby (St. Louis) .370

4. Author's correspondence with Furman Bisher, February 26, 2000.

5. "Hall of Famers Want Shoeless Joe in Cooperstown," *The Sporting News* web site, January 19, 1998.

6. There was one big mistake in *Field of Dreams*. In the film, Joe Jackson is depicted as a right-handed batter and a left-handed thrower.

7. *Cleveland Plain Dealer*, October 5, 1919, page 2-A.

8. *New York Times*, October 7, 1984.

9. Ted Williams, "Shoeless Joe: It's Time to Open the Door," Society for American Baseball Research (SABR) web site, March 1998.

10. Happy Felsch would also have had to rehearse his interview with Harry Reutlinger of the *Chicago American*.

11. Williams.

12. Author's conversation with Eliot Asinof, March 16, 2000.

13. Jackson's grand jury testimony of September 28, 1920.

14. *New York Times*, September 29, 1920.

15. One of the honest White Sox, Dickie Kerr, had little sympathy for Weaver, Jackson, and the others. "If I had been approached," said Kerr, "I would have gone straight to Mr. Comiskey, the owner of the White Sox. Not getting any response there, I would have gone to Ban Johnson. Then, maybe, it would never have happened." *New York Times*, October 7, 1984.

Bibliography

Books

Alexander, Charles C. *John McGraw* (New York: Viking Penguin, 1988).
_____. *Our Game: An American Baseball History* (New York: Henry Holt, 1992).
_____. *Ty Cobb* (New York: Oxford University Press, 1984).
Allen, Lee. *The American League Story* (New York: Hill, 1962).
Asinof, Eliot. *Eight Men Out* (New York: Holt, Rinehart, and Winston, 1963).
Broeg, Bob. *Super Stars of Baseball* (St. Louis: The Sporting News, 1971).
Brown, Warren. *The Chicago White Sox* (New York: G. P. Putnam's Sons, 1952).
Burns, Ken, and Geoffrey C. Ward. *Baseball: An Illustrated History* (New York: Alfred A. Knopf, 1994).
Cataneo, David. *Peanuts and Crackerjack: A Treasury of Baseball Legends and Lore* (Nashville, Tenn.: Rutledge Hill Press, 1991).
Cobb, Ty, with Al Stump. *My Life in Baseball: The True Record* (Garden City, New York: Doubleday, 1961).
Daley, Arthur. *Inside Baseball* (New York: Grosset and Dunlap, 1950).
Danzig, Allison, and Joe Reichler. *The History of Baseball* (Englewood Cliffs, New Jersey: Prentice-Hall, 1959).
Dickson, Paul. *Baseball's Greatest Quotations* (New York: Edward Burlingame Books, 1991).
Einstein, Charles. *The Third Fireside Book of Baseball* (New York: Simon and Schuster, 1968).
Frommer, Harvey. *Shoeless Joe and Ragtime Baseball* (Dallas: Taylor Publishing, 1992).
Golenbock, Peter. *Fenway: An Unexpurgated History of the Boston Red Sox* (New York: G. P. Putman's Sons, 1952).

Graham, Frank. *The New York Giants: An Informal History* (New York: G. P. Putnam's sons, 1952).

Gropman, Donald. *Say It Ain't So, Joe!* (Secaucus, New Jersey: Carol Publishing Group, 1999).

Honig, Donald. *Baseball America* (New York: Macmillan, 1985).

_____. *The Man in the Dugout* (Chicago: Follett, 1977).

Hynd, Noel. *The Giants of the Polo Grounds* (Dallas: Taylor, 1988).

Lieb, Fred, *Baseball as I Have Known It* (New York: Coward, McCann, and Geoghegan, 1977).

_____. *Connie Mack: Grand Old Man of Baseball* (New York: G. P. Putnam's Sons, 1945).

Longert, Scott. *Addie Joss: King of the Pitchers* (Cleveland: Society for American Baseball Research, 1998).

Murdock, Eugene C. *Ban Johnson: Czar of Baseball* (Westport, Connecticut: Greenwood Press, 1982).

_____. *Baseball Players in Their Times: Oral Histories of the Game, 1920–1940* (Westport, Connecticut: Meckler, 1991).

1920 Reach Baseball Guide.

Okrent, Daniel, and Harris Levine, eds. *The Ultimate Baseball Book* (Boston: Houghton Mifflin, 1980).

Perry, Thomas. *Textile League Baseball* (Jefferson, North Carolina: McFarland, 1993).

Pietrusza, David. *Judge and Jury: The Life of Kenesaw Mountain Landis* (South Bend, Indiana: Diamond Communications, 1998).

Reichler, Joseph. *The Great All-Time Baseball Record Book* (New York: Macmillan, 1981).

Ritter, Lawrence. *The Glory of Their Times* (New York: Morrow, 1966).

Robinson, Ray. *Matty: An American Hero* (New York: Oxford Press, 1993).

Seymour, Harold. *Baseball: The Golden Age* (New York: Oxford University Press, 1971).

Spink, J.G. Taylor. *Judge Landis and Twenty-Five Years of Baseball* (St. Louis: The Sporting News, 1974).

Bill Veeck. *The Hustler's Handbook* (New York: Simon and Schuster, 1965).

Newspapers

Atlanta Journal-Constitution

Boston Herald

Chicago American

Chicago Daily News

Chicago Herald-Examiner

Chicago Tribune

Cleveland News

Cleveland Plain Dealer

Cleveland Press

Detroit Free Press

Greenville (SC) News
New York Evening World
New York Sun
New York Times
New York World-Telegram and Sun

Philadelphia Evening Telegraph
Philadelphia Evening Times
Savannah (GA) Morning News
Toledo Blade
Washington Post

Magazines

Baseball Digest
Baseball Magazine
Baseball Research Journal
Collier's
Coronet

Literary Digest
The National Pastime
Sport
The Sporting News
Sports Illustrated

Internet sites

National Baseball Hall of Fame and Museum (http://www.baseballhalloffame.org)
Shoeless Joe Jackson's Virtual Hall of Fame (http://www.blackbetsy.com)
Society for American Baseball Research (SABR) (http://www.sabr.org)
The Sporting News (http://tsn.sportingnews.com)
Total Baseball (http://www.totalbaseball.com)

Index

309